Supply Chain Management and Knowledge Management

Also by Ashish Dwivedi

HEALTHCARE KNOWLEDGE MANAGEMENT

Also by Tim Butcher

GLOBAL LOGISTICS AND SUPPLY CHAIN MANAGEMENT
(with John Mangan and Chandra Lalwani)

Supply Chain Management and Knowledge Management

Integrating Critical Perspectives in Theory and Practice

Edited by

Ashish Dwivedi
Lecturer in Information Sciences, University of Hull, UK

Tim Butcher
Lecturer in Operations and Project Management, University of Hull, UK

First published 2009 by
PALGRAVE MACMILLAN

Palgrave Macmillan in the UK is an imprint of Macmillan Publishers Limited,
registered in England, company number 785998, of Houndmills, Basingstoke,
Hampshire RG21 6XS.

Palgrave Macmillan in the US is a division of St Martin's Press LLC,
175 Fifth Avenue, New York, NY 10010.

Palgrave Macmillan is the global academic imprint of the above companies
and has companies and representatives throughout the world.

Palgrave® and Macmillan® are registered trademarks in the United States,
the United Kingdom, Europe and other countries.

ISBN-13: 978–0–230–57343–7
ISBN-10: 0–230–57343–6

This book is printed on paper suitable for recycling and made from fully
managed and sustained forest sources. Logging, pulping and manufacturing
processes are expected to conform to the environmental regulations of the
country of origin.

A catalogue record for this book is available from the British Library.

Library of Congress Cataloging-in-Publication Data
Supply chain management and knowledge management : integrating
    critical perspectives in theory and practice / edited by Ashish
    Dwivedi, Tim Butcher.
        p. cm.
    Includes bibliographical references and index.
    ISBN 978–0–230–57343–7 (alk. paper)
    1. Business logistics.   2. Knowledge management.   I. Dwivedi,
    Ashish.   II. Butcher, Tim.
    HD38.5.S896045   2009
    658.7—dc22   2008029932

10   9   8   7   6   5   4   3   2   1
18   17   16   15   14   13   12   11   10   09

Printed and bound in Great Britain by
CPI Antony Rowe, Chippenham and Eastbourne

Contents

Part I   Supply Chain Management: Transforming Supply Chains into Integrated Knowledge Value Chains

Part II   Approaches, Frameworks and Techniques for Integrating Knowledge Management in the Supply Chain

List of Figures

List of Tables

Acknowledgements

This book would not have been possible without the cooperation and assistance of many people: the authors, reviewers, our colleagues and the staff at Palgrave Macmillan. In particular, we would like to thank Virginia Thorp for inviting us to produce this book, and for managing this project and answering our many questions as well as enabling us to keep this project on schedule. We would also like to thank the authors of the chapters in this book and the reviewers for their support and cooperation.

We also acknowledge our respective research groups at Hull University Business School (Centre for Systems Studies and Centre for Logistics Research) for enabling us to have the time to work on this exciting project and also to our colleagues for the many stimulating discussions on the manuscript. Finally, we would like to acknowledge our respective families for their support throughout this project.

ASHISH DWIVEDI
TIM BUTCHER

Preface

Advances in information technologies have transformed the way organizations interact with each other, and with their customers. Customers and organizations have become more demanding, desiring customized products and services that are made to their precise needs, at comparatively cheaper costs, and within a time-compressed environment. The last two decades have also witnessed a constantly changing business environment wherein revolutionary technologies are resulting in the creation of innovative products with shorter product life cycles, while being under constant pressure to reduce lead times.

In response, best practice organizations have recognized that they cannot compete alone. Today supply chains compete. Furthermore, the exploitation of knowledge across the supply chain is fundamental to business optimization. Organizations have accepted and recognized that in the dynamic modern-day business environment, knowledge is the prime resource for providing an organization with a sustainable competitive advantage. Consequently, to enable organizations to respond to this dynamic environment, new management paradigms such as knowledge management and supply chain management have evolved.

In this text, we seek to explore the role of knowledge management in the supply chain. We explore the current trends in supply chain management, the efficacy of current knowledge creation/acquisition, and transfer mechanisms among supply chain partners, key drivers for supply chain modelling and simulation. We also focus on new approaches and skills for supply chain management.

The purpose of this book is to: (a) contribute to building bridges between supply chain management and knowledge management paradigms and (b) to extend critical thinking in the supply chain management and knowledge management domains. This books does this by bringing together contributions from supply chain management and knowledge management theorists and practitioners in a manner so as to enable researchers not only to identify and discuss key issues for research in supply chain management and knowledge management, but also to allow others interested in supply chain management and knowledge management to acquire fresh perspectives. In doing so, we hope that knowledge in these fundamental business disciplines will be extended and combined to forge new domains.

ASHISH DWIVEDI
TIM BUTCHER

Organization of the Book

Part I, Supply Chain Management: Transforming Supply Chains into Integrated Knowledge Value Chains, has five chapters that present the case for incorporating knowledge management concepts into supply chain management. This section also looks at how knowledge management concepts can transform supply chains into integrated knowledge value chains.

Chapter 1, Innovation in Distributed Networks and Supporting Knowledge Flows, by Petrick and Pogrebnyakov examines how innovation happens in distributed supply networks that are by nature complex and adaptive. They argue that traditional IT information transfer is inadequate to support the knowledge flows required in networked innovation. This chapter draws insights from two studies of supply chain coordination conducted over a decade with companies involved in supply chain innovation.

Chapter 2, The Role of Knowledge Sharing in a Supply Chain, by Hadaya and Cassivi expands our understanding of the role knowledge sharing in a supply chain by integrating the literature from supply chain management, information systems and knowledge management. They argue that knowledge sharing positively influences IOISs' use of and process innovation in both perspectives, and that process innovation is a critical factor in improving firm performance in a supply chain environment.

Chapter 3, A Conceptual Model of Knowledge Management for Strategic Technology Planning in the Value Chain, by Suárez-Núñez, Monahan and Vojak develops, for the first time, a detailed conceptual model of knowledge management for strategic technology planning in the value chain. The authors argue that strategic technology planning in the value chain shares many key features with order quantity planning in the supply chain, including such knowledge management issues as the communication of demand between multiple levels of a supply chain and the observation of 'bullwhip' as demand is distorted when one moves upstream in the chain.

Chapter 4, Ontology Engineering for Knowledge Sharing in Supply Chains, by Smirnov, Levashova and Shilov presents a novel approach in developing an ontology for enabling knowledge sharing in supply chains. They argue that modern companies have to form supply chain networks to provides maximum flexibility and optimally respond to changes in their environment. However, when dealing with multiple organizations and multiple processes within a complicated production network, identifying and locating a member that has responsibility and/or competence in a particular part of the network can be a laborious, time-consuming process. They argue that their proposed ontology is one possible solution for this problem.

Finally in this part, Chapter 5, Supply Chain Design: In An Outsourcing World, by Byrne, Liston and Heavey starts with the premise that supply chains are becoming increasingly complex, elongated and ultimately more competitive and that most organizations today do not compete with each other directly but instead compete supply chain to supply chain. They contend that to succeed in such an environment, many organizations have focused their scarce resources on core competencies and outsourced all other activities to third parties. They present critical insights into a study that examined how seven outsourced global supply chains were initialized.

Part II, Approaches, Frameworks and Techniques for Integrating Knowledge Management in the Supply Chain, has six chapters, which build upon the preceding section and present novel approaches, frameworks and techniques for integrating knowledge management in the supply chain.

Chapter 6, Modelling Supply Chain Information and Material Flow Perturbations, by Wu and Blackhurst presents a novel approach of using Petri nets to model supply chain systems. They note that little work has been done to study problems related to information flows such as unexpected order changes from the customer. They model supply chain systems using Petri nets with incidence matrices to conduct material flow analysis. They argue that potential benefits of this approach include the ability to determine the root cause of material flow disruptions and will allow quicker response times to the customer and a reduced bullwhip effect.

Chapter 7, Linking Product, Supply Chain, Process and Manufacturing Planning and Control Design, by Olhager analyzes the relationships among the design aspects of products, supply chains, manufacturing processes and manufacturing planning and control (MPC) systems. Olhager presents the result of a questionnaire survey with data from 128 manufacturing firms.

Chapter 8, Decision Frontiers in Supply Chain Networks, by Pearson outlines a new approach to the analysis of supply chains that uncovers a duality between networks as knowledge structures and networks as decision-making structures. The work incorporates a network transformation that introduces, under fairly general conditions, uncorrelated phase planes, which enable the investigation of changes in variability and network design both at a 'global' and 'local' decision-making level.

Chapter 9, Supply Chain Management: A Multi-Agent System Framework, by Li, Sikora and Shaw discusses the use of a multi-agent approach for supply chain management. They discuss coordination structures, information sharing policies, privacy and security, business environment and agent architecture. This chapter also presents results of a multi-agent simulation study comparing the effects of different information sharing strategies on the performance of a supply chain.

Chapter 10, Delivery Supply Chain Planning Using Radio Frequency Identification (RFID)-Enabled Dynamic Optimization, by Yee, Tew, Tang, Kim and Kumara looks into why many companies still have been struggling to gain a return on investment (ROI), despite the fact that there are a wide number of successful reports of radio frequency identification (RFID) technology applications for supply chains. They present a step-by-step procedure for an RFID-enabled decision-making framework development, which they argue leads to a high ROI.

Chapter 11, A Generalized Order-Up-To Policy and Altruistic Behaviour in a Three-Level Supply Chain, by Hosoda and Disney studies the benefit of the order coordination in a serially linked three-level supply chain. The authors show that, to minimize the total supply chain cost, the attitude of the first-level player to cost increases is essential. This type of order coordination is called 'altruistic behaviour' herein and can produce a significant cost reduction (more than 20 per cent) to the overall supply chain. A coordination model that may be more applicable in practical settings is also introduced.

Part III, Knowledge Management-Led Supply Chain Management: Innovations and New Understanding, comprising five chapters, builds upon the preceding sections and presents lessons from current and previous supply chain management implementations, and discusses how these would lead to new innovations and understanding.

Chapter 12, Electronic Integration of Supply Chain Operations: Context, Evolution and Current Practices, by Matopoulos, Vlachopoulou and Manthou analyzes the concept of supply chain integration and proposes an overall framework. The authors note that in the automotive, computer and grocery sector, companies seem to perform better in terms of the integration achieved, both supply chain and electronic, due to the structure of these sectors.

Chapter 13, Collaborative Cultural Space: Disciplines for Inter-Organizational Collaborative Learning Behaviour, by Sun and Childerhouse posits that repetitive interaction creates a collaborative cultural space where organizational learning takes place. This chapter provides practitioners with guidance on how to maximize and leverage learning from personnel involved in boundary-spanning roles.

Chapter 14, Innovative Information and Communication Technology for Logistics: The Case of Road Transportation Feeding Port Operations and Direct Short Range Communication Technology, by Mondragon, Mondragon and Mondragon notes that information and communication technology (ICT) has become an important element of the infrastructure required to support complex supply chain management and logistics operations. They note that there are several limitations associated with current ICT solutions in logistics, including reliability and connectivity problems, not to mention problems associated with limited range, scalability and security.

Chapter 15, An Evaluation of Electronic Logistics Marketplaces within Supply Chains, by Wang, Potter and Naim argues that, in recent years, the growth in electronic marketplaces has had a significant impact on business-to-business transactions. Using evidence from an international empirical study of six marketplaces, they critically review the use of closed ELMs within knowledge-driven supply chains.

Chapter 16, Environmental Management in Product Chains, by Jørgensen and Forman focuses on the topical theme of environmental management in supply chain management. They present an overview of environmental issues and initiatives in environmental management in product chains. They also critique a number of international schemes and standards that have a focus on environmental management in product chains.

We have collated chapters that we hope validate the coming of age of knowledge management in the supply chain. We hope that academics, practitioners, managers and students will find the issues highlighted herein of interest and value, to take our disciplines forward.

List of Abbreviations

4PL	fourth-party logistics provider
ABC	activity-based costing
AO	application ontology
APO	advanced planning and optimizing
APS	advanced planning systems
AR	AutoRegressive
ATO	assemble-to-order
AVE	average variance extracted
AVL	approved vendor listing
B2B	business to business
B2C	business to consumer
BOM	bill of materials
BSCI	Business Social Compliance Initiative
BTO	build-to-order
CA	certification authorities
CAD	computer-aided design
CCS	collaborative cultural space
CEC	cost estimation centre
CFA	confirmatory factor analysis
CM	contract manufacturer
COP	community of practice
CPFR	collaborative planning, forecasting and replenishment
CVIS	Cooperative Vehicle-Infrastructure Systems
DES	discrete event simulation
DIP	desired inventory position
DSRC	direct short range communication
EDI	electronic data exchange
ELM	electronic logistics marketplace
EM	electronic marketplace
EM	empirical
ERP	enterprise resource planning
ESPO	European Sea Ports Organization
ETI	Ethical Trading Initiative
EWMA	exponentially weighted moving average
FFE	fuzzy front end
FMCG	fast-moving consumer goods
FSC	Forest Stewardship Council
GPRS	general packet radio service
GPS	global positioning system

GSM   global supplier management
HMI   human machine interface
ICT   information and communication technology
IOIS   inter-organizational information system
IP   internet protocol
IT   information technology
ITS   intelligent transport systems and services
JIT   just-in-time
JV   joint venture
KMP   knowledge management platform
LHS   left hand side
LO   learning organization
LTF   lead-time focus
MA   moving average
MAC   media access control
MAS   multi-agent system
MF   manufacturing focus
MMSE   minimum mean square error
MOQ   minimum order quantity
MP   materials planning
MPC   manufacturing planning and control
MRP   manufacturing resource planning
MRP   material requirements planning
MS   map server
MS   master scheduling
MSP   minimum spanning tree
MSW   message switch
MTO   make-to-order
MTS   make-to-stock
NDA   non-disclosure agreement
NM   network management
NOC   network operation centre
NP   non-deterministic polynomial time
OBU   on-board unit
OEM   original equipment manufacturer
OUT   order-up-to
PAB   product attribute bullwhip
PAC   production activity control
PAYG   pay as you go
PC   process choice
PCB   printed circuit board
PLAN   Swedish Production and Inventory Management Society
POD   proof of delivery

POS   point of sale
PP   primary purpose
PTH   pin through hole
RAS   Russian Academy of Sciences
RFID   radio frequency identification
RFQ   request for quotation
RHS   right-hand side
ROI   return on investment
RO-RO roll on-roll off
RSU   roadside unit
SA   situational awareness
SAS   statistical analysis software
SC   supply chain
SCM   supply chain management
SCN   supply chain network
SCOR   Supply Chain Operations Reference
SEM   structural equation modelling
SHOE   simple HTML ontology extensions
SMT   surface mount technology
S&OP   sales and operations planning
STP   strategic technology planning
TQM   total quality management
TSP   travelling salesman problem
V2I   vehicle to infrastructure
V2V   vehicle to vehicle
VE   virtual enterprise
VII   vehicle infrastructure integration
VMI   vendor managed inventory
VRO   vehicle routing optimization
WIP   work in progress
WLAN   wireless local area network
WSM   Wireless Access for Vehicular Environment (WAVE)
       short messages
WWRE   worldwide retail exchange
XML   Extensible Markup Language

Notes on the Contributors

Jennifer Blackhurst is Assistant Professor of Logistics and Supply Chain Management in the College of Business at Iowa State University. Her research interests include supply chain risk and disruptions, supply chain coordination and supplier assessment. Her publications have appeared or been accepted in such journals as *Decision Sciences Journal*, *Journal of Operations Management*, *Production and Operations Management*, *IEEE Transactions on Engineering Management* and *International Journal of Production Research*.

Tim Butcher is Lecturer in the University of Hull Logistics Institute, where he is the Director of the MSc Logistics and Supply Chain Management Programme. His areas of expertise are in human factors and new technologies in logistics and supply chain management.

P. J. Byrne is Lecturer of Operations/Supply Chain Management in Dublin City University Business School, having formerly worked as a senior research fellow at the University of Limerick. His research interests are supply chain design, analysis and optimisation, environmental impacts of supply chain construction, company outsourcing, decision-making and costing, and industrial simulation applications.

Luc Cassivi is Associate Professor in the Department of Management and Technology at the Université du Québec à Montréal, Canada. His research interests include information systems, innovation management and supply chain management.

Paul Childerhouse is Associate Professor in the Waikato Management School, University of Waikato, New Zealand. His main research interests are supply chain management and logistics management, and he has published widely in many international refereed journals. He has undertaken research in the automotive, aerospace, construction, as well as health service sectors, to investigate how supply chain can become fully integrated and market-orientated.

Adrian E. Coronado Mondragon is RCUK Academic Fellow in Logistics at the Logistics Institute, the University of Hull Business School, UK. He has had the opportunity to collaborate in projects with companies in different sectors looking at how to extend build-to-order production upstream, increase synchronization in the supply chain, reduce the amplification of demand fluctuations, reduce pipeline inventory levels and reduce supply chain throughput time. His current research interests cover schedule and information visibility downstream in the supply chain, finished vehicle logistics, performance measures and audit tools for supply chain performance and information and communication technology in logistics.

Christian E. Coronado Mondragon is product design engineer at NewFlyer Industries in Winnipeg, Manitoba, Canada. He is also a PhD candidate at the École Polythechnique de Montréal, in the Department of Mathematics and Industrial Engineering, and holds an MSc in Engineering Management of Production from Chalmers University of Technology, Gothenburg, Sweden. He has worked as an automotive product/project design engineer and sales engineer for several OEMs. His research interests are: innovation management, technology transfer and product development in the automotive industry.

Etienne S. Coronado Mondragon is a researcher and a PhD candidate in the Department of Electrical and Computer Engineering at the University of Sherbrooke, Sherbrooke, Quebec, Canada. He holds an MSc in Digital Communication Systems and Technology from Chalmers University of Technology, Gothenburg, Sweden. His current research interests are focused on information service provisioning for vehicular ad hoc networks, wireless communication protocols and IP converged networks for next generation networks.

Stephen M. Disney is Senior Lecturer in Operations Management with the Logistics Systems Dynamics Group in the Logistics and Operations Management section of Cardiff Business School, UK. His current research interests involve the application of control theory and statistical techniques to supply chains in order to investigate their dynamic and economic performance.

Ashish Dwivedi is Lecturer in Information Sciences at the University of Hull, UK. His research areas of expertise are knowledge and healthcare management. He has published a book on *Healthcare Knowledge Management* and is working on a number of other texts.

Marianne Forman is Senior Researcher at the Danish Building Research Institute, Aalborg University, Denmark. Her research area encompasses innovation, user driven innovation, environmental management in companies and product chains, project management and change processes, working environment, and cooperation inside companies and among companies.

Pierre Hadaya is Professor in the Department of Management and Technology at the École des Sciences de la Gestion de l'Université du Québec à Montréal, Canada. He holds a PhD in Management of Technology from the École Polytechnique de Montréal. His main research interests lie at the intersection of information technology management, business strategy, and interorganizational design.

Cathal Heavey is Senior Lecturer in the Manufacturing and Operations Engineering Department in the College of Engineering at University of Limerick, Ireland. He lectures in the areas of operations research, information technology, supply chain modelling and discrete event simulation. He is Joint Director of the Enterprise Research Centre. His research interests include simulation modelling of discrete event systems, modelling and analysis of supply chains and manufacturing systems and enterprise modelling. In his research he has specialized in the area of modelling and optimization of manufacturing and supply chain systems using both analytical and simulation techniques.

Takamichi Hosoda is Lecturer in Operations Management at Cardiff Business School, UK. Considering the fact that application of supply chain integration schemes to industries has not brought supply chain participants to higher stages as promised by the literature, and where the benefit comes from and whether this benefit is large enough to support the integrated relationships is not yet well-understood, his research seeks to provide rigorous principles that can help managers and management researchers understand the source of the true benefit coming from supply chain integrations.

Michael Søgaard Jørgensen was one of the co-founders of the Science Shop at the Technical Universtiy of Denmark (DTU) in 1985 and has been one of its co-ordinators since then. Since 1989 he has held an Associate professorship at DTU in user participation in technology assessment and technology development, now at the department DTU Management. He is the author of around 110 publications within environmental management in companies and product chains, sustainable transition, technology assessment and technology foresight, developmental work, community-based research strategies, organic food production and consumption, and food system innovation. He is a chairman of the Society of Green Technology within the Danish Society of Engineers and a member of the Danish Board of Technology appointed by the Danish Ministry of Science, Technology and Innovation.

Jindae Kim is Logistics Research Engineer at the Expeditors International of Washington, Inc., USA. His current research interests include decentralized dynamic control using market-based mechanisms, multiagent-based information systems, and dynamic control for RFID-enabled computational models, all in the context of supply chain and logistics, communication and sensor networks, and service engineering study, he was employed as a Research Assistant in the Laboratory for Intelligent Systems and Quality (LISQ).

Soundar Kumara is Allen, E., and Allen, M., Pearce Chaired Professor of Industrial Engineering at the Pennsylvania State University, USA. He also holds joint appointments with Computer Science and Engineering, and School of Information Sciences and Technology. He is an elected fellow of the International Institution of Production Research (CIRP) and the Institute of Industrial Engineers (IIE). His research interests are in sensor networks, logistics networks and complexity and large scale networks. He has published more than 150 articles, and co-edited five books.

Tatiana Levashova is a leading programmer at Computer Aided Integrated Systems Laboratory of SPIIRAS, St Petersburg, Russia, Her current research is devoted to knowledge-related problems such as knowledge representation, knowledge management, ontology and context management. She has published more than 50 papers in reviewed journals and proceedings of international conferences.

Jingquan Li is Assistant Professor of Accounting and Computer Information Systems at the College of Business Administration at Texas A&M University-Kingsville, USA. His research focuses on privacy and security, economics of information technology, data mining and business intelligence, agent technology, and supply chain management. He received the Seymour Sudman Award and College of Commerce Fellowship from the University of Illinois at Urbana-Champaign.

Paul Liston is Postdoctoral Researcher at the Enterprise Research Centre in the University of Limerick, Ireland. His research interests include web-based discrete event simulation, supply chain design and analysis, environmental impact performance metrics, decision support and knowledge management systems, non-hierarchical networks, and outsourced services modelling.

Vicky Manthou is Professor of Information Systems & Logistics at the University of Macedonia, Department of Applied Informatics, Thessaloniki, Greece, and Visiting Research Professor at Loyola University, USA. Her professional expertise and research interests are analysis and design of management information systems, supply chain management, and logistics information systems. She has participated in European projects in the above fields (e-business forum, ISIS project) and has published papers and reports in Greek and international journals and books. She acts as a reviewer for the *International Journal of Production Economics*, the *International Journal of Logistics Systems and Management*, and the *International Journal of Enterprise Information Systems*.

Aristides Matopoulos is Scientific Associate at the University of Macedonia's Department of Marketing and Operations Management in Thessaloniki,

Greece. He is currently teaching supply chain management and business logistics and is also involved as a Researcher in the University of Macedonia for the European Project 'e-Trust', which deals with the exploration and analysis of trust factors in electronic relationships in food chains. His current research interests include sustainable supply chain management, E-business adoption and E-business impact on supply chain operations.

George E. Monahan is Professor of Business Administration and former Co-Director of the Technology & Management Program at the University of Illinois at Urbana-Champaign, USA. His research deals with the analysis of strategic issues in manufacturing, operations, and marketing management. This research has been published in major scholarly journals such as *Operations Research, Management Science, Naval Research Logistics, Journal of Operations Management, IIE Transactions, Manufacturing & Service Operations Management, Games and Economic Behavior*, and *Marketing Science*.

Mohamed Naim is Professor in Logistics and Operations Management at Cardiff Business School, UK. He is a Director of the Logistics Systems Dynamics Group and the EPSRC funded Cardiff University Innovative Manufacturing Research Centre. Mohamed is a former Editor-in-Chief of the *International Journal of Logistics* and is an Advisory Committee Member for the International Symposium on Logistics. He has published over 80 journal papers including publications in International *Journal of Logistics Management, OMEGA: International Journal of Management Science* and *International Journal of Production Economics*.

Jan Olhager is Professor of Production Economics at Linköping University, Sweden. He has authored two books on operations management, and on manufacturing planning and control. He has published in international journals such as *European Journal of Operational Research, International Journal of Operations and Production Management, International Journal of Production Economics, International Journal of Production Research, OMEGA*, and *Production Planning and Control*. He is the Director of the Production Strategy Centre at Linköping University, and has been a consultant to Scandinavian industry for more than two decades. His research interests include manufacturing strategy, operations and supply chain management, flexibility, manufacturing planning and control systems, and modelling and analysis of operations management systems.

Michael Pearson is Reader in the Centre for Mathematics and Statistics at Napier University Business School, UK. Research interests are in the fields of supply chain networks and social network analysis. His work on supply chain networks began as a result of a major consultancy programme for a large commercial newspaper distributor where he developed software for the distribution of newspaper and magazines across a retail network in the UK. He is chairman of the Operational Research Group of Scotland.

Irene J. Petrick is Professor of Practice at Penn State University, USA and is the director of the Enterprise Informatics and Integration Center in the College of Information Sciences and Technology. She is an active researcher, teacher and consultant, having published over 85 articles and presentations. In addition to her academic work, she advises companies on technology strategy, product and systems development, supply chain collaboration, and strategic roadmapping. She is an internationally recognized expert on roadmapping and has made presentations in the UK and to government experts and scientists in Taiwan and Korea.

Nicolai Pogrebnyakov received his PhD from the College of Information Sciences and Technology at the Pennsylvania State University, USA. He holds an MS in Computer Science and Mathematics from the Belarusian State University for Informatics and Radioelectronics in Minsk, Belarus. Before entering the graduate school he worked as a software developer and analyst. His research interests include international firm strategy in technology industries and IT use, coordination and innovation in supply networks.

Andrew Potter is Lecturer in Transport and Logistics at Cardiff University, UK. His research has particularly focused on how freight transport can become more integrated within supply chains. This research has considered process, people and technology-based approaches, and more recently, environmental performance in addition to traditional supply chain performance measures. His PhD thesis was highly commended in the Emerald/EMDF Outstanding Doctoral Research Awards 2006. He has published in a wide range of journals including *Transportation Research Part* E and *International Journal of Production Economics*.

Michael J. Shaw is Professor/Hoeft Endowed Chair of Information Technology and Management, the Director of Center for Information Systems and Technology Management, and the Director of Graduate Studies, at the University of Illinois at Urbana-Champaign, USA. He has published more than 100 research papers in academic journals and proceedings on topics focused on intelligent systems, decision support, network theory, complex systems, electronic commerce, and information technology. Dr. Shaw has edited five books and is currently on the editorial board of more than ten journals. He is the co-editor of the journal *Information Systems and e-Business Management*.

Nikolay Shilov is Senior Researcher at the Computer Aided Integrated Systems Laboratory of SPIIRAS, St Petersburg, Russia. His current research interests belong to areas of virtual enterprise configuration, supply chain management, knowledge management, ontology engineering and Web-services.

Riyaz T. Sikora is Associate Professor of Information Systems at the College of Business at the University of Texas at Arlington, USA. His current research interests include multi-agent systems and data mining. He has published refereed scholarly papers in journals such as *Management Science, Information Systems Research, INFORMS Journal of Computing, IEEE Transactions on Engineering Management, Decision Support Systems, EJOR, IEEE Transactions on Systems, Man, and Cybernetics,* and IEEE *Expert.* He is on the editorial board of the *Journal of Information Systems and e-Business Management* and the *Journal of Database Management.*

Alexander Smirnov is Deputy Director for Research and a Head of Computer Aided Integrated Systems Laboratory at the St Petersburg Institute for Informatics and Automation of the Russian Academy of Sciences (SPIIRAS), and a full Professor of St Petersburg State Electrical Engineering University, Russia. His current research interests belong to areas of corporate knowledge management, Web-services, group decision support systems, virtual enterprises, and supply chain management.

Carlos A. Suárez-Núñez is a consultant in the Business Integration and Optimization group of the Technology Integration area of Deloitte Consulting LLP in Chicago, USA. He is a PhD candidate in Systems and Entrepreneurial Engineering in the College of Engineering at the University of Illinois at Urbana-Champaign. His primary research interest has been in developing models of the strategic technology planning process. His research has been published in *Transactions on Engineering Management* and *Journal of Technology Intelligence and Planning.*

Peter Y. T. Sun is Senior Lecturer in the Waikato Management School, University of Waikato, New Zealand. His primary research interests are in the areas of organizational learning, knowledge management, innovation, leadership, and he has published in many international refereed journals. He consults for multinational organizations in the areas of assessing an organization's innovation and knowledge management capabilities.

Kaizhi Tang is Senior Research Scientist at Intelligent Automation, Inc., Rockville, USA. He has over a decade of experience in operations research and its related applications. He has been working on research and development into the methodologies of optimization, mathematical programming, distributed information systems, data mining, artificial intelligence, statistical analysis, game theory, and simulation, and the applications of mechanical design optimization, image processing and image recognition, supply chain dynamic control and optimization, dynamic and real-time sensor management on satellites, manufacturing cost evaluation and optimization, bioscience data mining and decision support, health and biology informatics.

Jeffrey Tew is Group Manager of Global Manufacturing Strategy and Planning at General Motors R&D Center, USA. He is Adjunct Professor of Supply Chain Management at Georgia Tech University and a Visiting Professor of Industrial Engineering at Tsinghua University in Beijing, China. He has published numerous articles in many operational and supply chain management journals. Besides being in the forefront of research in the theory of supply chain management, he also has extensive practical experience in implementing supply chain structure for different industries. He has lectured extensively on supply chain management, Six Sigma implementations, and quality control at many universities including Stanford University and MIT.

Maro Vlachopoulou is Professor of e-Marketing/Business at the University of Macedonia, Department of Applied Informatics, Thessaloniki, Greece, and Visiting Research Professor at the University of Sunderland, UK. Her professional expertise and research interests are marketing information systems, e-business, ERP/CRM systems, supply chain management, knowledge management, e-supply chain management, virtual organization. She acts as a reviewer in the *International Journal of Production Economics*, the International Journal of Business Information Systems, and the *European Journal of Operational Research*.

Bruce A. Vojak is Associate Dean for Administration in the College of Engineering, and Adjunct Professor of both Electrical and Computer Engineering and Industrial and Enterprise Systems Engineering, University, of Illinois, USA. Previously he held technical and management positions at MIT Lincoln Laboratory, Amoco, and Motorola, where he was Director of Advanced Technology for Motorola's frequency generation products business. His research in electronic materials, components and subsystems and, more recently, in innovation management has been published in such journals as *Applied Physics Letters, Journal of Applied Physics, Solid State Communications, Electron Device Letters, Physical Review Letters, Physical Review B, Journal of Engineering Education, Transactions on Engineering Management, R&D Management*, and *Journal of Product Innovation Management*.

Yingli Wang is Lecturer in Logistics and Operations Management at Cardiff Business School, UK. She joined Cardiff University in 2004, and her three-month field research with a leading European retailer has been published by the EPSRC *Newsline Magazine* as a good example of collaboration with industry. She also recently secured funding from the Department for Transport and Welsh Assembly Government for research into electronic logistics marketplaces. Her current research interests focus on the use of information and communication technology in B2B logistics and transport management.

Teresa Wu is Associate Professor in the Industrial Engineering Department at Arizona State University, USA. Her current research interests include distributed decision support, distributed information system, supply chain modelling and disruption management. She has articles published (or accepted) in such journals as *International Journal of Production Research, Omega, Data and Knowledge Engineering and Journal of Computing and Information Science in Engineering.* She serves on the Editorial Review Board for *Computer and Standard Interface: International Journal of Electronic Business Management.*

Shang-Tae Yee has over 20 years' experience in supply chain and logistics. He has been leading a research program at General Motors that develops and implements real-time enterprise decision systems framework using wireless, advanced software, and decision technology. He has led several wireless initiatives, including RFID, at GM that include finished vehicle tracking, inbound material tracking, and container & part traceability. He has published numerous papers and articles in archived journals and had presentations at professional workshops and conferences. He has served as a reviewer for several academic journals and is now on the Editorial Board for *International Journal of Services Operations and Informatics.* Since 2003, he has been a Visiting Professor at Penn State University IE Department, USA, and he is now serving as an adjunct faculty at the University of Michigan-Dearborn School of Management, USA and SungKyunKwan University Management of Technology Department, Korea.

Part I
Supply Chain Management: Transforming Supply Chains into Integrated Knowledge Value Chains

1

Innovation in Distributed Networks and Supporting Knowledge Flows

Irene J. Petrick and Nicolai Pogrebnyakov

Introduction

At a recent gathering of 30 top executives from non-competing customer-facing firms at an innovation summit, discussions centred on how to innovative more effectively (Petrick 2007a). These companies are struggling with how to identify the best talent, how to fund and manage the innovation process, and how to measure its effectiveness. Without exception, these executives believe that leveraging their company's supply chain and the talent and technologies located within it are a key to success. A major barrier to this, however, was captured by one executive's comment, 'Within our company, and even outside of it, information gets shared. Insight doesn't.' This chapter focuses on the theoretical understanding and practical realities of networked innovation. We specifically explore the challenges of creating and sharing insights in supply chain networks.

In our conceptual model (see Figure 1.1), we portray innovation as a contact sport that occurs between individuals, acting within firms. In this model, information flows between firms that the individual can access. Moreover, the individual – acting as an expert – is particularly well suited to scan his or her environment for additional relevant information. Situational awareness is created at the individual level when the network and firm share information about goals and objectives through formal channels; network situational awareness, on the other hand, develops when the individual shares his or her expert knowledge with others in the network. In the context of supply network innovation, we see traditional information technology (IT) systems as the primary conduit for information flow and emerging Enterprise 2.0 platforms as the primary tool for the more content-rich and context-specific knowledge flows.

Today's complex products require expertise in multiple scientific, engineering and manufacturing fields. Thus, the ability of any one firm to take an idea into the marketplace by itself is limited. For example, Boeing engineers often comment that an aeroplane is a collection of components flying in

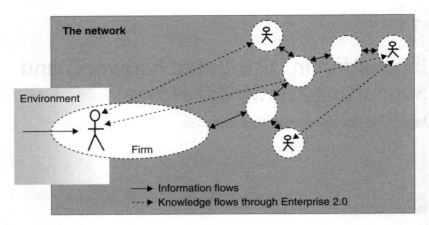

Figure 1.1   Information and knowledge flows needed to create situational awareness and support innovation in distributed networks

formation. For the 737, the number of parts that need to come together approaches nearly 3 million, and for the 777, the number is closer to 6 million. These components are supplied by over 27,000 firms from 100 countries, and many of these firms innovate only with respect to the component they supply.

Throughout our discussion, we focus on technology and product innovation. We consider the way that IT can support the knowledge flows needed to enable innovation to occur in a network. Here we argue that many of today's challenges result from the inadequacies of IT to support the underlying knowledge flows between a diverse set of actors within and across organizational boundaries. Because of this, IT is not seen as a strategic asset by many firms and thus receives little to no attention in the boardroom as a strategic enabler. Our presentation emphasizes our belief that emerging Web 2.0 approaches can provide a meaningful alternative to existing knowledge IT systems by more naturally supporting the realities of innovation in supply networks.

Overview of concepts

To fully appreciate the linkage between networked innovation and knowledge sharing, we begin with the innovation process as it occurs within a firm and a network. This perspective naturally yields to a discussion of knowledge flows within the innovation cycle from sensing through sense-making to action. Then we must understand the way that supply networks are structured and how structure influences supply network collaboration. Finally, all

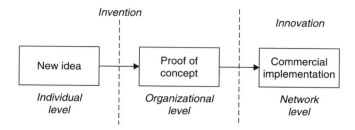

Figure 1.2 Innovation as a process that occurs through several levels of analysis

of these concepts must be linked to consider the implications for knowledge flows, and roles and responsibilities within the network.

Innovation in the context of the firm and network

We view innovation as a multi-phased process that leads from an idea to its commercial implementation (Schumpeter 1942, Brown and Karagozoglu 1989, Utterback 1971). When superimposed on the supply network, we see that innovation permeates several levels of analysis. Innovation starts with a new idea by an individual or a group of individuals, is transformed into the proof of concept by the firm or organization and this invention is finally implemented as a commercial application by the supply network. This process is shown in Figure 1.2, and emphasizes the interplay between the individual, the firm and the network.

Innovation is often characterized as resulting from market pull or technology push (Narayanan 2001). In the first case, innovation occurs when there is a market demand for it; in the second case, it is the availability of a new technology that drives innovation. For example, market pull innovations in battery technology have resulted due to the surge in the number of portable electronic devices used by an average person, which in the first decade of the 21st century often includes a personal audio player, a mobile phone, a laptop, a handheld computer and a camera.

Market pull innovations require that the customer-facing firm in the network (often an original equipment manufacturer [OEM]) has a deep understanding of the customers' needs and wants. Winsor (2006, p. 270) explains innovation through a co-creating process between customers and firms directly interacting with them, observing that 'innovation can spring from any part of the company-customer community [of individuals], but ONLY if the support and encouragement for this environment exists at every level of the business'.

By contrast, technology push innovation occurs when breakthroughs in technology promote innovation in search of new applications of this technology. For example, the continuing development of faster computer processors (Moore's law) allows software developers to create applications that use this increasing processing power by being more functionally versatile or having a better user interface. Our own studies in manufacturing supply chains indicate the importance of supplier-held knowledge in creating compelling products in the market. One supplier of plastic components commented on the way that his company leverages its knowledge of resins and manufacturing to help a consumer products OEM develop new products:

> If a customer brings us a unique product [idea], we can take it and do three designs. We can have a prototype made up in a similar material, and [our customer] can try it out and see if they like it. This gives them a realistic feel of what the product is going to look like. Then we can take it and we can design the tooling around it. We can build the tooling and we can do the production of the plastic [resin]. (Taken from an interview conducted for the study, 'Pennsylvania Plastics Initiative – Supply Chain Effectiveness,' Funded by the PA Plastics Initiative, I.J. Petrick and C.M. Maitland, Principal Investigators. May 2006–December 2007.)

Technology push and market pull innovations suggest different roles and responsibilities for different firms within the supply chain, based on their proximity to the end customer or their specialized expertise. Firms that are distant from the end product market (e.g. raw materials processors or component makers) are more likely to innovate around technology product features, while in firms that manufacture the final product or its subassemblies innovation are often driven by both market demands and technological advances (Petrick 2007b). We believe that this sharing of responsibility leverages the individual knowledge within those firms.

Innovation cycle

Technological innovation occurs across stages that are increasingly deterministic, where earlier stages are characterized by high uncertainty (see Figure 1.3).

An organization does not have an idea; an individual does. Thus the first challenge to innovation is for the individual expert to understand the organization's goals in such a way as to comprehend the needs and priorities of the organization (Stage 1). In the context of innovation, the individual expert must have a deep enough understanding of the organization's intent as to be able to distinguish relevant information from otherwise interesting, but irrelevant information. In essence, the individual acts as a sensor of environmental changes for the organization. The human as a sensor, linked by informal communication channels to other humans as sensors, has enabled terrorist cells to rapidly respond and take advantage of changing situational dynamics in ways that outstrip traditional military command and control

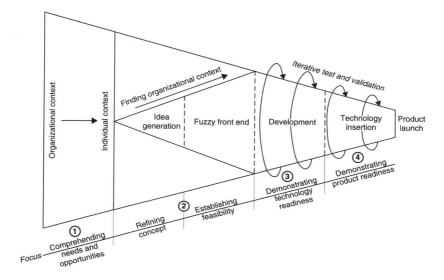

Figure 1.3 Stages of the innovation cycle

patterns. We suggest that this same rapid detection and communication be deployed in a more positive manner to promote networked innovation.

Sternberg (2003) identifies the responsibilities of the individual in sensing and sense-making activities as selective encoding (locating relevant information in context), selective combination (combining this information into a meaningful whole) and selective comparison (interrelating the information to what the expert already knows). Individual insight can then be shared with the group, in a transition from individual effort to organizational effort.

During Stage 2 of the innovation process, the back and forth dialogue between group members helps to refine the concept so that the organization can begin to judge its usefulness. Here we transition into what is typically known as the fuzzy front end (FFE) of the innovation process, where the group downselects from possible applications of the idea to identify the best or most appropriate target application. In this stage, conditions are highly unpredictable and ill defined (Reid and de Brentani 2004, Montoya-Weiss and O'Driscoll 2000). The focus of the FFE is establishing the feasibility of the idea to actually meet organizational needs and priorities.

Once feasibility and application target are established, the group begins the development process where the technology goes from a concept to a prototype. In Stage 3, we are trying to demonstrate the technology's readiness. Technology readiness levels generally include analytical, experimental and prototype-testing assessments to determine whether or not the technology is sound, reliable and repeatable. The curved arrows in the Development phase of Figure 1.3 indicate this iterative process. Also during this stage the technology begins to be linked to other technologies that are typically required in a complex innovation. A colleague at Boeing refers to the challenges of combining technologies into a solution as the 'Problem of the Dog Polisher', commenting:

> If we want to develop a dog polisher, we have to think about all of the components that go into it – a washer, a motor, a dryer, a polisher ... any one of these alone is only a partial solution, leaving the customer with a wet dog or a dirty polished dog.

In networked innovation, this is particularly challenging as the technology developments for these complex solutions often occur at different firms. For example, Toyota gets about half of its technology innovations from its supply base, and Proctor & Gamble hopes to use this open innovation model to yield similar percentages of supplier innovation.

For a technology to reach a commercial market we must place it into the larger product architecture. During Stage 4, technology insertion, the interfaces between the technology and its surroundings within the product are established. Once again, iterative test and validation are required to fully accomplish this. In the technology insertion phase, the team establishes product readiness – in other words, not only does the technology solution work as intended, but in the larger product architecture it contributes to a desired set of features and performs as intended.

Supply networks as complex adaptive systems

A supply network is a collection of firms that possess diverse knowledge and manufacturing or assembly capabilities that acts as a complex adaptive system – it is an interconnected network of multiple entities, each of which can change its actions in response to changes in the environment and the system (Choi, Dooley and Rungtusanatham 2001). Because of this, collective network performance results from individual and firm actions, interactions and adaptations, many of which occur in parallel. Complex adaptive systems tend to co-evolve with their environment and the rules of behaviour within these systems are typically non-linear.

Firms in the network are linked to one another through actions, but these actions are often supported by information and knowledge flows and integrated decision-making. The degree to which this occurs between firms is often constrained by the structure of the network (Samaddar, Nargundkar and Daley 2006). We identify three common network structures based on their degree of hierarchy and centrality (see Figure 1.4).

Hierarchical networks are characterized by the top-down influence from the OEM, strong-tiered structure and limited interactions within tiers horizontally and between firms in non-adjacent tiers. This conceptualization is the

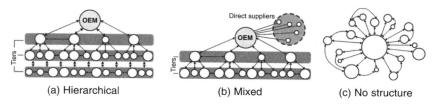

Figure 1.4 Supply network structures

closest to the traditional notion of a supply chain and is commonly associated with the automotive industry and other heavy manufacturing industries. In a hierarchical network, the OEM has the greatest knowledge of the end consumer due to its close proximity. In this hierarchical structure, the OEM translates its understanding of the customers' needs and wants into product features that are then produced by subsequent layers in the supply hierarchy. Tier 1 firms interact directly with the OEM, but non-tier 1 firms do not.

By comparison, *mixed* networks possess multiple paths to the OEM and a less rigid tier structure. Additionally, the influence of some lower-tiered companies (labelled direct suppliers in Figure 1.4b) may be higher than those in hierarchical networks. In this type of structure, some non-tier 1 firms interact directly with the OEM, thus gaining more direct knowledge of customer needs and wants, and frequently working as a co-designer. A comment from a plastics resin moulder highlights the unique role that specialized knowledge plays in linking a non-tier 1 supplier to an OEM, noting, 'Molding is a skill ... that has to be learned through experience because there are so many different resins ... every resin requires special handling, special drying, special temperatures.'

In the medical products industry, understanding resin options in medical devices is a competitive differentiator for products that can extend their useful life and enhance the ease of sterilization. Moreover, OEMs are now beginning to search for plastic resins that are robust and can be used in a variety of applications, thus reducing the inventory of multiple plastics (Weber 2008).

Finally, networks with *no structure* are characterized by distributed leadership, little tier structure and multiple paths from individual companies to the market. In a no-structure network the influence of an individual company is not always related to its size or tier position and leadership often accrues to the company that has unique intellectual property or capabilities or unique access to distribution channels. Some supply networks in the medical devices industry act in this fashion, for example.

The structure of a particular supply network can affect the motivation for innovation at the network level. Networks with reduced hierarchy and fewer tiers, or with a group of direct suppliers that exist outside the tier hierarchy, may be more apt at absorbing radical technological breakthroughs and finding new uses for them. In other words, such networks are more likely to excel at technology-push innovation. By contrast, networks with more rigid hierarchy may be more capable of innovating through market pull.

Supply network collaboration

Collaboration can occur at many levels, including network and firm level. However, while internal firm collaboration can be a significant source of knowledge generation and adoption and ultimately innovation (Narula 2004), in this chapter our interests primarily focus on external collaboration – between individuals of different firms.

Supply network collaboration has its roots in a variety of collaboration strategies, such as collaborative planning, forecasting and replenishment (CPFR) (Barratt 2004), vendor-managed inventory, continuous replenishment (Holweg *et al*. 2005, Skjoett-Larsen, Thernøe and Andresen 2003), as well as the Japanese manufacturing model, which encourages member network firms to openly share knowledge and reduces costs of finding knowledge (Dyer and Nobeoka 2000, Langfield-Smith and Greenwood 1998). The common goal of these formal cross-firm collaboration strategies is to increase transparency and synchronization across the entire supply network (Holweg *et al*. 2005, Skjoett-Larsen, Thernøe and Andresen 2003).

Information sharing, while an important part of collaboration, is not its ultimate objective. It is acting on the information that is at the heart of collaboration (Skjoett-Larsen, Thernøe and Andresen 2003). Even though passive sharing of information reduces costs and decreases uncertainty, synchronization of plans and activities and coordinated decision-making between network firms is even more beneficial (Sahin and Robinson 2005, Fiala 2005).

In our studies of collaboration between firms (Petrick, Maitland and Pogrebnyakov 2007, Petrick *et al*. 2008) in different types of supplier networks, we observe that mixed networks tend to have a higher level of collaboration between firms than the other two types of networks we identify. We believe this can be explained in part by the network's structure in the case of hierarchical networks, where the hierarchy itself establishes roles and responsibilities for individuals and firms as well as establishing the formally accepted channels of communication. In non-structured networks we believe there are two possible reasons for a lower level of collaboration between firms. First, firms in non-structured networks may be engaging in one-off interactions with customers or suppliers where the need for repeated interaction is limited to the transaction or project at hand. Second, firms in these networks may simply not see themselves as being in a network of trusted and/or predictable relationships and thus act independently.

Situational awareness: from the individual to the firm to the network

Because supply networks are complex adaptive systems that are constantly evolving, the actions of any single individual, team, or firm can influence both local decisions and global network behaviours (Choi, Dooley and Rungtusanatham 2001). Since it is the global network behaviour that differentiates the performance of one supplier network from another, we can further appreciate the link between individual situational awareness and network behaviours.

Situational awareness (SA) can be simply described as the knowledge of the environment and prioritization of elements in the environment according to their importance, which often includes analysis of the way that the actions of the individual or entity will affect the environment (Endsley 2000). Individuals vary in their ability to acquire SA given the same data input. SA builds up over time, and is frequently reliant on the individual's ability to relate emerging information to past experience.

Here we present Endsley's three levels of SA in the context of supply networks.

- At the basic level, an individual within a firm in the supply network develops a perception of fundamental information relevant to the firm's position in the network and the surrounding environment. Because of this level of SA, the individual is able to begin identifying information about changes to the environment that might be important or relevant.
- The second level of SA includes the combination and interpretation of fundamental information. The difference between the first and second level can be the difference between reading words and comprehending the text. At this level, information about the environment is more actively and systematically used for decision-making and problem-solving than at the first level. Here is where we begin to see the expansion from the individual to the firm, since the firm must internalize the individual's insights for immediate use.
- At the highest level of SA, the individual (and by extension, the firm) is able to forecast future events based on information from current events. It is this third level of SA that plays the most important role in innovation for the supply network. The firm's ability to forecast and plan future events may allow it to anticipate possible market trends and offer its customers products that are aligned with these trends.

Supply network innovation changes the roles and responsibilities of not only the firm, but also the individuals within the firm, primarily due to the specialized knowledge of individuals and the fairly limited view of the value stream that the individual has in a supply network. One key to network effectiveness is the ability to use tacit knowledge, or intuition and 'subjective insights' (Nonaka 1991) to understand and expand explicit, or articulated, knowledge, and to transfer this newly created knowledge to others who can understand it and who have the strategic experience to make use of it. Spender (1996) decomposes explicit and tacit knowledge into the following four classifications: conscious knowledge (facts, figures and frameworks that can be stored and retrieved); automatic knowledge (theoretical and practical knowledge that people possess due to their unique skills); objectified knowledge (distributed knowledge that can be placed into a common framework, thus expanding the use of facts and figures by the relationships between these facts and figures); and collective knowledge (knowledge that is fundamentally embedded in the organization's practices and which is sustained by interactions). In the context of a network, a key distinction between the four types is the ability to be captured and/or transferred.

Innovation and knowledge flows in supply networks

One oft-cited advantage of IT when it is used to support collaboration is that it enhances information sharing (Gunasekaran and Ngai 2004, McDermott 2000, Scott 2000), quickly and at a low cost (Mukhopadhyay, Kekre and Kalathur 1995). Walmart, for example, shares point-of-sale information with its suppliers, directly transmitting orders electronically. Motorola combines product life cycle models and component reuse strategies to project demand for critical components in its mobile phones and shares this with suppliers to reduce out of stocks. Increased network performance is often achieved through closer customer–supplier relationships that emerge as a result of more intensive information sharing (Subramani 2004).

When information is translated into knowledge and shared, IT can play a critical role, especially during the early stages of the innovation cycle (Orlikowski 1992). Articulating tacit knowledge is one of the goals of knowledge management in the firm and the network. Here we seek to capture automatic knowledge of the individual and reflect it as conscious knowledge for use by the firm and then transfer this through meaningful exchanges into objectified knowledge for use at the network level (Petrick and Maitland 2007). Two other major goals include creating a knowledge-oriented culture by encouraging knowledge seeking and sharing and contextualizing existing knowledge and building a network of connections among individuals (Alavi and Leidner 2001).

Networks with frequent and well-established knowledge exchanges between firms tolerate higher specialization within the network and promote innovation in participating firms (Narula 2004). Knowledge management at the supply network level therefore is a foundation for collaboration and innovation in the network. It may be used to make knowledge that resides within the network visible and articulated, as well as foster collaboration to contextualize knowledge.

While the benefits of IT in information sharing have been well documented, its role in sharing of knowledge is still contested. This is due in part to the fact that the development and interpretation of tacit and explicit knowledge rely on the context in which it is being used (Siesfeld 1998). Knowledge loses value if it cannot be transferred to another context. However, many widely used IT applications are not context-aware. These systems do not foster proactive collaboration and contextualization of knowledge or building a network of knowledge sharing between individuals and, instead, often reinforce existing patterns of documenting and information sharing.

In our observations, workers, particularly at the FFE, frequently modified and adapted various technologies to support their work; the modifications were often beyond the scope of the technology's intent. Hence, information technologies that successfully supported one group's activities could not always be reused by other groups or even the same group over time. More importantly, technologies used to capture and transfer new ideas and concepts were limited in their ability to capture and express critical tacit knowledge (Ayoub and Petrick 2008). This limitation is particularly challenging when sharing and transferring concepts with individuals and groups outside the group that generated them – a critical need in supply network innovation.

Finally, existing IT systems often require formal yet close relationships between their adopters, for example, between customers and suppliers (Kim, Cavusgil and Calantone 2005). The formality of relationships refers to common technologies, data structures and practices that are used throughout the supply network. Establishment of such common technologies requires close links between firms in the network in order for the firms to reach agreement on these standards (Smith and Weil 2005), and may often require large-scale investments to harmonize IT systems (Gunasekaran and Ngai 2004).

In a nationwide study of coordination in manufacturing supply networks that we conducted in 2006–8 (Petrick, Maitland and Pogrebnyakov 2007, Petrick *et al.* 2008), 23 per cent of the 175 respondents reported formal inter-firm coordination on IT issues. These respondents indicated that IT coordination enhanced their position in the supply network (42 per cent), and some also noted that they were able to keep other companies from entering their supply network because of their IT coordination practices (12 per cent).

Yet software compatibility as an information transfer issue remains a problem. In a 2005 survey, more than 570 computer-aided design software engineers and managers reported 42 different formats for CAD files received from customers (Wong 2006). And even within different locations of a firm, software incompatibility remains a challenge: Airbus traces delays in its A380 product development and delivery to incompatible software, where two of its key installations were using Catia V4 (versus V5), thus causing configuration management issues with the electrical system.

The promise of Enterprise 2.0 for supply network collaboration and innovation

Emerging participatory distributed technologies and approaches, often referred to as Web 2.0 (O'Reilly 2005), may overcome some drawbacks of the more traditional approaches to IT use in collaboration. These Web 2.0

technologies include blogs, wikis and online shared documents, as well as instant-messaging software, and in the context of supply network collaboration we refer to them as Enterprise 2.0 (McAfee 2006). Participants in Enterprise 2.0 knowledge creation and sharing do not have to be identified *a priori*, but rather self-identify based on common interest or other individual motivation. Because of this, the IT solution more closely resembles the social network and community aspects of individual collaboration.

A particularly prominent feature of these technologies lies in their ability to capture not only knowledge, which is done by many existing specialized knowledge management systems (McDermott 2000), but also the actual processes in which the knowledge was used and the output of these processes (McAfee 2006). In other words, it allows more contextualized knowledge to be captured, something existing knowledge management systems fail to deliver.

Furthermore, by capturing knowledge in a less formal manner, Enterprise 2.0 technologies allow innovation to spontaneously emerge at any point in the supply network and quickly disseminate to other points throughout the network where it may be considered relevant (Swan, Newell and Robertson 1999). Individuals and firms in the network will benefit because of the lower need to create formal links with other firms to tap into the knowledge and innovation potential of the network (Ahuja 2000). This outcome is similar to what professional associations offer to their members. They effectively recreate the so-called 'small-world' effect (Watts and Strogatz 1998), or a community where the levels of knowledge are high, the variation in knowledge is substantial and knowledge diffuses quickly (Cowan and Jonard 2004). This increases the rate of innovation diffusion. Additionally, knowledge can be more easily reused over time and across different contexts. In fact, Enterprise 2.0 is predicated on the notion of the network as a complex adaptive system.

A very good example of Enterprise 2.0 and its role in supply network formation and operations is PM Gear, a start-up manufacturing and merchandizing company, completely organized around the internet, that provides high-end ski equipment and related apparel. The company's management and operations is coordinated virtually through the web, and is the result of online social networking types of interactions that bring need together with opportunity. The company grew out of an online community referred to as the Powder Maggots, a group of ski enthusiasts associated with powdermag.com message boards.

Enterprise 2.0 also offers technical advantages over existing IT systems. Typically implementation of IT systems across organizations, as discussed above, requires agreement on standards and close links between companies (Gunasekaran and Ngai 2004). By contrast, many Enterprise 2.0 technologies rely on a thin client, such as a web browser, and established standardized web services. This alleviates the technical challenge of IT implementation across the network (Gunasekaran and Ngai 2004, Nambisan and Wilemon 2000, McAfee 2006), while fostering seamless knowledge exchange within the firm and between firms (Swan *et al.* 1999).

We see Enterprise 2.0 technologies as the next level of technological sophistication in firms, which nevertheless decreases the level of formality required in some earlier technologies, thus offering more potential for collaboration. Technologies used to support collaboration have progressively allowed for more complex types of interaction (Danese 2006), from very basic information sharing tools such as faxes to more rich and at the same time more formal electronic data interchange to knowledge management systems and technologies to support collaboration. This decreased level of formality may lead to increased adoption at the individual, firm and network levels.

Conclusion

Throughout this chapter we have emphasized important distinctions in the way that innovation occurs within a supply network as compared to within a single organization. Two factors combine to challenge the ability of a network to effectively innovate. First, as a complex adaptive system, the supply network is evolving over time in response to its environment while simultaneously influencing its environment. Because of this, individuals within the network who are closest to the environment are more likely to be aware of relevant changes. Second, with increased fragmentation and specialization within the supply network, the knowledge that any one firm or individual possesses is inadequate to independently drive the process of idea creation through to product launch. This creates interdependencies between firms and the individuals within them that traditional IT systems either ignore or serve only marginally. As Enterprise 2.0 expands knowledge sharing, we believe that the environment for networked innovation will be improved. We note, however, that this will not come without a cost. The potential for leakage of intellectual property beyond the network may be increased, and certainly organizational and IT security policies will need to be adapted to these new realities.

References

Ahuja, G. 2000 'Collaboration networks, structural holes, and innovation: A longitudinal study', *Administrative Science Quarterly*, 45(3): 42–55.
Alavi, M. and Leidner, D.E. 2001 'Knowledge management and knowledge management systems: Conceptual foundations and research issues', *MIS Quarterly*, 25(1): 107–36.
Ayoub, P.J. AND Petrick, I.J. 2008 'From industrial to knowledge work: Five challenges in strategic fit for supporting creativity and innovation at the fuzzy front end', Paper

presented at 9th International Symposium on Human Factors in Organizational Design and Management, Guarujá, Brazil, 19–21 March.

Barratt, M. 2004 'Understanding the meaning of collaboration in the supply chain', *Supply Chain Management*, 9(1): 30–42.

Brown, W.B. and Karagozoglu, N. 1989 'A systems model of technological innovation', *IEEE Transactions on Engineering Management*, 36(1): 11–16.

Choi, T.Y., Dooley, K.J. and Rungtusanatham, M. 2001 'Supply networks and complex adaptive systems: Control versus emergence', *Journal of Operations Management*, 19(3): 351–66.

Cowan, R. and Jonard, N. 2004 'Network structure and the diffusion of knowledge', *Journal of Economic Dynamics and Control*, 28(8): 1557–75.

Danese, P. 2006 'Collaboration forms, information and communication technologies, and coordination mechanisms in CPFR', *International Journal of Production Research*, 44(16): 3207–26.

Dyer, J.H. and Nobeoka, K. 2000 'Creating and managing a high-performance knowledge-sharing network: The Toyota case', *Strategic Management Journal*, 21(3): 345–67.

Endsley, M.R. 2000 'Theoretical underpinnings of situation awareness: A critical review', in M.R. Endsley and D.J. Garland (eds), *Situation Awareness Analysis and Measurement*, Mahwah, NJ: Lawrence Erlbaum Associates.

Fiala, P. 2005 'Information sharing in supply chains', *Omega*, 33(,): 419–23.

Gunasekaran, A. and Ngai, E.W.T. 2004 'Information systems in supply chain integration and management', *European Journal of Operational Research*, 159(2): 269–95.

Holweg, M., Disney, S., Holmström, J. and Småros, J. 2005 'Supply chain collaboration: Making sense of the strategy continuum', *European Management Journal*, 23(2): 170–81.

Kim, D., Cavusgil, S.T. and Calantone, R.J. 2005 'The role of information technology in supply-chain relationships: Does partner criticality matter?', *Journal of Business and Industrial Marketing*, 20(4/5): 169–78.

Langfield-Smith, K. and Greenwood, M.R. 1998 'Developing co-operative buyer–supplier relationships: A case study of Toyota', *Journal of Management Studies*, 35(3): 331–53.

McAfee, A.P. 2006 'Enterprise 2.0: The dawn of emergent collaboration', *MIT Sloan Management Review*, 47(3): 21–8.

McDermott, R. 2000 'Why information technology inspired but cannot deliver knowledge management', in E. Lesser, M.A. Fontaine and J.A. Slusher (eds), *Knowledge and Communities*, Woburn, MA: Butterworth-Heinemann: 21–36.

Montoya-Weiss, M.M. and O'Driscoll, T.M. 2000 'From experience: Applying performance support technology in the fuzzy front end', *Journal of Product Innovation Management*, 17(2): 143–61.

Mukhopadhyay, T., Kekre, S. and Kalathur, S. 1995 'Business value of information technology: A study of electronic data interchange', *MIS Quarterly*, 19(2): 137–56.

Nambisan, S. and Wilemon, D. 2000 'Software development and new product development: Potentials for cross-domain knowledge sharing', *IEEE Transactions on Engineering Management*, 47(2): 211–20.

Narayanan, V.K. 2001 *Managing Technology and Innovation for Competitive Advantage*, Upper Saddle River, NJ: Prentice-Hall.

Narula, R. 2004 'R&D collaboration by SMEs: New opportunities and limitations in the face of globalisation', *Technovation*, 24(2): 153–61.

Nonaka, I. 1991 'The knowledge creating company', *Harvard Business Review*, 69(6): 96–104.

O'Reilly, T. 2005 'What is Web 2.0', accessed 15 March 2008, <http://oreillynet.com/pub/a/oreilly/tim/news/2005/09/30/what-is-web-20.html>

Orlikowski, W.J. 1992 'The duality of technology: Rethinking the concept of technology in organizations', *Organization Science*, 3, (3): 398–427.

Petrick, I.J. 2007a Personal participation in the 'Future Forum', an innovation summit hosted by Proctor & Gamble and Boeing, 2–4 October.

Petrick, I.J. 2007b 'Tipping the balance of power: The case of large scale systems integrators and their supply chains', *International Journal of Foresight and Innovation Policy*, 3(3): 240–55.

Petrick, I.J. and Maitland, C.F. 2007 'Economies of speed: A conceptual framework to describe network effectiveness', in GI Susman (ed.), *Small and Medium-Sized Enterprises and the Global Economy*, Cheltenham, Glos.: Edward Elgar.

Petrick, I.J., Maitland, C.F. and Pogrebnyakov, N. 2007 *Effective Supply Network Practices: Final Report to Manufacturing Extension Partnership Program, National Institute of Standards and Technology, United States Department of Commerce*. University Park, PA: Pennsylvania State University.

Petrick, I.J., Maitland, C.F., Pogrebnyakov, N. and Ayoub, P.J. 2008 *Pennsylvania Plastics Manufacturing Industry – Profile and Supply Chain Coordination Practices: Final Report to Pennsylvania Workforce Development*, University Park, PA: Pennsylvania State University.

Reid, S.E. and de Brentani, U. 2004 'The fuzzy front end of new product development for discontinuous innovations: A theoretical model', *Journal of Product Innovation Management*, 21(3): 170–84.

Sahin, F. and Robinson, E.P. 2005 'Information sharing and coordination in make-to-order supply chains', *Journal of Operations Management*, 23(6): 579–98.

Samaddar, S., Nargundkar, S. and Daley, M. 2006 'Inter-organizational information sharing: The role of supply network configuration and partner goal congruence', *European Journal of Operations Research*, 174(2): 744–65.

Schumpeter, J.A. 1942 *Capitalism, Socialism and Democracy*, New York: Harper & Row.

Scott, J.E. 2000 'Facilitating interorganizational learning with information technology', *Journal of Management Information Systems*, 17(2): 81–113.

Siesfeld, G.A. 1998 'The measurement of knowledge', in D. Neef, G.A. Siesfeld and J. Cefola (eds), *The Economic Impact of Knowledge*, Woburn, MA: Butterworth-Heinemann: 189–202.

Skjoett-Larsen, T., Thernøe, C. and Andresen, C. 2003 'Supply chain collaboration: Theoretical perspectives and empirical evidence', *International Journal of Physical Distribution and Logistics Management*, 33(6): 531–49.

Smith, M.H. and Weil, D. 2005 'Ratcheting up: Linked technology adoption in supply chains', *Industrial Relations*, 44(3): 490–508.

Spender, J.-C. 1996 'Making knowledge the basis of a dynamic theory of the firm', *Strategic Management Journal*, 17(2): 45–62.

Sternberg, R.J. 2003 *Wisdom, Intelligence and Creativity Synthesized,* New York: Cambridge University Press.

Subramani, M. 2004 'How do suppliers benefit from information technology use in supply chain relationships?', *MIS Quarterly*, 28(1): 45–73.

Swan, J., Newell, S. and Robertson, M. 1999 'Central agencies in the diffusion and design of technology: A comparison of the UK and Sweden', *Organization Studies*, 20(6): 905–31.

Swan, J., Newell, S., Scarbrough, H. and Hislop, D. 1999 'Knowledge management and innovation: Networks and networking', *Journal of Knowledge Management*, 3(4): 262–75.

Utterback, J.M. 1971 'The process of technological innovation within the firm', *The Academy of Management Journal*, 14(1): 75–88.

Watts, D.J. and Strogatz, S.H. 1998 'Collective dynamics of "small-world" networks', *Nature*, 393(6684): 440–2.

Weber, A. 2008 'Medical Plastic Trends', accessed 15 March 2008, <http://www.assemblymag.com/Articles/Web_Exclusive/BNP_GUID_9-5-2006_A_100000000000 00226273>

Winsor, J. 2006 *Spark: Be More Innovative Through Co-Creation*, Chicago, IL: Deaborn Trade Publishing.

Wong, K. 2006 'Small manufacturers, big file-exchange issues', accessed 15 March 2008, <http://manufacturing.cadalyst.com/manufacturing/article/articleDetail.jsp?id= 326841>

2
The Role of Knowledge Sharing in a Supply Chain

Pierre Hadaya and Luc Cassivi

Introduction

To improve their performance and respond to market pressures such as international competitiveness, outsourcing and harder to please customers, manufacturing firms are now being forced to develop closer relationships with their suppliers and customers (Corbett, Blackburn and Van Wassenhove 1999, Kotabe, Martin and Domoto 2003). These new inter-organizational structures have resulted in the emergence of tightly coupled networks, also called supply chains, within many sectors (Andersen and Christensen, 2005).

A supply chain encompasses the following three functions: (1) the supply of materials to a manufacturer; (2) the manufacturing process; and (3) the distribution of finished goods through a network of distributors and retailers to a final customer (Canadian Supply Chain Sector Council 2008). At the operational level, a supply chain supports three types of flows: financial flows, material flows and information flows (Akkermans *et al.* 2003). These flows require careful planning, collaboration and close coordination between the partners as well as the efficient use of IT by the members of the network to support those fluxes. Managing financial flows within a supply chain is quite straightforward as norms and standards exist to support these fluxes. Managing material flows within a network, notably through logistics management to reduce the high costs associated with inventories and transportation, is also quite straightforward as firms can usually quickly identify what they buy from their suppliers and what they sell to their customers. Managing information flows within a supply chain is, however, much more complex due to the vast array of information being exchanged (Mentzer, Min and Zacharia 2000). Even though some pertinent information flows are tied to both monetary and material flows, it becomes difficult for member firms to manage these fluxes without having a framework to help them capitalize on the numerous information exchanges. Indeed, the communication of critical and proprietary information between partners (Monczka *et al.* 1998) must be undistorted and up to date throughout the supply chain in order to be useful (Cassivi 2006, Towill 1997) and become source of competitive advantage (Li *et al*. 2005).

Properly managing information, material and financial flows between members of a network is of critical importance, as these fluxes can become knowledge that can be used to optimize supply chain relationships. Indeed, some authors argue that if the information is contextualized so that partners know how to react to the information they receive, then supply chain knowledge is exchanged between partners (Ke and Wei 2007). However, in order to do so, firms have to express their objectives, requirements and understanding of the relationship to their partners in order to optimize future supply chain operations. In short, firms must extend their intra-enterprise processes to their supply chain partners in order to form inter-enterprise processes. For example, when a firm receives a sales forecast from one of its supply chain partners, to fully understand the short- and long-term impact of these numbers on their business, this forecast must be contextualized using complementary information (such as inventory level and plant capacity) and be part of a 'framework' that translates into discussion/decision-making communications between the partners. The exchanged forecast, as well as the contextual information tied to it, can then become a fully documented process with the necessary requirements. As Ke and Wei (2007: 297) put it: 'Knowledge sharing allows trading partners to orchestrate the operation of supply chain and capture positions of advantage. Yet, lack of knowledge sharing has been consistently found to be the most critical failure factor in supply chain management.'

Knowledge sharing in a supply chain thus allows partners in the chain to integrate their knowledge to identify opportunities in the market and develop a potential competitive advantage (Gavirneni *et al*. 1999, Sambamurthy *et al*. 2003). It is also a critical factor in supply chain management (Elmuti 2002, Welker, van der Vaart and van Donk 2008), as it plays an important part in the orchestration of various supply chain activities such as joint business plans and demand forecasts (Welker, van der Vaart and van Donk 2008). Despite its importance, the literature on the subject is scarce and mainly limited to uncovering whether or not knowledge should be shared in the supply chain and if so how member firms should manage a sharing relationship. For instance, Levinson and Asahi (1995) focus on the knowledge sharing and knowledge management processes, while Gerard and Marshall (2000) attempt to uncover the impact and benefits of knowledge sharing. Unfortunately, to date, the literature on the subject does not provide much information on how knowledge should be shared between supply chain partners (Welker, van der Vaart and van Donk 2008).

To partially address this gap in the field, this study attempts to expand our understanding of the role of knowledge sharing in a supply chain. More specifically, by integrating the literature from supply chain management, information systems and knowledge management, the objective of this research is to measure the influence of *knowledge sharing* on *interorganizational information systems (IOISs) use*, supply chain *process innovations* and *firm output performance*. The path model proposed in this study also posits that IOISs use positively affects process innovation and firm output performance, while process innovation positively affects firm output performance. This model is tested on data collected concerning two sets of relationships (upstream and downstream) within the supply network of a large Canadian OEM (system integrator) in the telecommunications equipment industry.

In the context of this research, *knowledge sharing* comprises actions executed by supply chain partners in order to contextualize the information they share between each other throughout the relationship. IOISs use captures the extent to which inter-organizational information systems are used to support a set of inter-firm coordination processes. IOISs are computer networks that support information exchanges across organizational boundaries (Choudhury 1997) and enable the electronic integration of business transactions and processes carried out by two or more organizations. Electronic data interchange (EDI) is probably the most commonly used technology allowing the exchange of information between business partners. However, in today's digital economy, more and more firms are turning to web-based approaches to support their inter-organizational activities (Elgarah *et al.* 2005). Process innovation captures the extent to which inter-organizational processes have been improved or created to better support supply chain relationships. Finally, firm output performance captures the firm's ability to improve the number of on-time deliveries, customer satisfaction and product quality.

The next section presents the research model and hypotheses. It is followed by a description of the supply network investigated and an explanation of the research methodology. Next, the research results are presented and discussed. The chapter concludes with the research limitations, and the prospects for future research.

Research model and hypotheses

The research model comprises the following seven variables (three for upstream relationships, three for downstream relationships and one for both upstream and downstream relationships): knowledge sharing with suppliers/customers; IOISs use with suppliers/customers; supply chain process innovation with suppliers/customers; and firm output performance (see Figure 2.1).

The six research hypotheses concerning the relationships between these seven variables are presented below. Each of these hypotheses takes into account both upstream (with suppliers) and downstream (with customers) supply chain relationships.

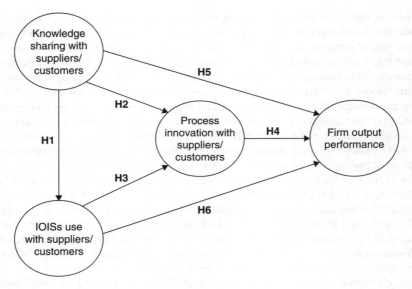

Figure 2.1   Research model

Knowledge sharing and IOISs use

As previously defined, knowledge can be shared when the information exchanged between supply chain partners is contextualized so that partners know how to react to the information they receive. This better understanding of the information exchanged should, in turn, entice supply chain members to increase their use of IOISs to better orchestrate the network. The positive relationship between knowledge exchange and IOISs use has already been implied by Dyer and Nobeoka (2000) in their case study on Toyota's network and is congruent with the numerous studies that have argued that information and communication technology (ICT) can be used to generate information and facilitate information sharing between supply chain members (Barua *et al.* 2004. Byrne and Heavey 2006, Cachon and Fisher 2000, Chae, Yen and Sheu 2005, Saeed, Malhotra and Grover 2005, Srinivasan, Kekre and Mukhopadhyay 1994, Ward and Zhou 2006).

The arguments provided above lead to the first hypothesis:

> Hypothesis 1:   Knowledge sharing activities will positively influence IOISs use.

Knowledge sharing and process innovation

Knowledge sharing involves the preparation and development of information to be shared and discussed with supply chain partners (Welker, van der Vaart and van Donk 2008). As such, knowledge sharing may force firms involved in these networks to modify and innovate in the way they do business (Mason-Jones and Towill, 1999). One way to innovate in such environments is to create or improve the processes supporting the relationships (Subramani, 2004). Indeed, knowledge sharing and information sharing between supply chain members transform the way business activities are conducted since business processes are no longer simply viewed as a means to integrate corporate functions within the firm but also used to structure the activities between members of a network (Croxton *et al.* 2001, Lambert, García-Dastugue and Croxton 2005).

These arguments are the basis of the second hypothesis:

> Hypothesis 2: Knowledge sharing will positively influence process innovation.

IOISs use and process innovation

The adoption and use of IT in a supply chain often translates into the elaboration of new or revised inter-organizational processes (Auramo Kauremaa and Tanskanen 2005, Bhatt 2001, Cagliano, Caniato and Spina 2003, Riggins and Mukhopadhyay 1994). Indeed, some authors have demonstrated that IOISs adopters can succeed in their implementation and/or achieve above normal performance improvements only if the assimilation of the technology initiates inter-firm process re-engineering (Lee and Clark 1996, Lee, Clark and Tam 1999, Power and Simon 2004). These arguments lead to the third hypothesis:

> Hypothesis 3: IOISs use will positively influence process innovation.

Process innovation and firm output performance

A process innovation is a new or significantly improved process (method) that may require changes in equipment and personnel, sometimes resulting from the use or availability of new knowledge (OECD/Eurostat 1997). Numerous researchers have demonstrated that a process innovation in a supply chain context, through the reform of inter-organizational processes, can significantly improve member firms' output performance. For example, Sahay, Gupta and Mohan (2006) have demonstrated how Indian organizations, through improvements of inter-organizational processes with their supply chain partners, have significantly improved their number of on-time deliveries. Other authors have also demonstrated how process enhancements with their supply chain partners have allowed firms to improve customer satisfaction (Zokaei and Simons 2006) and product quality (Sehgal, Sahay and Goyal 2006). The arguments provided above lead to the fourth hypothesis:

> Hypothesis 4: Process innovation will positively influence firm output performance.

Knowledge sharing and firm output performance

Despite the fact that some authors have demonstrated through model simulation that seamless knowledge sharing between partners does not result into better performance (Raghunathan 2001, Sohn and Lim 2008), there seems to be a general consensus in the literature that better information and knowledge sharing can have a positive impact on firm output performance. For example, Cai *et al.* (2006) and Spekman, Kamauff and Myhr (1998) have respectively shown that information sharing contributes positively to on-time delivery and customer satisfaction. Sasson and Douglas (2006), Liu and Tsai (2007) and Sila, Ebrahimpour and Birkholz (2006) have also respectively demonstrated that knowledge sharing can improve on-time delivery, customer satisfaction and product quality. These arguments lead to the fifth hypothesis:

Hypothesis 5: Knowledge sharing will positively influence firm output performance.

IOISs use and firm output performance

In the field of diffusion and assimilation of information technology innovations, researchers have demonstrated the significant relationship between technology use and firm performance (McAfee 2002, Simatupang and Sridharan 2005). Some authors have also proven that there is a significant relationship between IOISs use and firm operational performance measures. For example, Iyer, Germain and Frankwick (2004) have demonstrated that that the use of IOISs, can significantly improve on-time deliveries. Lefebvre *et al.* (2005) also demonstrated that business-to-business e-commerce can positively impact on-time deliveries and customer service, while Wang, Tai and Wei (2006) have shown that virtual integration with supply chain partners can improve a firm's product quality. These arguments lead to the sixth and final hypothesis:

Hypothesis 6: IOISs use will positively influence firm output performance.

Methodological issues

Units of analysis and supply network selected

To date, most studies on inter-organizational relationships have validated their conceptual models by gathering data on manufacture (OEM)–distributor, manufacturer–customer or manufacturer–supplier relationships within a particular sector or group of sectors (e.g. Cannon and Perreault 1999, Ganesan 1994, Janda, Murray and Burton 2002). In an attempt to extend the results obtained in the field, this study's model is tested on data collected from two sets of relationships within the supply network of a large Canadian

OEM (system integrator) in the telecommunications equipment industry: (1) the relationships between the first-tier suppliers (mostly assemblers) of the supply network and the second-tier suppliers of the network (mainly sub-assemblers); and (2) the relationships between those same first-tier suppliers and their customers (mainly OEMs). The decision to choose those two types of relationships as the units of analysis rests mainly on the fact that these relationships are key to the success of an effective supply network since, as Lee, Padmanabhan and Whang's (1997) bullwhip effect illustrates, demand volatility increases the further upstream a firm is in the supply chain because information distortion is amplified.

Population and data collection

As a first step, the research constructs were developed or adapted based on a literature review in the fields of operations, information systems and buyer–seller relationships and a set of interviews conducted with supply chain managers from first-tier and second-tier suppliers in the selected supply chain network. The complete instrument was then validated by members of the OEM's Supply Management, Supplier Collaboration and eSourcing groups, as well as three of the OEM's strategic first-tier suppliers. Some minor adjustments were then made to the questionnaire, based on their remarks and suggestions. Finally, the survey instrument was distributed via e-mail to supply chain managers at 130 first-tier suppliers (76 per cent in the United States, 12 per cent in Canada and 12 per cent in the rest of the world) identified by the OEM. The request to answer the electronic questionnaire was sent out twice over a two-month period. A total of 53 companies participated in the web survey, for a 40.8 per cent response rate. This high response rate can be explained by the fact that the request to answer the questionnaire was sent directly by the OEM, since one of the main objectives of this joint research initiative between the OEM and academia was to improve the OEM's supply chain.

Research variables

The survey instrument comprised seven latent variables (knowledge sharing with suppliers/customers, IOISs use with suppliers/customers, process innovation with suppliers/customers, firm output performance). Table 2.1 presents the operationalization of the research constructs.

For the first two constructs, knowledge sharing with suppliers/customers, five items were derived from the set of actions included in the first two steps of the CPFR methodology (VICS 1998). CPFR is a method created by the Voluntary Interindustry Commerce Standards Association (VICS) to facilitate collaboration between supply chain partners. The items selected were those that could contextualize information sharing and could serve in the orchestration of the supply chain relationship.

Visits to the OEM's and three suppliers' manufacturing sites enabled us to identify how IOISs were used to share knowledge between supply chain

Table 2.1 Constructs, items and sources

Constructs (number of items)	Items description	Items abbreviation	Sources
Knowledge sharing with suppliers/customers (5 items)	*Do you develop and share the following knowledge with your suppliers/customers?* – An agreed-upon partnership strategy – Periodic business goals and objectives – Roles, objectives, goals for specific categories of items – Individual plans based on previous shared information between partners – Business plans and a joint business plan	KS1s/KS1c KS2s/KS2c KS3s/KS3c KS4s/KS4c KS5s/KS5c	VICS-CPFR (1998)
IOIS use with suppliers/customers (6 items)	*When dealing with your suppliers/customers, do you use inter-organizational information systems to support the following activities?* – Procurement – Replenishment – Shortages – Delivery and tracking – Forecasting – Capacity planning	IOIS1s/IOIS1c IOIS2s/IOIS2c IOIS3s/IOIS3c IOIS4s/IOIS4c IOIS5s/IOIS5c IOIS6s/IOIS6c	Field research observations
Process innovation with suppliers/customers (3 items)	*To what extent has your relationship with suppliers/customers led you to:* – Gear processes to customer requirements? – Improve logistic processes? – Design new production processes?	PI1s/PI1c PI2s/PI2c PI3s/PI3c	Hawkins and Verhoest (2002)
Firm output performance (3 items)	*To what extent has your relationships with your supply chain partners led you to improve:* – Number of on-time deliveries? – Customer satisfaction? – Product quality?	OP1 OP2 OP3	Beamon (1999), Shin, Collier and Wilson (2000)

partners. Overall, IOISs were used to support five supply chain activities: procurement/sales, replenishment, shortages, delivery and tracking, forecasting, and capacity planning. As such, each of the next two constructs, IOISs use with suppliers/customers, comprised those five items.

Process innovation with suppliers/customers was operationalized with three items. The first two are tied to two critical activities in the telecommunication equipment supply chain, namely production and logistics (Hawkins and Verhoest 2002), whereas the third relates to the partners' ability to gear processes to customer requirements.

Finally, the three items used to capture firm output performance were adapted from Beamon (1999) and Shin, Collier and Wilson (2000): on-time deliveries, customer satisfaction and product quality.

Analytical procedure

In order to reach our research objective, structural equation modelling was used to test our model on both the supplier and customer perspectives. This validation process required four steps: (1) assessing the unidimensionality and convergent validity of the constructs; (2) assessing the internal consistency of the constructs; (3) assessing the discriminant validity between the constructs; and (4) assessing the relationship between the research constructs with the structural model.

Model estimation and results

Unidimensionality, convergent validity, internal consistency and discriminant validity

Unidimensionality refers to the existence of one latent trait or construct underlying a set of indicators and convergent validity examines the magnitude of the correlation between item measures of a construct (Gerbing and Anderson 1988). For both models (i.e. the supplier and customer perspectives), we assessed unidimensionality and convergent validity of each dimension at the mono-method level of analysis since the sample size was small (Venkatraman 1989). Table 2.2 summarizes the results of assessments for unidimensionality for the seven latent variables of the research model. It provides the four model statistics for the assessment of goodness-of fit: the chi-square statistic, its associated degrees of freedom, the p-level of significance and the Bentler and Bonett index. Based on the findings, one can conclude that each of variables of the model achieves unidimensionality and convergent validity at the mono-method level of analysis (Venkatraman 1989). Table 2.2 also shows that standardized CFA loadings for all scale items are above or very close to the recommended threshold of 0.707 (Hair *et al.* 1998, Segars 1997). This also provides evidence of convergent validity.

Table 2.2 Unidimensionality, convergent validity and internal consistency

	Supplier perspective					
	Knowledge sharing with suppliers		IOIS use with suppliers		Process innovation with suppliers	
	Items	Loadings[1]	Items	Loadings	Items	Loadings
	KS1s	0.748	IOIS1s	0.723	PI1s	0.822
	KS2s	0.910	IOIS2s	0.840	PI2s	0.725
	KS3s	0.821	IOIS3s	0.822	PI3s	0.654
	KS4s	0.823	IOIS4s	0.837		
	KS5s	0.893	IOIS5s	0.681		
			IOIS6s	0.662		
χ^2	0.101		6.59		0.213	
df	3		7		1	
p-level	0.992		0.473		0.645	
Bentler-Bonett	1.00		0.952		0.992	
Cronbach's alpha	0.912		0.883		0.761	
Internal consistency	0.923		0.893		0.779	
AVE	0.707		0.584		0.543	

	Customer perspective				Process innovation with customers		Both perspectives	
	Knowledge sharing with customers		IOIS use with customers				Firm output performance	
	Items	Loadings	Items	Loadings	Items	Loadings	Items	Loadings
	KS1s	0.689	IOIS1s	0.737	PI1s	1.00	OP1	1.00
	KS2s	0.778	IOIS2s	0.824	PI2s	0.659	OP2	0.837
	KS3s	0.740	IOIS3s	0.752	PI3s	0.691	OP3	0.703
	KS4s	0.625	IOIS4s	0.823				
	KS5s	0.836	IOIS5s	0.750				
			IOIS6s	0.722				
χ^2	1.932		5.988		0.049		0.234	
df	3		7		1		1	
p-level	0.587		0.541		0.823		0.628	
Bentler-Bonett	0.984		0.954		0.998		0.996	
Cronbach's alpha	0.875		0.886		0.713		0.809	
Internal consistency	0.855		0.897		0.835		0.889	
AVE	0.543		0.591		0.637		0.732	

[1] All loadings are significant at p < .001.

The internal consistency of each dimension is assessed by computing the Cronbach's alpha, composite reliability and average variance extracted (AVE) (Hair *et al.* 1998). Table 2.2 also shows that all Cronbach's alpha and composite reliabilities exceed the 0.70 threshold (Nunnally 1978), while the AVE of each construct exceeds the variance attributable to its measurement error (i.e. 0.50) (Hair *et al.* 1998).

Discriminant validity is defined as the degree of uniqueness achieved from item measures in defining a latent construct (Gefen 2003). The constructs are distinct since the correlations between all pairs of variable were below the 0.8 threshold proposed by Venkatraman (1989) (see Table 2.3). To further assess discriminant validity, McKnight, Choudhury and Kacmar (2002) suggest using a constrained analysis method, which involves setting the correlations between each pair of variables at unity (1.0) and running the models again. Discriminant validity between a pair of constructs is established if the chi-square value of the unconstrained model is significantly lower than the chi-square value of the constrained model. Table 2.4 shows strong evidence of discriminant validity.

Structural model

The significance and strength of hypothesized effects in the structural model were analyzed using the EQS 6.1 for Windows program. Due to our small sample size, a path analysis model for directly observed variables was used to test the research hypotheses. This multivariate regression technique considers the model as a system of equations and estimates all the structural coefficients directly (Jöreskog and Sorbom 2001). Thus, each variable comprised in the structural models was equal to the mean of the construct's items. Figure 2.2 and Figure 2.3 summarize the results for the supplier and customer perspectives respectively.

Hypothesis 1 tested whether knowledge sharing positively influenced IOIS use. This hypothesis was confirmed. Results also show that knowledge sharing explains 59 per cent of the variance of IOIS use in the supplier perspective and only 9 per cent in the customer perspective. Hypotheses 2 and 3 tested whether knowledge sharing and IOIS use positively affected process innovation. H2 was confirmed but H3 only partly confirmed, as IOIS use positively affected process innovation only in the customer perspective. Results also show that knowledge sharing and IOIS use explain 52 per cent of the variance of process innovation in the supplier perspective and 36 per cent in the customer perspective. Hypotheses 4, 5 and 6 tested whether process innovation, knowledge sharing and IOIS use positively affected firm output performance. H4 was confirmed, while H5 and H6 were not supported. Results also show that process innovation, knowledge sharing and IOIS use explain 29 per cent of the variance of process innovation in the supplier perspective and 23 per cent in the customer perspective.

Table 2.3 Means, standard deviation and the Pearson correlation matrix

	Mean	Standard deviation	Pearson correlation matrix			
			Knowledge sharing	IOIS use	Process innovation	Firm output performance
Supplier perspective						
Knowledge sharing with suppliers	5.14	1.15	1.00			
IOIS use with suppliers	5.23	1.14	0.54****	1.00		
Process innovation with suppliers	5.36	1.00	0.52****	0.51****	1.00	
Firm output performance	5.30	0.86	0.31**	0.36**	0.48***	1.00
Customer perspective						
Knowledge sharing with customers	4.99	1.17	1.00			
IOIS use with customers	4.89	1.37	0.286**	1.00		
Process innovation with customers	5.32	1.03	0.532****	0.445***	1.00	
Firm output performance	5.30	0.86	0.181	0.149	0.507****	1.00

p = level of two-tailed significance based on a chi-square distribution.
*p < .10, **p < .05, ***p < .01, ****p < .001.

Table 2.4 Assessment of discriminant validity

Constructs	Supplier perspective			Customers perspective		
	Constrained model χ^2 (df)	Unconstrained model χ^2 (df)	$\Delta\chi^2$	Constrained model χ^2 (df)	Unconstrained model χ^2 (df)	$\Delta\chi^2$
Knowledge sharing						
IOIS use	113.06(40)	78.33(39)	34.73****	99.12(40)	55.48(39)	43.64****
Process innovation	41.67(19)	31.13(18)	10.54***	50.34(19)	35.51(18)	14.83****
Firm output performance	80.74(19)	31.93(18)	48.81****	45.95(19)	9.43(18)	36.52****
IOIS use						
Process innovation	61.83(26)	51.66(25)	10.17***	54.97(26)	42.96(25)	12.01****
Firm output performance	104.41(26)	48.10(25)	56.31****	75.46(25)	34.57(24)	40.89****
Process innovation						
Firm output performance	30.96(11)	10.33(10)	20.63****	24.93(10)	9.39(9)	15.54****

*p < .10, **p < .05, ***p < .01, ****p < .001.

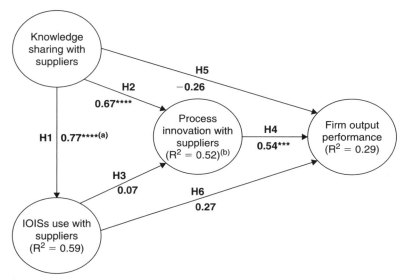

(a) Coefficients of estimation and level of significance, one-tailed t-test where *p < 0.05, **p < 0.01 and ***p < 0.001.

(b) R^2 values of dependent constructs.

Figure 2.2 Estimated model (supplier perspective)

Discussion of the results

This ultimate intent of this study was to improve our understanding of the role of knowledge sharing in a supply chain, make a theoretical contribution at the intersection of the fields of supply chain management and knowledge management, as well as improve managers' understanding of the critical role played by process innovations in supply chains.

In pursuing this objective, we found that knowledge sharing positively influences IOISs use in both perspectives (i.e. upstream and downstream). These results corroborate previous research findings that have argued that information technology can be used to facilitate information sharing between supply chain members (Barua *et al.* 2004, Byrne and Heavey 2006, Cachon and Fisher 2000, Chae, Yen and Sheu 2005, Saeed, Malhotra and Grover 2005, Srinivasan, Kekre and Mukhopadhyay 1994, Ward and Zhou 2006). These results also revealed that the percentage of variance explaining IOISs use is much higher in the upstream perspective than in the downstream perspective (59 per cent versus 9 per cent). These findings may be explained by the fact that firms are more willing to share knowledge and use IOISs with their suppliers than with their customers, as knowledge management activities and IT use are often dictated by the member in the relationship that has the most bargaining power.

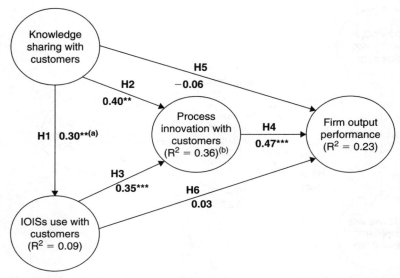

(a) Coefficients of estimation and level of significance, one-tailed t-test where $^*p < 0.05$, $^{**}p < 0.01$ and $^{***}p < 0.001$.

(b) R^2 values of dependent constructs.

Figure 2.3   Estimated model (customer perspective)

The path model proposed in this study also showed that knowledge shar-ing will encourage process innovation in both perspectives. These findings emphasize the importance of knowledge sharing and its role of orchestrating the supply chain at the very beginning of the relationship. As Croxton *et al.* (2001) and Lambert, García-Dastugue and Croxton (2005) have previously stated, business processes, through knowledge and information sharing, structure the activities between members of a network. Our results empirically confirm these arguments.

Results also show that that IOISs use positively influences process innova-tion only in the downstream perspective. The difference between these two perspectives may be explained by the fact that, again because of the power structure in the supply chain, firms generally use their own IOISs when deal-ing with their suppliers, whereas they are often forced to use their customers' IOISs when dealing with their downstream partners. By using their counter-part IOISs, firms are more likely to change their inter-organizational processes than if they were to use their own system.

Finally, data analyses revealed that in both perspectives, process innovation positively influences firm output performance whereas knowledge sharing and IOISs use do not. These very interesting findings seem to indicate that the performance improvements tied to the use of a technology or a work method are more likely to be the result of the process innovation that will ensue than the adoption per se of the innovation. These results corroborate previous research findings that have demonstrated that inter-firm process innovations, through re-engineering or process creation, can improve supply chain performance (Lee and Clark 1996, Power and Simon 2004). Our results, by demonstrating that process innovation is a catalyst to enhance supply chain performance, also complement previous findings in the literature that have demonstrated that knowledge sharing does not improve performance in the supply chain (Raghunathan 2001, Sohn and Lim 2008). We hope these findings will provide a baseline to continue studying knowledge sharing and process innovations in supply chain environments.

Limitations and future research avenues

There are three main limitations on this study. The first is that the research model was tested with data collected from a small sample, which evidently limits the scope and generalizability of our results. Nonetheless, this limitation is understandable as the information we gathered originated in relationships between members of a single supply network. Second, because of the sample size constraint, a path analysis model for directly observed variables was used to test the research hypotheses. This method for data analysis is less powerful than the structural equation modelling (SEM) technique. Finally, the supply chain relationships were investigated only from the first-tier supplier's perspective. Evidently, it would have been interesting to also investigate the points of view of the second-tier suppliers and the OEMs, but that would have been very difficult to do.

Numerous research avenues stem from this research initiative. Indeed, more research effort should be undertaken to better understand the critical role played by knowledge sharing and process innovation in supply chains. For example, investigating the impact of knowledge sharing and process innovation on other critical supply chain variables, including different types of performance measures (e.g. resources and flexibility) could lead to interesting findings. More research is also required to better understand how the characteristics of supply chain relationships can influence the characteristics of IOISs adopted to support those relationships.

References

Andersen, P.H. and Christensen, P.R. 2005 'Bridges over troubled water: Suppliers as connective nodes in global supply networks', *Journal of Business Research*, 58(9): 1261–73.
Akkermans, H.A., Bogerd, P., Yucesan, E. and Wassenhove, L.N. 2003 'The impact of ERP on supply chain management: Exploratory findings from a European Delphi study', *European Journal of Operational Research*, 146(2): 284–301.
Auramo, J., Kauremaa J. and Tanskanen, K. 2005 'Benefits of IT in supply chain management: An explorative study of progressive companies', *International Journal of Physical Distribution and Logistics Management*, 35(2): 82–100.

Barua, A., Konana, P., Whinston, A.B. and Yin, F. 2004 'An empirical investigation of net-enabled business value', *MIS Quarterly*, 28(4): 585–621.

Beamon, B.M. 1999 'Measuring supply chain performance', *International Journal of Operations and Production Management*, 19(3): 275–92.

Bhatt, G.D. 2001 'Business process improvement through electronic data interchange (EDI) systems: An empirical study', *International Journal of Supply Chain Management*, 6(2): 60–74.

Byrne, P.J. and Heavey, C. 2006 'The impact of information sharing and forecasting in capacitated industrial supply chains: A case study', *International Journal of Production Economics*, 103: 420–37.

Cachon, G.P. and Fisher, M. 2000 'Supply chain inventory management and the value of shared information', *Management Science*, 46: 1032–48.

Cagliano, R.F., Caniato, G. and Spina, G. 2003 'E-business strategy, how companies are shaping their supply chain through the Internet', *International Journal of Operations and Production Management*, 23(10): 1142–62.

Cai, S., Jun, M. and Yang, Z. 2006 'The impact of interorganizational internet communication on purchasing performance: A study of Chinese manufacturing firms', *Journal of Supply Chain Management*, 42(3): 16–30.

Canadian Supply Chain Sector Council, accessed February 2008, <http://www.supplychaincanada.org>

Cannon, J.P. and Perreault Jr, W.D. 1999 'Buyer–seller relationships in business markets', *Journal of Marketing Research*, 36(4): 439–60.

Cassivi, L. 2006 'Collaboration planning in an electronic supply chain', *International Journal of Supply Chain Management*, 11(3): 249–58.

Chae, B., Yen, H.R. and Sheu, C. 2005 'Information technology and supply chain collaboration: Moderating effects of existing relationships between partners', *IEEE Transactions on Engineering Management*, 52(4): 440–8.

Choudhury, V. 1997 'Strategic choices in the development of interorganizational information systems', *Information Systems Research*, 8(1): 1–24.

Corbett, C.J., Blackburn, J.D. and Van Wassenhove, L.N. 1999 'Partnerships to improve supply chains', *Sloan Management Review*, 40(4): 71–82.

Croxton, K.L., Garcia-Dastugue, S.J., Lambert, D.M. and Rogers, D.S. 2001 'The supply chain management processes', *International Journal of Logistics Management*, 12(2): 13–36.

Dyer, J.H. and Nobeoka, K. 2000 'Creating and managing a high-performance knowledge-sharing network: The Toyota case', *Strategic Management Journal*, 21(3): 345–67.

Elgarah, W., Falaleeva, N., Saunders, C.S., Ilie, V., Shim J.T. and Courtney, J.F. 2005 'Data exchange in interorganizational relationships review through multiple conceptual lenses', *The DATA BASE for Advances in Information Systems*, 36(1): 8–29.

Elmuti, D. 2002 'The perceived impact of supply chain management on organizational effectiveness', *Journal of Supply Chain Management*, 38(3): 49–57.

Ganesan, S. 1994 'Determinants of long-term orientation in buyer–seller relationships', *Journal of Marketing*, 58(2): 1–19.

Gavirmeni, S., Kapuscinski, R. and Tayur, S. 1999 'Value of information in capacitated supply chains', *Management Science*, 45(1): 16–24.

Gefen, D. 2003 'Assessing unidimensionality through LISREL: An explanation and example', *Communications of the Association for Information Systems*, 12: 23–47.

Gerard, P.C. and Marshall, F. 2000 'Supply chain inventory management and the value of shared information', *Management Science*, 46(8): 1032–48.

Gerbing, D.W. and Anderson, J.C. 1988 'An updated paradigm for scale development incorporating unidimensionality and its assessment', *Journal of Marketing Research*, 25(2): 186–92.

Hair, J.F., Anderson, R.E., Tatham, R.L. and Black, W.C. 1998 *Multivariate Data Analysis*, 5th edn, Prentice Hall, Upper Saddle River, NJ.

Hawkins, R. and Verhoest, P. 2002 'A transaction structure approach to assessing the dynamics and impacts of business-to-business electronic commerce', *Journal of Computer-Mediated Communication*, 7(3).

Iyer, K.N.S., Germain, R. and Frankwick, G.L. 2004 'Supply chain B2B e-commerce and time-based delivery performance', *International Journal of Physical Distribution and Logistics Management*, 34(7/8): 645–61.

Janda, S., Murray, J.B. and Burton, S. 2002 'Manufacturer–supplier relationships: An empirical test of a model of buyer outcomes', *Industrial Marketing Management*, 31(5): 411–20.

Jöreskog, K.G. and Sorbom, D. 2001 LISREL 8: *User's Reference Guide*. Lincolnwood, IL: Scientific Software Inc.

Ke, W. and Wei, K.K. 2007 'Factors affecting trading partners' knowledge sharing: Using the lens of transaction cost economics and socio-political theories', *Electronic Commerce Research and Applications*, 6: 297–308.

Kotabe, M., Martin, X. and Domoto, H. 2003 'Gaining from vertical partnerships: Knowledge transfer, relationship duration, and supplier performance improvement in the US and Japanese automotive industries', *Strategic Management Journal*, 24(4): 293–316.

Lambert, D.M. García-Dastugue, S.J. and Croxton, K.L. 2005 'An evaluation of process-oriented supply chain management frameworks', *Journal of Business Logistics*, 26(1): 25–51.

Lee, H.G. and Clark, T.H. 1996 'Market process reengineering through electronic market systems: Opportunities and challenges', *Journal of Management Information Systems*, 13(3): 113–37.

Lee, H.G., Clark, T.H. and Tam, K.Y. 1999 'Can EDI benefit adopters?', *Information Systems Research*, 10(2): 186–96.

Lee, H.L., Padmanabhan, V. and Whang, S. 1997 'Information distortion in a supply chain: The bullwhip effect', *Management Science*, 43(4): 546–58.

Lefebvre, L., Lefebvre, É., Elia, É. and Boeck, H. 2005 'Exploring B-to-B e-Commerce adoption trajectories in manufacturing SMEs', *Technovation*, 25(12): 1443–56.

Levinson, N.S. and Asahi, M. 1995 'Cross-national alliances and interorganizational learning', *Organizational Dynamics*, 24(2): 50–63.

Li, S., Subba Rao, S., Ragu-Nathan, T.S. and Ragu-Nathan, B. 2005 'Development and validation of a measurement instrument for studying supply chain management practices', *Journal of Operations Management*, 23(6): 618–41.

Liu, P.L. and Tsai, C.H. 'Effect of knowledge management systems on operating performance: An empirical study of hi-tech companies using the balanced scorecard approach', *International Journal of Management*, 24(4): 734–45.

Mason-Jones, R. and Towill, D.R. 1999 'Using the information decoupling point to improve supply chain performance', *International Journal of Logistics Management*, 10(2): 13–26.

McAfee, A. 2002 'The impact of enterprise information technology adoption on operational performance: An empirical investigation', *Production and Operations Management*, 11(1): 33–53.

McKnight, D.H., Choudhury, V. and Kacmar, C. 2002 'Developing and validating trust measures for e-Commerce: An integrative typology', *Information Systems Research*, 13(3): 334–61.
Mentzer, J.T., Min, S. and Zacharia, Z.G. 2000 'The nature of inter-firm partnering in supply chain management', *Journal of Retailing*, 76(4): 549–68.
Monczka, R.M., Petersen, K.J., Handfield, R.B. and Ragatz, G.L. 1998 'Success factors in strategic supplier alliances: The buying company perspective', *Decision Science*, 29(3): 5553–77.
Nunnally, J.C. 1978 *Psychometric Theory*, New York: McGraw-Hill.
OECD/Eurostat 1997 'The measurement of scientific and technological activities', proposed guidelines for collecting and interpreting technological innovation data, OSLO Manual, Paris.
Power, D. and Simon, A. 2004 'Adoption and diffusion in technology implementation: A supply chain study', *International Journal of Operations and Production Management*, 24(5/6): 566–81.
Raghunathan, S., 2001 'Information sharing in a supply chain: A note on its value when demand is nonstationary', *Management Science*, 47(4): 605–10.
Riggins, F.J. and Mukhopadhyay, T. 1994 'Interdependent benefits from interorganizational systems: Opportunities for business partner reengineering', *Journal of Management Information Systems*, 11(2): 37–57.
Saeed K.A., Malhotra, M.K. and Grover, V. 2005 'Examining the impact of interorganizational systems on process efficiency and sourcing leverage in buyer-supplier dyads', *Decision Sciences*, 36(3): 365–97.
Sahay, B.S., Gupta, J.N.D. and Mohan, R. 2006 'Managing supply chains for competitiveness: The Indian scenario', *International Journal of Supply Chain Management*, 11(1): 15–25.
Sambamurthy, V., Bharadwaj, A. and Grover, V. 2003 'Shaping agility through digital options: Reconceptualizing the role of information technology in contemporary firms', *MIS Quarterly*, 27(2): 237–263.
Sasson, J.R. and Douglas, I. 2006 'A conceptual integration of performance analysis, knowledge management, and technology: From concept to prototype', *Journal of Knowledge Management*, 10(6): 81–102.
Segars, A.H. 1997 'Assessing the unidimensionality of measurement: A paradigm and illustration within the context of information systems research', *Omega – The International Journal of Management Science*, 25(11): 107–21.
Sehgal, S., Sahay, B.S. and Goyal, S.K. 2006 'Reengineering the supply chain in a paint company', *International Journal of Productivity and Performance Management*, 55(8): 655–73.
Shin, H., Collier, D.A. and Wilson, D.D. 2000 'Supply management orientation and supplier/buyer performance', *Journal of Operations Management*, 18(3): 317–33.
Sila, I., Ebrahimpour, M. and Birkholz, C. 2006 'Quality in supply chains: An empirical analysis', *International Journal of Supply Chain Management*, 11(6): 491–520.
Simatupang, T.M. and Sridharan, R. 2005 'The collaboration index: A measure for supply chain collaboration', *International Journal of Physical Distribution and Logistics Management*, 35(1): 44–62.
Sohn S.Y. and Lim, M. 2008 'The effect of forecasting and information sharing in SCM for multi-generation products', *European Journal of Operational Research*, 186(1): 276–87.

Spekman, R.E., Kamauff Jr, J.W. and Myhr, N. 1998 'An empirical investigation into supply chain management: A perspective on partnerships', *International Journal of Supply Chain Management*, 3(2): 53–67.

Srinivasan, K., Kekre, S. and Mukhopadhyay, T. 1994 'Impact of electronic data interchange technology on JIT shipments', *Management Science*, 40(10): 1291–304.

Subramani, M. 2004 'How do suppliers benefit from information technology use in supply chain relationships?', *MIS Quarterly*, 28(1): 45–74.

Towill, D.R. 1997 'The seamless chain – the predator's strategic advantage', *International Journal of Technology Management*, 13(1): 37–56.

Venkatraman, N. 1989 'Strategic orientation of business enterprises: The construct dimensionality and measurement', *Management Science*, 35(8): 942–62.

VICS –(Voluntary Interindustry Commerce Standards Association) 1998 *Collaborative Planning, Forecasting and Replenishment Voluntary Guidelines*, Uniform Code Council.

Wang, E.T.G., Tai, J.C.F. and Wei, H.L. 2006 'A virtual integration theory of improved supply-chain performance', *Journal of Management Information Systems*, 23(2): 41–64.

Ward, P. and Zhou, H. 2006 'Impact of information technology integration and lean/just-in-time practices on lead-time performance', *Decision Sciences*, 37(2): 177–204.

Welker, G.A., van der Vaart, T. and van Donk, D.P. 2008 'The influence of business conditions on supply chain information sharing mechanisms: A study among supply chain links of SMEs', *International Journal of Production Economics*, 113(2): 706–720.

Zokaei, A.K. and Simons, D.W. 2006 'Value chain analysis in consumer focus improvement: A case study of the UK red meat industry', *International Journal of Logistics Management*, 17(2): 141–63.

3
A Conceptual Model of Knowledge Management for Strategic Technology Planning in the Value Chain

Carlos A. Suárez-Núñez, George E. Monahan and Bruce A. Vojak

Introduction

The development of the field of supply chain management (SCM) has led to the realization of significant, firm-level and industry-wide financial efficiencies, as inventory levels are managed through the application of a variety of knowledge management techniques to logistics management. Independently, the field of strategic technology planning (STP) has grown, addressing the longer-term needs of firms as they develop options for current investment and potential future return.

Our work over the past several years has led us to observe that, while on the surface, SCM and STP are quite different, some important similarities exist. As a result, we have considered how insights from each of these apparently distinct fields can be leveraged to the benefit of the other. While this book specifically addresses issues of knowledge management in the supply chain, we have chosen to address the corollary problem of knowledge management in the value chain, focusing on STP issues of long-term, strategic concern, rather than SCM issues of near-term, tactical concern. It is our expectation that, by introducing this analogy to knowledge management researchers and practitioners in SCM, additional contributions to both SCM and STP might be stimulated and enabled. Our specific goal for this chapter is to illustrate some of the similarities and differences between SCM and STP through the development, for the first time, of a detailed conceptual model of knowledge management for STP in the value chain.

Description of the problem

Knowledge management challenges of strategic technology planning in the value chain

The speed and accuracy with which a technology-based firm implements knowledge management techniques can mean the difference between that firm's success and failure (Spender and Grant 1996, Hitt, Ireland and Lee

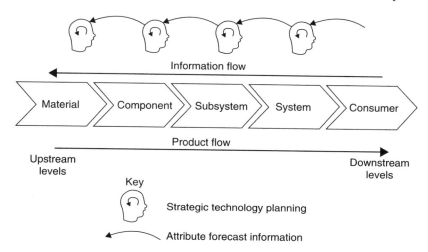

Figure 3.1   Information and product flows in the technology planning process
Sources: Vojak and Suárez-Núñez 2004; Vojak and Suárez 2004.

2000, Susman and Majchrzak 2003). As such, technology-based firms invest significant effort in such activities as marketing research (Churchill 1991, Kotler 2000, Davenport, Harris and Kohli 2001), competitor benchmarking (Porter 1980, 1985), technology forecasting (Cetron 1969, Bright and Schoeman 1973, Millett and Honton 1991, Porter *et al.* 1991, Martino 1993) and roadmapping (Willyard and McClees 1987, Groenveld 1997, Garcia and Bray 1998, Galvin 1998, Kappel 1998, Peet 1998, Phaal, Farrukh and Probert 2001, Kostoff and Schaller 2001, Schaller 2004). Nevertheless, firms regularly fail in these activities. Some technologies are developed but never commercialized and, conversely, other technologies are not ready when they are demanded in the marketplace. As a result, it is important for technology-based firms to identify failure mechanisms in these knowledge management processes and find ways to address them.

In our earlier work (Vojak and Suárez-Núñez 2004, Vojak and Suárez 2004), we described one such form of failure in the value chain, summarized in Figure 3.1, in which information flows upstream, while products flow downstream. In this figure, product attribute forecast information is shared between firms, while technology planning decisions are made within firms.

The knowledge management problems faced by upstream suppliers in their pursuit of product attribute forecast information are manifold, including that system-level suppliers typically are not entirely transparent regarding the details of their future needs, that inadvertent miscommunication occurs as information makes its way through the lower levels of the supply chain to

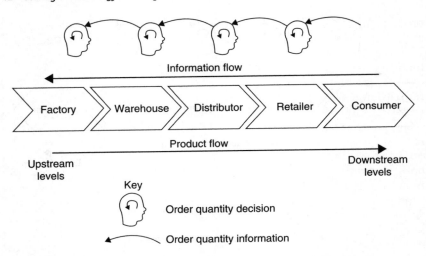

Figure 3.2   Information and product flows in supply chain management
Sources: Vojak and Suárez-Núñez 2004; Vojak and Suárez 2004.

these higher levels, and that downstream firms make incorrect translations (as part of their technology planning processes) of product attribute information that they receive from their customers into product attribute information that they pass on to their suppliers. A confounding problem is that the upstream suppliers typically have only intermittent contact with downstream customers regarding their demand for next generation, strategic product attributes.

As a result of these problems, upstream suppliers often either do not invest sufficiently in strategic technology development in support of attributes that are later required by downstream customers or do invest in strategic technology development in support of attributes that are never commercialized by downstream customers. All of this occurs because the upstream suppliers focus their technology planning efforts in response to the expressed needs of their downstream, system-level customer. To the extent that system-level firms accurately interpret market trends, upstream suppliers succeed. On the other hand, if system-level firms misread future market demand or miscommunicate that demand to their upstream suppliers, the upstream suppliers pay the price in the form of poor financial performance or, in the extreme, financial failure.

Analogy to supply chain management

Fortunately, an analogous problem already has been considered in the field of supply chain management, as shown schematically in Figure 3.2 (Mason-Jones and Towill 1997). As is commonly known within SCM, distortion of order quantity demand, known as the 'bullwhip effect' (Lee, Padmanabhan and Whang 1997a, 1997b), is often observed upstream in the supply chain. The bullwhip effect is believed to be the source of significant financial inefficiencies in the supply chain, empirically estimated, for example, to be of the magnitude of $30 billion in excess inventory in the grocery industry (Kurt Salmon Associates 1993) and to have $25 billion annual costs associated with supply chain inefficiencies in the apparel industry (Blackburn 1991).

Several similarities have been noted between the STP problem observed in the upstream environment, as described above, and order quantity bullwhip observed in SCM. These similarities include that: planning is involved in both (order quantity in SCM vs. technology in STP); inventory is managed in both (physical inventory in SCM vs. technology capability in STP); and variance or distortion of demand increases as one moves upstream (Vojak & Suarez-Nunez 2004; Vojak & Suarez 2004). Because of these similarities, we have referred to this technology planning problem as *product attribute bullwhip* (PAB). We do so because misunderstanding or miscommunication of attribute forecasts, or wrong decisions regarding technology plans or product attribute needs, along the value chain 'cracks the whip' on upstream technology developers.

The need for a conceptual model of knowledge management for strategic technology planning in the value chain

Having recognized the importance of information flow, and thus knowledge management, in the process of strategic technology planning in the value chain, we also recognize a key limitation of the current state of the art in this field. Although the literature is replete with examples of how technology planning knowledge management tools, such as technology roadmapping, are applied to both internal STP within a company (Willyard and McClees 1987, Barker and Smith 1995, Albright and Kapel 2003, McMillan 2003; Phaal *et al.* 2003, Grossman 2004) and external STP between suppliers and customers within an industry (Richey and Grinnell 2004, Phaal, Farrukh and Probert 2004, Schaller 2004), there is no generalized, conceptual discussion or model of how such activities occur.

The needs for a conceptual model are manifold. First, such a framework can be used by first-time industry practitioners who need to learn about, and have a global overview of, knowledge management in the STP process, and understand the issues that affect their firms and other participants' organizations. Second, a detailed conceptual model could be used by experienced practitioners to better understand the STP process and gain insights on how it might be optimized, for example, by seeking ways to reduce the PAB effect described above. Finally, such a model is critical in order to begin to consider how to analyze these issues in a quantitative manner, as has already been successfully accomplished in the SCM literature (Metters 1997, Xu, Dong and Evers 2001, Dejonckheere *et al.* 2004).

The specific goal of this chapter, then, is to develop a conceptual model of knowledge management for STP in the value chain. In the next section, we note some of the exceptions to the analogy to SCM. It is such exceptions that make the development of such a model both challenging and important, since, although providing great insight to the issues under consideration, existing SCM models cannot be readily applied to the problem at hand. We then present the results of our modelling effort. The final section provides our concluding comments.

Some exceptions to the analogy to supply chain management

As noted above, our understanding of knowledge management for STP has been aided by identifying similarities to analogous counterparts in SCM. However, as will be explained next, some important differences exist that must be understood before a detailed conceptual model can be developed.

Direction of the information flow

In our initial considerations of knowledge management in STP, we believed that the direction of the information flow in the STP process was similar to that observed in SCM, with information flow unidirectional and upstream, as described above. This unidirectional and upstream characteristic occurs in SCM because that is the nature of the distribution of finished goods. End-user market demand drives order quantities of finished goods transmitted in the supply chain and, thus, it works under a *market pull* scheme. However, this is not always the case in the technology planning process. A *technology push* scenario can also take place where one of the upstream-level firms in the value chain drives or pushes new technology developments downstream towards the end-user. Information can travel bidirectionally, increasing the complexity of knowledge management (Figure 3.3). In addition to information flowing either upstream or downstream, an intermediate firm or level may behave as the *dominant* firm or level in the value chain, one that drives technology developments more than others.

The nanotechnology industry provides an example of a technology push scenario. This industry is dominated by the prediction of new developments at the materials level. Downstream firms expect new materials with the potential to enable new components, subsystems and systems. To the extent that downstream firms adjust their strategic technology plans and forecasts in anticipation of nanotechnology industry forecasts becoming a reality – and to the extent that such forecasts are, or are not, realized – the potential for PAB exists.

Intel provides an example of a dominant firm at the subsystem level. Intel has been driving technology developments in the electronics industry for decades with smaller and faster integrated circuits. As a result, materials-level

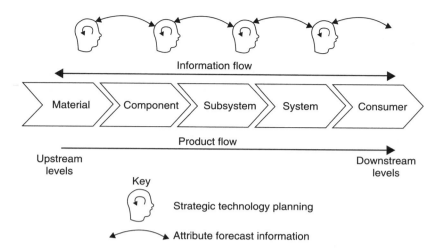

Figure 3.3   Bidirectional information flow in technology planning
Source: Vojak and Suárez 2004.

suppliers (for example, silicon wafer manufacturers) and systems-level suppliers (for example, computer manufacturers) respond to technology forecasts from Intel.

This potential for PAB in either direction represents a significant departure from the case found in SCM.

Interdependence between elements

Because SCM deals with the distribution of finished products, forecasts shared between different *supply chain* levels involve order quantities (number of units) demanded at each level. Although this number needs to be forecast with a level of uncertainty, it is related to a unique finished product that can be calculated in a straightforward manner and then easily transferred to the next level. However, this is not the case in the STP process in the *value chain* since the product attribute forecasts and information shared between value chain levels can be interrelated to each other and not simple to calculate.

In the typical process of transferring product attribute information, a system-level firm develops a forecast of the product attributes that they require from their suppliers at some future date. This information is then passed to the subsystem level. Next, the subsystem-level firm converts that forecast into their technology development projects. These, in turn, are converted into product attribute forecasts for products that they will need from their suppliers (Vojak and Suárez-Núñez 2004). This forecast is usually given

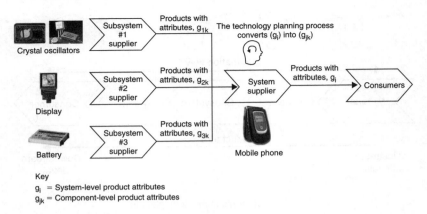

Figure 3.4   Example of interdependence between firms in the value chain

in the form of a technology roadmap and the process continues until it reaches the extreme upstream level of the value chain.

To illustrate how the interdependency between elements increases complexity, consider the example of Figure 3.4 for the development plans of a mobile phone handset. First, assume that end-users are interested in phones with a high operational reliability. The system-level supplier (phone manufacturer) converts this requirement into their technology development plans. These plans then are converted into forecasts for crystal oscillators (subsystem #1 supplier) with specific characteristics, for example, in temperature tolerance and frequency jitter, so that they can comply with the desired reliability. Although not depicted, the subsystem #1 supplier would then develop their own technology plans and request other characteristics from their suppliers. This example shows that the information shared in the STP process is not as simple in SCM and, more important, that the product attribute itself is not always unique; it can change from level to level (Vojak and Suárez-Núñez 2004).

To illustrate how product attribute inter-relationships can be even more complex, assume now that the end-user is interested in mobile phones that are smaller and have longer battery life. The system-level supplier (phone manufacturer) converts these requirements into their technology development plans. These plans then are used to create forecasts for the size and characteristics of the display (subsystem #2 supplier) and the battery (subsystem #3 supplier). Even though the attribute of size remains the same in the three firms involved, that is not the case with battery life. A longer battery life may translate for subsystem #2 into which display technology to choose (for example, liquid crystal versus light-emitting diode), since the amount of power needed to operate each technology is different. Similarly,

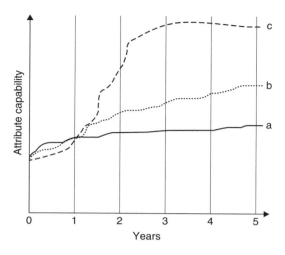

Figure 3.5   Possible forecast options

for subsystem #3, the technology used in the battery (for example, lithium-ion versus nickel-cadmium) is a key determinant of battery life. However, if battery size is decreased, battery life likely will decrease (Croce 2004). In addition, the size and type of technology used in the subsystem display affect the amount of power that it requires from the battery and thus influence battery life.

These examples illustrate the high level of interdependence between different elements of a finished product that need to be considered when forecasting product attributes and developing strategic technology plans in the value chain.

The strategic nature of technology planning

In SCM, the forecasts that are shared between levels are conveniently summarized in a single number, a *scalar*, which represents the order quantity for the upcoming time period. However, in STP there is a strategic component that must be considered. Instead of single, next time-period plans, STP involves developing forecasts, multiple, several years into the future, regarding where product attributes and technology capabilities are desired to be. These yearly forecasts are typically updated annually, creating a *vector* of product attribute forecasts, which can be represented in the form of a technology roadmap. The strategic nature and inherent uncertainty present in the STP process can be depicted by the roadmaps shown in Figure 3.5; each is created in year 0, each has forecast information for the next five years of a single attribute. Now, consider a firm that needs to make a technology investment decision on a certain technology utilizing one of these roadmaps. If a decision were made only by looking at the forecasts of year 1, the three roadmaps would not be different from each other from a decision-making point of view. However, it is evident that roadmap 'c' requires a larger investment since every attribute forecast is more aggressive than roadmaps 'a' and 'b'. In addition, the long-term goal of each roadmap in five years is different. Thus, when making a decision in the present, all five years in the forecast should be considered.

A conceptual model of knowledge management for strategic technology planning in the value chain

Model development methodology

The methodology used to develop the conceptual model presented herein was based on a review of the literature and input gathered in two sets of open-ended discussions with five industry experts in STP in the value chain. The experts had extensive experience in a variety of technology-based industries such as aerospace, automotive, communications, electronic components and systems, medical equipment, and manufacturing.

As noted, the literature includes many examples of applications of technology roadmapping in a single firm (Willyard and McClees 1987, Barker and Smith 1995, Albright and Kapel 2003, McMillan 2003, Phaal *et al.* 2003, Grossman 2004) and also cases where it extends from a single firm to include external suppliers and customers (Richey and Grinnell 2004, Phaal, Farrukh and Probert 2004, Schaller 2004). Based on a review of these examples, an initial, high-level conceptual model of the STP process was developed. Using this initial model, the first set of open discussions with industry experts was performed to obtain their feedback.

Building on these insights, the authors considered how the first, high-level conceptual model would have to be expanded in order to develop a more complete analytic model. Through this process, the detailed conceptual model presented in the coming section so titled was constructed. The external industry experts then were probed a second time in order to test the validity of the proposed detailed conceptual model and to obtain final feedback as to how else the model could be further developed, as discussed in the section following that.

High-level conceptual model

The first model was a high-level representation of the STP process between two firms in a value chain: a customer and its supplier (Figure 3.6). First, each firm creates its own roadmaps and technology plans using a wide range of sources of information, such as those identified in previous studies (Vojak and Suárez 2002, Vojak and Suárez-Núñez 2005, Vojak *et al.* 2005). Once the roadmaps are developed, both firms meet and exchange their perspectives and forecasts about the future. During this communication, the customer and the supplier may reach agreement, resulting in a mutually agreed roadmap.

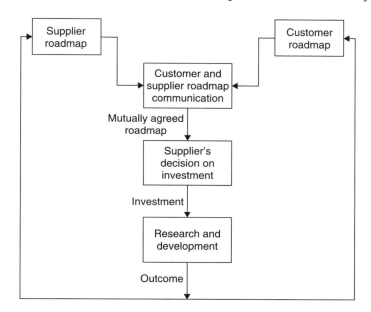

Figure 3.6 STP process using roadmaps between two firms

Based on this outcome, the supplier makes a decision regarding how much of its resources will be invested in achieving its technology plan in support of the customer's needs, at which point an investment is made towards relevant research and development (R&D) projects to fulfil the technology plan. After a certain period of time, normally one year, the outcomes of the R&D projects are realized and the supplier knows whether or not they are on target to reach the plan's long-term goal. At this point, the process is repeated, creating an iterative STP process using technology roadmaps.

Detailed conceptual model

While the model described above was limited to two firms, one objective of the second model was to develop a conceptual framework of the STP process in the value chain using three levels: a firm, its supplier and its customer. A conceptual framework that considers three levels (Figure 3.7) can be generalized to a value chain with n firm levels due to its symmetry. The purpose was to understand the interactions and constraints that a firm has to manage when it works towards fulfilling its customer's requirements and is dependent on the technology developments provided by its supplier.

The firm needs to align the inputs supplied to it with the outputs required by its customer (both of which are out of the firm's control) by making decisions about its expectations regarding its external relationships with its

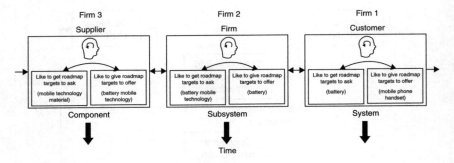

Figure 3.7 Value chain representation for conceptual framework

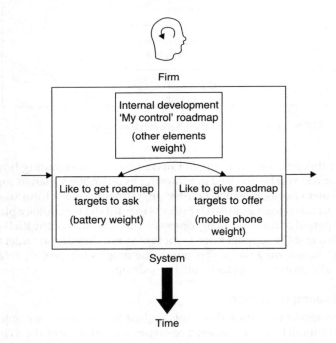

Figure 3.8 STP inside a firm

supplier and customer and about its own internal technology development (Figure 3.8). The firm's external planning with its supplier involves preparing a roadmap of target product attributes that it seeks to receive from its suppliers products ('Like to get' roadmap), while its external planning with its customer involves preparing a roadmap of target attributes that it seeks to provide in its products to its customers ('Like to give' roadmap).

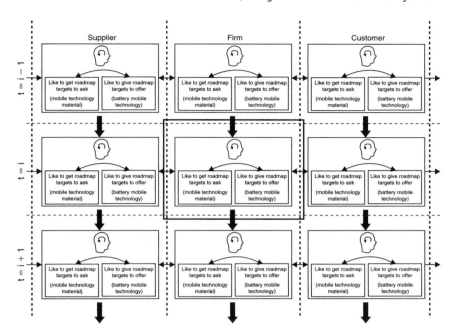

Figure 3.9   STP over time for three firms in the value chain

To illustrate the internal planning process, consider a system-level firm developing technology plans for a mobile phone handset. For simplicity, assume that there is only one supplier, the battery producer, and that the phone manufacturer controls the rest of the elements in the phone. As a result, if the firm is working on reducing the weight of the phone to satisfy customer requirements, it needs to manage the weight of the battery provided by its supplier and the weight of the other elements inside the phone by making appropriate investment decisions.

When the three firms and time are included in the model, the STP process in the value chain is as depicted in Figure 3.9. Here, the three firms are linked to their immediate neighbours with whom they interact. Also, over time, firms are linked to themselves by their own technology development outcomes.

It is important to mention that the linkages are not as simple as presented here. In reality, a firm interacts and exchanges information with many customers and suppliers at the same time. A firm can have different suppliers for one element or a single supplier for all of the elements. Thus, in practice, the STP process occurs in a complex network of firms, suppliers and customers. However, for ease of the analysis in this chapter, the models are developed assuming a single supplier and a single customer for each firm at every level.

As a result of these characteristics, and due to the symmetry in the representation observed in Figure 3.9, it is only necessary to examine the internal processes of one firm in order to develop the conceptual model of Figure 3.10. In this model, the firm gathers information about its internal technology capability as well as insights about its supplier and its customer. The firm then processes that information to develop technology roadmaps and gain technical and non-technical insights. This is performed in the 'Technology planning process "design process"' box. Afterwards, the firm negotiates with its customer and its supplier, separately, by communicating and exchanging plans in the form of technology roadmaps. The goal of this negotiation is to find ways to achieve a mutually agreed-upon roadmap about future developments. Next, the firm processes all the new information generated and obtained in the preceding steps and makes an investment decision about its technology developments. In this step, the firm also updates its technical and non-technical insights as well as the insights about its supplier and its customer, all used in the next time period. Following the investment decision, the R&D projects are executed for the rest of the time period. However, they may be influenced by external factors and physical limitations, which could affect their outcome. Finally, at the end of the time period, the outcome of the technology development is realized and a new technology capability is obtained, which is used as an input in the next time period and the whole cycle repeats itself.

A more detailed description of the main steps and elements contained in the conceptual framework is presented next.

Inputs, insights and sources of information

The first step in the conceptual framework is gathering all relevant inputs and information needed to execute the rest of the STP process in the value chain. However, distinctions were made between categories of information; hence the inputs were categorized in three groups, inputs about: the supplier, the customer and the firm itself.

Inputs about the supplier include expected technology to be provided, current technology capability and R&D projects, past history about the relationship with the firm, and performance on previous roadmaps. Inputs about the customer include expected requirements and preferences, current R&D projects (if any), past history with the firm and previous requested roadmaps and trends. Inputs about the firm include all the information necessary to determine the actual technology capability of the firm with the available resources.

Technology planning process box

The two technology planning process 'boxes' in the conceptual framework have similar characteristics and represent complex processes in themselves. The main activities inside each box are depicted in Figure 3.11. Existing

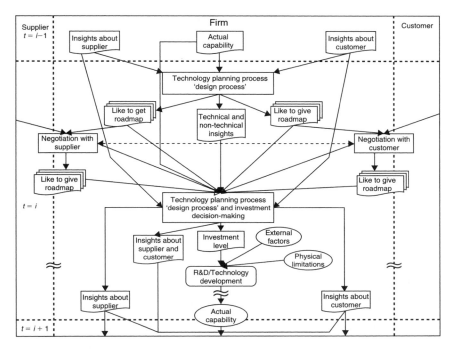

Figure 3.10   Conceptual model of STP

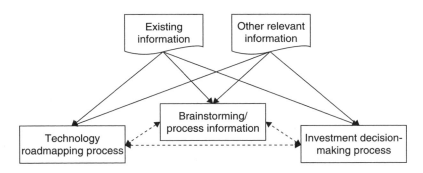

Figure 3.11   The technology planning process 'black box'

information, as described in the previous subsection, is utilized in addition to any other relevant supplemental information. Then a combination of the three sub-processes shown in the lower half of the figure is executed. For example, in the brainstorming process, both technical staff (such as

R&D engineers, technical visionaries and applications engineers) and non-technical staff (such as marketing and sales staff, non-technical visionaries and finance staff) gather and process information to generate an updated set of technical and non-technical insights. The main activity in the first technology planning 'box' is the technology roadmapping process, which generates roadmaps needed for subsequent negotiations with both customer and supplier.

Meanwhile, in the second, later technology planning 'box', besides the brainstorming process described above, the main activity is the investment decision-making process. Since the firm already has had its communication and exchange of information with the customer and supplier by this point, it has an idea of its supplier's current and future technology capabilities as well as its customer's current and future expectations. Therefore, the firm is in a position to evaluate the different technology investment alternatives and make a decision on the level of investment required to achieve its strategic technology development goals.

Negotiation processes

From the firm's perspective, two negotiation processes take place, one each with the customer and supplier. As one of the industry experts commented, the inner workings of these boxes is a highly complex process that can be seen as a 'black box', where many different activities occur but are hard to define explicitly. Nevertheless, an overview of this process is given next. When the firm meets with its customer or supplier, the first activity is the sharing of their technology roadmaps. This includes reviewing the status of the current technology capability of each participant and their product attribute forecasts for the following years. To the extent to that the firm's technology capability is dependent on the supplier's capability, updates or adjustments to their technology roadmaps may be needed. For example, a significant change of direction in what the supplier expects to provide the firm may result in a change to what the firm expects to provide to its customer. Likewise, a significant change of direction in the customer's requirements may affect what the firm expects to need from its suppliers. Since there can be considerable interdependence between the three firms involved, their future forecasts and technology roadmaps may need to be updated. Another issue to consider is negotiation order. The firm or level in the value chain that drives the technology developments has more power on how these negotiations are resolved and the order they take place. That is, the dominant firm or level determines whether this process follows a technology push or market pull scheme and, thus, the direction of any bullwhip that might occur. At the end of the negotiation process, a negotiated roadmap emerges and affects the investment-level decision taken in the next step of the process.

R&D and technology development

After making the investment-level decision, the technology development process starts. As shown in Figure 3.10, this process and its outcome may be affected by external factors outside the firm's control (for example government regulations, the emergence of disruptive technologies and competition) and unforeseen physical limits, previously thought to be feasible. Both can affect the outcome of the technology development projects and the new technology capability realized at the end of the period.

Other considerations to more fully develop the conceptual model

The feedback from industry experts about the conceptual model was positive and encouraging. All agreed that while the process in practice is highly complex, the framework provided a good model of the STP process. However, the experts noted other factors that come into play in a real-world setting that could be incorporated to obtain an even more complete framework. Some of these factors are listed below.

Interdependence of elements

The model could be expanded to two or more product attribute forecasts so that their tradeoffs are considered when making decisions. These elements could come from different suppliers not competing with one another, thus creating a complex network of firms.

Competition

More than one supplier, firm and customer competing with each other could be added. This will affect the negotiations and outcomes of the whole strategic technology planning process since new considerations would be taken regarding how the process is executed and decisions are made. Again, this would result in a complex network of firms.

Breakthrough technology

Radical innovations and new technologies coming from new or existing firms could be included to analyze their impact on the STP process. This would cause rapid and abrupt change in the customer requirements and roadmaps, and would complicate the negotiation process.

Other drivers of development

Forces other than dominant levels or firms, such as government regulations, could be analyzed as the drivers of the process. For example, a new environmental regulation, like engine emissions, is causing changes in the automotive industry and engine technologies.

Multilevel communication

The current model represents a nearest neighbour communication model. However, a multilevel communication model, where a supplier communicates directly with the customer or with the customer's customer, could bring more insights and completeness to the negotiation process.

Multi-industry applicability

Finally, it should be noted that the model described here is more relevant to industries that tend to be technology driven; it should be remembered that this research was entirely performed in technology-based industries. Therefore, special care should be taken when applying it to a different industry. A replication of this study to other industries could also be performed.

Conclusions

STP in the value chain shares many key features with order quantity planning in the supply chain, including such knowledge management issues as the communication of demand between multiple levels of a chain and the observation of 'bullwhip' as demand is distorted when one moves upstream in the chain.

Encouraged by the observation of these similarities, in this work we developed a new conceptual model of knowledge management for strategic technology planning in the supply chain. The needs for such a model are manifold, including its potential to guide first-time industry practitioners in their navigation of STP, challenge experienced industry practitioners in their optimization of STP and enable scholars to analyze STP in a quantitative manner, as has already been successfully accomplished in the SCM literature.

In developing this model, we first noted how, while similar, STP in the value chain and order quantity planning in the supply chain differ in some important respects. Next, with guidance from industry experts, we built off of both these similarities and differences to develop the detailed conceptual model. This model is symmetric relative to both level in the value chain and time. As a result of this symmetry, it can be applied to systems of any number of value chain levels and time periods. Moving beyond our present model, we note that additional refinements are possible, with the potential to open even more options of analysis.

In closing, since the level of process detail identified for STP in this work is considerably greater than that observed in SCM, which is characterized by relatively simple order quantity decisions, we expect that new avenues of value and supply chain research, and, thus, new insights, should become available as a result of the development of this model.

References

Albright, R.E. and Kappel, T.A. 2003 'Roadmapping in the corporation', *Research Technology Management*, 42(2): 31–40.

Barker, D. and Smith, D.J.H. 1995 'Technology foresight using roadmaps', *Long Range Planning*, 28(2): 21–8.

Blackburn, J.D. 1991 'The quick response movement in the apparel industry: A case study in time-compressing supply chains', in J.D. Blackburn (ed.), *Time-Based Competition: The Next Battleground in American Manufacturing*, Ch. 11, Homewood, IL: Irwin.

Bright, J.R. and Schoeman, M.E.F. (eds) 1973 *A Guide to Practical Technological Forecasting*, Englewood Cliffs, NJ: Prentice-Hall.

Cetron, M.J. 1969 *Technological Forecasting*, New York: Gordon and Breach.

Churchill Jr, G.A. 1991 *Marketing Research: Methodological Foundations*, Chicago: Dryden Press.

Croce, W. 2004 'Cell phones demand better battery life', *Wireless System Design Magazine*, July/August, accessed March 2008, <http://www.wsdmag.com/Articles/ArticleID/8629/8629.html>

Davenport, T.H., Harris, J.G. and Kohli, A.K. 2001 'How do they know their customers so well?', *MIT Sloan Management Review*, Winter edition: 63–73.

Dejonckheere, J., Disney, S.M., Lambrecht, M.R. and Towill, D.R. 2004 'The impact of information enrichment on the bullwhip effect in supply chains: A control engineering perspective', *European Journal of Operational Research*, 153(4): 727–50.

Galvin, R. 1998 'Science roadmaps', *Science*, 280: 803.

Garcia, M. and Bray, O. 1998 'Fundamentals of technology roadmapping', Sandia National Labs, Albuquerque, NM, SAND97-0665.

Groenveld, P. 1997 'Roadmapping integrates business and technology', *Research-Technology Management*, 40(5): 48–55.

Grossman, D.S. 2004 'Putting technology on the road', *Research Technology Management*, 47(2):pp 41–44.

Hitt, M.A., Ireland, R.D. and Lee, H. 2000 'Technological learning, knowledge management, firm growth and performance: An introductory essay', *Journal of Engineering and Technology Management*, 17(3–4): 231–46.

Kappel, T.A. 1998 'Technology roadmapping: An evaluation', PhD thesis, Northwestern University, Evanston, IL.

Kostoff, R.N. and Schaller, R.R. 2001 'Science and technology roadmaps', *IEEE Transactions on Engineering Management*, 48(2): 132–43.

Kotler, P. 2000 *Marketing Management*, Upper Saddle River, NJ: Prentice Hall.

Kurt Salmon Associates 1993 *Efficient Consumer Response: Enhancing Consumer Value in the Grocery Industry*, Atlanta, GA: Kurt Salmon Associates.

Lee, H.L., Padmanabhan, V. and Whang, S. 1997a 'Information distortion in a supply chain: The bullwhip effect', *Management Science*, 43(4): 546–58.

Lee, H.L. Padmanabhan, V. and Whang, S. 1997b 'The bullwhip effect in supply chains', *Sloan Management Review*, 38: 93–102.

Martino, J.P. 1993 *Technological Forecasting for Decision Making*, New York: McGraw-Hill.

Mason-Jones, R. and Towill, D.R. 1997 'Information enrichment: Designing the supply chain for competitive advantage', *Supply Chain Management*, 2(4): 137–48.

McMillan, A. 2003 'Roadmapping: Agent of change', *Research Technology Management*, 42(2): 40–7.

Metters, R. 1997 'Quantifying the bullwhip effect in supply chains', *Journal of Operations Management*, 15: 89–100.

Millett, S.M. and Honton, E.J. 1991 *A Manager's Guide to Technology Forecasting and Strategy Analysis Methods*, Columbus, OH: Battelle Press.

Peet, C.S. 1998 'Technology road mapping: A tool for the formulation of technology strategy', MSc thesis, University of Manchester Institute of Science and Technology, Manchester.

Phaal, R., Farrukh, C.J.P., Mitchell, R. and Probert, D.R. 2003 'Starting-up roadmapping fast', *Research Technology Management*, 36(2): 52–8.

Phaal, R., Farrukh, C.J.P. and Probert, D.R. 2001 'Characterization of technology roadmaps: Purpose and format', *Proceedings of the 2001 Portland International Conference on the Management of Engineering and Technology (PICMET)*.

Phaal, R., Farrukh, C.J.P. and Probert, D.R. 2004 'Collaborative technology roadmapping: Network development and research prioritization', *International Journal of Technology Intelligence and Planning*, 1(1):.pp 39–55

Porter, A.L., Roper, A.T., Mason, T.W., Rossini, F.A., Banks, J. and Wiederholt, B.J. 1991 *Forecasting and Management of Technology*, New York: John Wiley and Sons.

Porter, M.E. 1980 *Competitive Strategy*, New York: Free Press.

Porter, M.E. 1985 *Competitive Advantage*, New York: Free Press.

Richey, J.M. and Grinnell, M. 2004 'Evolution of roadmapping at Motorola', *Research Technology Management*, 47(2):pp 37–41.

Schaller, R. 2004 'Technological innovation in the semiconductor industry: A case study of the International Technology Roadmap for Semiconductors (ITRS)', PhD thesis, George Mason University, Fairfax, VA.

Spender, J.-C. and Grant, R.M. 1996 'Knowledge and the firm: Overview', *Strategic Management Journal*, 17, special issue: Knowledge and the Firm: 5–9.

Susman, G.I. and Majchrzak, A. 2003 'Research issues in knowledge management and virtual collaboration in new product development: An introductory essay', *Journal of Engineering and Technology Management*, 20(1–2): 1–5.

Vojak, B.A. and Suárez, C.A. 2002 'Sources of information used in new product and process technology planning within the electron device industry', *Proceedings of the 2002 IEEE International Engineering Management Conference*, 2: 623–8.

Vojak, B.A. and Suárez, C.A. 2004 'Technology planning "bullwhip" in the electronics industry supply chain', *Proceedings of the 2004 IEEE International Engineering Management Conference*, 3: 1190–4.

Vojak, B.A. and Suárez-Núñez, C.A. 2004 'Product attribute bullwhip in the technology planning process and a methodology to reduce it', *IEEE Transactions on Engineering Management*, 51(3): 288–99.

Vojak, B.A. and Suárez-Núñez, C.A. 2005 'Sources of information used in technology planning in the upstream environment of the electronics industry', *International Journal of Technology Intelligence and Planning*, 1(4): 441–55.

Vojak, B.A. and Suárez, C.A., Peters, L. and Sundararajan, M. 2005 'Sources of information used in technology planning within the nanotechnology industry', *Proceedings of the 2005 IEEE International Engineering Management Conference*, 1: 53–7.

Willyard, C.H. and McClees, C.W. 1987 'Motorola's technology roadmap process', *Research-Technology Management*, 30(5): 13–19.

Xu, K., Dong, Y. and Evers, P.T. 2001 'Towards better coordination of the supply chain', *Transportation Research Part E*, 37: 35–54.

4
Ontology Engineering for Knowledge Sharing in Supply Chains

Alexander Smirnov, Tatiana Levashova and Nikolay Shilov

Introduction

Networked organization structures have become common practice for companies to strengthen their competitive position. Examples of such networks include temporary project-based cooperations (e.g. in product design or system development projects), marketing organizations and industrial clusters sharing expensive resources. Such networks can take form of supply chains (SC) integrating enterprises based on their contribution to the value chain. SC are typically governed by common economical and value-creation objectives and proactively form cooperations for a given demand. These cooperations are geographically distributed, respond quickly and are flexible to market demands. The life cycle of SC, including a description of needs and services of the cycle phases, is presented in Figure 4.1 and Table 4.1.

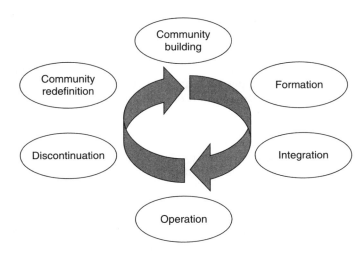

Figure 4.1   Life cycle of enterprise networks

Usually it is not fully obvious to the SC members, which competence and resources are available from which partner in which quantity to which expenses and how to access them. In this context, efficient support for configuration of cooperations and efficient reuse of existing knowledge is a critical success factor. Configuration includes selection of suitable partners based on their competences and integration of work processes and existing knowledge sources in order to ensure a common level of knowledge, understanding and commitment. Ontological modelling of knowledge representation provides a way to achieve this common level.

We propose to use ontologies as a basis for SC configuration. Ontologies are widely considered as a technique for representing knowledge in an application domain. They also have been successfully applied in modelling competences of enterprises. The approach presented here consists of four major elements: (1) capture all relevant characteristics of the overall application domain of SC with a domain ontology; (2) represent the competences of SC members with enterprise ontologies; (3) identify candidates for SC networks based on matching between enterprise ontologies and domain ontology; (4) configure the SC network by matching enterprise ontologies of the identified candidates. This chapter covers development methodologies for both, domain ontology and enterprise ontologies.

The second and third sections introduce the general framework of the approach and the application-driven methodology used. The fourth section describes the process of application ontology engineering in detail. The usage example of the created ontology is given in the fifth section. The sixth section summarizes findings and gives some conclusions.

Framework

The framework is based on an analysis of research in ontology area. The framework shares the idea of the referred research and proposals concerning interdependency of the application area and the knowledge domain. The methodology deals with the creation of ontologies of two types: an ontology describing knowledge of a certain domain (domain ontology) and an ontology describing what domain knowledge is required to achieve a task (application ontology) (Figure 4.2).

The architecture presented in Figure 4.2 includes three levels corresponding to different types of knowledge. The domain level describes domain knowledge; the task level represents task knowledge, it contains sets of tasks that are to be achieved and methods of achieving them; the application level provides knowledge that is a combination of knowledge of the previous two levels, depending on the task under consideration. Knowledge of all the levels is supposed to be described by means of common knowledge representation formalism.

Table 4.1 Characteristics of SC life cycle phases

Life cycle phase	Needs	Services
Community building	Community builder Common understanding (language, concepts, view) Common/shared objectives and goals Criteria for identification of potential members (location, competence, size, skill ...) Community rules (risk sharing, value sharing, membership) Work processes and roles during community building Community promotion	Modelling goals and objectives Identification, qualification, registration of members Common knowledge representation Competence modelling for community members Communication, coordination, collaboration methods Common infrastructure
Formation	Formation is initiated by a project Project definition model (goals/objectives, preliminary experience, requirements, expected results, logistics, business rules for risk sharing and value sharing) Project manager Partner selection	Tool for modelling project definition Tool for partner selection Match-making between member competence models based on project definition
Integration	Negotiating business agreements Exploiting existing systems and experiences Project execution modelling (work processes, teams, roles, management ...) Integration of existing systems Interoperable, scalable, secure solutions	Integration of partner systems Tool for project execution modelling Configuration management Change management

(Continued)

62

Table 4.1 Continued

Operation	Work management (dynamic resource assignment, reporting)	Tool for work management
	Feedback of experience to project execution modelling	
	Relationship management (customer, community, partners, conflict ...)	Relationship management support (e.g. views for different target groups)
	Performance measurement	Tools for performance measurement
Discontinuation	Disintegration of solutions	Reconfiguration of integrated systems
	Assessment of lessons learned, achieved results, created assets, performance ...	Evaluation tools, methods, measurement scales
	Application of business agreements from Integration phase	
Community redefinition	Application of rules from Community building phase	Same services as for community building
	Community manager	
	Re-evaluation of community criteria	

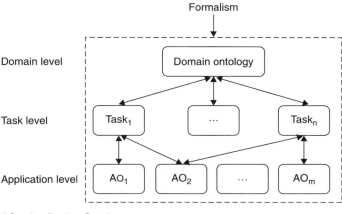

Figure 4.2   Multilevel framework architecture

Within the framework domain knowledge is described by a domain ontology. Task knowledge represents sets of tasks and methods formalized by means of the common formalism. Domain knowledge that is used in the task-achieving in conjunction with the task knowledge makes up an application ontology (AO). Every AO can represent knowledge involved in achieving one or more tasks.

Application-driven methodology

For the proposed methodology the formalism of object-oriented constraint networks is used as the common formalism for ontology representation. According to the formalism, ontology is described by sets of classes, class attributes, attribute domains and constraints. The set of constraints includes those describing attributes needed to belong to a class and the domains these fall into; those representing structural relations as hierarchical relationships 'part-of' and 'is-a', class compatibility and associative relationships; and those describing functional dependencies.

According to the framework the methodology allows for the development of a domain ontology and an application ontology. The methodology includes the stages of task analysis, domain ontology building, task formalization, mapping specification, checking sufficiency of the domain ontology, AO composition and AO consistency checking (Figure 4.3). These stages are described in detail below.

The starting point of the ontologies development is a task at hand. Based on an analysis of the task a domain ontology is created. Methodologies for

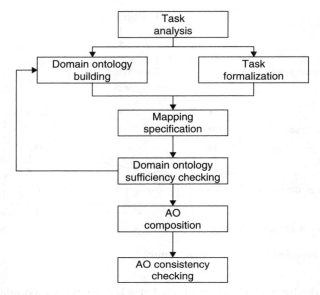

Figure 4.3 Methodology phases

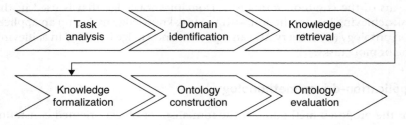

Figure 4.4 Domain ontology building

a domain ontology creation include following main phases: requirement specification, knowledge extraction, knowledge formalization and ontology evaluation. Within the proposed methodology the implementation of the phases is as follows (Figure 4.4). First, the domain of knowledge is to be identified; second, knowledge representing the domain in question is to be retrieved from knowledge sources (as many knowledge sources as possible should be found); third, the retrieved knowledge is to be represented by means of the common formalism; fourth, a domain ontology is to be constructed through the integration of the formalized knowledge; and, last, the resulting ontology is to be validated and evaluated.

Referring to the validation and evaluation phase, it has been decided that at the domain level the ontology is validated and checked for its sufficiency to the target task only, the ontology consistency is checked at the application level. This is for two reasons:

- there is a hypothesis, not proven yet, that a large ontology represented by means of the formalism of object-oriented constraint networks could be inconsistent on the whole because of a network of the constraints. Various constraints within the ontology could disagree. It is a problem similar to the problem described by the authors of Cyc ontology. Instead of trying to maintain some sort of global consistency Cyc maintains local consistency. This was made possible by introduction of contexts/microtheories. For the framework described above, AOs play the role of the contexts/microtheories;
- ontology evolution produces ontology changes – in the case of a large domain ontology, small changes make it necessary to check consistency of the whole ontology, which is a time-consuming process.

According to the above, AOs are checked for the consistency. If AO holds disagreeing constraints they are to be corrected within both ontologies: this AO and the domain ontology.

Besides the identification of knowledge sources describing the domain, knowledge sources holding knowledge about methods for task-achieving are to be identified, the provided knowledge is to be retrieved and formalized. Within the formalism tasks and methods are represented as ontology classes. The listed steps result in formalized task knowledge providing for a hierarchy of methods to achieve the task. Alternative methods are represented by different hierarchy branches. The phases of the domain knowledge identification and the task knowledge identification can be carried out simultaneously.

As the domain ontology has been built and the task knowledge has been formalized, the mapping between domain and task knowledge is specified. The methods' input and output parameters are mapped onto domain knowledge elements. By means of the accepted formalism, the attributes of task knowledge represent methods' parameters. Thereby, the mapping is indicated by associative relations between attributes of task knowledge and attributes (in some cases, classes) of the domain ontology.

If, for the given task, a branch of the methods hierarchy with mapping for all the parameters exists, the domain ontology is considered as sufficient for the task-achieving. The next step consists of AO composition for the task. If the domain ontology does not provide sufficient knowledge it means that the ontology should be refined and the process of ontology development is taken back to the knowledge retrieval phase.

The AO composition consists of forming slices of the domain ontology based on the mapping between domain and task knowledge. Domain knowledge that can serve as the method parameters is considered as relevant to the task. This relevant knowledge serves as basic knowledge or the 'seeds'

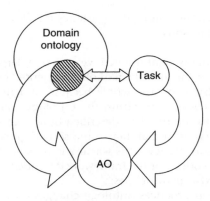

Figure 4.5   Application ontology constituents

for the slicing operation. The operation assembles knowledge related to the basic knowledge using an algorithm. The resulting slice and the hierarchy of methods used in the task-achieving are integrated into AO (Figure 4.5). The resulting AO is validated and checked for consistency.

The methodology allows for ontology modularization and consequently its reusability, since the resulting AO represents modular knowledge. Later on, this AO can be reused in different contexts.

As the application-driven methodology is proposed, the ontology development strategy cannot be restricted by the ontology itself. Accordingly, the methodology in the phases leading to ontology building includes a maintenance phase. The phase has to provide strict rules for ontology modification operations as update/insert/delete, merging/splitting of concepts, taking into account ontology evolution, allowing for propagation of changes and enabling ontology versioning. Ontology storage and access can be placed in this phase.

Development of supply chain management ontology

The section describes the application of the methodology to the supply chain management (SCM) area. The purpose of the methodology in this case lies in the building of a domain ontology for SCM and AO representing a task knowledge. It is illustrated through a number of pre-assembled stages.

Task analysis

The starting point for the development of the SCM ontology was work on the discovery of a list of tasks pertinent to the area of SCM. For the purpose of this chapter, the task of supply chain configuration has been chosen. Generally

Table 4.2 Supply chain management tasks

- Supply chain configuration
- Tasks on evaluation of supply chain
  performance attributes as reliability,
  responsiveness, flexibility, efficiency,
  response time, management cost, and so on
- Forecasting
- Planning
- Scheduling
- Logistics
- Supply chain decision-making

speaking, this task is a complex one including most of the other SCM tasks presented in Table 4.2.

Within the chapter the configuration task is assumed to be parameterized by sector and specialization as the input parameters, and time and cost as the output parameters. Sector describes an industry sector the supply chain belongs to; specialization indicates what kind of production the supply chain deals with, for example, mass production, mass customization, small branch production, piece production and so on. The parameters of time and cost are to return lead time of supply chain configuring and cost of the configuration respectively.

Task formalization

In part of the formalization, the configuration task is represented by the class 'Configuration', having a hierarchy of methods configuring the supply chain and evaluating it. The input and output task parameters and the methods' parameters (not presented in the scope of this chapter) are represented by classes' attributes, with domains specified by data types.

Domain ontology building

The domain ontology was built by an expert. The main principle for knowledge sources identification was the search for knowledge sources containing already developed and potentially reusable ontologies.

Reference could be made to a most clearly structured representation of the SCM domain UNSPCS taxonomy (UNSPSC 2001) (Table 4.3). But the taxonomy cannot be accepted as a fundamental ontology since it does not provide any characteristics or attributes for the taxonomy nodes and considers SCM from the logistics point of view only.

Another effort was made by the *MIT Process Handbook* project. The MIT business model includes three perspectives (Table 4.4) on how to manage supply chain.

Table 4.3   Supply chain management taxonomy in UNSPCS code

Research- and science-based services
  Manufacturing technologies
    Supply chain management
      Logistics
      Transit analysis
      Transport facilitation
      Transport finance or economics
      Transport infrastructure
      Transport planning

Table 4.4   Supply chain management views in the *MIT Process Handbook* (adapted)

Management
  Business management
    Business management views
      ...
      Typical business management
      ...
      Supply chain management
        SCOR model
        Stage model
        Systems approach

The top level of Supply Chain Operations Reference (SCOR) model is made up of five key activities: *plan, source, make, deliver* and *return.* Management activities mapped onto these key activities include management of business rules; capital assets; data collection and maintenance; equipment; facilities; information; inventories; network of suppliers and production; incoming and in-process products; performance of supply chain, production, access delivery and return processes; regulatory requirements and compliance; transportation; and warehouses.

The stage model considers SCM in a logical progression of development in logistics management and experiencing in four phases (Table 4.5). Every stage is characterized by a set of functions. The following stages include and extend the functions of the previous ones. SCM is considered as a set of interacting functions being managed in coordination to bring out the best overall performance. Functions like material flow functions of receiving raw material or subassemblies, manufacturing, distributing and delivering; information-processing and decision-making functions; funds-handling functions can be considered as a specialization of those top-level functions. In addition to the

Table 4.5 Multistage supply chain

Stage	Number of functions
1. Physical distribution stage Transportation Warehousing	2
2. Logistics stage Manufacturing Ordering Procurement	5
3. Integrated supply chain management stage Supplier Customer	7
4. 'Super' supply chain management Product development Marketing Customer service	10

top-level functions presented in Table 4.5, key SCM drivers are introduced. They are information, manufacturing and transportation.

The systems approach defines supply chain as a number of entities, interconnected for the primary purpose of supply of goods and services required by the end customer. It clearly postulates that SCM domain is described by two concepts: supply chain as a structural organization of business and management process. Depending on the way supply chain entities are organized SCM is related to different systems levels. These levels are identified as the internal supply chain, the dyadic relationship, the external supply chain and the inter-business network.

The MIT business model (2001) considers SCM as a business function. Main activities of SCM, according to this business model, are presented in Figure 4.6. Some of the activities are analyzed in depth. For instance, management of other external relationships consists of management of regulatory relationships, competitor relationships, societal relationships, environmental relationships and stakeholder relationships.

One more structured representation of the SCM domain considers SCM consisting of three main constituents (Table 4.6): supply chain structure (structure dimensions are given in parentheses), supply chain business processes and management components.

An examination of many other sources dealing with the SCM domain did not reveal any ontologies of the domain in question. The ontology building was based on a definition of SCM, the postulate that SCM consists of the supply chain and its components and management processes, the structures above and an analysis of concepts used in publications on SCM problems.

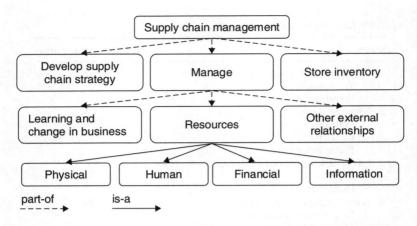

Figure 4.6 Activities of supply chain management in the *MIT Process Handbook*

Table 4.6 Framework of supply chain management

1. Supply chain structure (supply chain length, number of suppliers, number of customers)
    1.1 Pipeline
    1.2 Tree
2. Supply chain business processes
    2.1 Management
        2.1.1 Customer relationship
        2.1.2 Customer service
        2.1.3 Demand
        2.1.4 Manufacturing flow
    2.2 Product flow
    2.3 Order fulfillment
    2.4 Procurement
    2.5 Product development and commercialization
3. Management components
    3.1 Structure
    3.2 Management
        3.2.1 Work
        3.2.2 Organization
        3.2.3 Product flow facility
        3.2.4 Information flow facility
        3.2.5 Product
        3.2.6 Power and leadership
        3.2.7 Risk and reward
    3.3 Planning and control
    3.4 Management methods
    3.5 Culture and attitude

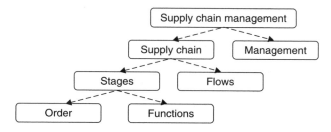

Figure 4.7 Supply chain management domain ontology: top-level classes view

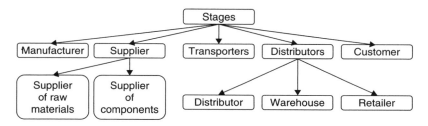

Figure 4.8 Supply chain stages: taxonomy

Summing up definitions of SCM, it can be defined as management of flows of products and services, finances and information between different stages of supply chain from a supplier to a consumer/customer and managing operational activities of procurement and material releasing, transportation, manufacturing, warehousing and distribution, inventory control and management, demand and supply planning, order processing, production planning and scheduling, and customer service across a supply chain.

The resulting SCM domain ontology is given in Figure 4.7. The figure presents the class hierarchy for the taxonomy level following the root. SCM concepts are constructed to cover various supply chain stages, functions, decisions and flows.

Taking into account the current tendency towards the creation of an integrated supply chain that is the integration of separate supply chain stages based on the communication flow between the intermediate stages as well as the alignment of the goals of the intermediate stages with overall supply chain objectives (IBM Business Solution 2002), supply chain is considered as running through different stages linked by material and information flows.

The supply chain *stages* are: supplier, manufacturer, transporters, distributors and customer (Figure 4.8). Later, every stage can be specialized and characterized by a set of attributes based on the developed ontologies representing these particular concepts. For instance, a description of supplier and manufacturer (SHOE 2000) can be found in SHOE ontology library.

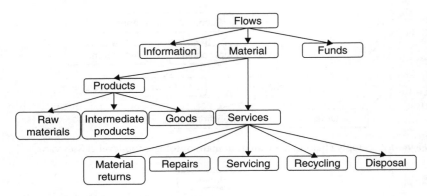

Figure 4.9   Supply chain flows: taxonomy

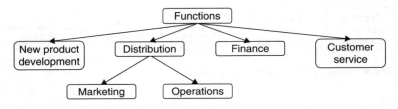

Figure 4.10   Supply chain functions: taxonomy

Supply chain activities include *flow* of information, materials and finances between different stages of a supply chain from suppliers to customer (Figure 4.9). *Information flow* includes capacity, promotion plans, delivery schedules, sales, orders, inventory, quality; *material flow* contains raw materials, intermediate products, finished goods, material returns, repairs, servicing, recycling, disposal; *finances flow* is made up of credits, consignment, payments. Detailed specializations for products and services can be found in various product ontologies and classification systems (e.g. UNSPSC 2001, NAICS 2002, UNSD 2004) and mapped onto the presented classification level of the material flow.

SCM is a mechanism to integrate supply chain functions taking place at the separate stages. Most of the *functions* (Figure 4.10) happen within various stages, some of them cross the boundaries among several stages. The functions operate on the supply chain flows.

Stages of the supply chain exchange the flows above through *orders*. *Orders* on *sale, replenishment, procurement, manufacturing, transportation,* or *customer order* can take place within every stage. An order within a certain stage is characterized by a set of properties pertinent to orders of this stage and the order cycle representing different states of the order. Basically, an order cycle is described by initialization, planning, execution and disposition phases. Every order cycle within its stage has its own triggering events.

Management concept refers to the coordination activities between supply chain components focusing on the planning and execution issues involved in managing the supply chain. These activities are represented as SCM tasks (Table 4.2). The main purpose of management is to make and distribute the right product at the right time to the right location at a minimum cost, while maintaining desired level of service. The set of the characteristics listed influences performance of the supply chain. Four key drivers of supply chain performance are facilities, inventory, transportation and information.

Application ontology for supply chain configuration

Since the supply chain configuration problem complex, this chapter only deals with a part of AO describing the task given. The phase of bridging the whole domain ontology and supply chain configuration is left out due to the great number of concepts, attributes and constraints of the domain ontology involved. The result of the bridging is partially illustrated within AO.

The aim is to find a feasible configuration with which the supply chain can achieve a high level of performance. Usually, there are two categories of configuration decisions: (1) structural decisions dealing with location, capacity and distribution channel and (2) coordination decisions focusing on supplier selection, partnership, inventory ownership, sharing information about sales, demand forecast, production plan and inventory.

Figure 4.11 focuses on the supplier selection task as a subtask of a logistics problem, which is a part of the supply chain configuration problem. As a characteristic influencing supply chain performance, supply chain cost is considered. In fact, many cost items make up the total costs of the product required by the customer and the supply chain cost, among them manufacturing costs and shipping costs. This means that the complete AO includes all domain ontology classes that have an influence on supply chain cost. To simplify, interrelations between the domain ontology and the set of supply chain configuration tasks are illustrated by the example of putting together an order for bill of materials (BOM). This task defines a set of materials and components that compose the product ordered by the customer.

The supplier selection task follows the BOM definition task and has the set defined as input parameters. The task also takes into account maximal cost of the product that the customer is ready to pay, if any. Within the limits of the considered example the supplier selection task and the domain ontology are interrelated by the following set of functional constraints:

[Supplier selection].[component (material)] = F ([BOM definition]. [component (material)])
[Supplier selection].[maximal cost] = F([Customer].[price])
[Supplier selection].[location] = F([Supplier].[address])

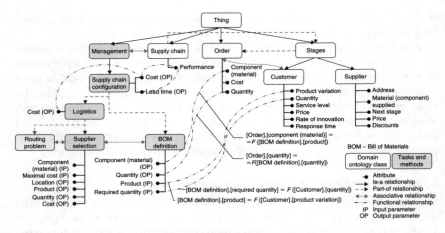

Figure 4.11   AO (slice) for supply chain configuration problem

[Supplier selection].[product] = F([Supplier].[material (component) supplied])
[Supplier selection].[quantity] = F_1([Supplier].[next stage]) ∪
$\qquad\qquad\qquad\qquad F_2$([Distributor].[availability])
[Supplier selection].[cost] = F_1([Supplier].[price]) ∪
$\qquad\qquad\qquad\qquad F_2$([Supplier].[discounts]) ∪...

Analogously, the supply chain performance depends on supply chain configuration cost combined with other influencing items:

[Supply chain].[performance] = F_1([Supply chain configuration].[cost]) ∪ F_2...

SCM focuses on understanding and improving the coordination of multiple firms that compose a supply chain. It is supposed that every firm is described by its ontology. In this connection the next issue addressed in this chapter is the question of integration of SCM ontology and SME ontologies.

Example of the ontology-based knowledge management platform usage

This section represents a simple but illustrative example of usage of the knowledge management platform (KMP) based on the developed ontology. One of the possible scenarios of using the KMP knowledge content component is presented in Figure 4.12. In accordance with this scenario, the user (a representative of an assembly plant) is trying to find a possible build-to-order (BTO) supplier of an engine.

At the first step, the user logs into the KMP and finds the engine required. This can be done by two ways: using an external link or finding the required class/instance in the KMP manually (e.g. using the search function).

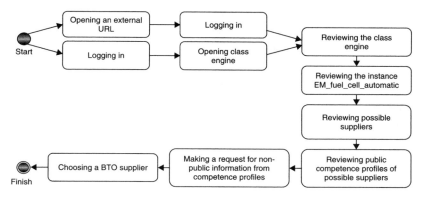

Figure 4.12 UML diagram of a sample KMP usage scenario

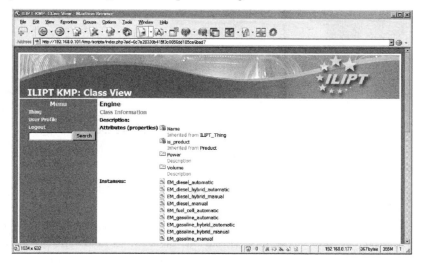

Figure 4.13 An example of the screen of the KMP: engine

After reviewing the class (Figure 4.13), the user can proceed to its instances by clicking their names (hyperlinks). For example, the user might want to check the *EM_fuel_cell_automatic* (Figure 4.14) and related documents (e.g. specifications).

Then, the user can open the instance *Plant_Magdeburg_Module_Assembly* of the class *plant* (Figure 4.15), since it is related to the *EM_fuel_cell_automatic* by the relationship *produced_by*. To get additional information the competence profile of the company should be open (Figure 4.16). For security reasons the 'online' competence profile contains only public (for SC members) information. To get additional information, the user sends a request

Figure 4.14   An example of the screen of the KMP: EM_fuel_cell_automatic

from the KMP to a representative of the corresponding company. The representative can review the request, fill out pre-defined fields and send the response to the user (the user's e-mail is taken from his/her profile). Based on this information, the user can decide if the corresponding plant can be qualified as a BTO supplier or not and decide on future collaboration.

Conclusions

This chapter proposes an approach to ontology engineering for representation of a supply chain. The process of ontology engineering was based on analysis of other existing ontologies modelling related domains. It was shown that using ontology repositories that are the results of application of semantic web technologies, models for specification of a problem at hand can be composed from the ontologies found in these repositories. Application of the approach was an integrated project with industrial partners from the area of

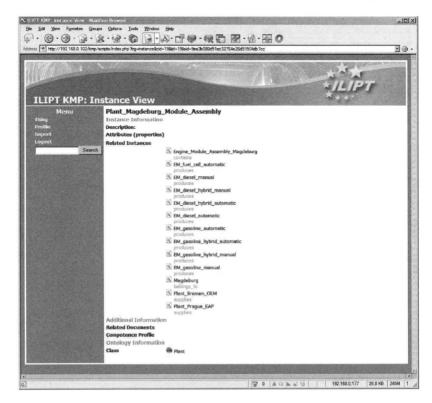

Figure 4.15 An example of the screen of the KMP: Plant_Magdeburg_Module_Assembly

automotive supply chains. Possible applications of the presented approach are in the areas of intelligent decision support in flexible supply networks, automotive logistics systems and competence management networks.

Planned future work is mostly oriented to development of more substantial competence profiles than those presented in this chapter. This would complement the ontology-based knowledge sharing, since application of profiles makes it possible to organize personalized support of supply chain members.

Acknowledgements

The research described in this chapter is supported by grants from following projects: Integrated Project FP6-IST-NMP 507592-2 'Intelligent Logistics for Innovative Product Technologies', sponsored by the European Commission; projects funded by grants # 08-07-00264 and # 06-07-89242 of the Russian Foundation for Basic Research; projects funded by grants # 14.2.35 of the

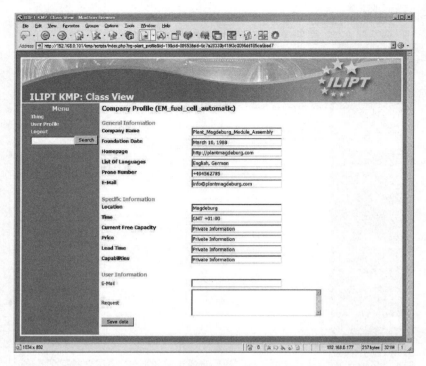

Figure 4.16   An example of the screen of the KMP: competence profile example

research programme 'Mathematical Modelling and Intelligent Systems' and # 1.9 of the research programme 'Fundamental Basics of Information Technologies and Computer Systems' of the Russian Academy of Sciences (RAS) and the project of the scientific programme of St Petersburg Scientific Centre of the RAS.

References

Chandra, C. and Tumanyan, A. 2003 'Supply chain system taxonomy: Development and application Conference Proceedings', *Proceedings of the 12th Annual Industrial Engineering Research Conference (IERC 2003)*, http://www.isye.gatech. edu/faculty/-Leon_McGinnis/8851/Sources/Ontology/Chandra/Supply chain system taxonomy – development and application.doc, accessed June 2008.

Chaudhri, V.K., Lowrance, J.D., Stickel, M.E., Thomere, J.F. and Wadlinger, R.J. 2000 'Ontology construction toolkit: Technical note ontology', AI Center Report, January, SRI Project No. 1633.

Chopra, S. and Meindl, P. 2001 *Supply Chain Management: Strategy, Planning, and Operation*, New Jersey: Prentice Hall.

Chopra, S. and Mieghem, J. 2000 'Which e-business is right for your supply chain?', *Supply Chain Management Review*, July/August: 32–40, <http://www.kellogg. northwestern.edu/faculty/chopra/-htm/research/scm.pdf>, accessed June 2008.

Chopra, S., Dougan, D. and Taylor, G. 2001 'B2B e-commerce opportunities', *Supply Chain Management Review*, May/June: 50–8.

Cisco Systems 2001 'What you need to implement a supply-chain management solution', white paper, http://www.cisco. com/-application/pdf/en/us/guest/netsol/ ns451/c129/-cdccont_0900aecd800 e492a.pdf, accessed May 2003.

Cooper, M.C., Lambert, D.M. and Pagh, J.D. 1997 'Supply chain management: More than a new name for logistics', *The International Journal of Logistics Management*, 8(1): 1–14.

Ding, Y., Fensel, D., Klein, M. and Omelayenko, B. 2002 'The semantic web: Yet another hip?', *Data and Knowledge Engineering*, 41(3): 205–27.

eCl@ss 2001 *Standardized Material and Service Classification*, Cologne Institute for Business Research, <http://www.eclass-online.com/>, accessed June 2008.

FIPA 2008 *Ontology Service Specification*, Geneva, Switzerland, Foundation for Intelligent Physical Agents, <http://www.fipa.org>

Gattorna, J. (ed.) 1998 *Strategic Supply Chain Alignment*, Gower, UK.

Gennari J. et al. 2002 'The evolution of protégé: An environment for knowledge-based systems development', SMI Technical Report, No. SMI-2002-0943, http://www.smi.stanford.edu/pubs/-SMI_Reports/SMI-2002-0943.pdf, accessed May 2003.

Guarino N. 1998 'Formal ontology and information systems', *Proceedings of FOIS '98*, IOS Press: 3–15.

Harland, C.M. 1996 'Supply chain management: Relationships, chains and networks', *British Journal of Management*, 7: 63–80.

Fully integrated, scalable supply chain management solution', *Solution Blueprints* (IBM Business Consulting Services), http://www.intel. com/business/bss/solutions/ blueprints/pdf/-sb_ibmbcs0252.pdf, accessed May 2003.

Klein, M. and Fensel, D. 2001 'Ontology versioning on the semantic web',*Proceedings of the 1st Semantic Web Working Symposium*: 75–91, <http://informatik.uibk.ac.at/ users/ c70385/ftp/paper/SWWS01.pdf>, accessed June 2008.

Lau, J.S.K., Huang, G.Q. and Mak, K.L. 2001 'A web-based collaborative order life cycle management in supply chain', *Proceedings of International Conference on Supply Chain Management and Information Systems in the Internet Age (SCMIS2001)*: 359–70, http://147.8.86.56/Downloads/OLC.pdf, accessed May 2003.

Lee, Y.T. and Umeda, S. 2001 *Management Data Specification for Supply Chain Integration*, NISTIR 6703, National Institute of Standards and Technology, Gaithersburg, MD, <http://www.nist.gov/msidlibrary/doc/mgtdata.pdf>, accessed June 2008.

Lenat, D.B. 1998 'From 2001 to 2001: Common sense and the mind of HAL', in D.G. Stork (ed.), *HAL's Legacy: 2001's Computer as Dream and Reality*, MIT Press.

Levashova, T.V., Pashkin, M.P., Shilov, N.G. and Smirnov, A.V. 2003 'Ontology management', *Journal of Computer and System Sciences International*, Part II, 42(5): 744–56.

Maedche, A., Motik, B., Stojanovic, L., Studer, R. and Volz, R. 2002 'Managing multiple ontologies and ontology evolution in ontologging', *Proceedings of the Conference on Intelligent Information Processing*, Kluwer Academic Publishers, The Netherlands: 51–63.

Maedche, A., Motik, B., Stojanovic, L., Studer, R. and Volz, R. 2003 'Ontologies for enterprise knowledge management', *IEEE Intelligent Systems*, March/April: 26–33.

Malone, T.W., Crowston, K. and Herman, G.A. (eds) 2003 *Organizing Business Knowledge: The MIT Process Handbook*, MIT Press, USA:.

Metz P.J. 1998 'Demystifying supply chain management', *Supply Chain Management Review*, Winter, http://www.manufacturing.net/-scm/index.asp?layout= articleWebzine&articleid=CA159708, accessed May 2003.

MIT Process Handbook 2001 Version N-3 (1.22), http://process.mit.edu, accessed June 2008.

Motik, B., Maedche, A. and Volz, R. 2002 'A conceptual modeling approach for semantics-driven enterprise applications', *Proceedings of CoopIS/DOA/ODBASE2002 Confederated International Conferences DOA, CoopIS and ODBASE 2002*: 1082–99.

Motta, E. and Zdrahal, Z. 1998 'A principled approach to the construction of a task-specific library of problem solving components', *Proceedings of the Eleventh Workshop on Knowledge Acquisition, Modeling and Management (KAW '98)*, http://spuds.cpsc.ucalgary.ca/KAW/KAW98/motta/, accessed May 2003.

The North American Industry Classification System, http://www.census.gov/epcd/ www/naics.html, accessed December 2002.

Noy, N.F. and Musen, M.A. 2002 'PromptDiff: A fixed-point algorithm for comparing ontology versions', *The Eighteenth National Conference on Artificial Intelligence (AAAI-02)*, AAAI Press: 744–50, http://www.smi.stanford.edu/pubs/SMI_Reports/SMI-2002-0927.pdf, accessed May 2003.

Oberle, D., Staab, S., Studer, R. and Volz, R. 2004 'Supporting application development in the semantic web', *ACM Transactions on Internet Technology*, 4 (4), <http://www.aifb.uni-karlsruhe.de/WBS/dob/pubs/acm2004.pdf, accessed May 2003.

On-To-Knowledge Methodology 2002 *On-To-Knowledge: Content-driven Knowledge Management Tools through Evolving Ontologies*, Final Version, Deliverable 18, http://www.ontoknowledge.org/downl/del18.pdf, accessed June 2008.

Perez, A.G. and Benjamins, V.R. 1999 'Overview of knowledge sharing and reuse components: Ontologies and problem-solving methods', in V.R. Benjamins, B. Chandrasekaran, A. Gomez-Perez, N. Guarino and M. Uschold (eds),*Proceedings of the IJCAI-99 Workshop on Ontologies and Problem-Solving Methods (KRR5)*, http://sunsite.informatik.rwth-aachen.de/Publications/CEUR-WS/Vol-18/, accessed June 2008.

Sandkuhl, K., Smirnov, A. and Henoch, B. 2004 'Towards knowledge logistics in agile SME networks: Technological and organisational concepts', in A. Dolgui, J. Soldek and O. Zaikin (eds), *Supply Chain Optimisation: Product/process Design, Facility Location and Flow Control*, Kluwer Academic Publishers, The Netherlands.

Schreiber G. et al. 1999 *Knowledge Engineering and Management: The CommonKADS Methodology*, MIT Press,

SCOR 2008 SCOR Model. Supply Chain Council. http://www.supply-chain.org/cs/root/scor_tools_resources/scor_model/scor_model, accessed June 2008.

SHOE Commerce Ontology, Version 1.0, http://www.cs.umd.edu/-projects/plus/SHOE/onts/commerce1.0.html, accessed June 2008.

Simchi-Levi, D., Kaminsky P. and Simchi-Levi, E. 2000 *Designing and Managing the Supply Chain: Concepts, Strategies, and Case Studies*, Boston: McGraw-Hill.

Smirnov, A., Pashkin, M., Chilov, N. and Levashova, T. 2001 'Agent-based support of mass customization for corporate knowledge management', *Engineering Applications of Artificial Intelligence*, 16(4): 349–64.

Smirnov, A., Pashkin, M., Chilov, N., Levashova, T. and Haritatos, F. 2003 'Knowledge source network configuration approach to knowledge logistics', *International Journal of General Systems*, 32(3) (Taylor & Francis Group): 251–69.

Staab, S., Schnurr, H.-P., Studer, R. and Sure, Y. 2001 'Knowledge processes and ontologies', *IEEE Intelligent Systems*, 16(1), Special Issue on Knowledge Management: 26–34, <http://www.aifb.uni-karlsruhe.de/~sst/Research/Publications/-isystems-knowledgeprocess.pdf, accessed June 2008.

Stojanovic, L., Maedche, A., Motik, B. and Stojanovic, N. 2002 'User-driven ontology evolution management', *Proceedings of the 13th European Conference on Knowledge Engineering and Knowledge Management (EKAW)*: 285–300.

Sure, Y., Erdmann, M., Angele, J., Staab, S., Studer, R. and Wenke, D. 2002 'OntoEdit: Collaborative ontology development for the semantic web', *Proceedings of the 1st International Semantic Web Conference – ISWC2002, Lecture Notes in Computer Science* (Springer): 221–35, http://www.aifb.uni-karlsruhe.de/~sst/Research/Publications/iswc2002sub.pdf, accessed June 2008.

Swartout B., Patil R., Knight K. and Russ, T. 1996 'Toward distributed use of large-scale ontologies', *Tenth Knowledge Acquisition for Knowledge-Based Systems Workshop (KAW '96)*, http://www.isi. edu/isd/banff_paper/Banff_final_web/-Banff_96_final_2. html, accessed June 2008.

Trent, R.J. 2004 'What everyone needs to know about SCM', *Supply Chain Management Review*, March, <http://www.manufacturing.net/scm/-index.asp?layout= article&articleID= CA409514, accessed September 2005.

Truong, T.H. and Azadivar, F. 2003 'Simulation based optimization for supply chain configuration design', in S. Chick, P.J. Sánchez, D. Ferrin and D.J. Morrice (eds), *Proceedings of the 2003 Winter Simulation Conference*, Vol. 2: 1268–75, http://ieeexplore. ieee.org/iel5/8912/28189/01261560.pdf, accessed June 2008.

UN Classifications Registry, United Nations Statistics Division, <http://unstats.un. org/unsd/cr/registry/default.asp>

The UNSPSC Code (Universal Standard Products and Services Classification Code), DAML Ontology Library, Stanford University, <http://www.ksl.stanford.edu/projects/DAML/-UNSPSC.daml, accessed December 2002.

Wielinga, B.J. and Schreiber, A.T. 1994 'Conceptual modelling of large reusable knowledge bases', in K. von Luck and H. Marburger (eds), *Management and Processing of Complex Data Structures, Lecture Notes in Computer Science*, 777, (Springer): 181–200, http://www.swi.psy.uva.nl/usr/wielinga/postscript/Wielinga:94a.ps, accessed June 2008.

5
Supply Chain Design: In An Outsourcing World

P.J. Byrne, Paul Liston and Cathal Heavey

Introduction

Supply chain management as a formal technique has been in existence since the mid- to late 1980s. It evolved in the western world from the concept of mass customization in the 1950s and 1960s, through to the use of manufacturing resource planning in the 1970s, to the concept of continuous improvement techniques, such as JIT (just-in-time) and TQM (total quality management) in the 1980s. Since its inception, supply chain management has evolved and adapted to the continually accelerating needs of what is today a truly global economy. With modern supply chains, globalization plays a significant role in their complexity. There is no agreed starting point for globalization, as it can be traced back through the centuries in different guises. Nevertheless, globalization has been rapidly increasing in the last 15 years or so. This has been facilitated greatly by vast improvements in transport, removal of trade barriers (such as the sustained expansion of the European Union and the continued implementation of multilateral trading systems, e.g. GATT/WTO) and the vast advancements of ICT (information and communications technology) (Ethier 2005, Ngowi *et al.* 2005, Morrissey and Filatotchev 2000).

One significant difference between the globalization of today and that of the late 19th century is the density and interdependence of networks. These networks have formed and developed due to the increasingly widespread use of outsourcing on both a national and international level. With this continual expansion of global markets in combination with reduced product life cycles, supply chains are becoming increasingly elongated and complex.

Fundamental to any supply chain are the customers that it serves. Customer expectations and needs are continuing to change, at an ever-increasing rate. For example, customers expect better quality, increased choice, enhanced customizability, reduced lead times, reduced cost, reduced time-to-market and/or better after-sales service for the products and services that they receive. Ultimately, present-day supply chain customers are more demanding than in the past. As supply chains continue to evolve to satisfy this customer demand, one critical emerging characteristic is their dynamic nature. Successful supply chains need to be able to adapt as required in an ever-changing environment.

With this in mind many organizations have focused their scarce resources on core competencies and outsourced all other activities to third parties. Outsourced (or contract) manufacturing is now one of the fastest-growing industries in a broad range of business sectors, including pharmaceuticals, medical devices, electronics and automotive. Plambeck and Taylor (2005) report that firms that traditionally manufactured their own products are outsourcing production and, instead, focusing on product design, development and marketing. For example, in a recent online report, Friedlos (2007) notes that the total value of outsourcing deals during the first quarter of 2007 increased in Europe by 67 per cent to 7.7 billion euros compared to the same period in 2006. In most instances such outsourcing activities are governed by legal contracts exchanged between the parties involved.

Getting the supply chain design right from the outset is now more than ever an integral component of success, as supply chain durations decrease. Historically, supply chains were designed to remain in place for a significant period of time, with the expectation of evolution. In many instances, this is no longer the case and errors in modern supply chain design can be extremely expensive and may ultimately erode the competitiveness of the business. This chapter presents a study that has been carried out to look at this issue with Irish-based global networks. As part of this study, current supply chain design practice is evaluated in seven global networks (with a base in Ireland). One of these networks is then examined in more detail, including a number of its design parameters. These design factors include supplier selection and parameter setting in a real-world outsourcing example using simulation.

Field study

As noted previously, the practice of outsourcing is globally prevalent and has led to formalized relationships between networks of independent companies. These relationships are typically controlled by contractual agreements, which specify how information, finance and goods are exchanged between the relevant parties. Prior to establishing these contracts the companies go through what is widely known as the request for quotation (RFQ) process whereby the service buyer will issue a document specifying the work on offer to a number of appropriate service providers. These suppliers must then calculate a cost for undertaking the work and compete against one another to secure the business. In this section, the details of a number of companies working in such outsourcing scenarios are described.

In order to maintain consistency across the case studies, a decision was made prior to selecting and engaging with companies, to confine the research to a particular industrial sector. The electronics manufacturing sector was selected for this purpose because it is known to have a successful and growing outsourcing market (Carbone 2005), thus making it a well-suited domain for requirements gathering and field testing. The supply chains associated with electronics production invariably contain many echelons (due primarily to repeated outsourcing activity) with independent companies working in series/parallel to complete the manufacturing process, as depicted in Figure 5.1.

In order to gain a balanced understanding of current outsourcing practice, field study participants were selected from across the supply chain spectrum, as denoted in Figure 5.1. [Note: Figure 5.1 is provided for illustrative purposes, to describe the relative positioning of companies in a supply chain. The selected companies do not necessarily participate in the same supply chains.] In all, seven different organizations are included in this case study evaluation, varying in size from a network coordinator with only four direct employees to a large multinational OEM with over 50,000 employees.

Prior to receiving any of the company-specific data used in this report, NDAs (non-disclosure agreements) were signed with each company, protecting their privacy. In order to adhere to these agreements each participant has been assigned an identifying number, which is used in place of their actual business name. The case study participants are listed accordingly in Table 5.1 together with the role they play in their respective supply chains and a general overview of each participant in terms of their RFQ-related activity. Each field study participant was visited between two and eight times for on-site data collection, while further clarification, explanation and supplementary data was gained through additional telephone and/or e-mail conversations.

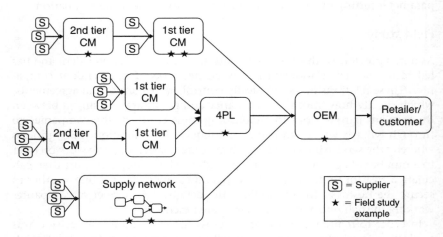

Figure 5.1   Supply chain nodes

Table 5.1 Summary of field study participant details

	Participant One	Participant Two	Participant Three	Participant Four	Participant Five	Participant Six	Participant Seven
Company's Main Area of Business	Low Volume Assembly and Manufacturing (2nd Tier CM)	Electronics Manufacturing (1st Tier CM)	Electronics Manufacturing (1st Tier CM)	Warehousing, Kitting and Supply Chain Management (4PL)	Supply Chain Management (Network Coordinator)	Manufacturing Related Services (Supply Network)	Electronics Manufacturing (OEM)
Number of Employees in Company (Approx.)	130	50	600 (Irish Facility)	400	4	46 Independent Companies	>50,000 (Globally)
Number of RFQs processed in a week (Approx.)	5	6–12	8	5–10	4–5	Still in initial stages of business development	n/a
Tools used to process RFQs	MS Excel Spreadsheet	MS Excel Spreadsheet	MS Excel Spreadsheet with Macro	MS Excel Spreadsheet	MS Excel Spreadsheet	MS Excel Spreadsheet	Ariba and MS Excel Spreadsheets
Tools developed in-house or purchased	In-House	In-House	In-House	In-House	In-House	In-House	Purchased and In-House
Typical turn around time for responding to an RFQ	2 Weeks	10–15 Working days	8–10 Working days	1–6 Weeks	2 Weeks	Still in initial stages of business development	n/a
Format of RFQs sent/received	email, telephone, hardcopy	email, CD, hardcopy	email, CD, hardcopy	email, hardcopy	telephone, email	email, telephone, hardcopy	email
Format of RFQ responses sent/received	email, hardcopy, telephone	email, hardcopy	email, hardcopy	email, hardcopy	email, hardcopy, telephone	email, hardcopy	email, hardcopy

As shown above, a broad range of companies has been consulted and consequently a selection of vastly different outsourcing scenarios has been examined. Some of these contracts resulted in long-term relationships with close cooperation between the parties involved, while other contracts were borne of very specific requirements and ceased once the work was completed. Regardless of their scale, there were many similarities between the reviewed outsourcing contracts themselves and the manner in which they are handled at the RFQ stage.

When a company is formulating a response to an RFQ they are essentially conducting a cost analysis on their business operations for a given set of conditions, that is, the terms of the contract on offer. To achieve this, the company has to first determine the system required to successfully carry out the tasks requested of them. It is already a difficult task to ensure that the correct systems are in place for current work, with which the analyst is familiar, but it is even more complicated when dealing with work due to occur in the future. The uncertainties and difficulties associated with this task can stem from a lack of knowledge on the part of the analyst in relation to the work to be carried out and the complications that can possibly occur, but they can also be a result of specific clauses in the contract. These contract terms are included to protect the customer's ability to adapt to changes in the market but they prevent details such as order quantity and timing from being stated in precise figures. The following section describes some specific details for one of the field study participants (Participant Three) and presents a typical RFQ scenario.

Case study example

Participant Three is a high-volume first-tier CM, which provides a range of integrated, value-added services. These include the design and development of, multilayered PCBs, custom-designed backplane assemblies (electronic circuit boards containing circuitry and sockets into which additional electronic devices on other circuit boards or cards can be plugged), memory modules, optical modules, electronic enclosure systems and cabling/wiring harness assemblies. Participant Three also conducts subsystem and system-level assembly, final system testing and manages distribution of finished goods for its customers. Participant Three has flexible manufacturing facilities in more than 20 countries on five continents, making it a truly global organization. The particular manufacturing facility studied in this analysis currently employs over 600 people and primarily serves the computing, medical and communications markets.

When completing a quotation, Participant Three has an established set of information requirements, some of which are deemed critical to the development of the RFQ response, while others are simply desirable, as they can improve the accuracy of the final quote figures. This information has been categorized by Participant Three under three headings as follows:

- Assembly – In the case of assembly-related information, critical requirements include a bill of materials (BOM), which gives specifications for each component, such as the part number, the quantity and the manufacturer. Participant Three also prefers to receive Gerber files, assembly drawings and, if possible, sample units or prototypes.
- Test – With regard to the testing of parts, Participant Three considers schematics, board drawings, a BOM and a test process flow to be critical. Desirable information includes CAD data, test times, test yields, part programming information, test platform details, rework times, debug times and special customer requirements.
- Materials – In addition to the BOM listed above, Participant Three usually receives an approved vendor listing (AVL), which details the preferred vendors that the customer has chosen for Participant Three to purchase from. Where a strict AVL policy applies, only suppliers on the list may be used, otherwise the CM may choose alternative vendors once they can guarantee that the same quality standards will be met. This provides an opportunity to make cost savings but it also requires more administrative effort to find and negotiate with the alternative suppliers.

The first step when responding to an RFQ is to perform a preliminary check for the required information as described above. Participant Three notes that there can be many difficulties at this point. There can be difficulty in getting technical details from the OEM because one rarely deals directly with design engineers at the quotation stage. Alternatively, the opposite problem can occur where too much information is supplied and it has to search through it to identify the elements that have an impact on their costs. This can happen when a product has been outsourced for a considerable length of time; the OEM becomes unfamiliar with the process and is no longer able to identify the relevant data.

The following data has been taken from a sample RFQ (for the provision of populated PCBs), which is considered typical of the several hundred received by Participant Three each year. This RFQ documentation comprises a descriptive section, a BOM with 115 components and an AVL with 31 suppliers. In the descriptive section (which appears to be based on a generic template) the customer first gives a brief company overview and states the objectives of issuing the RFQ. These goals include reducing cost, establishing long-term supplier relationships and gathering information relevant to the 'make versus buy' decision. The customer then outlines their qualitative and quantitative supplier evaluation criteria under the following headings:

- Quality products
- Service excellence

- Competitive pricing
- Technology capabilities and technical service
- Information management
- Partnership
- Continuous improvement
- Dedicated programme manager and support team
- On-time delivery
- Rapid repair/rework turnaround
- Fast action on samples/prototypes
- Inventory management
- Responsiveness to customers' needs
- R&D support
- Transportation cost management

The contract on offer in this RFQ can be classed as a rolling horizon flexibility contract (see Anupindi and Bassok 1999) due to the nature of the planned forecasting method and because of the commitment revision flexibility terms that have been stipulated. Explicitly, the customer will provide a 13-week rolling forecast, but specifies that if Participant Three wins the contract, it must adhere to one of the three flexibility models shown here in Table 5.2, depending on the country they will be supplying to.

The RFQ documentation provided by the customer did not specify at any point how the product was to be produced. Participant Three had to determine this from the BOM and their experience in working with PCBs, and then calculate their costs accordingly. At a corporate level, Participant Three has a

Table 5.2   Flexibility models specified in sample RFQ

Time frame	Upside flexibility	Downside flexibility
Flexibility Model 1		
0–4 Weeks	Demand Fixed	Demand Fixed
5–8 Weeks	20%	20%
9–12 Weeks	40%	40%
13 Weeks	100%	100%
Flexibility Model 2		
1 Month	15%	15%
2 Months	30%	100%
3 Months	50%	100%
Flexibility Model 3		
0–2 Weeks	Demand Fixed	Demand Fixed
2–4 Weeks	50%	0%
4–6 Weeks	100%	0%

number of centralized cost estimation centres (CECs) that aid local plants in responding to RFQs. When an RFQ is received, the BOM and AVL are loaded into the CEC computer system, which then assigns established pricing figures to each component based on either customer-provided pricing, prices negotiated by the GSM (global supplier management) department, quote history, or open purchase orders. Suppliers are then approached for quotations for any remaining components that have not yet been priced. By centralizing these activities Participant Three benefits from the advantages of 'economies of scale' and realizes cost reductions at the local manufacturing facility level.

While the CEC is responsible for material costs, other costs such as labour, tooling and testing are still calculated at a local level. For Participant Three there are four main processes that can be combined to configure a production line; these are SMT (surface mount technology), PTH (pin through hole), manual assembly and testing. For each of these processes there is a list of parameters that have an affect on the cost of completing the task. Participant Three uses a spreadsheet to calculate the combined production costs based on these parameters; however, its system is more sophisticated than those reviewed at the other CMs in this study, as it is macro-enabled. This added level of automation aids the cost-generation process by only presenting the user with the fields that they are required to complete for the particular product at hand.

The user first chooses from a list of different line configurations to get the combination of machines and processes necessary to produce the product. Then, depending on this selection, certain cells in the spreadsheet are hidden by the macro, so that only those related to the process parameters of interest are left. Most of these fields are completed by the user but some are filled automatically based on the entered data. For instance, the labour requirement is calculated according to the mix of machines in the production line and the direct labour costs are then deduced by multiplying this requirement by the hourly rate. The spreadsheet also incorporates a line-balancing capability based on cycle times, which allows to user to assess the various line configurations.

The macro-enabled Excel system is a useful aid when calculating the cost of providing a new manufacturing service but Participant Three does have a number of issues with it. Although it supports the inclusion of shop floor details such as production-line configurations, the existing system does not take into consideration the outsourcing contract, which will govern how and when the production will be undertaken. This means that demand volumes, changes to this demand (as permitted by commitment revision terms) and inventory costs associated with meeting contractually required service levels are not directly provided for in the existing costing process. The static spreadsheet analysis currently in place can only deal with deterministic cost drivers that can be stated in terms of defined equations and is therefore unable to cope with factors that vary unpredictably over time. Currently, cost analysts include additional margins to cover the financial consequences of this uncertainty, but without the ability to quantify these costs they must rely on experience to determine the adjustments they make.

Furthermore, the time required to populate the current system makes it impractical to conduct quick analyses on proposals such as alternative supplier selection criteria. Even when the details of a different supplier are added, only the direct cost elements of the change have a bearing on the output of the analysis. Other factors, such as the true effect of shorter/longer lead times on storage costs and overall supply chain performance remain difficult to quantify.

These shortcomings, coupled with technical difficulties related to maintaining and updating the in-house developed system, strengthen Participant Three's interest in new methodologies for designing outsourcing networks. It desires a tool that can capture a broader range of relevant cost drivers and profile the risk involved in agreeing to a new outsourcing contract but to date it has not found anything on the software market that can meet these requirements.

Field study synopsis

Based on the CMs reviewed, the scope of current cost calculations is limited to material, labour and overheads. Average demand figures are used to cost the activities conducted within the 'four walls' of their manufacturing facility (or facilities where more than one company is involved in the bid). To these manufacturing costs they add the cost of materials (as quoted by their suppliers), plus any other directly assignable costs (e.g. machinery or tooling purchases). Although CMs are adept at costing these manufacturing activities, they are unable to take into account other incidental costs due to material shortages, supplier unreliability or poor quality products. By focusing on the cost incurred inside the 'four walls' of the factory, further expenses influenced by the design of a supply chain, such as those of logistics, are often neglected. These expenses and other overheads (e.g. storage, heating, or maintenance) are included in quoted prices but often using percentage-based or arbitrary values.

Based on the examples reviewed during the field study, it is clear that many lower complexity contracts are adequately supported by current practice or at least they could be with further refinement of the ubiquitous Excel spreadsheets. However, it is argued that there are several factors in supply chain design and costing that justify more in-depth analysis (especially when dealing with high-value contracts or those with time frames that extend from one or two months up to 12 months or more, thereby demanding greater commitment and posing a larger risk if the associated costs are miscalculated). These include operational details that are either specified directly in the RFQ or are unavoidable real-life constraints on the system and therefore govern how the outsourcing solution is executed. These factors and other important considerations for outsourced supply chain design have been categorized as follows:

- Operational details
- Inventory costs
- Supplier selection
- Supply chain configuration
- Structured costing methodology
- Confidence in outsourcing solutions.

Contractually specified operational details include the commitment revision flexibility terms (example shown earlier in Table 5.2). Such contract terms undoubtedly have implications for the CM intending to provide the service. For instance, if the OEM dramatically reduces their purchase order quantity after the CM has committed to purchasing the necessary raw materials, the CM will be faced with costly storage problems. This effect is accentuated if the product has already been produced at the time of the order change, as the components cannot be readily used in any other products. Conversely, if the OEM increases their purchase order quantity the CM will have to be capable of producing the extra product within the time left to the due date. This may require the expedited acquisition of the necessary material, labour and capacity requirements, and consequently result in higher expenditure for the CM.

Other operational details include the minimum order requirements that must be satisfied according to purchasing agreements. This is a particularly important consideration in the electronics sector, where many components are purchased on reels containing thousands of parts. This does not pose a great problem for high-running components that are common to a number of products, but for more specific high-cost products this situation can entail a considerable risk, especially if the end product experiences highly fluctuating demand.

From discussing this issue with representatives from the case study companies, it is clear that they are aware of the existence of these cost implications but they do not possess a convenient means of quantifying the financial impact. In general, companies deduce whether the terms appear to be excessive or not based on previous experience with similar contracts. If deemed excessive, these contract terms are then contested as the CM aims to negotiate a more favourable scenario. Since neither side of the alliance has a true monetary measurement of these contract terms and because the lifespan of these transient agreements inhibits lengthy assessment, cost-benefit analyses have proven difficult during the negotiation period.

To extend the scope of current contract analysis and allow it to capture more of the cost drivers, which are inherent to an outsourcing scenario, a combination of activity-based costing (ABC) and discrete event simulation (DES) has been employed and is described next.

Design modelling

When a contractor responds to an RFQ, they are essentially bidding to become part of a supply chain and therefore need to consider the implications of forming such an alliance when forming their cost quotation. Taking the example described in the section 'Case study example', the resultant supply chain will take the form shown in Figure 5.2. The rate of consumption of the finished product at the end-customers will have a direct influence on the rate of production at the OEM and consequently at the CM facility. These production rates will then, in turn, determine when and how much material is acquired from suppliers. The stock levels, production capacities and processing times and the various nodes, plus the transportation times between these nodes, will influence the successful delivery of goods to the customer in a timely manner.

To calculate the costs involved in these types of supply chains, an ABC approach has been selected that assigns costs to each of the activities that must be undertaken. To represent these activities, analytical mathematical modelling techniques were considered but they were found to have limited application to the type of supply chain designs under consideration. Huang, Lau and Mak (2003) note that analytical models can be used successfully to model dyadic structures (i.e. structures consisting of two entities; a buyer and a vendor, for example), but they have difficulty in handling either serial or

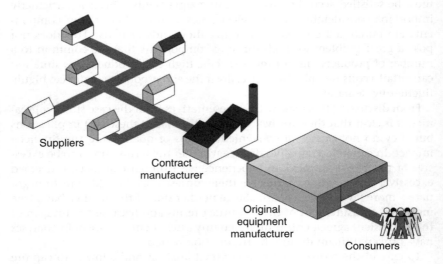

Suppliers

Contract manufacturer

Original equipment manufacturer

Consumers

Figure 5.2 Example supply chain structure

convergent structures. The supply chain analyzed here is a convergent supply chain.

As an alternative approach to formally investigating these more complex supply chain structures, Huang, Lau and Mak (2003) suggest the use of simulation. Simulation has long been used to support decision-making in manufacturing environments by analyzing planned changes such as the addition of production lines or reconfiguration of current shop floor layouts. It is proposed that the decisions that must be made when responding to an RFQ are comparable to these manufacturing decisions, as the exact system required to carry out the work on offer may not be in place but deductions can be made based on current systems or past experience. It is therefore suggested that the proven benefits of simulation can also be realized during the RFQ process if the respondents have access to appropriate models.

Figure 5.3 shows the main screen of a DES model, which has been built using eM-Plant (www.emplant.com) to understand the benefits of using simulation to design a supply chain at the RFQ phase of an outsourcing relationship. This model has been built in an object-oriented manner and custom objects have been designed and developed for each distinct node of the supply chain. These objects are added to the model and populated with

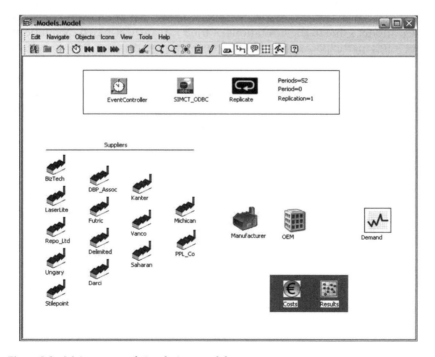

Figure 5.3 Main screen of simulation model

company-specific values to build the scenario. Forecasted demand information is used to drive the simulation and as material passes through the various modelled activities the cost of the activity is recorded. For instance, the model records an administration charge when handling the release of a work order to production and again when processing sales orders amended under the commitment revision flexibility terms of the contract. The following specifies the complete list of cost drivers catered for in the model:

- Receiving an order
- Amending a previous order
- Purchasing components
- Shipping components
- Storing components
- Processing goods (setup: per batch, build: per unit)
- Storing finished goods (per pallet or part thereof)
- Shipping finished goods (per pallet or part thereof)
- Penalty for late delivery.

A significant advantage of using discrete event simulation in place of spreadsheets is that it allows variability to be incorporated into the analysis. For instance, Figure 5.4 shows an example of a demand profile simulated in the model – due to the limitations of their spreadsheet-based calculations, field study participants were found to use average demand figures even in cases where demand was known to be as erratic as that shown here.

In the model, the relay of demand information from the contract manufacturer to relevant suppliers is controlled by a simulated MRP system. This system is based on forecasted orders, revised order quantities (as allowed in the

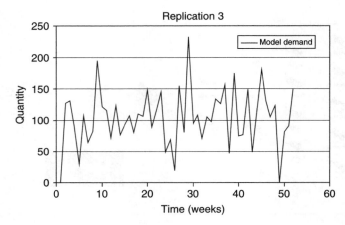

Figure 5.4 Example of modelled demand

contract), finished goods stock levels, component classification (inexpensive commodities are purchased in larger quantities) and purchasing constraints (such minimum order quantities). Further details of this reordering technique are provided by Liston *et al.* (2008).

When developing a quotation based on a particular supply chain design there are many factors that a contractor must consider. They must determine the manufacturing processes that are required and calculate the time taken to complete each production step. They must select suppliers to provide the materials that are required and consider the tradeoffs between low/high component costs, long/short lead times, different batch sizes and any material holding or transport costs incurred. The contractor must also consider the overall effect of these individual factors on their ability to supply the product within specified turnaround times. Under current practice, the most expensive components, or those with the longest lead times, often receive most attention because they are seen to be constraining factors. However, because of the high level of interaction in a manufacturing system, this may not necessarily be so. It will be shown here that the broader scope of a simulation-based analysis can support the decisions made when designing and pricing an outsourcing solution.

It will also be shown that simulation can help the user to explore the affect that altering the contract terms may have on their costs and thereby place them in a position where they can offer a more enriched quotation to the customer. Specifically, three different objectives are examined:

1. Relax system constraints – When analyzing a contract for a given supply chain design, the simulation model can highlight potential constraints in a proposed system.
2. Examine cost reduction opportunities in the system – In addition to relaxing known constraints, the cost analyst can also explore other ways of reducing the cost of their outsourcing solution by experimenting with cost drivers and establishing their affect on overall performance.
3. Establish possible avenues of negotiation – Once the cost analyst is satisfied with the system they have designed, they can then begin to look at elements of the contract that, if changed, would allow for further cost savings. These options can then be put to the customer, who (depending on the possible savings) may be willing to negotiate the contract terms.

The following sections present experimentation that can be conducted in an effort to achieve these goals and are therefore representative of the type of analysis that CMs are most interested in conducting on a regular basis. Note, it is the reaction of the model and the insight that can be gained through the use of simulation that is put forward as significant to the advancement of RFQ analysis, rather than the exact values and results presented here in these case study examples.

Table 5.3   Details of the top four constraining components

Item number	Quantity	Manufacturer name	Price $	Lead time	Minimum order quantity	Multiple order quantity	Days between orders
Blog07338400	1	INTEL	16.24	100	10	10	5
Blog07125300	1	C&D TECHNOLOGY	7.57	75	15	15	5
Blog07505100	2	CHIPS AND TECHNOLOGY	20.60	90	240	24	5
Blog07337600	1	MAXIM	7.12	70	12	12	5

Relaxing system constraints

A list of the components that constrained production during the simulation run is included in the model output and it is typically found that only a minority of the components causes the majority of the problems. The salient data for the top four constraining components has been extracted from a Participant Three example and is presented here in Table 5.3. Interestingly, these are not the components with the longest lead times (measured here in working days) and, while they do have relatively long lead times, there were many other components on the BOM with equally long or longer times. They are, however, among the more expensive components and all are in fact A-class components (meaning that under Participant Three's reordering policy only one week's worth is ordered at a time). The other commonality between these components is that they all have relatively low minimum and multiple order quantities associated with them (making them more susceptible to forecast inaccuracies). It is suggested that it is the combination of all three of these factors that causes the stock-out problems, since other components with comparable values for any one of the parameters, but not the others, do not experience the same problems.

Taking these four components, three experiments have been conducted, which look at different possible ways of alleviating the constraint they place on the outsourcing system. The selected experiments are described in the following points.

1. Supplier selection – The first experiment looks at the effect of reducing the lead times for the constraining products by selecting alternative suppliers. It is rare in the electronics-manufacturing sector that a component/material can only be obtained from a single source, as there is a high level of standardization associated with such goods. The choice between potential suppliers is often based on a tradeoff between cost and

lead time (this is particularly true for western companies who can locally source goods but must pay for the higher operating expenses that these suppliers incur; conversely they can source the goods from the lower cost economies of Eastern Europe or Asia but must suffer longer lead times as a consequence). In this experiment the lead times have been reduced by 50 per cent but, to acknowledge the associated costs, the prices are raised by 50 per cent (as shown in Table 5.4).

2. Purchasing constraints – The second experiment explores the option of keeping the current suppliers but increasing the minimum and multiple order quantities to ascertain if the consequential increases in material stock levels will alleviate the production constraints. Once quantity changes are kept to multiples of the original figures (i.e. kept in line with the suppliers' carton quantities), a manufacturer could implement this system adjustment without the need for renegotiations or supplier involvement.

3. Reorder policy – In the third experiment the components are reclassified. All of the four components are currently categorized as A-class, which means that purchasing is reviewed each week (signified in Table 5.3 and Table 5.4 by the number of (working) days between orders). By reclassifying these components as B-class items, they will be handled differently by the modelled MRP system and a longer planning horizon (four weeks) will be considered when placing purchase orders.

Looking at the results for Experiment 1 in Figure 5.5 and Figure 5.6, it can be seen that selecting alternative suppliers did improve the on time delivery performance but, as expected with the options given, it had a substantial cost implication. What is useful here is that by simulating the different options, performance values are assigned to the choices that can be used in further cost-benefit analyses. This allows for more holistic supplier selection decisions to be made based on the influence each supplier has on the supply chain rather than comparing supplier details (e.g. lead time) in isolation.

Figure 5.5. and Figure 5.6 also show that both Experiment 2 and Experiment 3 gave similar improvements in performance but each had a less pronounced affect on cost than Experiment 1. The reason for the similarity in the performance of both these experiments is that the fundamental effect of both is to increase the purchase order quantities for the components. Although similar, it can be seen upon closer inspection that the on time delivery results for Experiment 3 are skewed upwards (i.e. there is a higher median value) and that this is achieved at a marginally lower per unit cost (approximately one dollar less). This improved performance owes to the fact that altering the reorder policy (i.e. the classifications) is a more refined approach to increasing order quantities as it follows trends in the forecasted demand rather than blindly ordering larger quantities (i.e. increasing the MOQ). However, when changing the classifications, consideration must be

Table 5.4 Experimental settings for 'what-if' analysis

	Item number	Quantity	Manufacturer name	Price $	Lead time	Minimum order quantity	Multiple order quantity	Days between orders
Original	Blog07338400	1	INTEL	16.24	100	10	10	5
	Blog07125300	1	C&D TECHNOLOGY	7.57	75	15	15	5
	Blog07505100	2	CHIPS AND TECHNOLOGY	20.60	90	240	24	5
	Blog07337600	1	MAXIM	7.12	70	12	12	5
Experiment 1	Blog07338400	1	Other	24.36	50	10	10	5
	Blog07125300	1	Other	11.35	37.5	15	15	5
	Blog07505100	2	Other	30.90	45	240	24	5
	Blog07337600	1	Other	10.68	35	12	12	5
Experiment 2	Blog07338400	1	INTEL	16.24	100	100	100	5
	Blog07125300	1	C&D TECHNOLOGY	7.57	75	150	150	5
	Blog07505100	2	CHIPS AND TECHNOLOGY	20.60	90	2400	240	5
	Blog07337600	1	MAXIM	7.12	70	120	120	5
Experiment 3	Blog07338400	1	INTEL	16.24	100	10	10	20
	Blog07125300	1	C&D TECHNOLOGY	7.57	75	15	15	20
	Blog07505100	2	CHIPS AND TECHNOLOGY	20.60	90	240	24	20
	Blog07337600	1	MAXIM	7.12	70	12	12	20

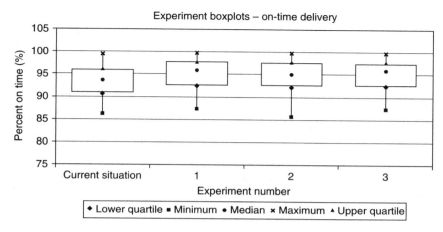

Figure 5.5 On-time delivery results for constraints experiments

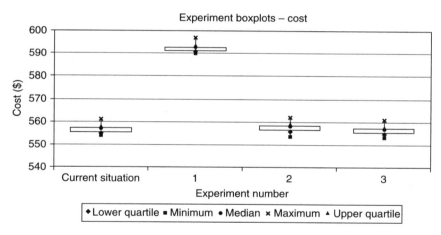

Figure 5.6 Cost per unit results for constraints experiments

given to any other decisions that are based on this component attribute, as the current categorization may be the most suitable in those cases.

Examining cost reduction opportunities

Apart from highlighting constraints in the system, the simulation model can also be used to explore other ways of making the outsourcing solution more efficient – so that either the contract will be more profitable or a lower quotation can be offered to the customer. There are many cost reduction ideas that could be simulated to test their feasibility, but as material purchases can form over 80 per cent of the cost for some products, the example shown here focuses on making savings in this area. In the example used in the last section, there was one component in the BOM that was significantly more expensive than any of the others, so it would be beneficial for a contractor to know if the parameters of such an item could be changed without affecting overall performance.

At $80.30, the microprocessor 'Blog07580500' costs almost 53 dollars more than the second most expensive item in the BOM. Since this item was not tagged as a potentially troublesome component it may be possible to source it from another supplier without affecting production. Making the assumption that this component could be sourced elsewhere at a lower cost but with a longer lead time, an experiment was run (see Table 5.5) to see the effect of choosing such an option.

Figure 5.7 compares both the cost and on-time delivery results for the current situation and the experimental run outlined in Table 5.5. These cost results reflect the material cost saving as inputted for the experiment and do

Table 5.5   Experiment with the most expensive component in Blog32

	Item number	Quantity	Manufacturer name	Price $	Lead time	Minimum order quantity	Multiple order quantity	Days between orders
Original	Blog07580500	1	MOTOROLA	80.3	20	24	24	5
Experiment	Blog07580500	1	Other	40.15	60	24	24	5

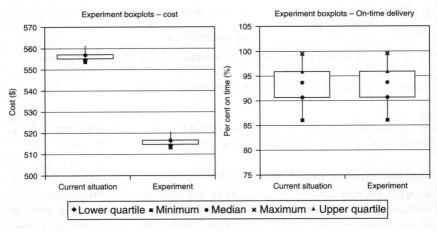

Figure 5.7   Results for cost reduction experiment

not indicate any further cost implications. Importantly, the on-time delivery results show that increasing the lead time of Blog07580500 did not affect overall performance, indicating that the supply of this component does not form a critical path in the current supply chain configuration. Therefore, the contractor can consider sacrificing lead time in order to avail of a lower price for this high-value item, without negative repercussions for the customer.

In this and the previous subsection, it has been shown that a contractor can quickly use the simulation model to test ideas as they arise when designing a supply chain. This allows for the development of more cost-effective and robust solutions to the contract on offer. It also gives confidence to both the contractor, in terms of understanding their cost drivers, and to the customer, who is given a more transparent view of the solution they are purchasing. In addition to this, the simulation model allows for further 'what-if' analysis to be carried out on the contract itself to determine if renegotiation of the terms is justified from an overall supply chain improvement perspective. This type of analysis is demonstrated in the next subsection.

Establish possible avenues of negotiation

As part of an outsourcing contract, many OEMs require the CM to hold a stock of finished goods to act as a buffer and ease the impact of sudden demand changes. To demonstrate how the developed simulation model can be used to experiment with this contractual requirement, a different sample RFQ has been chosen. There are two features of this contract that make it interesting to Participant Three from a stock-holding perspective:

1. Despite containing fewer components the product in this case is of greater physical dimension than the previous and only fits ten units per pallet rather than 40.
2. The customer in this case requires all their suppliers to hold four weeks' worth of finished goods at a hub near their manufacturing facility. At 6 dollars per pallet per week, the charge for this storage facility is considerably more expensive than that which Participant Three has negotiated ($3.20) with the local warehousing service they regularly use.

To establish the effect that buffer stock level has on the cost and performance of this contract, five different experimental simulation runs were carried out. In each of these experiments a different stock level was selected (zero, two, four, six and eight weeks' worth of stock) with all other parameters remaining constant. The results for 30 replications of each experiment are plotted in Figure 5.8 and Figure 5.9.

From these results it would appear that the current requirement of four weeks' worth of stock is a reasonable compromise between cost and performance. Reducing the stock level below this value would allow for cost savings

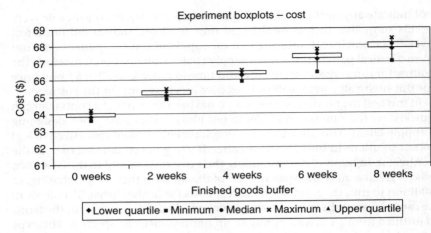

Figure 5.8   Cost results for increasing finished goods buffers

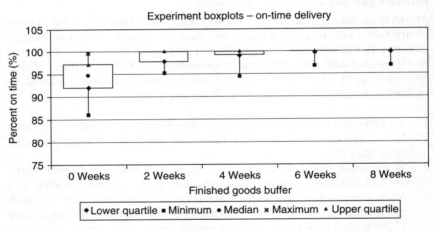

Figure 5.9   On-time delivery results for increasing finished goods buffers

to be made, but would also increase the risk of late delivery. The results show that increasing the buffer to six weeks will improve performance but increasing it further to eight weeks only serves to increase the cost of the product. In all, the experiments show that there is little merit in renegotiating the size of the finished goods buffer for this particular contract suggesting that other avenues of negotiation should be followed instead.

Conclusions

Outsourced (or contract) manufacturing is now one of the fastest-growing industries in a broad range of business sectors. Outsourced supply chains are formed through the RFQ process. A field study was carried out on seven enterprises involved in the establishment of outsourced supply chains with the purpose of understanding, in such cases, how supply chains are developed and what support tools are used. The seven enterprises ranged from small enterprises to large multinationals and were on different tiers in a supply chain. In all cases very limited analysis using spreadsheets that only captured the 'four walls' costs of the factory were used to design the supply chains. While this level of analysis may be appropriate in relation to some of the small enterprises, in several cases examined it is felt that a more detailed analysis at the supply chain initialization stage is merited.

To investigate this further a detailed simulation model of one outsourced supply chain, a first-tier high-volume CM, was developed. The simulation model, combined with ABC costing, allows the capture of the main cost drivers in the wider supply chain; costs such as inventory, reorder policies, supplier selection, contract conditions, etc. Hypothetical experiments on this real supply chain showed that major gains in terms of cost reduction and risk evaluation could be obtained by employing such tools.

However, to use simulation in the manner shown would require a high level of resources that would not be realistic for most companies. Simulation would need to be developed within an application that lowers the expertise required to use the tool and that would permit its deployment within a short time frame, as typically found in the RFQ process.

References

Anupindi, R. and Bassok, Y. 1999 'Supply contracts with quantity commitments and stochastic demand', in S. Tayur, R. Ganeshan and M. Magazine (eds), *Quantitative Models for Supply Chain Management*, Norwell, MA: Kluwer Academic Publishers: 198–232.

Carbone, J. 2005 'Worldwide outsourcing rises', *Electronics Purchasing*, accessed 12 December 2006, <http://www.purchasing.com/article/CA501253.html

Ethier, W.J. 2005 'Globalization, globalisation: Trade, technology and wages', *International Review of Economics and Finance*, 14(3): 237–58.

Friedlos, D. 2007 'Europe bucks outsourcing trend', accessed 25 June 2007, <http://www.computing.co.uk/computing/news/2188567/europe-bucks-outsourcing-trend>

Huang, G.Q., Lau, J.S.K. and Mak, K.L. 2003 'The impacts of sharing production information on supply chain dynamics: A review of the literature', *International Journal of Production Research*, 41(7): 1483–517.

Liston, P., Byrne, J., Heavey, C. and Byrne, P.J. 2008 'Discrete-event simulation for evaluating virtual organisations', *International Journal of Production Research*, 46(5): 1335–56.

Morrissey, O. and Filatotchev, I. 2000 'Globalisation and trade: The implications for exports from marginalised economies', *Journal of Development Studies*, 37(2): 1–12.

Ngowi, A.B., Pienaar, E. Talukhaba, A. and Mbachu, J. 2005 'The globalisation of the construction industry – a review', *Building and Environment*, 40(1): 135–41.

Plambeck, E.L. and Taylor, T.A. 2005 'Sell the plant? The impact of contract manufacturing on innovation, capacity and profitability', *Management Science*, 51(1): 133–50.

Part II

Approaches, Frameworks and Techniques for Integrating Knowledge Management in the Supply Chain

6
Modelling Supply Chain Information and Material Flow Perturbations
Teresa Wu and Jennifer Blackhurst

Introduction

It is well established that supply chains can be multitiered dynamic systems where each tier may have multiple entities (such as suppliers or manufacturers) and the linear flow of goods is uncommon (Riddalls, Bennett and Tipi 2000). This complexity is exacerbated when entities in the supply chain may be involved in a multitude of other supply chains, each with differing requirements or objectives (Sahin and Robinson 2002). In a supply chain system, there are forward flows of materials as product is moved from the supply base, to the manufacturers and eventually to the end customer. These material flows are triggered by information flows, which move in the reverse direction through the supply chain as shown in Figure 6.1.

Given the complex nature of today's supply chains, there is a need to understand the impact of perturbations on both the material and information flows. Perturbations can include a wide variety of disruptive events such as transportation delays, port stoppages, accidents and natural disasters, poor communication, part shortages, quality issues and operations issues (Cooke 2002, Machalaba and Kim 2002, Mitroff and Alpasan 2003). Supply chain networks are vulnerable to disruptions and failure at any point in the supply chain has the potential to cause the entire network to fail (Rice and Caniato 2003). Additionally, perturbations originating in a localized point of a supply chain have the potential to be passed onto subsequent tiers or branches of the supply chain, with possible amplification effects. In this research we seek to better understand how changes and disruptions in information being passed through the supply chain can actually be the root cause of disruptions to material flows. For example, an unexpected increase in demand (unexpected changes in information), poor forecasting (inaccurate information) or a delay in receiving information (late information) could lead to an inability to deliver product to the end customer.

One promising method to model flows within a supply chain is the use of Petri nets. In this chapter, we model supply chain systems using Petri

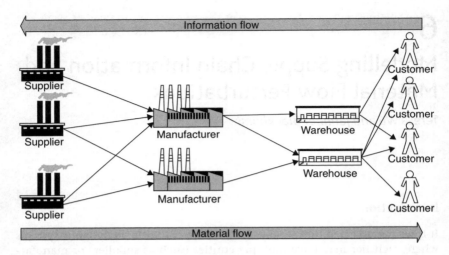

Figure 6.1   Simple supply chain example illustrating the forward flow of material and the backward flow of information
Source: Wu and O'Grady 2005.

nets with incidence matrices to conduct material flow analysis and inverse incidence matrices to conduct information flow analysis.

Literature review

In today's environment, supply chain performance has become a competitive edge for many firms. Well-performing supply chains are coordinated, in part, through the ability to share information. This ability to share information throughout the supply chain is enhanced by relatively recent advances in information systems technology and has had a significant impact on the evolution of supply chain management (Lee and Whang 2000). However, information technologies cannot be assumed to be flawless and information might be subject to undesirable effects, such as unpredictable or erroneous modifications. In fact, it is recognized that a major challenge in effective information sharing and supply chain management is the timeliness and accuracy of information (Lee and Whang 2000). Decisions at all points in the supply chain are determined based upon available information. Poor information quality can be detrimental in making good decisions.

The bullwhip effect is a well-known example of how changes in information being passed through the supply chain can have an impact on order size and fluctuation. The bullwhip effect was first recognized by Forrester (1961) and is described as small changes in demand becoming amplified as that demand is passed along a supply chain. Lee, Padmanabhan and Whang (1997a, 1997b) discuss causes and mitigation strategies for the bullwhip effect, including sharing information throughout the supply. It is interesting to note that typical amplification ratio between two echelons is 2:1; and between four echelons is 20:1 (Riddalls, Bennett and Tipi 2000). Recently, the quality of information has been recognized as having an impact on the bullwhip effect. Chatfield *et al.* (2004) conduct a simulation study to gain insights into the bullwhip effect and find that the quality of information used in the supply chain has a significant impact on the bullwhip effect at all levels of the supply chain. Results of the study indicate that better information quality reduces the bullwhip effect. Additionally, there has been other research that highlights the need for having correct and timely information in the supply chain. For example, Fleisch and Tellkamp (2005) study inventory information accuracy in a three-echelon supply chain and find that inventory inaccuracy leads to decreased supply chain performance. Lin, Huang and Lin (2002) use simulation experiments to show the more detailed information at all organizational levels leads to better operational performance and reduces supply chain costs. Similarly, Sahin and Robinson (2002) model a make-to-order supply chain and find that information sharing and coordinated decision-making improve operations and reduce costs.

While the examples presented above stress the need for using timely, reliable and accurate information, there is still a need for understanding (1) what information flows in the supply chain, (2) the design of the information flow path in the supply chain and (3) how the information flow errors or disruptions can affect material flow in a supply chain. Indeed, the ability to define the source and propagation path of information errors or inaccuracy in the supply chain has not yet been developed. A tool such as this could provide a supply chain manager with the ability to quickly identify sources of errors in the supply chain and could be used to mitigate information quality issues at the source, understand the propagation path of the inaccurate data flows allowing the users to reduce the use of the erroneous information, and redesign supply chain information flows for improved supply chain performance.

One potential approach to modelling a supply chain system and its disruptions is a Petri net-based methodology. This methodology has been shown to be an effective tool for modelling complex and dynamic systems due to its ability to illustrate precedence, concurrent and asynchronous events, its mathematical foundation and ability to graphically represent a system (Salimifard and Wright 2001, Zhou and Zurawski 1995, Zurawski and Zhou 1994).

Supply chain modelling and analysis using Petri nets

In this section, Petri net basics are introduced, followed by the proposed Petri net model with incidence matrices and inverse incidence matrices for supply chain material flow and information flow analysis.

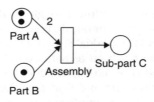

Figure 6.2   Petri net example

Petri net basics

The concept of Petri nets was first developed by Carl Petri in 1962. A Petri net is a bipartite directed graph that uses three objects to represent the system under study. Generally, resources and conditions (pre-conditions and post-conditions) of the system are represented by circles named *places*. A black dot, named *token*, inside of the circle indicates a resource or condition exists. The events or activities of the systems are represented by squares or by bars named *transitions*. Finally, arcs connect either a place to a transition or a transition to a place and show the direction of the flow in the network. Petri nets allow for a simulation of the dynamic and concurrent activities of systems by the use of moving tokens. A Petri net executes by firing transition nodes, which is controlled by the tokens residing in the place nodes. A transition node is enabled if, and only if, every place node directed to the transition node by the input arc has at least one token. Once the transition node is enabled, it may fire. A transition node fires by moving all of its tokens from the place node directed to the transition node and then deposits one token into each of the place nodes that is directed from the transition node. Petri nets, as a graphical tool, provide a visual communication medium between users. As a mathematical tool, Petri nets, embedded with mathematical algorithms, can offer a formal analysis of system properties (Zurawski and Zhou 1994, Murata 1989).

Figure 6.2 shows a simple example of a Petri net. In Figure 6.2, the activity 'Assembly' is ready to begin because we have the two 'Part A' parts and the single 'Part B' part required to produce the 'Sub-part C.'

A relevant property of Petri nets is the concept of reachability. Using reachability, we can find whether a determined state (condition or behaviour) is reachable from another state, through a series of other states. Related to this property is the one for reversibility, which is used to study the ability of systems for error recovery. In this chapter the property of reachability is extended to trace back errors that affect the quality of information in supply chains. Good introductory references to learn more about these and other important properties of Petri nets are Murata (1989), Zurawski and Zhou (1994) and Schneeweiss (1999).

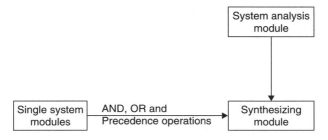

Figure 6.3   Proposed Petri net system architecture
Source: Wu and Blackhurst 2005.

Petri nets for supply chain modelling and analysis

The Petri net method presented in this chapter extends work by Wu and Blackhurst (2005) where three modules are defined, including the single system module, the synthesizing module and system analysis module. These modules are the basic building blocks for modelling a supply chain in a hierarchical manner and are illustrated in Figure 6.3. The *single system module* can model the key characteristics of a single entity in supply chain. The *synthesizing module* ties the individual entities together into an integrated system based on predefined synthesis operations, such as AND, OR, Precedence. The *system analysis module* evaluates system performance and analyzes the impact of supply chain perturbations such as inaccurate or distorted information. In this chapter, we introduce the use of incidence matrices and inverse incidence matrices to track the system performance over both material flow and information flow.

Single system modules

Single system modules can be used to represent single operations or entities within a system. These single systems are linked together in a hierarchical manner to form the structure of a supply chain. Definitions for creating the single system modules are shown below. Given a Petri net a 3-tuple *(M, A, L)* where $M = \{m_1, m_2, \ldots, m_p\}$ represents a finite set of places m_i in the network, $A = \{a_1, a_2, \ldots, a_q\}$ represents the finite set of transitions a_j in the network, $L \subseteq (M \times A) \cup (A \times M)$ is the set of arcs connecting places to transitions and transitions to places.

> **Definition 1 Input Place:** If an arc is from place node m_i to transition node a_j $(m_i \rightarrow a_j)$, m_i is called an input place.
> **Definition 2 Output Place:** If an arc is from transition node a_j to place node m_i $(m_i \leftarrow a_j)$, m_i is called output place.

Definition 3 Input Matrix (I): I is an input matrix mapping $M \times A \rightarrow \{0, 1\}$ corresponding to the set of directed arcs from M to A. If m_i is input place node for a_j, $I_{ij} = 1$, otherwise, $I_{ij} = 0$.

Definition 4 Out Matrix (O): O is an output matrix mapping $M \times A \rightarrow \{0,1\}$ corresponding to the set of directed arcs from A to M. If m_i is output place node for a_j, $O_{ij} = 1$, otherwise, $O_{ij} = 0$.

In this work, the nets used are self-loop free, that is, there is no place node m_i and transition node a_j such that there exists an arc from place node m_i to transition node a_j ($m_i \rightarrow a_j$), and an arc from transition node a_j to place node m_i ($m_i \leftarrow a_j$), that is, $O_{ij} \neq I_{ij} \neq 1$

Definition 5 Marking Vector (T): Let T^i be $[t_1^i, t_2^i, ...]$, T^i is called marking vector at stage i. In the graphical representation, a marking $t_q^i = t$ is indicated by t small tokens in the circle representing place m_q. Note that T^0 indicates the root or initial marking of the network.

Synthesizing module

The synthesizing module coordinates the individual system entities defined using the single system module into an integrated system. Formulating such an integrated system from multiple distributed entities requires the coordination among the single entities to be clearly identified. Therefore, operators need to be developed to explain the dependencies. We first identify the interface places that are places from each single system where the single system interfaces with another system or entity. We then define three operators (Wu and Blackhurst 2005), AND (Ψ_{And}), OR (Ψ_{OR}), Precedence(Ψ_{PRE}), to describe the relationships and synthesize single system modules into an integrated system.

Definition 6 AND Operator (Ψ_{And}): The AND Operation (Ψ_{And}) combines single entities' efforts into an integrated system requiring all operations from each single system to be performed. Given n single system modules, let us assume an AND relationship exists among the n single system modules, a synthesizing module is created with the AND operation. Given the interface places of the n single system modules having AND relations are explicitly listed, one transition named a_{and} is added and the arcs from all interface places to the a_{and} are added. Second, one place named m_{and} is added and the arc from a_{and} to m_{and} is added.

Definition 7 OR Operator (Ψ_{OR}): The OR Operation (Ψ_{OR}) allows single entities to be combined into an integrated system allowing the choice of operations from each single system to be performed based upon predetermined conditions. Given n single system module, let us assume an OR relationship exists among the single system modules, a synthesizing module is created with the OR operation. First, given all the interface places of the n single system module having OR relations are explicitly listed, one transition named $a_{\text{OR,i}}$ ($i = 1, \ldots, n$) is added to each of the interfaces and the arc from each interface place to the related $a_{\text{OR,i}}$ ($i = 1, \ldots, n$) is added. Second, one place named m_{OR} is added and the arcs from $a_{\text{OR,i}}$ ($i = 1, \ldots, n$) to m_{OR} are added.

Definition 8 Precedence Operator (Ψ_{Pre}): The Precedence Operation (Ψ_{Pre}) allows single entities to be combined into an integrated system in a specified order, which allows each single system to be triggered sequentially. Given n single system modules, let us assume a Precedence relationship exists among the single system modules, a synthesizing module is created with the Precedence operation. First, given all the interface places of the n single system modules having Precedence relations are explicitly listed, one transition named $a_{\text{Pre,i}}$ ($i = 1, \ldots, n$) is added to each of the interface place and the arc from each interface place to the related $a_{\text{Pre,i}}$ ($i = 1, \ldots, n$) is added. Next, the Precedence relationship output place named $m_{\text{Pre,i}}$ is added for each transition $a_{\text{Pre,i}}$ ($i = 1, \ldots, n$) . The arc from each transition $a_{\text{Pre,i}}$ ($i = 1, \ldots, n$) to each place $m_{\text{Pre,i}}$ is added respectively. Finally, to direct each single system to be integrated in the required sequence, one place named $m_{\text{Seq,i}}$ ($i = 1, \ldots, n$) is added to each of the transition named $a_{\text{Pre,i}}$ ($i = 1, \ldots, n$). The arc from each $m_{\text{Seq,i}}$ ($i = 1, \ldots, n$) to the related $a_{\text{Pre,i}}$ ($i = 1, \ldots, n$) is added and the arc from each $a_{\text{Pre,i}}$ ($i = 1, \ldots, n$) to each $m_{\text{Seq,i+1}}$ ($i = 1, \ldots, n - 1$) is added. By giving initial marking and placing sequence place nodes appropriately, each single system module will be triggered in the desired order.

System analysis module

Given a synthesizing module, the system analysis module is used to analyze how far-reaching the disruption impact is on given material flows and/or information flows based on incidence matrix and inverse incidence matrix.

Definition 9 Incidence Matrix (G): For a self-loop-free Petri net, the connectivity, that is, the links between places and transitions, is indicated by means of an integer matrix G, where $G = O - I$, G is called Incidence Matrix.

Definition 10 Enabled Transition: Given a synthesizing module, a transition node, a_{j}, is enabled if, and only if, every input place node for the transition node holds at least one token.

Definition 11 Transition Firing Matrix (H): At any time or stage s a transition a_{j} is enabled if, and only if, every input place for the transition holds at least one token. Any transition can fire if it is enabled, which leads to the next stage $s + 1$. The relation of such states for all the transitions in the network is kept in the firing vector $H^s = [h_1^s, h_2^s, \ldots, h_q^s]$. h_j^s is a binary parameter, where at stage s a value of zero means transition a_j is not ready to fire, otherwise a value of 1 means the transition a_j will operate at stage $s+1$.

Definition 12 Forward Flow Operation: After transitions are fired, the marking of the net updates according to the following relation, where the superscript s indicates the previous stage and $s+1$ for the new state:, E.G. $S+1$ TO $S+1$:

$$T^{s+1} = T^s + H^s * G$$

In this manner, it is possible to determine all sequences of firing and all sequences of marking in the net. A marking T^j is said to be reachable from marking T^i if there exists a sequence of firings that transforms T^i to T^j. The set of all possible markings reachable from T^i is called Reachability Set for T^i, denoted by $R(T^i)$. The forward flow operation may be used to analyze the flow of material.

Definition 13 Inverse Incidence Matrix: The inverse incidence matrix $W = I - O$. That is, the inverse incidence matrix W is the incidence matrix G times (-1).

Definition 14 Backwards Flow Operation: A new marking vector for the net is indicated by $J^s = \{j_1^s, j_2^s, \dots, j_q^s\}$. To determine the previous marking we use the following relations:

$$J^{s+1} = J^s + H^{s+1} * W$$

The backward flow operation may be used to analyze the flow of information.

A simple example is shown in Figure 6.4. It consists of four place nodes, $M = \{m_1, m_2, m_3, m_4\}$, two transition nodes, $A = \{a_1, a_2\}$ and a set of arcs, $L = \{(m_1 \rightarrow a_1), (m_2 \leftarrow a_1), (m_2 \rightarrow a_2), (m_3 \rightarrow a_2), (m_4 \leftarrow a_2)\}$, with an initial marking of $T^0 = \{1, 0, 1, 0, 0\}$. The input matrix, output matrix and incidence matrix are:

$$I = \begin{array}{c} \\ a_1 \\ a_2 \end{array} \begin{array}{cccc} m_1 & m_2 & m_3 & m_4 \\ \left| \begin{array}{cccc} 1 & 0 & 0 & 0 \\ 0 & 1 & 1 & 0 \end{array} \right| \end{array}$$

$$O = \begin{array}{c} \\ a_1 \\ a_2 \end{array} \begin{array}{cccc} m_1 & m_2 & m_3 & m_4 \\ \left| \begin{array}{cccc} 0 & 1 & 0 & 0 \\ 0 & 0 & 0 & 1 \end{array} \right| \end{array}$$

Transition firing matrices are $H^1 = [1,0]$ and $H^2 = [0,1]$

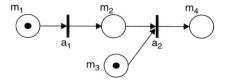

Figure 6.4   Another example of a Petri net model

First, we derive the incidence matrix $G = O - I$. Thus:

$$G = \begin{array}{c} \\ a_1 \\ a_2 \end{array} \begin{array}{cccc} m_1 & m_2 & m_3 & m_4 \\ \left| \begin{array}{cccc} -1 & 1 & 0 & 0 \\ 0 & -1 & -1 & 1 \end{array} \right| \end{array}$$

Given initial marking is $T^0 = [1, 0, 1, 0]$, we get:

$$T^1 = T^0 + H^{1*}G$$

$$= [1, 0, 1, 0] + [1, 0]^* \begin{bmatrix} -1 & 1 & 0 & 0 \\ 0 & -1 & -1 & 1 \end{bmatrix}$$

$$= [0, 1, 1, 0]$$

and

$$T^2 = T^1 + H^{2*}G$$

$$= [0, 1, 1, 0] + [0, 1]^* \begin{bmatrix} -1 & 1 & 0 & 0 \\ 0 & -1 & -1 & 1 \end{bmatrix}$$

$$= [0, 0, 0, 1]$$

Thus, we conclude $R(T^0) = (T^0, T^1, T^2)$. Assume we are interested in studying the impact of disruption from place m_1 on the material flow, we can easily summarize that places m_2 (from T^1) and m^4 (from T^2) will be affected.

Second, let us examine the information flow, with similar operation on inverse matrix; however, the marking will be changed to $J^0 = [0,0,0,1]$, we get:

$$J^1 = J^0 + H^{2*}W$$

$$= [0, 0, 0, 1] + [0, 1]^* \begin{bmatrix} 1 & -1 & 0 & 0 \\ 0 & 1 & 1 & -1 \end{bmatrix}$$

$$= [0, 1, 1, 0]$$

and

$$J^2 = J^1 + H^{1*}W$$

$$= [0, 1, 1, 0] + [1, 0]^* \begin{bmatrix} 1 & -1 & 0 & 0 \\ 0 & 1 & 1 & -1 \end{bmatrix}$$

$$= [1, 0, 1, 0]$$

Clearly, any inaccurate information from place m^4 (from J^0) will be passed to m_2 and m_3 (from J^1), which will be further passed onto m_1 (from J^1).

This simple example illustrates how properties of Petri nets, including incidence matrices, transition firing matrices and inverse incidence matrices can be used to study the path of both material flow and information flow. In the next section, we will use a more complex industry case to illustrate how the supply chain can be modelled from single components and synthesized into an integrated supply chain, and then analyzed.

Industry case study

In this section, we apply the Petri net model to an ice cream manufacturer supply chain located in the Midwestern USA.

Company background and case study setting

The manufacturer has been struggling with the impact of information flow disruption on its supply chain in recent years. The ice cream manufacturer plans orders using a continuously rolling four-week forecast. They are in an interesting situation in that their customer is not the ultimate end-user. The ice cream manufacturer sells to major retailers and grocery stores, while the end-users are individual consumers. Interestingly, the major retailers will give the ice cream manufacturer a forecast of their need, but will not give visibility of end-consumer demand. The ice cream manufacturer also is challenged by the fact that it is a highly seasonal business.

In recent years, the ice cream manufacturer has initiated a supplier coordination programme to improve communication and information quality with their supply base consisting of approximately 75 suppliers. However, its information is still shared manually to the supply base. Many of the products provided by the suppliers have an eight- to ten-week lead time and are perishable (possessing a short shelf life). Major categories of supply include:

- Dairy (milk and cream)
- Sugar
- Candy
- Flavourings (such as vanilla)
- Fruit
- Cones/wafers.

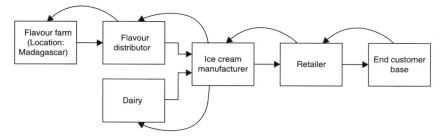

Figure 6.5 Ice cream supply chain

In the example we focus on a small portion of the supply chain as shown in Figure 6.5. The ice cream manufacturer has two suppliers: the flavour distributor and the dairy. These suppliers provide vanilla and cream. The flavour distributor purchases vanilla from a farm overseas. After the ice cream manufacturer produces the ice cream, it is sent to the retailer. End customers purchase directly from the retailer. Material flow is shown with blue arrows, while information flow is shown with red arrows. Note that the ice cream manufacturer does not have a direct link to end-customer information and must rely on the retailer to share that information.

The major issues for the ice cream manufacturer, in terms of information quality, are:

1. The ice cream manufacturer's customer will not give visibility of end-customer demand – only their own forecast. The result is that sudden changes in demand cannot be met due to the eight- to ten-week planning lead time on perishable materials like cream. Moreover, some suppliers such as flavouring and sugar are overseas, with long transportation lead times. In cases of large orders, the distributors of these products are not able to meet demand due to these long lead times. So, by the time the correct demand information reaches the ice cream manufacturer, it is too late for the supply base to respond.
2. To compound the problem, once the forecast data is received internally to the ice cream manufacturer, the sales and marketing departments are often overly optimistic and do not coordinate with the operations department.
3. Information from suppliers is often inaccurate, including incorrect inventory levels and lack of accurate estimate of delivery date.

Single system modules

The single system modules of the ice cream manufacturing supply chain are shown in Figure 6.6. There are five single system modules in this case study: the overseas flavour farm delivering to the flavour distributor, the flavour distributor delivering to the ice cream manufacturer, the

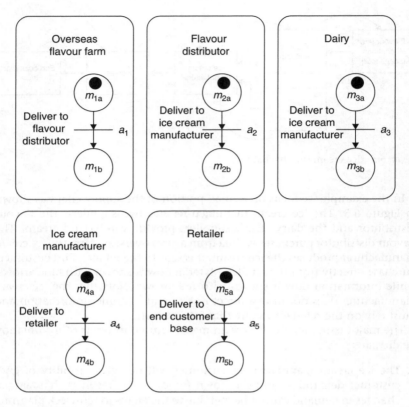

Figure 6.6   Single system modules

dairy delivering to the ice cream manufacturer, the ice cream manufacturer delivering to the retailer and the retailer delivering to the customer base.

These single system modules are next combined into an integrated supply chain system using the operators in the synthesizing module. Note that only the AND operator is used in this example. Interested readers are referred to a more complex industry application (aircraft communication equipment) in Wu and Blackhurst (2005), which uses AND, OR and Precedence operators.

Synthesizing module

In this section, the individual entities are synthesized into an integrated supply chain. The synthesized Petri net model of the ice cream supply chain is shown in Figure 6.7. In this example, the AND operator is used at transition node a_2 to indicate that the ice cream manufacturer needs both the milk from the dairy and the vanilla from the flavour distributor in order to manufacture the ice cream.

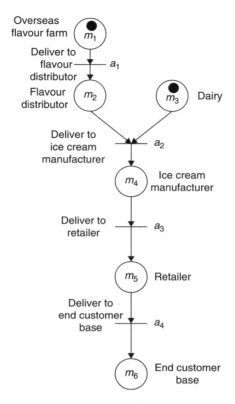

Figure 6.7 Synthesized Petri net model of the ice cream supply chain

System analysis module

The synthesized Petri net model consists of six place nodes, $M = \{m_1, m_2, m_3, m_4, m_5, m_6\}$, four transition nodes, $A = \{a_1, a_2, a_3, a_4\}$ and a set of arcs, $L = \{(m_1 \rightarrow a_1), (m_2 \leftarrow a_1), (m_2 \rightarrow a_2), (m_3 \rightarrow a_2), (m_4 \leftarrow a_2), (m_4 \rightarrow a_3), (m_5 \leftarrow a_3), (m_5 \rightarrow a_4), (m_6 \leftarrow a_4)\}$, with an initial marking of $T^0 = \{1, 0, 1, 0, 0, 0\}$.

In order to analyze how the impact of a disruption on information and material flows in the supply chain, the system analysis module is invoked. The system analysis module uses incidence matrices to analyze material and information flows.

The input matrix is:

$$
I = \begin{array}{c|cccccc}
 & m_1 & m_2 & m_3 & m_4 & m_5 & m_6 \\
\hline
a_1 & 1 & 0 & 0 & 0 & 0 & 0 \\
a_2 & 0 & 1 & 1 & 0 & 0 & 0 \\
a_3 & 0 & 0 & 0 & 1 & 0 & 0 \\
a_4 & 0 & 0 & 0 & 0 & 1 & 0
\end{array}
$$

The output matrix is:

$$
O = \begin{array}{c} \\ a_1 \\ a_2 \\ a_3 \\ a_4 \end{array}
\begin{array}{cccccc}
m_1 & m_2 & m_3 & m_4 & m_5 & m_6 \\
\left| \begin{array}{cccccc}
0 & 1 & 0 & 0 & 0 & 0 \\
0 & 0 & 0 & 1 & 0 & 0 \\
0 & 0 & 0 & 0 & 1 & 0 \\
0 & 0 & 0 & 0 & 0 & 1
\end{array} \right|
\end{array}
$$

The transition firing matrices are: $H^1 = [1, 0, 0, 0]$, $H^2 = [0, 1, 0, 0]$, $H^3 = [0, 0, 1, 0]$ and $H^4 = [0, 0, 0, 1]$

The incidence matrix is:

$$
G = \begin{array}{c} \\ a_1 \\ a_2 \\ a_3 \\ a_4 \end{array}
\begin{array}{cccccc}
m_1 & m_2 & m_3 & m_4 & m_5 & m_6 \\
\left| \begin{array}{cccccc}
-1 & 1 & 0 & 0 & 0 & 0 \\
0 & -1 & -1 & 1 & 0 & 0 \\
0 & 0 & 0 & -1 & 1 & 0 \\
0 & 0 & 0 & 0 & -1 & 1
\end{array} \right|
\end{array}
$$

And the inversed matrix $W = -G$

The matrices may be used to investigate a number of scenarios. In this example, the ice cream manufacturer is interested in better understanding the impact of unexpected changes on the information flows. In particular, the ice cream manufacturer is interested in understanding the impact of the bullwhip effect on its supply chain. The bullwhip effect is experienced, in part, due to the lack of information sharing from the retailer and the inability to rely of information being accurate from the supply base. Therefore, we use the inverse incidence matrix W with $J^0 = [0, 0, 0, 0, 1]$.

Following the backwards-flow operation, we get:
$J^1 = J^0 + H^4 W$, that is

$$
J^1 = [0\ 0\ 0\ 0\ 0\ 1] + [0\ 0\ 0\ 1]
\begin{bmatrix}
1 & -1 & 0 & 0 & 0 & 0 \\
0 & 1 & 1 & -1 & 0 & 0 \\
0 & 0 & 0 & 1 & -1 & 0 \\
0 & 0 & 0 & 0 & 1 & -1
\end{bmatrix}
$$

$$
= [0\ 0\ 0\ 0\ 1\ 0]
$$

We assume the information distortion will lead to the order amplification of 2:1 between tiers in the supply chain as discussed by Riddalls, Bennett and Tipi (2000). Therefore, as information is passed back through the supply chain from place node m_6 to place node m_5, actual customer information is from place node m_6 is amplified by a factor of two to place node m_5.

Similarly, each additional tier information is passed through amplifies the order by a factor of two. Therefore, when $J^2 = [0, 0, 0, 1, 0]$ (derived from H^3) the information will be distorted by a factor of four (from the original customer data) and when $J^3 = [0, 1, 1, 0, 0]$ (derived from H^2) the information will be distorted by a factor of eight. Finally, when $J_4 = [1, 0, 0, 0, 0]$ (derived from H^1) the information will be distorted by a factor of 16.

Using Petri nets to model material and information flows in the supply chain can aid supply chain managers in better understanding the impact of material disruptions and inaccurate information. The example from this section illustrates how the impact of inaccurate information manifesting itself through the bullwhip effect propagates through the supply chain and impacts multiple tiers. The example has illustrated how supply chains may be modelled using Petri nets and they analysis of the supply chain may be performed using the Petri net. In this example, the bullwhip effect has been modelled to illustrate how information is distorted as it moves back through the supply chain due to a lack of information sharing. In this example, the information is distorted by a factor of 16 from the end customer to the flavour farm.

Conclusions

Modelling supply chains to better understand their operation is certainly a timely and challenging topic, considering the dynamic and complex nature of today's global supply chains. In this chapter, we model supply chain systems using Petri nets. We have exploited some of the properties of Petri nets, such as incidence and inverse incidence matrices, to conduct supply chain material flow analysis (which we call forward-flow analysis and supply chain information flow analysis (backward-flow analysis). We have illustrated the use of this approach on an ice cream manufacturing supply chain where the impact of poor information sharing and inaccurate information has led to the manifestation of the bullwhip effect.

Tools such as this are of value to supply chain managers because information technologies cannot be assumed to be flawless and information might be subject to uncertainty or errors. Since good supply chain decisions require accurate and timely information, it is important to understand how inaccurate information might affect supply chain performance. We envision tools such as Petri nets to be of use to supply chain managers to assist in understanding the impact of information perturbations to supply chain performance, in particular material flows. Additionally, future extensions may involve the identification of sources of information errors, which could be used to stop them before they propagate through the supply chain.

Limitations of the Petri net model in this chapter include the limited number of supply chain operators as well as the inability to specifically measure and quantify supply chain performance metrics. For example, in the ice cream supply chain case study, information is distorted by a factor of 16, but that distortion is not quantified using real order data. Rather, it is simply a conceptual phenomenon in the model. Previous work has been done to include attributes of interest such as cost and lead time, which can be attached to each place node and transition node in a Petri net model (Wu and Blackhurst 2005). In doing so, the marking changes can be associated with the updates on the attributes, which can quantitatively study the impact of the imperfect information. This is certainly of interest in future extensions of this work. Other future extensions include the use of all three operators and an investigation into the need for developing additional operators to accurately model supply chain design and performance.

References

Chatfield, K., Kim, J., Harrison, T. and Hayya, J. 2004 'The bullwhip effect – impact of stochastic lead time, information quality, and information sharing: A simulation study', *Production and Operations Management*, 13: 340–53.

Cooke, J.A. 2002 'Brave new world', *Logistics Management and Distribution Report*, 41: 31–4.

Fleisch, E. and Tellkamp, C. 2005 'Inventory inaccuracy and supply chain performance: A simulation study of a retail supply chain', *International Journal of Production Economics*, 95: 373–85.

Forrester, J. 1961 *Industrial Dynamics*, New York: MIT Press.

Lee, H., Padmanabhan, V. and Whang, S. 1997a 'Information distortion in a supply chain: The bullwhip effect', *Management Science*, 43(4): 546–58.

Lee, H., Padmanabhan, V. and Whang, S. 1997b 'The bullwhip effect in supply chains', *Sloan Management Review*, 38: 93–102.

H. Lee, H. and Whang, S. 2000 'Information sharing in a supply chain', *International Journal of Manufacturing Technology and Management*, 1: 79–83.

Lin, F., Huang, S. and Lin, S. 2002 'Effects of information sharing on supply chain performance in electronic commerce', *IEEE Transactions on Engineering Management*, 49: 258–68.

Machalaba, D. and Kim, Q. 2002 'West Coast docks are shut down after series of work disruptions', *The Wall Street Journal (Eastern Edition)*, 30 September: A2.

Mitroff, I. and Alpasan, M. 2003 'Preparing for evil', *Harvard Business Review*, April: 109–15.

Murata, T. 1989 'Petri-nets: Properties, analysis and applications', *Proceedings of the IEEE*, 77: 541–80.

Petri, C. 1962 Kommunikation mit Autimaten, PhD dissertation, University of Bonn.

Rice, J. and Caniato, F. 2003 'Building a secure and resilient supply network', *Supply Chain Management Review*, 7: 22–30.

Riddalls, C., Bennett, S. and Tipi, N. 2000 'Modeling the dynamics of supply chains', *International Journal of Systems Science*, 31: 969–76.

Sahin, F. and Robinson, E. 2002 'Flow coordination and information sharing in supply chains: Review, implications and directions for future research', *Decision Sciences*, 33: 505–36.

Salimifard, K. and Wright, M. 2001 'Petri-net based modeling of workflow systems: An overview', *European Journal of Operation Research*, 134: 664–76.

Schneeweiss, W.G. 1999 *Petri Nets for Reliability Modeling: In the Fields of Engineering Safety and Dependability*, Hagen, Germany: Verlag.

Wu, T. and Blackhurst, J. 2005 'A modeling methodology for supply chain synthesis and disruption analysis', *International Journal of Knowledge-Based and Intelligent Engineering Systems*, 9: 93–106.

Wu, T. and O'Grady, P. 2005 'A network-based approach to integrated supply chain design', *Production Planning and Control*, 16: 444–53.

Zhou, M. and Zurawski, R. 1995 'Introduction to Petri nets in flexible and agile automation', in M. Zhou (ed.), *Petri Nets in Flexible and Agile Automation*, Dordrecht, NL: Kluwer Academic Publishers.

Zurawski, R. and Zhou, M. 1994 'Petri nets and industrial applications: A tutorial', *IEEE Transactions on Industrial Electronics*, 41: 567–83.

7
Linking Product, Supply Chain, Process and Manufacturing Planning and Control Design

Jan Olhager

Introduction

In order to improve upon competitive capabilities, firms need to understand how manufacturing and supply chain operations should be designed to better support market requirements. The interrelationships between product characteristics, supply chain design, process choice and the design of manufacturing planning and control principles is a complex problem generating increasing interest in industry and academia. How these decisions should be coordinated is an important issue for operational and supply chain performance. How product characteristics affect one or the other has previously been discussed in the literature. Three fundamental theoretical models are the product-supply chain model by Fisher (1997), the product-process matrix by Hayes and Wheelwright (1979a) and the systems-strategy model for linking manufacturing planning and control (MPC) system choices to product characteristics by Berry and Hill (1992). Other models have been proposed for linking product characteristics to supply chain design, process choice and MPC approaches, but all relate strongly to these three models. Thus, these three models can be considered as baseline reference models. They have been tested before, but only one at the time. Here, we provide a comprehensive analysis of all four factors.

This article investigates the relationships between these issues, using a survey to test the interdependencies empirically, using data collected from 128 Swedish manufacturing firms. Of special interest is the interaction between supply chain design aspects, process choice and MPC approaches. First, we discuss the research framework including a review of the fundamental theoretical models. Second, we present the research methodology in terms of the data and measurements used. Third, we investigate how the characteristics of products, supply chains, processes and MPC approaches interact. In the concluding section, we discuss managerial implications and suggestions for further research.

Framework

In this research, we are interested in all interrelationships between the four factors or decision areas. Figure 7.1 illustrates the research framework. In this section we will discuss the perspectives from literature on how product characteristics, supply chain design, process choice and MPC system approaches are interrelated. Product characteristics are market-related factors that need to be taken into account when deciding on supply chain design, process choice and the strategic choice of MPC principles. The literature is basically limited to how product characteristics affect one of the three other factors: the design of supply chains, processes, or MPC system. The interrelationships among these three decision areas will be explored later.

The relationships between product characteristics and supply chain design

Fisher (1997) proposed a model for the matching of product characteristics and supply chain design, which has attracted considerable attention both for practitioners and in academia. For example, Childerhouse, Aitken and Towill (2002) and Lee (2002) have proposed models that build upon the model by Fisher. Products that are innovative are characterized by, for example, variation in demand and short life cycles; they should therefore be transformed through a market-responsive supply chain that has extra capacity, capability of market information processing, and that is more flexible. On the other hand, products that are functional are characterized by, for example, a steady demand pattern and long product life cycles. A physically efficient supply chain that focuses on cost minimization and high utilization of resources should handle this kind of product. Thus, this model suggests that a certain

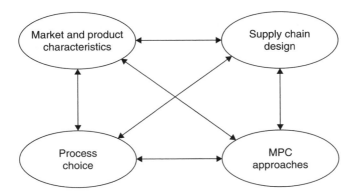

Figure 7.1 The research framework, in terms of the relationships that will be investigated

product type requires a specific type of supply chain design, whereas other choices will lead to a mismatch. This model is supported by cases such as Campbell Soup and Sport Obermeyer (Cachon and Fisher 1997, Fisher 1997, Fisher *et al*. 1994, 1997), and has been tested empirically in Selldin and Olhager (2007).

The relationships between product characteristics and process choice

The relationship between market and product characteristics and process choice has been described by Hayes and Wheelwright (1979a, 1979b, 1984) in the product-process matrix. The product-process matrix suggests that some combinations of product and process types are better than others, such that a more flow-oriented production process will be appropriate for increasing product demand volumes and a higher degree of standardization. At one end of the spectrum of product-process relationships we have one-of-a-kind production of customized products using an intermittent process. At the other end, high-volume standardized commodity products in continuous flow processes are found. Thus, this framework suggests that certain products should be produced using a specific type of manufacturing process in the firm. The type of unit depicted in this model is typically a plant or a manufacturing system, such as a plant within a plant. As a product matures and the sales volume increases, there is a need to shift from the initial low-volume and high-flexibility stage to a high-volume and low-cost manufacturing process. Thus, a life-cycle perspective can be employed, indicating that a product will need different process types for different stages in the product life cycle (Hayes and Wheelwright 1979a). This model is one of the most widely recognized concepts in the manufacturing strategy arena, and has been tested empirically in Spencer and Cox (1995), Safizadeh *et al*. (1996), McDermott, Greis and Fischer (1997) and Ahmad and Schroeder (2002).

The relationships between product characteristics and MPC approaches

The models for linking market characteristics to the design of MPC systems in the literature can basically be reduced to one, first presented in Berry and Hill (1992) and later included in Hill (2000) and Vollmann *et al*. (2005). In the Berry and Hill (1992) framework there are choices at three levels of the MPC system. At each level a set of market requirement attributes is used as a point of reference to make generic choices among a set of MPC design variables. At the master scheduling level, there are three choices; make-to-order (MTO), assemble-to-order (ATO), or make-to-stock (MTS). ATO covers for similar environments such as build-to-order, configure-to-order and finish-to-order, while MTO covers for engineer-to-order. At the materials-planning level the choices are rate-based or time-phased. Finally, at the shop floor control level the choices are MRP-type or JIT-type. It should be emphasized that the choices at these two planning levels are separate decisions (Berry and Hill

Table 7.1   The theoretical framework, linking product characteristics to supply chain design, process choice and the strategic choice of MPC approaches

Product characteristics			
Individual product volume per period	High	→	Low
Product variety	Narrow	→	Wide
Supply chain characteristics			
Primary purpose	Cost minimization	→	Quick response
Manufacturing focus	High utilization	→	Buffer capacity
Lead-time focus	Shorten lead times with respect to costs	→	Aggressive lead-time reduction
Process characteristics			
Process choice	Continuous processing	→	Project
MPC characteristics			
Sales and operations planning	Level	→	Chase
Master scheduling	MTS	→	MTO
Material planning	Rate-based	→	Time-phased
Production activity control	JIT-type	→	MRP-type

1992, Hill 2000, Vollmann *et al.* 2005). This framework provides theoretical normative guidelines for the choice of MPC approaches, wherefore these four variables are assumed to be the most important for choosing MPC approaches such that they align with the manufacturing environment. Firms with few high-volume standardized products would typically choose MTS, rate-based planning and JIT-type shop floor control, whereas firms with many low-volume, customized products would choose MTO, time-phased planning and MRP-type shop floor control. Olhager and Rudberg (2002) argue that a fourth, upper level should be added to the structure, that is, the sales and operations planning level. At this level two distinctly different planning strategies can be employed; chase and level. A chase planning strategy means that production output is changed to chase demand, whereas a level production strategy implies that production is at a constant uniform rate of output, with inventory build-ups and depletions (Vollmann *et al.* 2005). Theory suggests that a chase strategy should be used for low-volume, highly customized products, whereas a level strategy is more suitable for high-volume, standardized products (see Safizadeh and Ritzman 1997, Olhager and Rudberg 2002). This four-level framework linking product characteristics to MPC approaches has been tested empirically in Olhager and Selldin (2007).

Summarizing the relationships

The models for linking market characteristics to the designs of supply chains, processes and MPC approaches are summarized in Table 7.1, with respect to the expected relationships. Based on Table 7.1, which is developed from the models linking product requirements to the other three areas, the expected relationships between process, supply chain and MPC can be derived. The assumption is then that all three areas need to be designed to support the product characteristics in the marketplace. Thus, a cost minimization supply chain would typically include line or continuous manufacturing processes and level/MTS/rate-based/JIT-type approaches for manufacturing planning and control, to support high-volume, low-variety products. Also, a market-responsive supply chain would correspond well with a functional layout or project manufacturing and using chase/MTO/time-phased/MRP-type MPC approaches, to have the flexibility to support low-volume, high-variety products.

Methodology

Sample

The study is based on an extensive mail questionnaire survey among Swedish manufacturing firms. The survey includes responses from 128 manufacturing companies. The questionnaire is designed with respect to the guidelines and recommendations in Dillman (1998) and Forza (2002). The unit of analysis in this study is the main product line of a manufacturing plant and the corresponding supply chain. The sample was constituted of the entire body of PLAN members in a total of 511 different Swedish manufacturing companies; PLAN is the Swedish Production and Inventory Management Society. Thus, the respondents are all familiar with manufacturing and supply chain operations. After two reminders had been sent, usable responses from 128 companies were received. This represents a response rate of 25.0 per cent. Forza (2002) mentions that 20 per cent can be considered a minimum response rate for surveys in the operations research field.

Table 7.2 presents the characteristics of the respondents. The study includes small, medium-sized and large companies (see Table 7.2). Both consumer goods manufacturers (31 per cent) and industrial goods manufacturers (69 per cent) participated in the study. The companies represent the whole spectrum of the five generic process choices: project, jobbing, batch (flow shop), line and continuous processing. The different kinds of manufacturing environments with respect to size, product type and process type indicates that the sample is representative of the manufacturing sector in Sweden. An overview of the survey results in terms of the state of supply chain management practices in Sweden in general is presented in Olhager and Selldin (2004). Here, we focus on specific issues concerning product, supply chain, process and MPC approaches.

Non-response bias is estimated by comparing the responses from the first round with those received after the reminders, as suggested as an alternative method by Forza (2002) and by Lambert and Harrington (1990). No

Table 7.2 Characteristics of the respondents

Respondent's position	Per cent
Executive/general manager	5
Plant/operations manager	9
Materials/supply chain manager	39
Production planner	19
IS/IT manager	11
Purchasing manager	4
Other	13
Total sales revenue (in million euros)	
15 or less	25
16–50	27
51–250	30
251–750	13
750 or more	5
Number of employees	
150 or less	28
151–500	33
501–1,000	15
1,001–5,000	17
5,000 or more	7
Process choice	
Project	8
Jobbing	26
Batch (flow shop)	27
Line	29
Continuous processing	10

statistically significant differences were found on any study variable (at the 0.05 level).

Operational measures

In this section, we present the items and constructs that we use for this study. They all relate to the description in Table 7.1, such that a low value corresponds to the left-hand side and a high value to the right-hand side, captured or transformed to scales ranging from one to five. Items are captured through a five-step Likert scale or through the distribution among alternatives, which later was transformed to a scale ranging from one to five.

Product

The product characteristics that are used in the models mentioned above differ slightly. The product-process matrix by Hayes and Wheelwright (1979a) uses product volume and variety to describe product characteristics along a continuum from one-of-a-kind production to high-volume, standardized products. Fisher (1997) uses a number of characteristics to describe the type of product: product life cycle, contribution margin, product variety, average margin of error in the forecast at the time production is committed, average stock-out rate, average forced end-of-season markdown as percentage of full price, lead time required for made-to-order products. The variables linking market requirements to the MPC system design choices at the different levels are very similar (see Berry and Hill 1992, Hill 2000, and Vollmann *et al.* 2005). Four variables appear at all three levels, that is, product design, product variety, individual product volume per period and delivery speed. We use two product characteristics, product volume and product variety, as our measures, characterizing the type of product. Product variety is used in all three models, and product volume is central for choosing processes and MPC approaches. The operational measures for product characteristics are captured through questions related to product volume and variety using a five-step Likert scale and endpoints as depicted in Table 7.1. Thus, product volume ranges from 'very high' to 'very low' and variety from 'very low' to 'very high'.

Supply chain

Fisher (1997) distinguishes between two supply chain types: physically efficient and market-responsive, each having a certain set of characteristics. The operational measures are related to the three characteristics described in Table 7.1, that is, primary purpose, manufacturing focus and lead-time focus. In the survey, the respondents were asked to indicate the extent to which the companies included each aspect as a supply chain design criterion. We separated each aspect into two questions where each was given a five-step Likert scale from 'not important' to 'very important' with respect to supply chain design. For example, the manufacturing focus aspect was transformed into two questions concerning the importance of 'maintaining high average utilization rate' (associated with physically efficient supply chains) and of 'deploying excess buffer capacity' (associated with market-responsive supply chains). Thus, we have two items for every supply chain design aspect.

Process

The process types in Hayes and Wheelwright (1979a, 1979b, 1984) are (1) jumbled flow (job shop), (2) disconnected line flow (batch), (3) connected line flow (assembly line) and (4) continuous flow. However, many scholars regard project manufacturing as a fifth basic process choice (see e.g. Hill 2000), which in terms of degree of flow orientation would be positioned beyond job shop. These five process choices are typically regarded as the five basic and distinct choices for a manufacturing process, wherefore we use all five as our measures for process choice. The respondents distributed 100 per cent among the five choices. In principle, we use the same measure for process as Ahmad and Schroeder (2002), corresponding to the range in Table 7.1, such that a low value corresponds to a pure continuous processing situation and a high value corresponds to a pure project-manufacturing situation.

MPC approaches

We test the four levels of the MPC structure, and the structural choices at each level. Sales and operations planning (S&OP) is measured using a five-point scale ranging from a pure level planning strategy to a pure chase strategy. Master scheduling (MS) ranging from pure make-to-stock to pure make-to-order, materials planning (MP) ranging from pure rate-based to pure time-phased and production activity control (PAC) ranging from pure JIT-type to pure MRP-type are all measured using floating scales, where the respondents indicate the percentages of each approach. The floating scales were then transformed to a scale, ranging from one to five. The approaches were defined so that the respondents would not interpret them differently. The endpoints thus correspond to Table 7.1.

Results

In this section we divide the results into two parts. First, we analyze the relationships for product characteristics relative to the three decision variables, and then the relationships among the three decision variables.

Theory testing

Table 7.3 provides the Pearson correlations between, on the one hand, the product characteristics and, on the other hand, the process choice, supply chain design and the strategic choice of MPC approaches.

Table 7.3 The Pearson correlations between market and product characteristics and supply chain design, process choice and the strategic choice of MPC approaches

Market and product characteristics	Volume (high–low)	Variants (few–many)
Supply chain design aspects		
Primary purpose (cost minimum → quick response)	.015	−.061
Manufacturing focus (high utilization → buffer capacity)	.265**	−.009
Lead-time focus (cost-based → aggressive reduction)	.192*	.022
Process choice		
Process (line → project)	.332**	−.033
MPC approaches		
S&OP (level → chase)	.479**	.100
Master scheduling (MTS → MTO)	.330**	.228*
Material planning (rate-based → time-phased)	.028	−.030
Production activity control (JIT → MRP)	.078	−.022

* Correlation is significant at 0.05 level
** Correlation is significant at 0.01 level

The results in Table 7.3 show that the product volume has many more significant relationships with supply chain, process and MPC design than product variants does. The only instance where the number of variants is significantly related to any of the design issues is for the master scheduling, such that high product variety is significantly related to a make-to-order environment (at the 0.05 level). Product volume is significantly related to six out of eight design characteristics. All of these are in line with expectations.

The product-supply chain model by Fisher (1997) is partially supported. Two of the three aspects are significant in the expected direction for product volume, that is, manufacturing focus and lead-time focus, both implying that high volume corresponds to a cost focus. The primary purpose is not significant for either volume or variants. Selldin and Olhager (2007) recognized that many firms try to design the supply chain so as to provide both low cost and quick response. They identify an efficient frontier that includes those firms that exhibit the best combinations of physically efficient and market-responsive supply chains.

The relationship between product characteristics and process choice as suggested by Hayes and Wheelwright (1979a, 1979b, 1984) is supported. The results show that the degree of fit between product and process choice is good, that is, companies tend to choose the appropriate process type with respect to the product type, especially with respect to product volume. This is confirmed by the Pearson correlation of 0.332, which is significant at the 0.01 level.

The Berry and Hill (1992) model, expanded to include sales and operations planning, is partially supported. The results show that the two higher MPC levels, that is, sales and operations planning, and master scheduling, are significantly related to product characteristics, whereas the two lower levels (material planning and production activity control) are not related to either product volume or variety. Sales and operations planning is related to product volume, while master scheduling is related to both product volume and variety, in accordance with theoretical expectations. Thus, this study provides support for the conceptual framework by Berry and Hill (1992), but only at the master planning level. It should be noted that sales and operations planning, in addition, is strongly related to product volume. The strategic choice of MPC approaches is discussed further in Olhager and Selldin (2007).

Investigating the relationships between supply chain design, process choice and MPC approaches

The interrelationships between supply chain design, process choice and the strategic choice of MPC approaches are presented in Table 7.4, in terms of Pearson correlations between the items. For supply chain items, that are two per design aspect, the strongest Pearson correlation is provided.

Table 7.4 The Pearson correlations between supply chain design, process choice and the strategic choice of MPC approaches

Item	PP	MF	LTF	PC	S&OP	MS	MP
Supply chain design aspects							
Primary purpose (PP: cost minimum → quick response)	–						
Manufacturing focus (MF: high utilization → buffer capacity)	.208*	–					
Lead-time focus (LTF: cost-based → aggressive reduction)	.208*	.116	–				
Process choice							
Process (PC: line → project)	.068	−.110	.113	–			
MPC approaches							
Sales and operations planning (S&OP: level → chase)	.099	.343**	.266**	.339**	–		
Master scheduling (MS: MTS → MTO)	.111	.203*	.105	.159	.500**	–	
Material planning (MP: rate-based → time-phased)	−.023	.208*	−.022	.110	.086	−.149	–
Production activity control (PAC: JIT → MRP)	−.052	−.016	−.039	.004	.069	−.237*	.439**

* Correlation is significant at 0.05 level
** Correlation is significant at 0.01 level

Supply chain design and process choice

There is no significant relationship between process choice and any of the supply chain design aspect. This result suggests that these two design issues are independent. Thus, irrespective of supply chain type, there are opportunities for using any type of process choice at a particular position along the supply chain. At least, the results show that there are no dominating combinations in current practice.

Supply chain design and MPC approaches

There are significant relationships between supply chain design aspects and MPC approaches, such that four out of 12 combinations are significant at either the 0.05 or 0.01 level. The primary purpose of the supply chain type is not associated significantly with any MPC level, while manufacturing focus is significantly related to the three upper levels. Finally, lead-time focus is only significantly related to the sales and operations planning level. Overall, the strongest relationship is for the sales and operations planning level that is significantly related to both manufacturing focus and lead-time focus at the 0.01 level.

Process choice and MPC approaches

There is a very strong relationship between process choice and the type of planning strategy at the sales and operations planning level. The project-manufacturing end of the process type spectrum is significantly associated with a chase strategy. This also implies that continuous processing is associated with a level strategy. The other, three lower planning levels are not significantly related to the choice of process.

Conclusions

We have presented results from an empirical survey concerned with the relationships among product, supply chain, process and MPC characteristics. The results show that product volume influences some aspects of supply chain design, the process choice and the long-term manufacturing planning and control, that is, for sales and operations planning and master planning. The managerial implications are such that firms with low product volumes and many variants typically choose a supply chain with market-responsive characteristics, a project manufacturing or a job shop process for internal manufacturing operations, and MPC approaches that can manage variability, such as a chase planning strategy at the sales and operations planning level, and make-to-order at the master scheduling level. Firms with high product volumes and few variants, on the other hand, tend to choose a physically efficient supply chain, a line or continuous manufacturing process, level production and make-to-stock. Thus, the results are basically in accordance with theoretical expectations, and thereby provide support for the theoretical models.

Building on the results from the product characteristic perspective, one would expect that the three decision areas concerning the strategic choice and design of supply chains, processes and MPC approaches would be strongly interrelated. However, this is not the case. The supply chain design aspects and the process choice are uncorrelated. This indicates that there may be a difference between the internal perspective (manufacturing at the focal firm) and the external perspective (perceptions of the characteristics for supply chain partners). Another explanation might be that manufacturing firms have not yet fully developed their supply chain strategies. Yet another explanation is that some firms choose supply chains partners to compensate for particular weaknesses in their own operations. They have a particular manufacturing process, but may realize that the supply chain requires more cost efficiency or flexibility than they can offer themselves. The role of complementary competencies to address differences between internal and external perspectives of manufacturing firms needs further research.

The major connection between the three decision areas is through sales and operations planning, that is significantly related to supply chain design and process choice, as well as to master planning; the other long-term planning level. This result indicates that the choice of sales and operations planning approach is truly of strategic importance, having a significant relationship with supply chain design aspects as well as process choice.

A limitation of this research is that the sample is geographically restricted to Swedish manufacturing firms. For further research, it would be most interesting to test these relationships in other parts of the world. Since the sample consists of firms of different sizes and manufacturing processes, the implications for practice should nevertheless be generic and not restricted to any particular type of industry.

Acknowledgement

The contribution of Dr Erik Selldin in the research project is greatly appreciated.

References

Ahmad, S. and Schroeder, R.G. 2002 'Refining the product-process matrix', *International Journal of Operations and Production Management*, 20(1): 103–24.

Berry, W.L. and Hill, T. 1992 'Linking systems to strategy', *International Journal of Operations and Production Management*, 12(1): 3–15.

Cachon, G. and Fisher, M. 1997 'Campbell Soup's continuous replenishment program: Evaluation and enhanced inventory decision rules', *Production and Operations Management*, 6(3): 266–76.

Childerhouse, P., Aitken, J. and Towill, D.R. 2002 'Analysis and design of focused demand chains', *Journal of Operations Management*, 20(6): 675–89.

Dillman, D. 1998 *Mail and Internet Surveys: The Tailored Design Method*, 2nd edn, New York: John Wiley & Sons.

Fisher, M.L. 1997 'What is the right supply chain for your product?', *Harvard Business Review*, 75(2): 105–16.

Fisher, M.L., Hammond, J., Obermeyer, W. and Raman, A. 1994 'Making supply meet demand in an uncertain world', *Harvard Business Review*, 72(3): 83–93.

Fisher, M.L., Hammond, J., Obermeyer, W. and Raman, A. 1997 'Configuring a supply chain to reduce the cost of demand uncertainty', *Production and Operations Management*, 6(3): 211–25.

Forza, C. 2002 'Survey research in operations management: A process-based perspective', *International Journal of Operations and Productions Management*, 22(2): 152–94.

Hayes, R.H. and Wheelwright, S.C. 1979a 'Link manufacturing process and product life cycles', *Harvard Business Review*, 57(1): 133–40.

Hayes, R.H. and Wheelwright, S.C. 1979b 'The dynamics of process–product life cycles', *Harvard Business Review*, 57(2): 127–36.

Hayes, R.H. and Wheelwright, S.C. 1984 *Restoring our Competitive Edge: Competing Through Manufacturing*, New York: John Wiley & Sons.

Hill, T. 2000 *Manufacturing Strategy – Text and Cases*, 2nd edn, Basingstoke: Palgrave.

Lambert, D.M. and Harrington, T.C. 1990 'Measuring non-response bias in consumer service mail surveys', *Journal of Business Logistics*, 11: 5–25.

Lee, H. 2002 'Aligning supply chain strategies with product uncertainties', *California Management Review*, 44(3): 105–19.

McDermott, C.M., Greis, N.P. and W.A. Fischer, N.P. 1997 'The diminishing utility of the product/process matrix – a study of the US power tool industry', *International Journal of Operations and Production Management*, 17(1): 65–84.

Olhager, J. and Rudberg, M. 2002 'Linking manufacturing strategy decisions on process choice with manufacturing planning and control systems', *International Journal of Production Research*, 40: 2335–51.

Olhager, J. and Selldin, E. 2004 'Supply chain management survey of Swedish manufacturing firms', *International Journal of Production Economics*, 89: 353–61.

Olhager, J. and Selldin, E. 2007 'Manufacturing planning and control approaches: Environmental alignment and performance', *International Journal of Production Research*, 45(6): 1469–84.

Safizadeh, M.H. and Ritzman, L.P. 1997 'Linking performance drivers in production planning and inventory control to process choice', *Journal of Operations Management*, 15: 389–403.

Safizadeh, M.H., Ritzman, L.P., Sharma, D. and Wood, C. 1996 'An empirical analysis of the product-process matrix', *Management Science*, 42(11): 1576–91.

Selldin, E. and Olhager, J. 2007 'Linking products with supply chains: Testing Fisher's model', *Supply Chain Management: An International Journal*, 12(1): 42–51.

Spencer, M.S. and Cox III, J.F. 1995 'An analysis of the product-process matrix and repetitive manufacturing', *International Journal of Production Research*, 33(5): 1275–94.

Vollmann, T.E., Berry, W.L., Whybark, D.C. and Jacobs, F.R. 2005 *Manufacturing Planning and Control for Supply Chain Management*, 5th edn, New York: McGraw-Hill.

8

Decision Frontiers in Supply Chain Networks

Michael Pearson

Introduction

The chapter will start with a description of the background to the problem and related literature. The next section will provide a general outline of the proposed new methodology, which makes use of phase plane analysis to detect patterns and profiles associated with decision frontiers. The third section describes some of the theory underlying the new approach, as well as the applications where it can be used. The final section ends with a conclusion and indications of further research.

Background and literature

The classical approach to solving supply chain problems involving the flow of inventory has generally made use of some knowledge of the demand distribution. Such knowledge may be acquired through the fitting of an appropriate model using techniques such as regression. Other techniques such as time series analysis and generating processes (Makridakis, Wheelwright and Hyndman 1998) may also be used whereby patterns in historical data are identified in order to forecast future behaviour. A key feature of the methodology outlined in this article is the way in which we not only distinguish, but also uncover a duality, between *decisions* made about inventory, such as quantity and pricing, and *knowledge* of demand and supply distributions, as acquired by experienced statisticians acting as predictors or forecasters. Such forecasting skills are often highly specialized and it is frequently unreasonable to expect one agent to carry expertise in both forecasting and the management of logistics and inventory. Many operational research analysts (Carr and Lovejoy 2000, Tsay 1999, Cachon 2004) have adopted just such an approach, frequently with the result of a highly technical solution tailored to a particular product line in a particular market. Even so many assumptions, such as the convexity, piece-wise continuity and distribution of the demand function, are often made.

The barriers to effective supply chain management are of pressing concern (Storey, Emberson and Reade 2005). Methods of addressing the problems range from advances in technology such as the improved ability to track individual items of inventory and product manufacture (Butcher 2007) to closer collaboration between the decision-makers, through sharing information and policies (Disney *et al.* 2008, Pearson 2007). The nature of contractual arrangements also plays an important role in determining decision-making policy. Some contracts are based on buy-back principles and pricing in order to stimulate distribution (Lau, Lau and Wang 2007). Among the range of contractual solutions are those associated with push and pull policies (Cachon 2004, Krishnamurthy, Suri and Vernon 2000) and those tied to flexible quantity ordering to establish equilibrium (Tsay 1999).

New approach

Our approach (Pearson 2007) has been to recognize the specialist skills of forecasting as distinct from those acquired by decision-makers in operations management. We have therefore made the assumption that the forecaster is doing a good job and assume that the forecasting method is both unbiased and results in normally distributed forecasting errors. Although the latter assumption is somewhat restrictive (for instance, if the demand distribution is Poisson the errors also tend to be Poisson) it serves as a valuable starting point and gives important insight into extending the model to also handle skewed distributions.

The work proceeds on the rather obvious, but fundamental, observation that real strategic progress is only achieved when mistakes (errors) are acknowledged and shared and use is made of this cooperation. To date much research in this area has been based on the muscular principle that we should share our strengths. Recent research in the area of both supply chain and revenue management (Talluri and van Ryzin 2005) also recognizes the difficulties associated with censored or truncated data. This phenomenon is familiar in yield management where seat availability in a certain class, such as the economy class, operates restricted levels, producing truncated demand data (Zeni 2001). The modelling of such features increases the complexity of the problem by increasing uncertainty and hence the variability of the forecasting errors. This is one area where the phase plane methods we propose are useful, because forecasting with over-censored data tends to produce characteristic, and sometimes chaotic, patterns.

The approach we advocate is simple, while at the same time facilitating effective modelling of complex phenomena in complex structures. The methods identify phenomena of practical interest, such as the push and pull effects occurring in manufacturing systems and marketing strategies and the bullwhip effect, whereby variability is pushed upstream through a variety of transactional strategies and agreements. So, for instance, we are able to model the loss of profit to an organization that employs non-cooperative Nash strategies compared with the limited cooperation strategy and associated equilibrium solution, which we promote. We do this by utilizing newly developed phase plane analysis to model and predict characteristic behaviour in supply chain networks. The method is essentially distribution-free.

The objectives are to increase profit, reduce waste and improve customer service in a coordinated way related to current business practice. Pearson (2007) gives an example of a newspaper business where significant reductions in wastage were achieved while maintaining current levels of customer service and increasing profit levels. Similar methods can be used in contractual supply chain problems where decision-makers enter into contracts with others in the supply chain. Such contracts are especially interesting because non-cooperative solutions (Nash equilibriums) have been shown not to exist, even though such problems form the foundation of much econometric theory.

In terms of statistical process control the methods share some features with those described by Box and Lucerno (1997). The latter authors adopt mainly a specific type of forecasting (that is, exponentially weighted moving average, or EWMA) and apply it as a feedback mechanism in the control of inventory levels. One generalization we make is to extend this to any forecasting method. Another is to incorporate strategic and contractual considerations resulting from defining the two-echelon problem in a certain way (Figure 8.1). The problem we address is a specific case of a general type of mathematical problem, the primal-dual type, or bi-level type, or game-theory type, where the optimal solution or strategy to one problem depends on the decision variable adopted in another problem and the equilibrium solution under some assumptions about cooperation or information between the players is

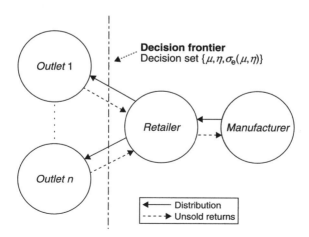

Figure 8.1 Distribution and unsold returns in a retail business

sought. There is a very general class of such problems and the multi-echelon newsvendor problem belongs to this class. The two-echelon problem is stated as: a manufacturer attempts to determine the cost to charge a retailer and the credit/unit to pay for unsold units returned. A retailer determines the amount of inventory to order from the manufacturer and the retail price to charge the customer. Both the manufacturer and the retailer attempt to maximize profit. The problem type is illustrated in Figure 8.1, where distribution and unsold returns in a retailer business are divided by the decision frontier line. The decision frontier divides the connected network into two components, which form a line-cut. Each component can then be treated as primal or dual. Initially, the line-cut shown in Figure 8.1 may have all n outlets as the primal component with the retailer forming the dual component. There can be as many decision frontiers as there are line-cuts in the graph representing the network. Each decision frontier generates a decision set and an efficient frontier.

Figure 8.2 illustrates other possible decision frontiers in the supply chain network. Approaching each problem then requires a profit-maximizing solution to the decision set $\{\mu, \eta, \sigma_e(\mu, \eta)\}$, which is derived from the variables D (amount of inventory demanded) and Q (amount of inventory supplied) by applying the primal–dual (sum–difference) transformation. Hence μ is the mean value of $Q - D$, while η is the mean value of $D + Q$, while σ_e is the standard deviation of the combined forecasting errors for D and Q. Furthermore, the variables D and Q are either stochastic variables representing states of nature, or decision variables, depending on which operator is viewing them. This latent duality, whereby an operator knows about his own distribution, but makes decisions about his partner's distribution (Pearson

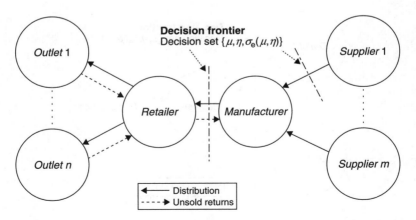

Figure 8.2   Distribution and unsold returns showing other possible decision frontiers

2007) enhances the traditional formulation of the newsvendor problem. Previously the demand, D, was viewed as a stochastic variable about which information was collected by the retailer for future forecasts and planning. At the same time, however, the supply variable, Q, was formulated as a decision variable, where the decision-maker is also the retailer. The primal operator, which in this case is the retailer, therefore has knowledge of his own distribution but makes decisions about the supply quantity, which is the manufacturer's distribution.

The types of decisions that can be made at a decision frontier are wide ranging. Contractual arrangements can be an important part of this process. Discussing contractual terms may be the first stage before negotiations over contractual details begin. There are various types of buy-back contract (Cachon 2004, Cachon and Lariviere 2001). It may even be that terms are agreed if a retailer estimates demand for some item and then reduces their order later on when demand falls short of the estimate (Tsay 1999). Another possibility that is currently causing concern is the issue of fair trade, where intermediaries may contract out to small manufacturing organizations in developing countries to get the lowest terms possible. In these circumstances a larger retailer with a reputation to uphold may not want adverse publicity if the source of manufacture were disclosed. A fair trade agreement might then become a priority. Another consideration may be taking into account the cost of losing customer goodwill (Pearson 2007). Maintaining a loyal or just a continuing customer base may be crucial to the success of the product.

Methods

Our model makes a number of assumptions, which are meant to be a starting point for subsequent models, rather than a rigid set of requirements. For instance, we start with the single period inventory model for the sake of simplicity. Such a model is readily extendible to others such as the periodic review or multi-period models.

Unbiased demand and supply fitting or forecast techniques are assumed to be applied and the prediction errors are normally distributed. The relationships between the standard deviation of the errors and the means of demand and supply are well behaved.

The stochastic model and problem formulation

The problem formulation on which we base our model is described in detail in Pearson (2003, 2007). Some of the methods associated with this approach, such as adaptive target control and the use of a target gain function (Pearson 2006) resemble those used by Box and Lucerno (1997). The decision set

$\{D, Q, \sigma_D, \sigma_Q\}$ is transformed into $\{\mu, \eta, \sigma_e(\mu, \eta)\}$ for the reasons explained in the following section. The primal–dual objective is to maximize:

$$E\{Profit\} = E\{Contribution\ from\ captured\ demand - Costs\ of\ overage$$
$$- Costs\ of\ underage\}$$
$$= \mu_D(c_{p_1} + c_{p_2}) - \{(\phi(k) - k(1 - \Phi(k)))c_p + (k\Phi(k) + \phi(k))(c_{o_1} + c_{u_2})$$
$$+ (\phi(k) - k(1 - \Phi(k)))(c_{u_1} + c_{o_2})\}\sigma_e \tag{1}$$

$$\text{subject to: } \mu - k\sigma_e = 0, \text{ (newsvendor constraint)} \tag{2}$$

where $\phi(k)$, $\Phi(k)$ are the normal distribution density and cumulative distribution functions, respectively, for safety factor, k. The contributions to profit of the retailer (downstream operator) and manufacturer (upstream operator) are c_{p_1} and c_{p_2} respectively. The overage and underage costs of the retailer are c_{o_1} and c_{u_1} respectively, while for the manufacturer they are c_{o_2} and c_{u_2}. An interesting feature of the problem and the way it is formulated is that the retailer's (primal) overage is the same as the manufacturer's (dual) underage. The associated costs, however, are not necessarily the same. For instance, the retailer may put a certain value on a disappointed customer that differs from that of the manufacturer.

The 'mix' (overage/underage) solution

The mix solution tracks the way in which partners across decision frontiers synchronize their efforts to reach optimality. The solution is described by the equation:

$$\Phi(k) + \frac{\partial \sigma_e}{\partial \mu} \phi(k) = Const\left\{= \frac{c_{u_1} + c_{o_2} + c_p/2}{c_{o_1} + c_{u_2} + c_{u_1} + c_{o_2} + c_p}\right\} \tag{3}$$

We see that the constant in equation (3) depends on the newsvendor costs and contribution to profit (where $c_p = c_{p_1} + c_{p_2}$) defined above. Equation (3) contributes to the generalization of the classical solution to the newsvendor problem (Silver, Pyke and Peterson 1998). The LHS has an additional term that measures the rate at which error variability changes with respect to the 'mix' variable μ. This assists in the identification of the optimal (maximum profit) solution.

The 'global' (volume) solution

The global ('volume of the total demand and supply output') solution is described by the equation:

$$\phi(k) \frac{\partial \sigma_e}{\partial \eta} = Const = \left\{\frac{c_p}{2(c_{o_1} + c_{u_2} + c_{u_1} + c_{o_2} + c_p)}\right\} \tag{4}$$

We see that the constant again depends on the newsvendor costs and contribution to profit defined above. Equation (4) also contributes to the generalization of the classical solution to the newsvendor problem. The LHS has a single term that measures the rate at which the error variability changes with respect to the 'global' variable. This also assists in the identification of the optimal (maximum profit) solution. The two equations (3) and (4) form a dynamic system of stochastic differential equations, which trace the optimal solution in circumstances where variability changes and uncertainty increases or decreases over time and with relation to differing contractual and marketing strategies. The sum and difference of equations (3) and (4) assist in the extraction of the primal and dual operator's (sub)optimal solutions to their own individual problems (Pearson 2003).

The formation of decision frontiers

Forming a line-cut in a graph in order to partition the graph into components is a well-established procedure (Harary, Norman and Cartwright 1965). We use this method in order to identify important decision components in a supply chain network. The flow of inventory between such components then forms the subject for a primal–dual process of knowledge transfer and decision management. We call the line-cut the decision (or knowledge transfer) frontier. We will use a simple example to illustrate the methodology. A retail product starts the season with average sales of 1,000 units distributed across (n =) ten retail outlets. We consider the link between the retailer and the manufacturer, which forms the first decision frontier shown in Figure 8.2. The sales increase due to seasonal factors as well as promotional activity and changing customer demand.

Figure 8.3 illustrates the period of increased sales for the market product (units are in 100 s). Demand rises sharply for a limited period. Supply quantity initially lags behind the demand, highlighting the way in which the market 'pulls' the product off the shelves creating shortages. Eventually supply quantities catch up with demand as demand falls away leading to surplus quantity due to the sluggish coordination between the supply and demand.

Figure 8.4 shows the 'mix' phase plane, which illustrates the way in which variability (and hence risk) varies as the retailer and supplier coordinate the flow of the product through the supply chain network. The variability we speak of here is not just demand variability (though frequently this is the cause of it) but the joint variability (or volatility) experienced by both decision-makers on either side of the decision frontier as influenced by many factors. Among these factors are such variables as uncertainty of supplies as well as demand, weak forecasting methods employed by both the retailer and the manufacturer/distributor etc. The variable used to encapsulate all of these factors is the best effort achievable by the joint decision-makers at the decision frontier, which is the joint variability of their combined forecasting

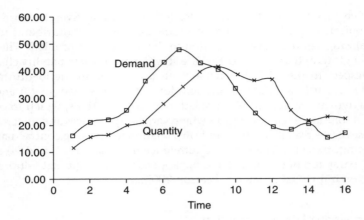

Figure 8.3   Quantity supplied lags behind demand

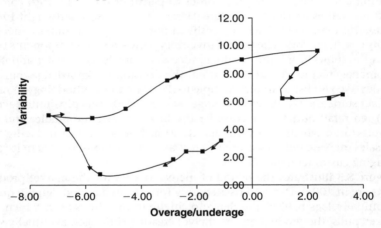

Figure 8.4   Clockwise movement indicates a 'pull' strategy

errors. This is σ_e, which is the standard deviation of the combined forecasting errors for the demand, D, and supply, Q (Pearson 2003). Figure 8.4 is a plot of this variability against the 'mix' or overage/underage variable, μ, which is the difference between the mean supply (Q) and the mean demand (D). We therefore get a visualization or profile of the way in which variability changes as the two decision-makers attempt to synchronize their business in the supply chain. Our example shows a clockwise profile in the 'mix' phase plane as time progresses. This is typical of a pull market strategy (Pearson 2008).

Figure 8.5 illustrates the way in which variability changes as the volume of trade increases and decreases. The profile typically increases in variability as the volume increases. Such a profile is not necessary, but decision-making

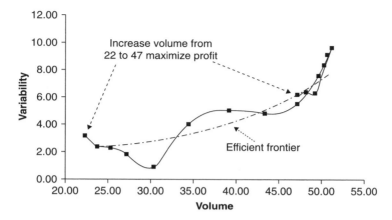

Figure 8.5 Preferred region of market operation

would actually be simplified if, for instance, the profile was decreasing in variability as volume increased. The decision-maker would simply increase the volume of supply knowing that the forecast error variability would decrease so that the process would become more reliable and, in general, more profitable. The efficient frontier for optimal allocation of stock volume can also be mapped onto this phase plane. The diagram shows a decision to operate in the more risky market where variability is higher but the prospects of greater profit for a short life cycle are improved.

The mix phase plane illustrates the relationship between the two operators functioning across a decision frontier and so acts as a decision tool used to establish healthy contractual agreement between such operators (Figures 8.6a, 8.6b, 8.6c). Generally, each decision-maker has superior *knowledge* of activity occurring on his side of the decision frontier. A decision-maker, however, is often required to make *decisions* about his partner's distribution variable. Suppose now we examine another decision frontier. We investigate the decision frontier between the retail distributor and the retail outlet 1 illustrated in Figure 8.1. Retail outlet 1 decides how much of the product to order from the retail distributor, while the distributor may have to make decisions about the promotional policy of the company which tend to determine the demand for the product (figures are in units where the average demand for the product is 50 units).

In the end some agreement needs to be reached concerning the way in which the product is marketed. In this situation the retail distributor may prefer a 'push' strategy in order to promote the product on the shelves. The safety factor would then be set rather higher than the retail outlet might prefer. This situation is reflected in Figure 8.6a, where the retailer's (sub)optimal solution would be to supply a higher level of produce by using a safety

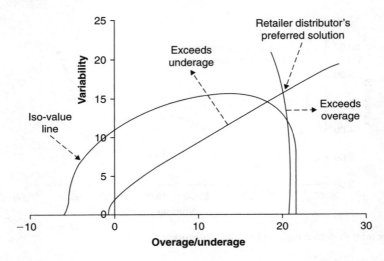

Figure 8.6a $k = 1.3$ Retail distributor wants to promote product and increase availability on the shelves

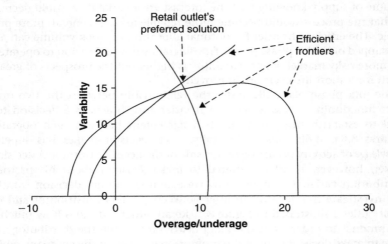

Figure 8.6b $k = 0.5$ Retail outlet wants the customer to demand the product and use shelf space more efficiently

factor of $k = 1.3$. This would be done at the expense of the retail outlet, however, given the present levels of uncertainty and variability associated with predicting demand and supply (Pearson 2007).

The retail outlet, on the other hand, may prefer to set the safety factor at a lower level in order to limit wastage and use shelf space more efficiently

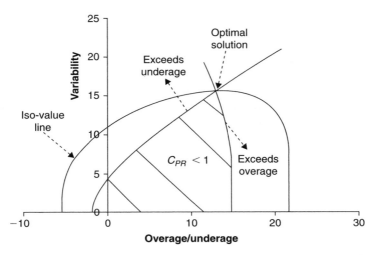

Figure 8.6c $k = 0.84$ Optimal solution occurs when efforts are coordinated and capability is achieved

(Figure 8.6b). The situation described in Figure 8.6a would now be reversed as reflected in Figure 8.6b, where the retail outlet's (sub)optimal solution would be to supply a lower level of produce by using a safety factor of $k = 0.5$. This would be done at the expense of the retailer, however, given the present levels of uncertainty and variability associated with predicting demand and supply. This may lead to a 'to and fro' ordering policy, which produces an increase in the bullwhip effect along the supply chain. Unless the operators can reach some consistent agreement concerning their ordering policy then the maximum profit solution cannot be achieved.

There are, in a sense, actually three efficient frontiers displayed in Figure 8.6b. One frontier, the iso-value line, refers to the maintenance of profit at a fixed value, while associated targets on overage and underage vary due to change in the decision parameter, k. Another frontier refers to the maintenance of the retailer's preferred level of customer service (underage), while profit and overage vary due to change in the decision parameter, k. The third frontier refers to the maintenance of the retailer's preferred level of overproduction (overage) while profit and underage vary due to change in the decision parameter, k.

The optimal solution is illustrated in Figure 8.6c. The iso-value line shows the efficient frontier for solutions that have the same profit level as that obtained by the maximum profit solution that achieves the desired target levels of overage and underage. The optimal solution occurs at the point where all three efficient frontiers meet, so that the agreed targets on customer service and overproduction match the maximum profit achievable in the area of market uncertainty where business is taking place. To achieve a more profitable solution would require the prediction capability with respect to the current targets to be less than 1 ($C_{PR} < 1$), which would occur if a lower level of risk (reduced error variability) could be identified, often through better forecasting and prediction. The decision-maker would also need to identify the position of the proposed solution on the volume chart and check for profitability by making use of the efficient frontier in that chart. In this way different scenarios of proposed market operation can be considered.

Conclusion

Supply chain networks are uniquely placed for research and development based on innovative operational research and management techniques. Both lean, but, more especially, agile supply chains are characterized by complexity due to the extended networks of different suppliers required for high product variety in volatile markets. Such complexity frequently leads to the employment of logistic specialists who take significant responsibility for managing the supply chains. In this context there are inherently high levels of uncertainty and risk. Consequently there is an increasing need for appropriate decision-making methods or models to better manage the risk and uncertainty associated with global supply chains.

The model we put forward can be used widely across lean and agile supply chain networks. The first step in the modelling process is to identify 'decision frontiers' where important decisions concerning the ordering of new products and prediction of demand take place through negotiation between retailers and distributors, as well as between retailers and their outlets, and between retailers and logistics specialists. The decision-making, though highly quantitative, can also be used to assist decisions made concerning qualitative information, such as customer preference and satisfaction, as well as loss of goodwill and loyalty. It is particularly powerful at shedding light on current practice methodology carried out in short life cycle products. Furthermore, the innovative facility to map changes in variability is a key proposed feature that should enhance research and understanding of the mechanisms occurring in supply chains.

The newsvendor problem is a generic one that forms the foundation for related areas of study in management science and operational research. One such area is revenue (or yield) management, which is based on the same class of problem. This is so because the single-leg revenue management problem is essentially equivalent to the single period newsvendor problem. There are therefore a whole set of commercial and business problems within such industries ranging from airline booking to hotel and catering (as well as many more recently employing revenue management principles) that might benefit from the methodology outlined here. Such problems can also occur in other disciplines, such as contract and econometric theory, where game theory and the establishment of Nash equilibrium solutions have been such important influences. Forming and evaluating partnerships across decision frontiers can stabilize network structures while maintaining the identity and freedom of each operator engaged in business activity.

Another aspect of the work outlined in this chapter is phase plane analysis, which is a well-established area of study used in, for example, chaos theory or fractals. Using such a tool can assist in identifying simple recurring patterns of behaviour, which can shed light on the way in which a process should be handled to achieve optimal results. Indeed, it may be more important to avoid making decisions that lead to extremely detrimental outcomes associated with high uncertainty. The use of phase plane analysis can assist through a greater understanding of the solution of stochastic differential equations associated with the formulation of these problems.

The main limitations of the modelling methods are associated with the assumptions underlying the modelling technique. One assumption is that the forecasting errors be normally distributed. This is because the solution is based on the mean values of the demand and supply variables, which in turn are used to identify target values for overage and underage. Unbiased forecasting with normally distributed errors becomes a difficult task, especially in circumstances where the mean demand is continuously changing. Although this assumption can be relaxed, particularly where skewed demand is involved, the formulation of the stochastic differential equations increases in complexity, so that other techniques, such as simulation become important. We note, however, that although the optimal solution may be subject to such a limitation imposed by the assumption, the mapping of progress using phase planes can still convey valuable information related to the control of the process when the assumption is breached.

The main limitation of the research outlined here, though, hinges on the assumptions made concerning cooperation and information exchange between the players in the decision-making process. Such cooperation is a risky business, but the decision-makers ultimately serve the customers and so depend on their goodwill, as well as the freedom and goodwill of those producing the goods. Indeed, one of the consequences of globalization is the way in which customers exercise their increased awareness concerning the conditions in which goods are produced and transported.

Acknowledgement

Do'n ghloir motha aig Dia. (To the greater glory of God)

References

Box, G., and Lucerno, A. 1997 *Statistical Control by Monitoring and Feedback Adjustment*, New York: Wiley.

Butcher, T. 2007 'Radio frequency identification: An enabler of agile supply chain decision-making', *Int. J. Agile Systems and Management,* 2(3): 1–17.

Cachon, G. 2004 'The allocation of inventory risk in a supply chain: Push, pull, and advance-purchase discount contracts', *Management Science,* 50(2): 222–38.

Cachon, G.P. and Lariviere, M.A. 2001 'Contracting to assure supply: How to share demand forecasts in a supply chain', *Management Science,* 47(5): 629–A.46.

Carr, S. and Lovejoy. W. 2000 'The inverse newsvendor problem: Choosing an optimal demand portfolio for capacitated resources', *Management Science,* 46(7): 912–27.

Disney, S.M., Lambrecht, M., Towill, D.R. and Van de Velde, W. 2008 'The value of coordination in a two echelon supply chain: Sharing information, policies and parameters', *IIE Transactions* 40(3): 341–56.

Harary, F., Norman, R. and Cartwright, D. 1965 *Structural Models: An Introduction to the Theory of Directed Graphs,* New York: Wiley.

Krishnamurthy, A., Suri, R. and Vernon, M. 2000 'Push can perform better than pull for flexible manufacturing systems with multiple products', proceedings of the Industrial Engineering Research Conference Cleveland, OH.

Lau, A.H.L., Lau, H.S. and Wang, J.C. 2007 'Some properties of buyback and other related schemes in a newsvendor-product supply chain with price-sensitive demand', *Journal of Operational Research Society,* 58: 491–504.

Makridakis, S., Wheelwright, S. and Hyndman, R. 1998 *Forecasting: Methods and Applications,* 3rd edn, New York: Wiley.

Pearson, M. 2003 'An equilibrium solution to supply chain synchronization', *IMA Journal of Management Mathematics,* 14(3): 165–85.

Pearson, M. 2006 'The application of prediction capability and adaptive target control to the newspaper business', *European Journal of Operational Research,* 168(2): 475–91.

Pearson, M. 2007 'Goodwill hunting and profit sharing: Decision-making in a newspaper chain' *European Journal of Operational Research,* 181(3): 1593–606.

Pearson, M. 2008 'Prioritizing edge over node: Process control in supply chain networks and push-pull strategies', *Journal of Operational Research Society,* 59: 494–502.

Silver, E., Pyke, F. and Peterson, R. 1998 *Inventory Management and Production Planning and Scheduling,* New York: Wiley.

Storey, JEmberson, C. and Reade, D. 2005 'The barriers to customer responsive supply chain management', *International Journal of Operations and Production Management,* 25(3): 242–60.

Talluri, K. and van Ryzin, G. 2005 *The Theory and Practice of Revenue Management,* New York: Springer.

Tsay, A.A. 1999 'The quantity flexibility contract and supplier–customer incentives', *Management Science,* 45(10): 1339–58.

Zeni, R.H. 2001 'Improved forecast accuracy in airline revenue management by unconstraining demand estimates from censored data', <http://www.Dissertation. com> accessed 17.6.08.

9
Supply Chain Management: A Multi-Agent System Framework

Jingquan Li, Riyaz T. Sikora and Michael J. Shaw

Introduction

A supply chain consists of a network of business units that procure raw materials, transform them into final products and distribute them to customers through a distribution system. The aim of supply chain management (SCM) is to manage these activities so that products go through the network in the shortest time and at the lowest costs (Lee and Billington 1995). For many companies the supply chain is the most crucial element in their entire value proposition to customers. A great deal of current commercial effort is being devoted to technology to support and manage supply chains.

The rapid growth of information and communications technologies (ICTs), especially the internet, wireless communication, peer-to-peer computing and agent technology, not only has an enormous potential for improving supply chain performance but also is shaping supply-chain structure and design. For example, attracted by large potential savings on product and transaction costs, businesses such as Caterpillar Inc. and General Motors Corp. use e-procurement capabilities to enhance their strategic management of competitive supply networks. Some leading companies even intend to complete their supply chains on the web. Ubiquitous computing, mainly enabled by the web and wireless communication, seems to be the inevitable trend for the near future.

Advances in embedded computing technology will allow the mass production of net-enabled objects, including everything from household appliances to transportation. Wireless communication will be the key to tying together the diverse functions of the many computers around us. Consumers and businesses will remain constantly connected, affording businesses a lot of new sales channels and giving consumers access to global services. Peer-to-peer computing naturally supports sharing of information and knowledge via direct exchange among individual systems in digital networks, enabling two or more systems to collabourate spontaneously in a network of peers by using distributed systems without the necessity for central control.

With increasing competition, more demanding consumers and growing uncertainties in the marketplace, it is not surprising to see that the various SCM methods in use today, such as just-in-time (JIT), which 'supplies the right things, at right time, at the right amount, to the right place', material requirements planning (MRP) in bucket style, enterprise systems, which are based on conventional centralized supply chain architecture, are facing many problems. First, the global information needed by a centralized system to make decisions is not always available in real supply chains. For example, many companies relocate labour-intensive production lines to developing countries. These factories may not have appropriate ICT infrastructure to provide accurate and timely data for making decisions.

Second, the centralized system is inadequate in processing information that grows at an explosive rate. The real-time information from the sites, such as goods in process or sales, has to be collected into the database located at the headquarters, and a demand forecast has to be worked out. As the marketplace becomes increasingly uncertain and requires quick responses, it has become impractical and very expensive for a centralized supply chain with limited information processing capability at the top of the hierarchy to keep up with the explosive growth of data. Also, the top management may not have the expertise to make the right decisions. Firms try to push down decision rights to lower levels in order to improve performance and encourage innovation (King, 1983).

Third, consumer behaviour cannot be precisely predicted using traditional analytic methods like forecasting or optimization. Instead, companies seeking a competitive edge have to investigate other analytic methods based on artificial intelligence techniques and good heuristics. More importantly, the traditional supply chain is unable to adapt to real-world situations quickly. Much of current commercial effort is oriented towards maintaining pre-existing relationships in the chain. Automated support for dynamically forming and dissolving business interaction is still a dream. When production and distribution lines are frequently modified in uncertain environments, it is impractical to centrally manage or plan the characteristics and the constraints of each site whenever a modification is made. Therefore, responding successfully to these challenges demands a new technology infrastructure for SCM.

A distributed, flexible, scalable and adaptive multi-agent SCM system represents a viable alternative to existing enterprise systems. By building on the distributed object foundation, agent technology models the supply chain as composed of very simple, intelligent software agents, each responsible for one or more activities in the supply chain and each interacting with other agents. The key aspects of intelligent agents are their autonomy and abilities to perceive, reason and act in their environments, as well as to interact with other agents. When agents interact with one another they form a multi-agent system (MAS). It is natural to model independent facilities in the supply chain as represented by autonomous agents and the supply chain as a multi-agent system because the supply chain is naturally distributed, involves a large number of autonomous commercial entities, which cooperate with each other to reach a common goal, while simultaneously pursuing individual objectives.

One of the major problems in the MAS is that the goals of the agents are not aligned with the overall goal of the chain. Agents usually have different goals and try to maximize their own good without concern for the global goal. Hence, the challenge is how to let the system reach global optima with selfish agents pursuing their own goals. In this chapter we highlight important issues that must be handled to make progress in the multi-agent SCM system. Specifically, we investigate the issues of coordination, information sharing, security and privacy, business environment and agent architecture.

The multi-agent system (MAS) paradigm

We have not seen a universally accepted definition of agent yet, but most researchers agree upon a weak notion of agency (Wooldridge and Jennings 1995). It views as an agent a computer system or a program that is characterized by the properties of autonomy, social ability, reactivity and proactiveness. Being autonomous means being able to act with no intervention by its principals (humans or computer systems) and control its own actions and internal state. Social ability is the capability to interact and communicate with other agents. When agents interact with one another and their environment they form a multi-agent system. An agent may take a reactive or proactive stance in their environment. An agent is reactive if it is equipped to perceive the environment around itself and is able to respond to its changes while an agent is proactive if it is able to anticipate an event and respond to it proactively.

All the above properties can be recognized in a business unit in a supply chain. Each business unit of a supply chain operates autonomously to achieve its own objectives, makes decisions on the basis of the available information, cooperates with other business partners to reach a common goal and acts reactively or proactively in its environment. A supply chain is a network of business units and manufacturing facilities working together to accomplish mutually beneficial goals. Therefore, if we keep in mind the above-mentioned analogies between a business unit in a supply chain and an agent, it becomes clearer that a MAS paradigm seems to be a natural choice for SCM.

Multi-agent SCM systems have several advantages over traditional enterprise systems (Lerman and Galstyan 2003), including (1) autonomy: the inherent autonomy of intelligent agents enables the different business units of a supply chain network to retain their autonomy of information and control; (2) adaptability: agents can modify their behaviour based on their learning experiences, the environmental dynamics and the actions of other agents; (2) local control: the desired collective behaviour can be achieved via local interactions between agents; (3) scalability: each agent has the same schemata (also known as internal model) whether the supply chain is composed of 30 or 100,000 agents; (4) robustness: system performance is robust to individual agent failure; (5) flexibility: agents can be dynamically added, removed, merged and split without significantly affecting the performance of the system.

There has been some work done on using multi-agent technology in supply chains. Intelligent agents are applied to SCM by using auction between agents as a method for resource allocation (Mori, Matsuo and Kosaka 1998). Sandholm (1998) develop technologies for automated negotiation and coalition formation among self-interested auction agents in electronic commerce. Lin, Tan and Shaw (1998) propose a multi-agent information system approach to model the order fulfilment process in supply chain networks (SCNs). Parkes (2000) proposes a model for the valuation problem of an agent that enables the derivation of optimal meta-deliberation and bidding strategies for auction agents. Papazoglou (2001) describes the use of agent technology in e-business application and the basic characteristics of e-business agents. Kaihara (2003) formulates the supply chain model as a discrete resource allocation problem under a dynamic environment, and demonstrates the applicability of the virtual market concept to this framework. Anthony and Jennings (2003) develop a decision-making framework for an agent to bid across multiple concurrent auctions with varying start and end times and with varying protocols (including English, Dutch and Vickrey). They employ a genetic algorithm to search for effective bidding strategies. Li *et al.* (2006) use information exchange in a supply chain as a representation of inter-organizational information sharing, and study five strategies for information sharing.

Despite the increasing number of cases on the multi-agent electronic commerce systems, such main issues of SCM as coordination structures, information sharing, privacy and security, business environment, have not been addressed in the multi-agent literature. This chapter advances the state of the art in the following ways. We first identify the severe restrictions of traditional enterprise systems and the restrictions that motivate the development of the multi-agent computing paradigm for SCM. We then highlight some strategic issues that must be tackled to make progress and provide a research framework in multi-agent SCM.

Elements of multi-agent supply chain management

A supply chain is a system composed of different business units working together to accomplish mutually beneficial goals. It has the following common properties. First, an electronic supply chain system is an aggregate system composed of a set of commercial entities that cooperate with each other to reach a common goal, while simultaneously pursuing individual objectives. An intelligent adaptive agent can represent each business entity in the multi-agent SCM system. Multi-agent SCM has to deal with the coordination and control structures that enable simple agents to form a highly adaptive supply chain aggregate. The aggregation property also allows the supply chain to be modelled in varying granularity. For example, at the industry level, enterprises form supply chains in the industry; an enterprise consists of one or more business processes; and a business process comprises several operation-level activities.

Second, the entire supply chain can be decomposed into building blocks. Each building block can be responsible for one or more supply chain functions and can be an independent firm or a group of firms. The building blocks have internal models, which can be translated into agents. Agents can be grouped by various ways, for instance, by type, speciality, or workflow. Efficiency can sometimes be improved if agents form groups. Consider, for instance, a supply chain in which one supplier is selling a package of items. One buyer wants part of the package and another buyer wants the remaining part. The sum of the amounts they are willing to pay separately exceeds the asking price for the entire package. Both the buyers and the seller benefit from forming a group. The coordination structures and strategies support this type of interaction of agents and agent groups working towards a common goal.

Third, agents interact with each other through information exchanges. Within supply chains, agents and agent groups are connected by and embedded in networks of interaction and knowledge, all of which change dynamically through an ecology of learning mechanisms. Effective management of information flows is among the most significant challenges of modern supply chains. In fact, the essence of any SCM technique is to enhance the value of information sharing across organizations. Furthermore, agents, like their principals, value their privacy and security and would not agree to open critical business data to a competitor. They may not share certain types of information with other agents unless they can benefit from the sharing.

Finally, the supply chain agents are of diverse form and capability, and interact with each other as well as the environment. When unpredictable factors such as customer demand, plant capacity, or the weather create a supply–demand imbalance, the multi-agent system needs to adapt to this

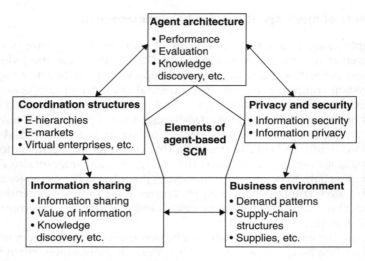

Figure 9.1　Element of multi-agent SCM

changing environment. It therefore becomes very important to understand the dynamic business environment in order to develop appropriate coordination structures and information-sharing strategies. Figure 9.1 summarizes the elements of multi-agent SCM.

Coordination structures

Economies have two basic coordination structures: markets and hierarchies. In an e-hierarchy, the organizations involved have a long-term contact and align their internal processes with one another. An example is series of legally separated firms along a static supply chain that are electronically connected to the neighbouring nodes. The primary reason for establishing an e-hierarchy is to improve the efficient exchange and sharing of information between firms. The emergence of e-hierarchies to link separate firms in the supply chain is also critical to maintaining product differentiation (also known as asset specificity) and represents a response to switching costs.

An e-market is designed to match buyers and sellers who generally do not share a long-term relationship. The participants in the market may benefit through economies of scale and specialization since the market is traditionally coordinated by pricing mechanisms. The main reason for establishing the market is to leverage the benefits of competition. Markets can be centralized or decentralized. Centralized markets use one or more intermediary, such as distributors or brokers. Buyers and sellers need only connect to one or more of these intermediaries to carry out a transaction; a stock exchange

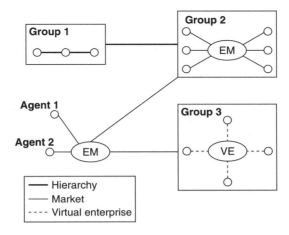

Figure 9.2   An example of a multi-agent SCM system

is a good example. In a decentralized market, all the participants can contact one another directly, and no intermediaries are present.

Although current literature overwhelmingly moves from one extreme – e-hierarchies, to another extreme – e-markets, we believe that both hierarchies and markets have their places in today's dynamic business environment. Virtual organizations are hybrid coordination structures that combine market and hierarchy elements simultaneously. Virtual enterprise (VE) is a temporary alliance of a variety of value-adding services in a dynamic supply chain. VEs are created to fill a window of market opportunity and are then dissolved to make way for restructuring to a new virtual entity when the window is closed. Under such a hybrid structure, business partners strategically form and reform coalitions to bid on contracts and leverage economies of scale – in essence creating dynamic partnerships that exist only as long as necessary. Hence, VE has the highest level of flexibility among all the coordination structures.

An electronic supply chain system by nature is composed of a set of agents or agent groups that cooperate with each other to reach a common goal. Each agent or agent group may have its own coordination structure. The system as a whole also has its own coordination structure. Figure 9.2 shows an example of a multi-agent SCM system. A major challenge in building a multi-agent SCM system is to coordinate the behaviour of the individual agents or agent groups to achieve the individual and shared goals of the participants. Agent or agent groups need to work in concert in order to quickly respond to changes in supply and demand. Developing novel coordination structures to improve dynamic supply chains is a fruitful area of research. The philosophy of the MAS paradigm values flexibility and adaptability over structure and predictability to facilitate the spontaneous formation of autonomous (sometimes temporary) supply chain networks.

Information sharing

Irrespective of whether the supply chain is an e-hierarchy or an e-market, or a VE, there exist different sources of uncertainties (Lee and Billington 1995). First, demand for most consumer products is subject to the whims of the customer. Hence by its nature it is random and uncertain in terms of volume and mix. Second, there is supply uncertainty. The uncertainty could be due to variations in lead time or the quality of the products. In addition, there is process uncertainty. This uncertainty could be due to transportation reliabilities, variations in yield, or machine downtimes. To account for these demand, supply and process uncertainties, safety stock is needed to ensure product availability and adequate customer service levels, but this is an expensive solution because inventory is often a company's largest single asset after capital equipment. In many cases, the value of inventory can be replaced by the value of timely information. Smart companies are finding ways to share information across organizations to drive decision-making, cut inventory costs, speed work processes and enhance customer service.

Companies may share the following major types of information: market and customer information (real-time demand, point-of-sale information, understanding of market trends, the things customers value most), product information (product designs and documentation), supplier information (quality, lead times, schedules, delivery specifications and price etc.), operational information (costs and schedules, inventory levels, shipments, production and transportation capacities), specialist knowledge and management information. All this information can be classified as either supply information (information from upstream sites) or demand information (information from downstream sites). Information sharing in supply chains could therefore be classified into one of the following four categories: no information sharing, supply information sharing, demand information sharing, or complete information sharing (Table 9.1).

The purpose of supply information sharing is to better coordinate an enterprise's activities with those of its suppliers, and also make better procurement decisions. Lack of supply information sharing can lead to significant misalignment of capacity and demand over time. Useful supply information includes lead times, schedules, capacity, response time, service level, availability and price etc. For example, lead times and their variability are important for the manufacturer to plan its production and inventory. With supply information sharing, the supply chain matches suppliers' capacity and schedules with the manufacturer's demand better.

In contrast, the purpose of demand information sharing is to better match the supply's activities to its downstream partners' needs. It has long been recognized that demand information and inventory are substitutes for one

Table 9.1 Types of information sharing

Type	Purpose	Driven by	Content
Supply information sharing	Coordinating an enterprise's activities with these of its suppliers and making better procurement decisions.	Uncertainties in lead time, the quality of the parts and supply process.	Sharing of schedules, lead times, capacity response time, service level, availability, product designs.
Demand information sharing	Matching the supply's activities to its downstream partner's needs and the market demand.	Uncertainties in the market, production and distribution systems.	Sharing of real-time demand, point-of-sale information, market trends, the things customer value most, costs and schedules, inventory levels, shipments, production and transportation capacities.
Complete information sharing	Maximizing the benefits of information sharing	Uncertainties in supply, demand, and process	Sharing of supply, demand, and operational information.

another. Real-time demand information, shipment data, inventory levels, service requirements, or customer buying patterns flow from downstream customers to upstream suppliers. Such information helps the suppliers forecast future demand more accurately, determine shipments and anticipate customer needs in order to cut production and inventory costs.

In order to achieve the maximum benefit of information sharing, complete information sharing, that is, simultaneous sharing of supply and demand information throughout the supply chain, is ideal. For example, to make production planning more efficient, it is worth the manufacturing firm being well informed about the market for certain products and its suppliers' possibilities. Accurate and real-time information sharing make it possible for each supply chain member to do a better job to match its supply with its demand and to coordinate its activities.

The multi-agent approach provides a straightforward way of implementing information sharing. Agents can communicate with each other through exchanging messages, web search and even mobile agents. However, agents need to determine what information they need to make good decisions. One of the important arguments for the multi-agent SCM approach is that the global information, needed by a centralized system to make decisions is not always available in complex supply chain systems. Hence, agents need to share the least amount of information that results in a most profitable decision. Therefore, a potential research question to investigate is how much information agents should share and how the strategic choices of information sharing depend on the characteristics of the dynamic business environment. Furthermore, prior research on the effect of information sharing on supply chain performance is mainly concerned with the hierarchy. From an economic theory point of view, freer flow of information will profoundly affect market efficiency since economic friction will be reduced significantly. Information sharing in the context of markets and VEs is still an open research area.

Privacy and security

Information sharing in SCM brings to the fore issues of privacy and security. Failure to protect customer data privacy can undermine customer confidence in the company, destroy its competitiveness in the market and expose it to lawsuits, while failure to protect critical business information causes a business to lose an economic advantage relative to its competitors. Even though ICTs now provide agents with the ability to share various types of information easily, firms may not want to share certain types of information because of concerns about privacy and security. Firms may not want to share sensitive information such as demand and inventory data with other firms, or may share information only with their neighbouring partners but not with other remote members in the supply chain.

Achieving security and privacy is fundamental for the successful deployment of the multi-agent SCM systems. The essence of security is the controlled use of information. Security is necessary to prevent unauthorized users from understanding the content of the data. Data encryption, as one of the primary methods for protecting data, is useful both for information exchanged on network and for information stored on the database.

Without privacy, however, the SCM solution is incomplete. Privacy refers to the ability of an agent to protect proprietary information about itself. The agent must implement sound privacy measures for two reasons: first, to protect vital organizational data, and, second, to safeguard its customers' and suppliers' private information, thereby encouraging a more stable customer and supplier base. Few enterprise systems, however, are designed from the outset with privacy in mind. Consequently, privacy policies are seldom fully effective, either because the organization's own system does not follow it, or because information 'leaks' to other organizations that are under no obligation to follow it. Instead, the guarantee and assurance of privacy must be included in the design of the multi-agent SCM from the onset.

Unfortunately, information sharing in a supply chain often conflicts deeply with individual agents' desires to be shielded from unauthorized use of their private data. As IT professionals, we are always searching for ways to providing agents the privacy they want while still allowing them to benefit from the value of information sharing. For privacy protection, there are three fundamental approaches, which are legislative, economic and technological. A legislative or regulatory solution may be the slowest and least effective way to address privacy concerns. An SCM system, with a complex web of interested parties, quickly becomes ill suited to a contract-based solution because of the high transaction costs involved in making and monitoring each agreement and controlling information exchange between parties.

Privacy protection through privacy-enhancing technologies seems to be a feasible approach. The multi-agent supply chain systems need to be guarded by specially designed agents that provide the security and privacy services required for the conduct of supply chain activities. For example, security agents should guarantee that eavesdroppers and interlopers cannot access the information sent over the internet and stored in servers. Open research questions are: can we implement sound data management and privacy measures to protect both critical organizational data and consumers' information without compromising the value of information sharing? Can we develop privacy agents that implement these measures to protect agent privacy while preparing high-quality information for effective sharing? Not limited to the field of SCM, privacy protection is an important concern of e-commerce world and emerging web services. If we can guarantee privacy protection through the laws of mathematics rather than the laws of politics and whims of bureaucrats, while still benefiting from the value of information, then we will have made a significant contribution to society. This potentially leads us to a new theory of information management that improves the understanding of the complexities of enterprise information management.

Business environment

A supply chain system is a self-evolving system composed of a set of active agents in a dynamic business environment. These agents are of diverse form and capability, and interact with each other as well as the dynamic business environment. The survival of an agent depends on its ability to fit itself into the environment through adaptation. The goal of multi-agent SCM is to enable these agents to form a highly adaptive supply chain. Therefore, one of the key issues in multi-agent SCM is to understand the dynamic business environment. Thanks to global competition enabled by new ICTs, such as the web, mobile computing and agent technology, today's business environment is becoming increasingly uncertain and complex. We look at the two most important characteristics of the business environment: supply chain structure and demand patterns.

A typical supply chain can be generally divided into a supplier network (upstream of final assembly) and a distribution network. Each subnetwork has its own distinct characteristics. The supplier network, in which products are in the raw or semi-finished state and have to be transformed and assembled at the manufacturer, is further away from the end consumer. Its inventories, including parts, components and subassemblies, have less value, greater commonality and greater flexibility than finished products. Collaboration and information sharing between suppliers and final assembly manufacturers are important, since a better knowledge of the supplier production schedules and part availability is of high value to the manufacturer in order to get the supplies in time for production. As different input factors are complementary, one part's shortage will halt the entire production line. So the objective of the supplier network is to improve availability and responsiveness to the manufacturer.

On the other hand, the distribution network is close to consumers. Finished products have a much higher value, greater differentiation and less flexibility than components. High inventory cost rates and high demand uncertainty require both the manufacturers and distributors to better forecast demands based on real demand. So the objective of the distribution network is to convey the right demand and lower inventories. In a volatile market demand may change in volume, product mix, or both.

For the multi-agent approach, agents of different form and capability generally take different supply chain positions and consequently are under different business situations. They need to understand their environment in order to choose the most appropriate coordination structures and strategies to deal with such problems as growing complexity of the supply chain, demand uncertainties, disturbances, supply changes, etc. For example, supply chains that supply customizable and innovative products are faced with increasing uncertainty in product mix. The managing of demand mix variability may be an important task for agent-based SCM and agents at different stages of the chain may share the information about the market trends in order to introduce new products to the emerging markets.

Consider another case: Dell Computer Corp. By sharing real-time demand information across the supply chain, Dell does not need to carry inventory until it is needed during production. Moreover, suppliers maintain convenient stocking points to guarantee reliable supplies. Information sharing and supplier availability enable Dell to manage inventory on a just-in-time basis. However, replication of the Dell model requires a careful consideration of environment-specific variables. For example, implementing the Dell model can be very difficult for General Motors because its supply chain is inherently more complex, with many stages. Since many suppliers, particularly the second-tier or third-tier suppliers, usually are smaller companies with limited financial resources and technical expertise, it is infeasible and very expensive to use real-demand information to drive decisions.

Agent architecture

Supply chain agents are of diverse form and capability. Depending on its capabilities, an agent has one or more of the following components: performance, evaluation and knowledge discovery system (Holland 1995). A performance system specifies how the agent behaves in different situations. It contains a knowledge base, which is a collection of decision rules (e.g. if-then clauses in the form 'if premise then conclusion') that determines what action to take under any given situation. The behaviour of an agent is a sequence of actions taken by the agent in response to a stimulus. An agent may take a proactive or reactive stance. A proactive behaviour is one that is made in anticipation of an event, such as in demand forecasting, when the firm tries to predict the demand for the future period. A reactive behaviour is in direct response to an outside stimulus. For example, a firm produces the required output upon receipt of an order.

A hybrid architecture involves closely integrated proactive and reactive subarchitectures. The evaluation system provides feedback from the environment by assessing the consequences of the decisions given by the agent. These experiences guide the agent to make changes to its structure or rules so that it makes better use of the environment for its own end. The knowledge discovery system builds and updates the knowledge base of the agent using its past experiences. In building its knowledge base, an agent uses two approaches: knowledge acquisition and machine learning. In the case of knowledge acquisition, the agent gets the decision rules about how the agent should behave under different situations from human experts, refines them and stores them in its knowledge base. In the case of machine learning, the agent acquires its knowledge from its memory of past experiences.

A suitable agent structure is one of basic concerns in multi-agent SCM. This involves the development of knowledge-based, analytically supported decision rules for disparate agents with differing capabilities. A critical item in this research is to create or identify the appropriate business model and policies for each individual agent. This includes appropriate coordination structures, policies of information sharing, and privacy and security measures. Agents should also strive to adapt themselves to the dynamic environment. The ability to learn and evolve is also important for them to increase their competence. Furthermore, agents can be organized into different agent groups. Coalition formation is an ideal behaviour in a multi-agent system, when a group of agents are needed in order to perform a task more efficiently. Each agent group may have its own coordination structure and information sharing and privacy policies. It is also important to have agent groups learn and evolve in the changing environment. Similarly, when the agents and agent groups interact with each other by following the global structures and policies, they form an adaptive SCM system.

From the different issues presented above we consider the issue of information sharing and present results of a multi-agent simulation done to study the effects of different information sharing strategies on the supply chain performance.

Effects of information sharing strategies: an example

We implemented a multi-agent simulation model to experiment with the effects of information sharing on the system performance under different demand pattern settings. The simulation design is based on our experience at an electronics manufacturer and series of plot runs. Although the parameters are chosen to reflect a particular problem setting, we tried to keep the model realistic enough so that the results hold for other general settings. We simulate a serial supply chain with four stages: retailer (stage 1), distributor (stage 2), manufacturer (stage 3) and supplier (stage 4). There may be multiple instances in stages 1 and 4, but only one manufacturer and one distributor. The manufacturer may transform an input component into a new product, or assemble several input components into a product according to a bill of materials, while other stages don't have manufacturing capabilities. We treat all the stages as inventory buffers. In addition to the above four stages, there exists a reliable exogenous source of inventory, called the source agent, and a market agent. The source agent receives orders from the supplier and ships products to it accordingly. The market agent generates the end demand to the retailer using a normal distribution and consumes the products shipped by the retailer. The average of the total demand is 10,000 units/period. The demand and cost parameters are chosen based on our industrial experience.

We model the inventory system at each stage of the supply chain as an order-up-to system with a fixed review time of one period. Each stage has a fixed lead time of two periods and a fixed safety factor of 1.645. Each stage determines its own safety stock based on the information shared rather than on the received orders, and uses a moving average over ten periods to forecast demand. When the demand in a period exceeds the on-hand inventory, the excess is backordered. But the backorder cost is not considered because it is a loss of goodwill and is very difficult to quantify. The unit holding cost rate, expressed as a percentage of the value of the product, is lowest at the supplier and increases towards downstream. The holding cost rates are 20 per cent, 15 per cent, 10 per cent, 5 per cent for stages 1, 2, 3, 4 respectively.

We consider four different information sharing strategies. In Model 0, each stage of the supply chain does not know the status of its downstream stages and forecasts are based only on the orders from its immediate downstream stage. The Beer Game is probably the most famous case of Model 0 in a traditional supply chain. Model 1 assumes total real demand visibility. The end demand is transmitted from the end consumer back through every stage in the supply chain. This means that any real change in demand can be known at all points in the supply chain. The sharing of POS data and collaborative planning and optimization are examples of Model 1. In Model 2, each stage of the supply chain shares information about its inventory levels with its adjacent supplier. This strategy is currently common in the grocery and fashion retailing industry. Vendor managed inventory (VMI), schedule sharing window and continuous replenishment belong to this type of information sharing. Model 3 assumes that each stage knows its downstream customer's shipment data. For instance, in the computer industry, manufacturers such as HP and IBM request sell-through data on withdrawn stocks from their resellers' central warehouse. Detailed analytical discussion and comparison of these models is presented in Li *et al.* (2006).

For each of the information sharing models in our experiments, we first conducted a pilot run of the simulation to estimate the steady-state safety stocks required at each of the stages. Figure 9.3 presents the simulation estimates of the standard deviation of orders across a four-stage supply chain. It shows that information sharing reduces the order variability dramatically and thus reduces the safety stocks. After initializing the system with a representative state, we generated ten independent runs of the model with length of 150 periods each. Statistics were collected over the ten runs. These choices are based on common simulation practices. We saved a different random seed for each different run so that we can use the same random seed across the models for a given run. We use the total inventory cost and the average fill rate across all stages to evaluate the system performance with each of the models. Using Model 0 as a base case, we defined as the value of information sharing the difference in each model's inventory cost and fill rate over

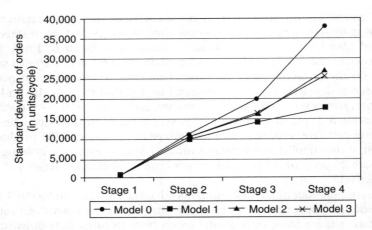

Figure 9.3 Standard deviation of orders placed across a 4-stage supply chain

Table 9.2 Results for low demand variability

Models	Inventory cost			Average fill rate		
	Inventory cost	% Benefit of inventory cost	p-value*	Percentage fill rate	% Benefit of fill rate	p-value*
Model 0	$906,568			88.12		
Model 1	$228,905	74.75	<0.0001	88.42	0.34	0.7204
Model 2	$595,471	34.32	0.0007	93.42	6.00	<0.0001
Model 3	$428,550	52.73	<0.0001	82.55	−6.33	<0.0001

*Based on the output generated by SAS using $\alpha = 0.05$

Model 0: that is (Model 0 cost – Model i cost)/Model 0 cost and (Model i fill rate – Model 0 fill rate)/Model 0 fill rate.

Results

We carried out two experiments to evaluate the system performance with the information sharing models under different demand pattern settings. We ran paired t-tests in SAS to test for statistical significance. In the first experiment, we studied the behaviour of the four models under low consumer demand variability. The end-demand process is specified by $\mu = 10,000$ and $\sigma = 866$. Table 9.2 reports the results for the first experiment. The pattern depicted in Table 9.2 can be summarized as follows. When demand is relatively stable, information sharing significantly reduces order variability, and thus reduces inventory and improve fill rate, except in Model 3.

Table 9.3 Results for high demand variability

Models	Inventory cost			Average fill rate		
	Inventory cost	% Benefit of inventory cost	*p*-value*	Percentage fill rate	% Benefit of fill rate	*p*-value*
Model 0	$2,308,440			88.59		
Model 1	$313,870	86.40	. <0.0001	71.99	−18.74	<0.0001
Model 2	$1,442,300	37.52	<0.0001	92.10	3.96	<0.0001
Model 3	$1,435,660	37.81	<0.0001	82.99	−6.32	<0.0001

*Based on the output generated by SAS using $\alpha = 0.05$

In the second experiment, we compared the performance of the four models under high consumer demand variability. Since products under volatile demand often have a fluctuating demand pattern, we consider a single product with demand fluctuating between two processes. The high-range demand is specified by $\mu = 15,000$ and $\sigma = 1,299$, the low-range demand is specified by $\mu = 5,000$ and $\sigma = 433$, and the high or low range is randomly selected every simulation period. Table 9.3 reports the results for the second experiment. Under high consumer demand variability, each stage of the supply chain needs to keep enough safety stock to buffer against high order variability. Model 1 lowers inventory cost by planning the safety stocks based on the end demand, but the resulting lower buffer gives lower fill rate. Model 2, on the other hand, gives the best customer service, but may drive inventory up. Under Model 3, each stage underestimates the downstream demand and thus results in a low fill rate.

Conclusion

Although companies and academic researchers have increasingly recognized the importance of agent technology in supply chain management, there has not been a representational multi-agent model of supply chains. We present such a strategic framework for multi-agent supply chain management that encompasses the issues of coordination structures, information sharing policies, privacy and security, business environment and agent architecture. We have analyzed the critical elements of the framework presented and identified open research questions. We have considered the issue of information sharing and presented results of a simulation study comparing the effects of different information sharing strategies on the performance of the supply chain.

Our supply chain example offers the following insights. First, information sharing helps counter the phenomenon of demand variability amplification, mainly caused by the time lag between channel partners in the supply chain. The sharing of demand information reduces the information distortion to a large extent, while the sharing of inventory data and shipment data reduces at least one level of information distortion. Second, the impact of information sharing on supply chain performance largely depends on demand patterns and the supply chain structure. No information sharing strategy is uniformly superior because each supply chain has its unique characteristics. We find that various information sharing schemes consistently improve supply chain performance under relatively stable demand. When the variance of consumer demand is high, however, the performance of information sharing strategies varies.

As mentioned earlier, there are many areas that require further investigation. One of the problems we want to investigate is the evolutionary path of coordination structures and the economic variables and conditions that drive the evolution. A second aspect that we are working on is the evolution of information sharing strategies in uncertain environments. While information is always beneficial, we want to investigate what types of information should be shared between partners and how the strategic choices of information sharing depend on the market characteristics, supply chain processes and structures. Finally, we are motivated to develop sound information management and privacy measures that protect crucial organizational data and consumers' privacy information without compromising the value of information sharing.

References

Anthony, P. and Jennings, N.R. 2003 'Developing a bidding agent for multiple heterogeneous auctions', *ACM Transactions on Internet Technology*, 3 (August): 185–217.

Holland, J. 1995 *Hidden Order: How Adaptation Builds Complexity*, New York: Addison-Wesley.

Kaihara, T. 2003 'Multi-agent based supply chain modelling with dynamic environment', *International Journal of Production Economics*, 85(2): 263–9.

King, J.L. 1983 'Centralized and decentralized computing: Organizational considerations and management options', *Computing Surveys*, 15(4): 319–49.

Lee, H.L. and Billington, C. 1995 'The evolution of SCM models and practice at Hewlett-Packard', *Interface 25*, 5 (September–October): 42–63.

Lerman, K. and Galstyan, A. 2003 'Agent memory and adaptation in multi-agent systems', *AAMAS '03*, (July): 797–803.

Li, J., Sikora, R., Shaw, M. and Tan, G.W., 2006 'A strategic analysis of inter-organizational information sharing', *Decision Support Systems*, 42(1): 251–66.

Lin, Fu-Ren, Tan, Gek Woo and Shaw, M.J. 1998 'Modeling supply-chain networks by a multi-agent system', *Proceedings of the HICCS*, 5 (January): 105–14.

Mori, M., Matsuo, H. and Kosaka, M. 1998 'Resource allocation using intelligent agent technology in supply chain management', *Transactions of the Society of Instrument and Control Engineers 34*, 11: 1675–83.

Papazoglou, M.P. 2001 'Agent-oriented technology in support of e-business', *Communications of the ACM 44*, 4(April).

Parkes, D.C. 2000 'Optimal auction design for agents with hard valuation problems', *Agent Mediated Electronic Commerce II: Towards Next-Generation Agent-Based Electronic Commerce Systems*, Berlin: Springer.

Sandholm, T. 1998 'Agents in electronic commerce: Component technologies for automated negotiation and coalition formation', *Proceedings of the International Conference on Multiagent Systems*, Los Alamos, CA.

Wooldridge, M. and Jennings, N.R. 1995 'Intelligent agents: Theory and practice', *The Knowledge Engineering Review 10*, 2:115–52.

10
Delivery Supply Chain Planning Using Radio Frequency Identification (RFID)-Enabled Dynamic Optimization

Shang-Tae Yee, Jeffrey Tew, Kaizhi Tang, Jindae Kim and Soundar Kumara

Introduction

For the past few years, many companies have investigated potential of radio frequency identification (RFID) technologies by conducting pilot project. Whereas successful cases were reported for supply chains, companies experienced under-achievement of their target on return on investment (ROI) due to various reasons. First of all, RFID hardware itself would be limited in satisfying functionality and performance of user requirements. The RFID hardware has been mature because RFID vendors have made a lot of effort to develop more robust RFID tags and readers. Except for harsh manufacturing environment, RFID hardware can be satisfactorily implemented right through RF design and calibration. Second, RFID would have been applied to inappropriate applications. In order to take a competitive advantage, some companies rushed to implement the RFID by selecting improper applications. The RFID is effective in an environment where materials, work-in-process and finished products are moving dynamically. Third, no sufficient planning and analysis would have been conducted as to the use of RFID data, the impact of RFID on other business processes and the connectivity to related information systems. This can lessen business benefits of the RFID capability.

An RFID pilot project could be unsuccessful when it merely focuses on the RFID implementation and is interested in collecting data more quickly. A real challenge is to achieve a reasonable ROI from the RFID implementation. A comprehensive understanding of the business processes the RFID is applied to is key to the success of the RFID project. This requires figuring out the right decision factors of the business processes where monitoring movement flow of an object in near real-time is important and how the business processes could be changed to improve performance using the RFID.

170

This chapter presents an approach to maximize the ROI of an RFID implementation using an RFID-enabled decision-making framework for finished vehicle delivery at an assembly plant from production release to shipment to dealers. The decision-making framework is based on a market-based multi-agent computational architecture that can take into account real-time data from the RFID, and the capability of the framework is validated using simulation.

Finished vehicles are moved from assembly plants to their adjacent shipping yards and then they are shipped to distribution centres or held until being ready for shipment to dealers. An automotive company in North America has numerous assembly plants and vehicle distribution centres where the vehicles reside for a few days for shipment mix and consolidation. The amount of time each vehicle stays at these facilities constitutes a big portion of the total lead time, and decreasing this time is crucial to achieve the lead-time reduction. In addition, the visibility of all the vehicles along the delivery chain can provide the customers with more reliable delivery dates as well as better order status.

This chapter is organized as follows. The second section briefly explains the general aspects of RFID and wireless technology. Then, the issues and problems in current delivery chain and the potential of wireless tracking are discussed in the third section. Next, the fourth section presents a solution approach consisting of five steps, which includes the details of a simulator emulating the real shipment yard environment and a dynamic optimization methodology using market-based algorithms with a multi-agent computational architecture. The fifth section provides numerical results obtained by simulation experiments. Finally, conclusions are given in the last section.

RFID and wireless technology in general

Radio frequency identification (RFID), one of the wireless technologies, has enlarged its application domain. Wal-Mart Stores Inc. and the US Department of Defense are drivers from retail and government side respectively. Since the 1980s, the automotive industry, an early adopter, has used RFID in manufacturing environments. EPCglobal consortium, transferred from the Auto-ID Center, proposed the EPCglobal Network that uses passive RF tag-based systems to construct the 'internet of things' by tagging objects. The RFID of products, the ability to identify a product or a part without physical handling, is becoming a basis for new supply chain management solutions (Karkkainen and Holmstrom 2002).

The RFID, leveraged with other wireless technologies like wireless local area network (WLAN), has been used for tracking assets. The RFID can enable obtaining higher granularity and visibility of supply chain operations. It can also improve data accuracy by tracking the events to item level. Once an item has an RF identification, seamless item tracking is possible from any tier of suppliers, through manufacturers, to retailers (Frontline Solutions 2001). Wireless technology can bring several benefits in how enterprises control and handle real-time data because, once connected to enterprise resource planning (ERP) system, hard-to-retrieve back-office data can be wirelessly transmitted to mobile users' fingertips (Grygo 2000). Demand will grow for wireless-to-ERP and wireless-to-supply chain integration solutions among shop floor groups, sales forces and field service workforces. Passing along the mobile devices on-the-spot specifics about shipment time, pricing, quotes and product availability brings a tremendous competitive advantage in the realm of supply chain management and e-business. All the facilities and computational systems are able to share real-time data and improve corporate productivity, throughput and efficiency (Department of Energy 2002).

In addition to the automotive industry, logistics and trucking companies have been using or implementing wireless solutions integrated with ERP systems. Supply chain management can benefit from emerging wireless technologies, such as smart sensor networks (IEEE 1451.5), mesh networks and wide area networks (IEEE 802.16 and 20). These new technologies will broaden the application space of the wireless for supply chain management.

Current delivery process problems and RF tracking potential

Every day, thousands of vehicles are produced at an assembly plant. As shown in Figure 10.1, once a vehicle is completely assembled, it is inspected and then, is deployed in a bay of buffer areas in the plant shipping yard for shipment according to two modes of transportation, namely, truck and rail (Kim *et al.* 2008). The deployment is an activity to put a vehicle in a particular bay of the yard and the shipment is to build shipment loads for delivering the vehicles. If the vehicle is transported by rail, it is deployed in RB1 or RB2, and loaded in RB3. If the vehicle is transported by truck, it is deployed in TB1, TB2, or TB4, and loaded in TB3. A certain portion of the vehicles deployed at the plant yard would be put on hold for some reason: bad parts from suppliers, production quality deviations, carrier unavailability and insufficient dealer lot. When the plant quality department needs to locate a range of vehicles to put on hold, it is time consuming and labour intensive. It is critical to quickly locate the vehicles before they are shipped out because it is much harder to resolve problems once they are off-site. When a vehicle is deployed in a wrong spot, called a misbay (several times a day), or is loaded in a wrong truck/rail, called a misload (several times a week), it becomes more difficult to know its exact location. These unexpected operational events can occur at the shipment yard, and cause prolonged vehicle dwell time (the time a vehicle stays at a facility, e.g. at the yard), shipment abnormality and labour cost increase. Due to lack of visibility of vehicle movements, delivery planning often fails to achieve optimality.

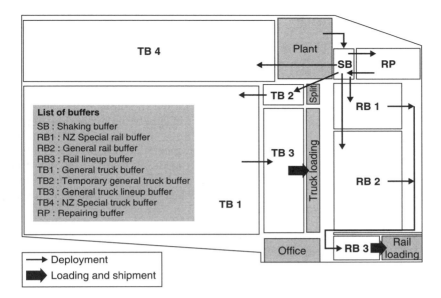

Figure 10.1   The shipping yard structure and layout

Note: The yard is split into two parts: one is for truck shipment, and the other for rail shipment. Vehicles released from plant are transferred to yard operators at the shaking buffer. Vehicles are deployed in the buffers according to transportation modes, that is, the vehicles transported using trucks are deployed in truck buffers and the vehicles delivered using rail are deployed in rail buffers. The vehicles are loaded at lineup buffers and then shipped out.

An RFID tracking system is expected to automatically detect the exact location of each vehicle upon request, emit an alarm to notify a misbay or a misload. Hence, the RFID system could be used as an enable to maintain continuous improvement of vehicle deployment and shipment.

In view of the visibility of the entire delivery chain, the RFID tracking system can keep track of a vehicle's location and provide dynamic flow information of the vehicle at each event point in real-time, such as when a vehicle comes to and leaves a point, and how much time a vehicle stays at the point. By collecting delivery time statistics, we can identify the bottleneck points that should be improved. The delivery chain involves several business partners like truck carrier, rail carrier and yard management company. Even though each partner uses its own reasonable practices, operational exceptions could occur at junction points where business events involve different parties. These exceptions could result in bottlenecks due to lack of information sharing between parties. Having RFID-enabled visibility for the entire distribution network can lead to shorter lead-time, better customer service, quality improvement and efficient delivery.

The solution approach

Prior to an actual RFID implementation that requires large investment, a detailed accurate value assessment and impact analysis should be conducted on how RFID tracking could help to improve the performance of vehicle delivery process. This chapter focuses on the plant shipping yard, the very starting point of vehicle delivery chain, as shown in Figure 10.1. Once the RFID tracking benefits at the shipping yard are clearly understood by developing appropriate metrics and analysis methods, a similar approach can be applied to distribution centres and other transportation routes. This chapter is intended to show how the RFID vehicle tracking system can change the delivery chain in terms of visibility and agility, and, consequently, how many savings can be obtained for specific benefit categories. The solution approach constitutes the following five steps:

1. Feasibility study and business case development
2. Value proposition of RFID tracking using simulation
3. Decision models development
4. RFID-enabled decision-making framework development
5. Performance analysis and recommendations.

The solution steps shown in Figure 10.2 are interrelated to each other. The feasibility study is conducted for investigating existing RFID/wireless technologies, and a business case was developed. The value proposition is to examine the value of each benefit item specified in the business case when we use the RFID tracking system. A simulator was developed to emulate the shipping yard environment and analyze the impact of the tracking system on yard operations. To maximize the benefits from the tracking system, it is important to have a thorough understanding of associated business processes, identify necessary operational decisions and develop the decision models accordingly. The decision models should consider all the dynamic nature of operational logics and practices, and provide optimal decisions related to vehicle deployment and shipment. Market-based decision algorithms were developed under a multi-agent computational architecture to accomplish optimization in this dynamic environment. Then, integrating the decision models with the simulator builds the RFID-enabled decision-making framework. We conducted a comprehensive performance analysis using the framework and made recommendations. Each step needs inputs from the previous step and the outcome of one step is fed back to the previous steps.

Step 1: Feasibility study and business case development

At the beginning of the RFID initiative, we conducted a feasibility study as to what RFID/wireless technology is the most appropriate for our business purposes and needs. We reviewed various technologies available in the market.

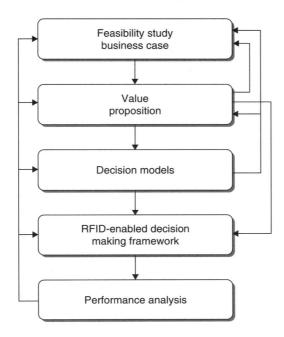

Figure 10.2 The solution approach consists of a series of steps
Note: Each step is correlated with others during the whole solution process. The outcome of one step is used as input to next step and it is updated with the feedback information of the next step.

We found that real-time location data of each vehicle is critical to track the vehicle's movement flow and selected active RFID-based system. A passive RFID-based system like EPCglobal Network is adversely affected by a harsh, metal environment and thus restricted in reporting the vehicle locations in real-time, not suitable for our needs. We also investigated the handheld device system based on the IEEE 802.11b wireless network. This system is advantageous in terms of low investment cost and ease of implementation. However, it does not provide continuously changing flow information of each vehicle. Similarly, a bar code system does not provide enough information of dynamic vehicle flow, and it is limited because of its line-of-sight requirement. To have the same level of visibility as active an RFID system for the vehicle flow, we have to scan many times and this causes significant increase in labour time. A real-time locating system, known as ANSI 371.1, was identified as the most appropriate technology for our case. The ANSI 371.1 captures RF signals from the tags attached to each vehicle using the readers installed in the ceiling or light post. It is not vulnerable to interferences and locates the vehicle within a range of 300 feet, with deviation of less than 10 feet.

Next, we developed a business case to justify the initiative by figuring out potential benefits and associated values. Through comprehensive discussions with the people working at the assembly plants, the shipping yards and the distribution centres, we identified several benefit categories, estimated their dollar values and defined metrics to be measured. The business case was reviewed with all the stakeholders involved in this initiative and approved by senior management.

Step 2: Value proposition of RFID tracking using simulation

The value estimation of the business case is a very high-level conjecture based on the experience and intuition of the people involved, not on the detailed analysis of business operations. Decision-makers want to have very accurate evidence, that is, whether or not the investment in the RFID system will be repaid with proper benefits on implementation (Chen 2001, Lee and Whang 1999). In other words, they want to know how much performance improvement would be expected from the RFID implementation. The senior management of a company is very careful about making a decision to implement, even a pilot project, until they can see obvious evidence of benefits; if it is successful, it will be rolled out to the entire corporation. Thus, we needed to conduct more detailed value analysis and developed a simulation model accordingly.

According to Huang, Lau and Mak (2003), the methods to model real-world operations are classified into two groups: analytical (mathematical model, mixed integer programming) and simulation (system dynamics, agent-based modelling and discrete event simulation). Analytical approaches, the mathematical model (Lee, So and Tang 2000) and mixed integer programming (Sterman 2000, Anderson, Gremban and Young 1997), due to their over-simplification and long computation time, would be intractable for the operational level of analysis. Three simulation-based approaches, system dynamics (Anderson, Fine and Deployer 2000, Souza, Zice and Chaoyang 2000), agent-based modelling (Brandolese, Brun and Portioli-Straudacher 2000, Gjerdrum, Shah and Papageorgiou 2001) and discrete event simulation (Beamon and Chen 2001, Banerjee *et al.* 2001) have been used in various supply chain environments. The complexity of shipping yard business processes lends itself to selection of a simulation-based approach. In particular, considering the operational characteristics of deployment and shipment process, the discrete event simulation was the best fit to our objectives.

The simulator for yard operations helps visualize all the processes and components. The processes, say events, include vehicle release from the plant, vehicle deployment in the yard, vehicle loading onto rail and truck, and vehicle shipment. The components, say entities, are yard personnel, loading personnel, plant personnel, vehicles, railcars and trucks. As shown in Figure 10.3, the simulator, part of the RFID-enabled decision-making framework, consists of four parts: (a) layout modelling of shipping yard; (b) operations

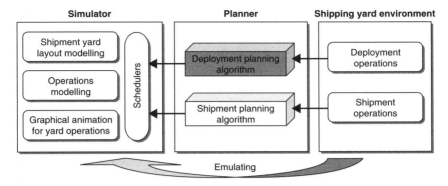

Figure 10.3   The structure of decision-making framework
Note: This consists of two components: simulator and planner. The simulator simulates the real shipping yard environment that relates to deployment and shipment of finished vehicles, and it is further decomposed into four subcomponents: (a) modelling the layout of shipping yard; (b) modelling the operations of yard; (c) graphical animations of yard operations; and (d) modelling the schedulers that are synchronized with the planner. The planner has algorithms for deployment and shipment, and is further classified into two parts: one is for deployment and the other for shipment. The connection between the simulator and the planner is achieved through the schedulers that control the time that these algorithms are invoked.

modelling of deployment and shipment; (c) graphical animations of yard operations; and (d) schedulers of deployment and shipment. The simulator also emulates real-time capabilities of the RFID tracking system, for example, providing current location of a vehicle in a given time. We conducted a value analysis using the simulation model (see Kim *et al.* 2008 for details).

Step 3: Decision models development

The RFID tracking system enables provision of real-time vehicle location data. Next a key question is how we can utilize the real-time data for better business decision-making. Companies have experienced several failures of IT-related projects in the past because they just adopted vendor solutions without carefully analyzing their unique business characteristics. Thus, this lesson led us to develop decision models by comprehensively capturing the business logics and practices of the shipping yard. As shown in Figure 10.3, the planner consists of two decision model components: one for deployment planning and the other for shipment planning.

Deployment planning

The deployment decision problem is how to deploy a vehicle released from the plant to a particular bay of the shipping yard to minimize the total distance for both putting the vehicle into a bay and loading it onto a truck or railcar. The difficulty of deployment planning is in calculating the exact distance from bays to lineup areas, RB3 and TB3, because we do not know ahead of time where trucks and railcars will be parked for loading vehicles. Vehicles can be located in any bay location, and trucks/railcars can be parked somewhere in lineup areas (see Figure 10.1). Two approaches can be used to calculate this distance: one is to make an approximation of the distance between two points, and the other is to predict the lineup sequence using advance notification of production schedule information. The former approach is termed as *distance-based deployment planning*. It approximates the distance from the central point of a bay to either of three points: the closest, middle, or longest point of rectangular lineup area. Whatever point we take, there will be an error in computing the exact distance. The second approach is termed *geography-based deployment planning*. It assumes that deployment area is clustered by destinations and loads are built accordingly. Thus, it maps the geographical clusters of vehicle destinations to the bay clusters in the deployment area. The performance mainly depends on the extent to which load building is done on the basis of destination-oriented deployment and the number of clusters.

Shipment planning

The shipment decision problem, also called the load makeup problem, is how to load a set of vehicles having different destinations onto either trucks or trains to minimize both total vehicle dwell time at the yard and total transportation cost. The load makeup planning is a two-layer non-deterministic polynomial time (NP)-hard problem with two conflicting objectives. That is, the yard manager wants to minimize the total transportation distance as well as to ship out the vehicles that have stayed longest first. The load makeup is now being done in a static manner, just using currently available vehicle inventory information at the yard. Three algorithms are applicable to build the shipment loads: empirical (EM), minimum spanning tree (MST) and vehicle routing optimization (VRO) algorithm.

In the EM algorithm, every morning, the yard manager obtains shipment truck and train schedules for the same day and vehicle inventory information of the yard. The yard manager uses this guaranteed information without considering the dynamics of the daily operations. The yard manager finds an oldest vehicle that will become the leading vehicle in load building. Starting from the leading vehicle, the manager starts to search for the vehicles having the closest destinations to the leading one. The vehicles going to the same dealer as the leading vehicle are selected first, then the vehicles having destinations in the same demand area are chosen, until the capacity of a truck or a train is used up.

In the MST algorithm, instead of using the rule of demand areas and their adjacency relationships, each load clusters its vehicles using the rule of minimum spanning tree, which is usually used to find a tree in a graph with the minimum summation of weights of connecting arcs (Cormen *et al.* 2001). Different from normal MST, the MST for load makeup is restricted such that the size of each tree is limited to the capacity of the corresponding truck. The algorithm starts from an oldest or a customized order vehicle. In the search process, the whole set of vehicles is divided into two exclusive sub-sets: one sub-set contains the vehicles already assigned to the load and the other contains the vehicles not assigned to the load. A priority queue stores all the pairs of vehicles with the enumeration of all the loaded vehicles and all the unloaded vehicles. The queue is sorted out by the distance of two vehicles in a pair and the vehicles just added into the loaded set. All the other unloaded vehicles are inserted into the priority queue. Then, the top pair is chosen and the relevant vehicle is moved from the unloaded set to the loaded set. Finally, the pairs related to the chosen vehicle are all deleted from the queue. After all the loads are built, a travelling salesman problem (TSP) is solved for each load. The MST algorithm is an approximate approach because the TSP is not directly used for clustering.

The VRO algorithm for load makeup has two distinctions compared to the generic vehicle routing problem: first, the capacities of trucks are different; second, there are more vehicles available than the scheduled number of trucks that can accommodate them. The VRO algorithm is a composite method that consists of two main steps. In the first step, multiple routes are constructed sequentially for all the available trucks. In the second step, the routes constructed are improved based on heuristic rules that exchange nodes between two routes.

Limitations of static shipment algorithms

Although the MST and VRO algorithm can improve the load makeup performance in one aspect or another, they are not as good as the EM algorithm in taking into account the most recently updated information, that is, real-time dynamic information of the vehicle and yard state. Between a load building and a truck arrival, yard conditions may change or unexpected events may occur. These unexpected circumstances can disrupt entire shipment plan. As shown in Figure 10.4, in the static environment, vehicles are deployed at the yard from t_1 to t_2. At t_2, loads are built only for the vehicles physically located in the yard. From t_3 to t_4, when trucks arrive at the yard, the vehicles are lined up. The vehicles are loaded on the trucks from t_4 to t_5 and shipped out from t_5 to t_6 in a given sequence. In other words, load makeup is being done in a structured, sequential manner based on the vehicle information available at t_2. However, during any time between t_1 to t_4 (even for the time from t_4 to t_5), the yard and vehicle status can be dynamically changed according to various regular and exceptional events, and these real-time changes should be captured in load planning and lineup process. Real-time information obtainable during this time period is the new vehicle arrivals, the vehicles redeployed from quality holds and repairs, the vehicles changed in bay locations and the schedule changes of trucks assigned to the yard. In addition, load building should consider other information, such as

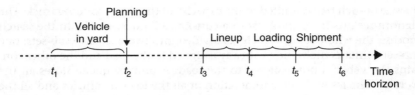

Figure 10.4 Static optimization limitations

Note: Under static optimization scenario, loads are built only for the vehicles physically located in the yard at t_2. When trucks arrive at the yard, the vehicles are lined up (from t_3 to t_4), loaded (from t_4 to t_5) and shipped out (from t_5 to t_6) in a sequential manner. However, during any time from t_1 to t_4 (even for the time from t_4 to t_5), various dynamic events regarding the yard and vehicle status can occur and static optimization cannot reflect these real-time changes in load planning and lineup process.

advanced production notifications, projected truck dispatching schedules, predicted future shipment schedules and yard personnel utilization status.

Even though the MST and VRO algorithm can use the RFID vehicle location data, it is very difficult or impossible to model this dynamic real-time behaviour using mathematical equations. More importantly, this real-time information needs to be monitored and captured continuously for robust decision-making.

When the RFID tracking system is in place, it enables consideration of these factors by making connectivity with different information sources, and then development of an intelligent decision-making system by comprehensively accommodating all the related data for shipment environment. More and reliable information will help make better decisions in real-time. Thus, we need a new method of shipment decision planning. It can help to either cluster the truck routes in a more compact way, so as to reduce the transportation cost, or fill more truck vacancies so as to reduce the dwell time at the planning instant. The load makeup can be done in an unstructured and non-sequential manner.

Dynamic optimization

We can have two strategies for load makeup planning. One strategy is to use the EM, MST, or VRO algorithm for building every load based on static environment information. This strategy can be prone to expensive computation, which requires a large amount of computation time that may be longer than the time gap between load makeups and, thus, might not produce the resulting loads within a given time. From an operational perspective, solving the whole problem again at every load building could totally change the previous solution, which can cause inconsistency for the shipment process, because too much change could occur in vehicle-destination pairs compared to the previous loads. Also, this strategy is not effective in capturing the difficult-to-model real-time information mentioned above.

The other strategy is to search for an optimal solution starting from an existing solution. This strategy is also termed as dynamic optimization or continual optimization (Bar-Noy *et al.* 2002). Instead of solving the entire problem again, a new solution is sought from the solution obtained by a static algorithm. This strategy could avoid the drawbacks of the first strategy: high computation time, solution inconsistency and real-time information modelling difficulty. The concept of dynamic optimization is, in a sense, similar to post-optimality analysis of linear programming using simplex method, in which the simplex pivot starts with an existing optimal solution before the parameters or constraints are changed (Vaserstein and Byrne 2003).

Our dynamic optimization of the load makeup uses the solution obtained from a static optimization as an initial solution; different from static optimization, any dynamic changes occurring between load planning periods are tracked and used to trigger incremental optimization.

Market-based multi-agent computational architecture

To capture and process the dynamic vehicle flows, we need a computational architecture to effectively collect and coordinate the dynamic events occurring among several operational players of the yard. The multi-agent system (MAS) has been suggested as a promising information infrastructure for distributed, complex and heterogeneous environments (Weiss 1999, Wooldridge 2002). Davidson *et al.* (2003) compared agent-based approaches to classic optimization techniques (including heuristic search) for dynamically distributed resource allocation. Agent-based approaches fit better in situations where the problem domain is large, node or link failure is high, frequency of decision-making is high, problem structure is frequently changed and private or local information is important. Our problem exhibits most of these characteristics, therefore MAS is a good choice. Because the shipping yard involves multiple parties and has the characteristics of a market, we can establish the MAS framework by defining a number of agents to which we assign different functions of the market. In addition, the concept of market equilibrium is analogous to the incremental optimality that can change the optimal solution according to the dynamics influencing the shipment processes. From the perspective of game theory, the equilibrium of a perfect market is reached at the point where no one is interested in selling and buying. This concept can be used to decide when the market heuristic process should stop (Tang and Kumara 2007).

As shown in Figure 10.5, three types of agents were designed: yard agent, truck scheduler agent and load agent. The yard agent represents the shipping yard. Its behaviour includes: monitoring and updating vehicle locations using the RFID system to detect newly shippable vehicles; deriving dwell time for a vehicle and lineup time for a load; predicting future production schedules; serving as a trading agent. The truck scheduler agent represents the transportation company that owns trucks for executing transportation.

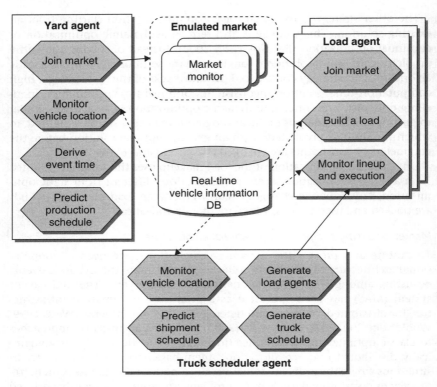

Figure 10.5 Agent design for market-based dynamic truck load makeup

It has the following behaviour: monitoring inventory level; generating truck schedules; predicting future shipment schedules; generating load agents. A load agent represents a truck and its main behaviour includes: building a load using vehicle information; monitoring lineup and execution of the load; serving as a trading agent.

To emulate a real market for the shipment environment, a yard agent and a group of load agents are designated as traders, vehicles as products and cost savings as profits. The yard agent and the load agents propose their selling or buying proposals based on their constraints, capabilities and interests. Market monitors collect these proposals, each of which is identified with a vehicle. The yard agent, truck scheduler agent, multiple load agents and market monitors constitute all the players of the emulated market.

In normal trading, double auction interactions take place, that is, a buyer has the ability to buy a vehicle from anybody who wants to sell. One round of interaction has two proposing steps. In the first step, the selling agents propose their asks; in the following step, the buying agents propose their bids based on the asks proposed in the first step. With the collected proposals, the monitors then decide the winners of double auction. A special interaction is designed to handle the situation of fully capacitated load agents. At the beginning of dynamic optimization, most load agents are full with vehicles and have no ability to buy any other vehicles. We design surplus trading to deal with this situation. In surplus trading, a fully capacitated load agent exchanges one of its vehicles with one of the vehicles of the yard agent. Since a fully capacitated load agent has no vacancy to include another vehicle in its routing plan, it is only interested in trading in a vehicle from the yard agent and trading out one of its own vehicles. The vehicle to trade out is called a surplus vehicle, which is left over and will be returned to the yard agent. The surplus trading between a fully capacitated load agent and the yard agent keeps the balance of the number of vehicles between the shipping yard and the scheduled trucks. The balance is one of the important constraints of the original load makeup planning problem. In surplus trading, the yard agent becomes passive and does not actively make decisions; it provides the vehicle requested by the load agent and always accepts the surplus vehicles unconditionally. The decision-making for the surplus trading can be deterministic or stochastic. The deterministic model addresses the self-interest of the load agent. The stochastic model makes the load agent possibly yield its self-interest to other load agents.

Step 4: RFID-enabled decision-making framework development

The planner developed in Step 3 reads in real-time location data from the tracking system and runs the decision models on user requests. It should be flexible enough to 'plug-and-play' to any type of wireless devices and systems. The simulator emulates the RFID real-time data for vehicle movements. The connection between the simulator and the planner can be accomplished through the schedulers that control the time to invoke these algorithms (Figure 10.3). Later, the simulator will be replaced by the real RFID tracking system. The decision-making framework can be reconfigurable and customizable to the other tracking system and yard environment.

Step 5: Performance analysis and recommendations

The decision-making framework allows us to evaluate both the impact of the decision models on the shipment yard decision-making and the real-time information value of the RFID tracking system. A comprehensive analysis was conducted for a variety of operational scenarios, and we measured the values for the metrics defined during the business case development of Step 1. The results showed that even RFID information alone can significantly enhance the performance of yard operations and, further, when the decision models are activated, more improvement can be attained as shown below.

Numerical results

Three types of practices were experimented using the decision-making framework: current practice, new practice 1 and new practice 2. Current practice represents the practice currently being used in the shipping yard. New practice 1 corresponds to the practice in which the RFID tracking system is in place. Basically, all manual errors are minimized and most waiting times in the yard are considerably shortened. However, deployment and load makeup practices are the same as in the current practice. They both use distanced-based algorithm for deployment planning and EM algorithm for shipment planning. New practice 2 is based on the same RFID information availability as new practice 1 and, in addition, employs a set of dynamic planning algorithms that fully utilize the RFID real-time information. It uses geography-based deployment planning algorithm and dynamic MST load makeup planning algorithm. The dynamic MST algorithm uses the MST algorithm for an initial solution first, then the MAS distributed algorithm for continual optimization.

Each simulation run produces a different number of vehicles; approximately 200,000 vehicles are produced at the manufacturer during 300 production days and shipped to 301 dealers, each having different demands. For each practice, five simulation runs were conducted to reduce random effects and simulation outputs were analyzed with 5 per cent significance. Simulation parameters, such as production volume, shipment frequency and number of yard operators were calibrated to make sure that simulated current practice reflects actual current yard operations. The average dwell time was 2.3878 days in current practice scenario, 1.9986 days in new practice scenario 1 and 1.7658 days in new practice scenario 2 (Table 10.1). The average labour consumption was 65.76 per cent in current scenario, 62.07 per cent in the first new scenario and 43.33 per cent in the second new scenario. The average labour consumption represents the proportion of average labour time spent out of the total labour time. New practice scenario 1 obtained 16.30 per cent improvement in dwell time and 5.62 per cent improvement in labour consumption, while new practice scenario 2 attained 26.05 per cent improvement in dwell time and 34.11 per cent improvement in labour consumption. In particular, new practice scenario 2 resulted in the smallest dwell time and the lowest labour consumption because it is the most intelligent practice, owing to the real-time information-enabled advanced planning algorithms. With new practice 2, dwell time reduction per vehicle of more than half a day can be accomplished and it can result in huge savings on inventory holding cost, considering the large annual volume of vehicle delivery. By delivering vehicles faster, we can have better cash flow and enhance customer satisfaction. In addition, more than 30 per cent savings in labour can provide the opportunity for economies in such labour-intensive shipping yards.

Table 10.1 Comparison of simulation results for three practices in dwell time and labour consumption in shipment yard

	Current practice	New practice 1	New practice 2
Dwell time (days)	2.3878	1.9986	1.7658
Labour consumption (per cent)	65.76	62.07	43.33

Note: New practice 2 resulted in maximum improvement because of combined benefit of RFID tracking information and advanced decision models.

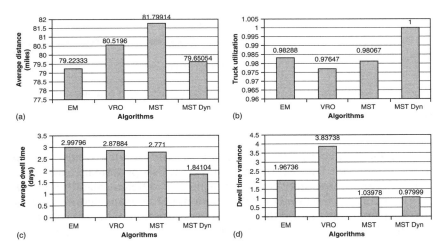

(a) (b) (c) (d)

Figure 10.6 The performance comparison of four algorithms for truck shipment
Note: Diagrams (a), (b), (c) and (d) compare the performance of average distance in miles, truck utilization, average dwell time in days and dwell time variance.

Because of the relative importance of truck shipment over rail shipment, we experimented with four algorithms of vehicle shipment via truck, namely EM, VRO, MST and MST Dyn (MST combined with dynamic optimization). Figure 10.6 summarizes the performance comparison. If we compare average travelling distance (see diagram (a)), MST algorithm produces the worst performance and EM algorithm the best; however, MST Dyn algorithm produces a slightly higher transportation cost than EM algorithm. For average dwell time (see diagram (c)), EM algorithm produces the worst performance and MST Dyn the best; VRO and MST algorithms are in-between. If we compare the variance of dwell time (see diagram (d)), VRO algorithm produces the worst performance and MST Dyn the best. Also, notice that only MST

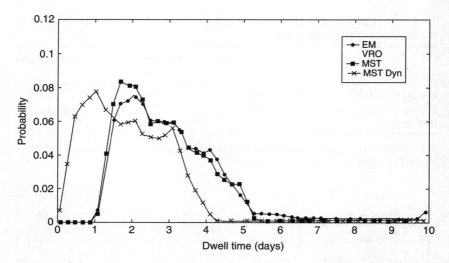

Figure 10.7 Comparison of dwell time distribution generated by four algorithms: EM, VRO, MST, MST Dyn
Note: The dynamic optimization algorithm, MST Dyn, showed the best performance.

Dyn produces 100 per cent truck utilization. Based on these results, we can conclude that MST Dyn algorithm produces the best performance overall.

In addition to the statistical performance of different algorithms, Figure 10.7 compares the dwell time distributions of these four algorithms. MST Dyn algorithm shifted most the dwell time distribution to the left because of the consideration of dynamic information and eliminated the long right tail.

Conclusions

Our analysis results proved that the RFID tracking system applied to current practice can significantly improve customer satisfaction by reducing average and variance of dwell time, decreasing labour cost by increasing labour utilization and, thus, lead to increased profits. The average dwell time was reduced by 16.30 per cent and the average labour consumption by 5.62 per cent. In addition, the real-time information of the RFID tracking system combined with advanced decision algorithms can facilitate better load building that helps to reduce the dwell time and transportation cost (the average dwell time was reduced by 26.05 per cent and the average labour consumption by 34.11 per cent). It was shown that dynamic decision algorithms based on the multi-agent-based computational architecture and market-based heuristics improved the performance of vehicle deployment and shipment much more, achieving 100 per cent truck utilization.

The experiment results demonstrated that the dynamic optimization approach produced better performance than any other static algorithms, which cannot capture the dynamics of the vehicle delivery environment. This research proved not only the value of real-time information of the RFID tracking system, but also the significant value of the dynamic optimization approach by taking advantage of the RFID data. The wireless-based information systems driven by intelligent algorithms can innovate supply chain operations with timely information and better decision-making.

The delivery chain can be influenced by exceptions and disruptions, such as truck or rail breakdowns, traffic accidents during delivery and logistics company strikes. The RFID-enabled decision system can mitigate the impact of these events on delivery performance by quickly sensing and responding to them. Finally, under a variety of circumstances, determining appropriate shipping yard management parameters, such as, ratio of holding, ratio of return-to-plant, number of crews, number and capacity of trucks and rails, and physical bay space, enables the shipping yard manager to optimize the performance of yard operations.

There are many other opportunities to leverage the benefits from RFID/wireless infrastructure, including manufacturing, sourcing, warehousing, distribution, retailing and after-sales. For example, in the automotive supply chain, the RF tags attached to raw materials by suppliers can be used for production scheduling and material replenishment in manufacturing plants and for delivery of finished products using logistics network, as well as for warranty management at the dealers. RFID/wireless visibility of raw materials and final products facilitates better control of the supply chain and it enables provision of real-time asset information to corporate information systems to better shape production and distribution structures. Further research needs to be done by investigating the RFID applicability to other business functions of the supply chain.

RFID-based location tracking is an innovative way that enables real-time connectivity and immediate decision-making. This leads us to transform data into information and information into knowledge for efficiently managing the delivery chain in real-time. The transition is not only to collect data, but also to connect to enterprise-wide information systems via corporate networks to react to operational exceptions. It can eliminate the 'information float' of traditional data collection methods because it fills the gap between when the transaction occurs and when the database is updated. Make-to-order environments can benefit from RFID tracking by ensuring visibility and data accuracy enhancement for all the stakeholders of a supply chain.

Transitioning to wireless infrastructure requires a paradigm shift in corporate and work force culture, not sticking to current practice. A rear-view focus will impede progress and the willingness to take risks is necessary to adapt to a changing world (Willis 2000). Involving all relevant stakeholders from the beginning is important to bring a success to this initiative. RFID/wireless adoption with the development of effective business decision-making models and seamless connectivity with existing enterprise IT infrastructure, considering the impact on other business processes like assembly process, material delivery, inventory control and quality control, are key considerations to maximize the resulting benefits from wireless investment.

References

Anderson, B.M., Gremban, K.D. and Young, B.A. 1997 'Shipyard operational improvement through process management', the National Shipbuilding Research Program, 1997 Ship Production Symposium, Bloomington, MN, USA.
Anderson, E.G., Fine, C.H. and Deployer, G.G. 2000 'Upstream volatility in the supply chain: The machine tool industry as a case study', *Production and Operations Management*, 9: 239–61.
Banerjee, S., Banerjee, A., Burton, J. and Bistline, W. 2001 'Controlled partial shipments in two-echelon supply chain networks: A simulation study', *International Journal of Production Economics*, 71: 91–100.
Bar-Noy, A., Bhatia, R., Naor, J.S. and Schieber, B. 2002 'Minimizing service and operation costs of periodic scheduling', *Mathematics of Operations Research*, 27: 518–44.
Beamon, B.M. and Chen, V.C.P. 2001 'Performance analysis of conjoined supply chains', *International Journal of Production Research*, 39: 3195–218.
Brandolese, A., Brun, A. and Portioli-Straudacher, A. 2000 'A multi-agent approach for the capacity allocation problem', *International Journal of Production Economics*, 66: 269–85.
Chen, F. 2001 'Market segmentation, advanced demand information, and supply chain', *Manufacturing and Service Operations Management*, 3: 53–67.
Cormen, T., Leiserson, C., Rivest, R. and Stein, C. 2001 *Introduction to Algorithms*, 2nd edn, Cambridge: MIT Press and McGraw-Hill.
Davidson, P., Johansson, S.J., Persson, J.A. and Wemstedt, F. 2003 'Agent-based approaches and classical optimization techniques for dynamic distributed resource allocation: A preliminary study', *AAMAS'03 Workshop on Representations and Approaches for Time-Critical Decentralized Resource/Role/Task Allocation*, Melbourne, Australia.
Department of Energy 2002 *Industrial Wireless Technology for the 21st Century*, accessed 15 June 2005, <http://www.wina.org/wina/files/1930.2226 vision.pdf>
Frontline Solutions 2001 'Supply chain meets the web', 2: 52–4.
Gjerdrum, J., Shah, N. and Papageorgiou, L.G. 2001 'A combined optimization and agent-based approach to supply chain modeling and performance assessment', *Production Planning and Control*, 12: 81–8.
Grygo, E. 2000 'Partnerships essential for wireless ERP links', *InfoWorld*, 22: 34.
Huang, G.Q., Lau, J.S.K. and Mak, K.L. 2003 'The impacts of sharing production informaton on supply chain dynamics: A review of the literature', *International Journal of Production Research*, 41(7): 1483–517.
Karkkainen, M. and Holmstrom, J. 2002 'Wireless product identification: Enabler for handling efficiency, customization and information sharing', *Supply Chain Management: An International Journal*, 7: 242–52.
Kim, J., Tang, K., Kumara, S., Yee, S.T. and Tew, J. 2008. 'Value analysis of location-enabled radio-frequency identification information on delivery chain performance', *International Journal of Production Economics* 112(1): 403–415.

Lee, H. and Whang, S. 1999 'Decentralized multi-echelon supply chains: Incentives and information', *Management Science*, 45: 633–40.

Lee, H.L., So, K.C. and Tang, C.S. 2000 'The value of information sharing in a two-level supply chain', *Management Science*, 46: 626–43.

Souza, R.D., Zice, S. and Chaoyang, L. 2000 'Supply chain dynamics and optimization', *Integrated Manufacturing Systems*, 11: 348–64.

Sterman, J.D. 2000 *Business Dynamics: System Thinking and Modeling for a Complex World*, Boston: McGraw-Hill.

Tang, K. and Kumara, S. 2007 'Double auction market mechanism: A distributed negotiation protocol to model an e-procurement problem', *IEEE Transactions on Automation Science and Engineering* (under review).

Vaserstein, L.N. and Byrne, C.C. 2003 *Introduction to Linear Programming*, Upper Saddle River: Prentice Hall.

Weiss, G. 1999 *Multiagent Systems: A Modern Approach to Distributed Artificial Intelligence*, Cambridge: MIT Press.

Willis, D. 2000 'Customers design online', *Purchasing*, 129: S53.

Wooldridge, M.J. 2002 *An Introduction to Multiagent Systems*, New York: Wiley.

11
A Generalized Order-Up-To Policy and Altruistic Behaviour in a Three-Level Supply Chain

Takamichi Hosoda and Stephen M. Disney

Introduction

An order coordination policy based on the order-up-to (OUT) policy that minimizes the *total* inventory costs for a three-level supply chain will be examined. For a single level of a supply chain, Vassian (1955) introduced an ordering policy with a work in progress (WIP) feedback loop and showed that this ordering policy minimizes the variance of the end of period net stock levels. In addition, Vassian showed that the minimized variance of the end-period net inventory level is identical to the variance of the error in the forecast of demand over the lead time plus review period. In this research, Vassian's ordering policy is called as *the traditional OUT policy*.[1] From Vassian's seminal contribution, it is obvious that in a single-level supply chain case, the traditional OUT policy is an optimal policy for minimizing the variance of the end of period net stock levels over time. In a multi-level supply chain scenario, however, it might be reasonable to assume that a sequence of traditional OUT policies may not be optimal any more as there is no guarantee that a succession of local minimizations will result in a global optimum, as shown in Hosoda and Disney (2006a). Since the traditional OUT policy does not provide much freedom to manipulate the dynamics of the ordering process, Hosoda and Disney (2006a) have investigated a two-level supply chain using the traditional OUT policy modified to include a proportional controller. This brings more flexibility to alter the dynamics of the ordering process, and shows that a sequence of traditional OUT policies is no longer optimal. They also show that to enjoy the cost saving, the attitude of the first level player to cost increases is an essential factor. They call this attitude 'altruistic behaviour'. In this chapter the model shown in Hosoda and Disney (2006a) will be extended to a three-level supply chain model, and the benefit of the altruistic behaviour and roles of the first- and the second-level players in a three-level supply chain will be analyzed.[2] In addition, as a benchmark for performance comparisons, a sequence of three traditional OUT policies supply chain model shown in Hosoda and Disney (2006b) will be used.

Literature review

As a type of supply chain coordination, information sharing has been studied by many researchers. However, counter-intuitively, not all results support the benefit of information sharing.

Graves (1999) studies a two-level supply chain with the OUT policy (termed 'adaptive base-stock policy' in his paper), a non-stationary demand process, IMA(1,1) process, with minimum mean square error (MMSE) forecasting.[3] Graves finds that sharing demand information brings no benefit to the upstream player, if the upstream player knows the coefficients of the customer demand process. Kim and Ryan (2003) analyze the value of demand information sharing using the model with an unknown demand process and an exponential smoothing forecast. They conclude that sharing demand data can significantly reduce the costs in upper-stream players of the supply chain. However, the benefit is limited when the upper-stream player has a large amount of historical order data, as by exploiting this data, the upper-stream player can improve its forecast accuracy. Assuming a known demand process and the MMSE forecast, Raghunathan (2001) reports similar results in that the set of order history data contains all the necessary information to allow the upper-stream player to reduce his costs. Assuming an AR(1) demand process, Lee, So and Tang (2000) develop a two-level supply chain model and investigate the benefit of demand information sharing. Under their assumption that the manufacturer uses only the latest observed demand information in its forecast, they conclude that the manufacturer can obtain inventory and costs reductions with information sharing. Hosoda *et al.* (2008) investigate the benefit of sharing the market demand information using a set of data obtained from a real retail supply chain. It is shown that there is a benefit of information sharing, and a source of such benefit is the error terms, which are originally hidden in the market demand process and difficult to extract without shared market demand information. In addition to information sharing, some researchers have analyzed operational coordination of supply chains, such as vendor managed inventory (VMI). This field of research has attracted abundant attention since the late 1990s. Disney and Towill (2003a) develop a two-level VMI supply chain model and compare the measured bullwhip with a traditional serially linked supply chain. They report that the VMI scheme can substantially reduce the bullwhip. In their VMI scheme, information about the first-level stock level, the goods in transit, the second-level stock level and the reorder point is used to determine the target inventory level. Using their VMI model, Disney and Towill (2003b) investigate each of the potential sources of the bullwhip proposed by Lee, Padmanabhan and Whang (1997). They show that two of the four causes – the rationing game and order batching – can be completely eliminated by the adoption of VMI scheme in a supply chain, and the other two causes also can be reduced significantly.

Aviv and Federgruen (1998) study the benefits of a VMI scheme using a two-echelon supply chain model consisting of a single supplier and J retailers. They study three scenarios: (1) a traditional decentralized system, (2) a VMI system and (3) a system with full information sharing between players. Under the VMI programme, the timing and magnitude of the replenishment shipments to the retailers are decided by the supplier on the basis of the full information given by all retailers. A comparison was made and they conclude that the VMI programme (where information on inventory levels is also shared) has much more potential and can reduce costs by 4.7 per cent on average. The benefits of VMI against the full information sharing scenario become larger when capacity is tight, since the VMI scheme enables the supplier to increase its utilization rate. Using a serially linked two-level supply chain with an AR(1) market demand, Hosoda and Disney (2006a) investigate the impact of altruistic behaviour on the overall supply chain cost. To realize altruistic behaviour at the first level, they introduced a traditional OUT policy with a single proportional controller in the system feedback loop. This proportional controller enables us to manipulate the order placed by the retailer to achieve lower total supply chain cost. The sum of the standard deviations of net stock levels at each level was used as an objective function to be minimized. It is suggested that altruistic behaviour by the first-level player mitigates the bullwhip effect, and this lower bullwhip is the source of the benefit at the second level. Also, the cost benefit at the second level is large enough to compensate the loss at the first level. It is shown that on average more than 10 per cent cost reduction can be achieved.

Some researchers assume that the second-level player can modify the first-level player's order pattern by offering incentives and find that the first-level player should be altruistic to achieve lower total costs. In his two-level supply chain model, Gavirneni (2006) assumes that the supplier can alter the pattern of orders placed by the retailer, by offering fluctuating prices. As the result of this incentive, the retailer's ordering pattern is not optimum for itself any more and thus the retailer's cost will increase. However, the benefit at the supplier is sufficient to compensate the increase at the retailer. The overall supply chain performance can be improved by 5 per cent on average with the aid of information sharing. Luo (2007) considers a coordination scheme in a two-level supply chain consisting of a vendor and a buyer. The vendor asks the buyer to change its order quantity to achieve lower setup, ordering and inventory holding costs for the vendor. To convince the buyer, a credit period incentive is offered by the vendor. It is shown that the benefit to the vendor is always greater than the loss to the buyer so that this cooperation scheme can bring the benefits to overall supply chain. From these two papers, it might be reasonable to conclude that the type of incentives for the first-level player affects the total amount of saving costs. Other incentives to encourage the first-level player to incur cost increase include quantity flexibility (Tsay

1999), quantity discounts (Weng 1995) and revenue sharing (Giannoccaro and Pontrandolfo 2004).

The literature review suggests some useful insights to our problem. First, sharing market demand information may bring benefits to a supply chain, but the amount of such benefit is not clear. In our model, therefore, to negate the benefit coming from sharing the market demand information, it is assumed that up-to-date market demand information is shared and common knowledge in the supply chain. This assumption enables us to focus on the benefits only from the altruistic behaviour. Second, it might be better to assume a centralized supply chain model to quantify the benefit of the altruistic behaviour. In the case of a decentralized supply chain, incentives and/or a way of redistribution of the generated benefits may significantly affect the behaviour of each player in a supply chain. The centralized supply chain assumption allows us to ignore such issues. Therefore, we will assume that in the supply chain there are no incentive conflicts, all necessary information is shared and all players will cooperate to minimize the total cost.

The model

A serially linked three-level supply chain system is analyzed. All three players exploit a periodic review system, and the replenishment lead time is constant and known. The ordering policy used herein is the OUT policy. The OUT level is adjusted each time period according to the latest updated demand forecast and the shared information. The knowledge about the market demand process captured by the first-level player is shared with all other players without delay. It is assumed that the true market demand process is correctly captured. The cost parameters and the ordering policies in the supply chain are common knowledge.

Sequence of events and costs

The sequence of events in any period at any level is as follows: the order placed earlier is received, and the demand is fulfilled at the beginning of the period, the net stock level is reviewed and ordering decision is made at the end of the period. We will now describe the three-level supply chain model where each level uses the OUT policy with the MMSE forecasting scheme. We assume a periodic review policy but do not assume a specific length of the review period. All of the results herein are consistent whatever review period is adopted (day, week, month, etc.). We will use the subscript n ($= 1$, 2, 3) to represent the level of the supply chain. It is assumed that the costs in the supply chain are directly proportional to the standard deviation of the net stock level at each level, as in Hosoda and Disney (2006a). Therefore, the objective function used in this research can be written as:

$$J = \sum_{n=1}^{3} \sqrt{V[NS_n]} = \sqrt{V[NS_1]} + \sqrt{V[NS_2]} + \sqrt{V[NS_3]} \qquad (11.1)$$

where $V[NS_n]$ represents the stable variance of the net stock level at nth level of the supply chain.

Market demand

Let us assume the demand pattern faced by the retailer is an AR(1) process. The AR(1) demand process assumption is common when autocorrelation exists among the demand process. Many researchers employ this assumption (see, Hosoda *et al.* 2008, for example). The formulation of AR(1) process is given by:

$$D_t = d + \rho D_{t-1} + \varepsilon_t$$

where D_t is the observed market demand at time period t, d is the constant term, ρ is the Autoregressive coefficient, $|\rho| < 1$ and ε_t is an i.i.d. white noise process with a mean of zero and a variance of σ_ε^2. The stable variance of D_t, $V[D_t]$, is $\sigma_\varepsilon^2/(1 - \rho^2)$. Detailed discussions about an AR(1) model can be seen in Box, Jenkins and Reinsel (1997).

Ordering policy

The traditional OUT policy for the player at level n in the supply chain can be described as follows (Vassian 1955):

$$O_{t,n} = S_{t,n} - (WIP_{t,n} + NS_{t,n})$$

$$S_{t,n} = \hat{O}_{t,n-1}^{L_n} + safety\ stock$$

where $O_{t,n}$ is the order rate at time t, S_t is the OUT level at time t and $WIP_{t,n}$ is the sum of orders that are already placed but not yet received at time t and can be expressed as $WIP_{t,n} = \sum_{i=1}^{L_n-1} O_{t-i,n}$. $NS_{t,n}$ is the end of period net stock level at time t, and $\hat{O}_{t,n-1}^{L_n}$ is the conditional estimate of the total demand from the $n-1$ level player over L_n time periods, which is the lead time plus review period. For $n = 1$, $\hat{O}_{t,n-1}^{L_n}$ is denoted as $\hat{D}_t^{L_1}$. To realize our generalized

OUT policy, let us begin by modifying the traditional OUT policy:

$$O_{t,n} = S_{t,n} - (WIP_{t,n} + NS_{t,n})$$

$$= \hat{O}_{t,n-1}^{L_n} - (WIP_{t,n} + NS_{t,n}) + safety\ stock$$

$$= \tilde{O}_{t,n-1}^{L_n} + \hat{O}_{t,n-1}^{L_n-1} - (WIP_{t,n} + NS_{t,n}) + safety\ stock$$

$$= \tilde{O}_{t,n-1}^{L_n} + (\hat{O}_{t,n-1}^{L_n-1} - (WIP_{t,n} + NS_{t,n})) + safety\ stock$$

$$= \tilde{O}_{t,n-1}^{L_n} + (DIP_{t,n} - (WIP_{t,n} + NS_{t,n})) + safety\ stock \tag{11.2}$$

where $\tilde{O}_{t,n-1}^{L_n}$ is $E[O_{t+L_n,n-1} \mid O_{t,n-1}]$, the conditional estimate of the demand in time period $t+L_n$ made at t. Therefore, $\tilde{O}_{t,n-1}^{L_n} + \hat{O}_{t,n-1}^{L_n-1} = \tilde{O}_{t,n-1}^{L_n}$. When $n=1$, $\tilde{O}_{t,n-1}^{L_n}$ is $E[D_{t+L_1} \mid D_t]$ and denoted as $\tilde{D}_t^{L_1}$. $DIP_{t,n}$ is a desired inventory position at time t and $DIP_{t,n} = \hat{O}_{t,n-1}^{L_n-1} = E\left[\sum_{i=1}^{L_n-1} O_{t,n-1} \mid O_{t,n-1}\right]$. Note that $DIP_{t,n} = 0$, if $L_n = 1$. Incorporating a proportional controller, F_n, into equation 11.2 yields the ordering policy, the generalized OUT policy:

$$O_{t,n} = \tilde{O}_{t,n-1}^{L_n} + F_n(DIP_{t,n} - (WIP_{t,n} + NS_{t,n})) + safety\ stock$$

where $0 < F_n < 2$ as shown in Hosoda and Disney (2006a). Obviously, if $F_n = 1$, the policy is identical to the traditional OUT policy. In what follows, for simplicity, we will set $d=0$ and *safety stock* $=0$ without loss of generality, since these values are time-invariant values and do not affect the value of J.

Scenarios

Three different scenarios will be considered herein, Scenario 1 is the three-level traditional OUT policy supply chain that was investigated in Hosoda and Disney (2006b). Scenario 1 will form the baseline scenario for the other scenarios to be compared against. Scenario 2 is the generalized OUT policy supply chain case where the first- and the second-level players exploit the generalized OUT policy and the third-level player adopts the traditional OUT policy. Scenario 3 is a special case of Scenario 2; here not only the third-level player, but also the first-level player, adopts the traditional OUT policy to minimize its own variance of the net stock. Only the middle-level player is concerned with minimizing the objective function by tuning its proportional controller, F_2. Scenario 3 is expected to bring enough benefit so that this scenario might be a more acceptable strategy for a retail supply chain where usually the unit cost of the net stock at the first level (retail store, for example) is the most expensive. If Scenario 3 is successful, the variance of net stock level at the first-level player, namely the retail store, is minimized due to the traditional OUT policy and, at the same time, the complete supply chain can also enjoy a cost reduction generated by the altruistic behaviour of the second-level player.

Scenario 1: The traditional OUT policy supply chain

In what follows $V[\overline{NS_n}]$ will be used to show the variance of net stock level in a traditional OUT policy supply chain. As shown in Hosoda and Disney (2006b), the expressions of the variances of net stock level at each level in a serially linked three-level supply chain model are expressed as:

$$V[\overline{NS_1}] = \frac{(L_1(1-\rho^2) + \rho(1-\rho^{L_1})(\rho^{L_1+1} - \rho - 2))}{(1-\rho)^2(1-\rho^2)}\sigma_\varepsilon^2$$

$$V[\overline{NS_2}] = \frac{(L_2(1-\rho^2) + \rho^{L_1+1}(1-\rho^{L_2})(\rho^{L_1+1} + \rho^{L_1+L_2+1} - 2\rho - 2))}{(1-\rho)^2(1-\rho^2)}\sigma_\varepsilon^2$$

$$V[\overline{NS_3}] = \frac{(L_3(1-\rho^2) + \rho^{L_1+L_2+1}(1-\rho^{L_3})(\rho^{L_1+L_2+1} + \rho^{L_1+L_2+L_3+1} - 2\rho - 2))}{(1-\rho)^2(1-\rho^2)}\sigma_\varepsilon^2$$

$$(11.3)$$

Therefore the objective function for Scenario 1, J_{S1}, becomes:

$$J_{S1} = \sqrt{V[\overline{NS_1}]} + \sqrt{V[\overline{NS_2}]} + \sqrt{V[\overline{NS_3}]}$$

$$= \sqrt{\frac{(L_1(1-\rho^2) + \rho(1-\rho^{L_1})(\rho^{L_1+1} - \rho - 2))}{(1-\rho)^2(1-\rho^2)}\sigma_\varepsilon^2}$$

$$+ \sqrt{\frac{(L_2(1-\rho^2) + \rho^{L_1+1}(1-\rho^{L_2})(\rho^{L_1+1} + \rho^{L_1+L_2+1} - 2\rho - 2))}{(1-\rho)^2(1-\rho^2)}\sigma_\varepsilon^2}$$

$$+ \sqrt{\frac{(L_3(1-\rho^2) + \rho^{L_1+L_2+1}(1-\rho^{L_3})(\rho^{L_1+L_2+1} + \rho^{L_1+L_2+L_3+1} - 2\rho - 2))}{(1-\rho)^2(1-\rho^2)}\sigma_\varepsilon^2}$$

Scenario 2: The generalized OUT policy supply chain

Scenario 2 assumes that the generalized OUT policy is used in the three-level supply chain. To minimize the objective function (equation 11.1), from the *Principle of Optimality* (Bellman 1957), the highest-level player must use the policy which minimizes his own variance of the net stock level, as shown in Hosoda and Disney (2006a). Thus, the third-level player should use the traditional OUT policy. As the result, only the first two players in the supply chain employ the generalized OUT policy.

The ordering process and MMSE forecasts

To obtain an MMSE forecast, knowledge of the structure of the order process is required. In the case of Scenario 2, the process of $O_{t,1}$ and $O_{t,2}$, the volume of orders placed by the first and the second players respectively, can be described as

$$O_{t+1,1} = (1 - F_1)O_{t,1} + \rho^{L_1}(\rho + F_1 - 1)D_t + (\rho^{L_1} + F_1 \cdot \Lambda_{L_1})\varepsilon_{t+1} \qquad (11.4)$$

$$O_{t+1,2} = (1 - F_2)O_{t,2} + (1 - F_1)^{L_2}(F_2 - F_1)O_{t,1}$$
$$+ (\rho^{L_1}(1 - F_1)^{L_2}(F_1 - F_2) + \rho^{L_1+L_2}(\rho + F_2 - 1))D_t + \xi \cdot \varepsilon_{t+1} \qquad (11.5)$$

where

$$\Lambda_{L_1} = \frac{1 - \rho^{L_1}}{1 - \rho}, \text{ and } \xi = \frac{(1 - F_1)^{L_2}(F_2 - F_1)(1 - \rho^{L_1}) + \rho^{L_1+L_2}(\rho + F_2 - 1) - F_2}{\rho - 1}$$

Hosoda (2005) provides details. Equations 11.4 and 11.5 yield expressions for the MMSE forecasts of $O_{t,n}$ over L_{n+1} time periods, $\hat{O}_{t,n}^{L_n+1}$ where $n = 1$ and 2:

$$\hat{O}_{t,1}^{L_2} = E\left[\sum_{i=1}^{L_2} O_{t+i,1} \mid D_t, O_{t,1}, \rho, F_1, L_1\right]$$
$$= \frac{(1 - F_1)(1 - (1 - F_1)^{L_2})}{F_1}O_{t,1} + \frac{\rho^{L_1}\left(\begin{array}{c}((1 - F_1)^{L_2+1} - 1)(\rho - 1) \\ + F_1(\rho^{L_2+1} - 1)\end{array}\right)}{F_1(\rho - 1)}D_t$$

$$\hat{O}_{t,2}^{L_3} = E\left[\sum_{i=1}^{L_3} O_{t+i,2} \mid D_t, O_{t,1}, O_{t,2}, \rho, F_1, F_2, L_1, L_2\right]$$
$$= \frac{(1 - F_1)^{L_2}\left((1 - F_1)^{L_3} - 1\right)(F_1 - 1)}{F_1}O_{t,1} - \frac{(1 - F_1)^{L_2}\left((1 - F_2)^{L_3} - 1\right)(F_2 - 1)}{F_2}O_{t,1}$$
$$+ \frac{((1 - F_2)^{L_3} - 1)(F_2 - 1)}{F_2}O_{t,2} + \frac{((1 - F_1)^{L_3} - 1)(1 - F_1)^{L_2+1}\rho^{L_1}}{F_1}D_t$$
$$+ \frac{((1 - F_2)^{L_3} - 1)(1 - F_1)^{L_2}(F_2 - 1)\rho^{L_1}}{F_2}D_t - \frac{((1 - F_2)^{L_3} - 1)(F_2 - 1)\rho^{L_1+L_2}}{F_2}D_t$$
$$+ \frac{(\rho^{L_3} - 1)\rho^{L_1+L_2+1}}{\rho - 1}D_t$$

Hosoda (2005) provides details. Note that if a sequence of the traditional OUT policies are used in the supply chain (that is $F_l = F_2 = 1$), then $\hat{O}_{t,1}^{L_2} = \frac{\rho^{L_1+1}(\rho^{L_2} - 1)}{\rho - 1}D_t$ and $\hat{O}_{t,2}^{L_3} = \frac{(\rho^{L_3} - 1)\rho^{L_1+L_2+1}}{\rho - 1}D_t$.

The objective function

From here, the expression $V[\overline{\overline{NS}}_n]$ will be used for the variance of net stock levels of the generalized OUT policy at the nth level. As shown in the appendix and Hosoda (2005), the net stock levels at the first and the second levels follow ARMA(1, $L_n - 1$) processes, where $n = 1$ and 2 respectively. By exploiting this property, we can have the following:

$$V[\overline{\overline{NS_1}}] = V[\overline{NS_1}] + \frac{\Omega^2\Psi^2}{(\rho-1)^2(1-\Psi^2)}\sigma_\varepsilon^2 \qquad (11.6)$$

$$\begin{aligned} V[\overline{\overline{NS_2}}] = V[\overline{NS_2}] + \frac{\sigma_\varepsilon^2}{(\rho-1)^2} & \left(\frac{(\Psi^{2L_2}-1)\Omega^2\Psi^2}{\Psi^2-1} \right. \\ & + 2\Omega\Psi\left(\frac{1-\Psi^{L_2}}{1-\Psi} - \frac{\rho^{L_1+1}((\rho\Psi)^{L_2}-1)}{\rho\Psi-1} \right) \\ & + \left. \frac{\left((1-(1-F_1)^{L_2})-\rho^{L_1}(\rho^{L_2}-(1-F_1)^{L_2})\right)^2(F_2-1)^2}{(2-F_2)F_2} \right) \qquad (11.7) \end{aligned}$$

where $\Psi = 1 - F_1$, $\Omega = \rho^{L_1} - 1$. Detailed steps to obtain equations 11.6 and 11.7 are shown in the appendix. Since the third-level player adopts the traditional OUT policy to contribute to the minimization of the objective function, the forecast error over the lead time plus review period can be used as an alternative:

$$\begin{aligned} V[\overline{\overline{NS_3}}] = E\left[\left(\hat{O}_{t,2}^{L_3} - \sum_{i=1}^{L_3} O_{t+i,2} \right)^2 \right] = \xi^2 \cdot \sigma_\varepsilon^2 + \sum_{r=2}^{L_3} & \left(\left(\sum_{i=2}^{r} \left(\frac{-1}{(F_1-1)(\rho-1)\rho} \right. \right. \right. \\ & \times ((1-F_2)^{i-1}((F_1-1)(F_2-1)(\rho-1)\rho^{L_1+L_2}(\rho/(1-F_2))^i \\ & - \rho F_1(1-F_1)^{L_2}((F_1-1)/(F_2-1))^i(F_2-1)(\rho^{L_1}-1) \\ & + \left. \rho F_2(F_1-1)\,(1-(1-F_1)^{L_2}+\rho^{L_1}((1-F_1)^{L_2}-\rho^{L_2}))) \right) + \xi \Bigg)^2 \Bigg) \sigma_\varepsilon^2 \end{aligned}$$

$$(11.8)$$

Details of the derivation of equation 11.8 are shown in Hosoda (2005). It should be noted that equation 11.8 cannot be used when $F_1 = 1$, $F_2 = 1$ and/or when $\rho = 0$ because of a singularity in the denominator. However, solutions do exist at the singularity, and they are also shown Hosoda (2005). In this section, equation 11.8 will be used in the analysis.

The objective function for the three-level generalized supply chain model is:

$$\begin{aligned} J_{S2} &= \sqrt{V[NS_1]} + \sqrt{V[NS_2]} + \sqrt{V[NS_3]} \\ &= \sqrt{V[\overline{\overline{NS_1}}]} + \sqrt{V[\overline{\overline{NS_2}}]} + \sqrt{V[\overline{\overline{NS_3}}]} \end{aligned}$$

$$= \sqrt{\left(\frac{\left(L_1(1-\rho^2) + \rho(1-\rho^{L_1})(\rho^{L_1+1} - \rho - 2)\right)}{(1-\rho)^2(1-\rho^2)} \sigma_\varepsilon^2 + \frac{(\rho^{L_1}-1)^2(F_1-1)^2}{(\rho-1)^2(2-F_1)F_1} \sigma_\varepsilon^2 \right)}$$

$$+ \sqrt{\left(\frac{\sigma_\varepsilon^2}{(\rho-1)^2} \left(\begin{array}{l} L_2 + \dfrac{((1-F_1)^{2L_2}-1)(\rho^{L_1}-1)^2(1-F_1)^2}{(1-F_1)^2-1} \\[2mm] + \dfrac{\rho^{L_1+1}(\rho^{L_2}-1)(\rho^{L_1+L_2+1}+\rho^{L_1+1}-2\rho-2)}{\rho^2-1} \\[2mm] +2(\rho^{L_1}-1) \\[2mm] \times(1-F_1)\left(\dfrac{1-(1-F_1)^{L_2}}{F_1} - \dfrac{\rho^{L_1+1}\left((\rho(1-F_1))^{L_2}-1\right)}{\rho(1-F_1)-1} \right) \end{array} \right) \\[2mm] + \dfrac{((1-(1-F_1)^{L_2})-\rho^{L_1}(\rho^{L_2}-(1-F_1)^{L_2}))^2(F_2-1)^2}{(\rho-1)^2(2-F_2)F_2}\sigma_\varepsilon^2 \right)}$$

$$+ \sqrt{\left(\begin{array}{l} \xi^2\sigma_\varepsilon^2 + \\[2mm] \displaystyle\sum_{r=2}^{L_3}\left(\left(\sum_{i=2}^{r}\left(\dfrac{-1}{(F_1-1)(\rho-1)\rho} \right. \right.\right. \\[2mm] ((1-F_2)^{i-1}((F_1-1)(F_2-1)(\rho-1)\rho^{L_1+L_2}(\rho/(1-F_2))^i) \\[2mm] -\rho F_1(1-F_1)^{L_2}((F_1-1)/(F_2-1))^i(F_2-1)(\rho^{L_1}-1) \\[2mm] \left.\left.\left.+\rho F_2(F_1-1)(1-(1-F_1)^{L_2}+\rho^{L^1}((1-F_1)^{L_2}-\rho^{L_2}))))\right)+\xi\right)^2\right)\sigma_\varepsilon^2 \end{array} \right)} \tag{11.9}$$

Scenario 3: The generalized OUT policy supply chain when $F_1 = 1$

In Scenario 3, a special case of scenario 2, where $F_1 = 1$, will be considered. In this scenario, only the second player employs the generalized OUT policy in the supply chain in order to manipulate the dynamics of the supply chain.

In Scenario 3, from equation 11.5, the ordering process can be expressed as:

$$O_{t+1,2} = (1-F_2)O_{t,2} + \rho^{L_1+L_2}(\rho+F_2-1)D_t + \frac{F_2-\rho^{L_1+L_2}(\rho+F_2-1)}{1-\rho}\varepsilon_{t+1}$$

From equation 11.7, by setting $F_1 = 1$, the variance of the net stock level at the second in Scenario 3, $V[\overline{\overline{NS}}_2 \,|\, F_1 = 1]$ can be expressed as:

$$V[\overline{\overline{NS}}_2 \,|\, F_1 = 1] = \frac{\left(L_2(1-\rho)^2 + \rho^{L_1+1}(1-\rho^{L_2})(\rho^{L_1+1}+\rho^{L_1+L_2+1}-2\rho-2)\right)}{(1-\rho)^2(1-\rho^2)}\sigma_\varepsilon^2$$

$$+ \frac{(1-\rho^{L_1+L_2})^2(F_2-1)^2}{(\rho-1)^2(2-F_2)F_2}\sigma_\varepsilon^2 \tag{11.10}$$

The variance of the net stock level at the third level in Scenario 3, $V[\overline{\overline{NS}}_3 \mid F_1 = 1]$, can be written as:

$$
V[\overline{\overline{NS}}_3 \mid F_1 = 1]
$$

$$
= \sum_{r=1}^{L_3} \left(\left(\frac{(1-F_2)^r + \rho^{L_1+L_2}(\rho^r - (1-F_2)^r) - 1}{\rho - 1} \right)^2 \right) \sigma_\varepsilon^2
$$

$$
= \frac{\sigma_\varepsilon^2}{(\rho - 1)} \left(L_3 - 1 + \frac{2((1-F_2)^{L_3} - 1)(F_2 - 1)(\rho^{L_1+L_2} - 1)}{F_2} \right.
$$

$$
+ \frac{((1-F_2)^{2(L_3+1)} - 1) + ((1-F_2)^{2L_3} - 1)(F_2 - 1)^2 \rho^{L_1+L_2}(\rho^{L_1+L_2} - 2)}{(F_2 - 2)F_2}
$$

$$
+ \frac{\rho^{L_1+L_2+1}(\rho^{L_3} - 1)(\rho(\rho^{L_1+L_2} + \rho^{L_1+L_2+L_3} - 2) - 2)}{(\rho^2 - 1)}
$$

$$
+ \left. \frac{2\rho^{L_1+L_2+1}(F_2 - 1)((\rho - F_2\rho)^{L_3} - 1)(1 - \rho^{L_1+L_2})}{1 + (F_2 - 1)\rho} \right) \tag{11.11}
$$

Details are shown in Hosoda (2005). By using equations 11.3, 11.10 and 11.11, J_{S3}, the objective function for Scenario 3 can be described as:

$$
J_{S3} = \sqrt{V[NS_1]} + \sqrt{V[NS_2]} + \sqrt{V[NS_3]}
$$

$$
= \sqrt{V[\overline{NS}_1]} + \sqrt{V[\overline{\overline{NS}}_2 \mid F_1 = 1]} + \sqrt{V[\overline{\overline{NS}}_3 \mid F_1 = 1]}
$$

$$
= \sqrt{\frac{(L_1(1-\rho^2) + \rho(1-\rho^{L_1})(\rho^{L_1+1} - \rho - 2))}{(1-\rho)^2(1-\rho^2)} \sigma_\varepsilon^2}
$$

$$
+ \sqrt{\left(\frac{(L_2(1-\rho^2) + \rho^{L_1+1}(1-\rho^{L_2})(\rho^{L_1+1} + \rho^{L_1+L_2+1} - 2\rho - 2))}{(1-\rho)^2(1-\rho^2)} \sigma_\varepsilon^2 \atop + \frac{(1-\rho^{L_1+L_2})^2(F_2-1)^2}{(\rho-1)^2(2-F_2)F_2} \sigma_\varepsilon^2 \right)}
$$

$$
+ \sqrt{\left(\begin{array}{l} \dfrac{\sigma_\varepsilon^2}{(\rho-1)^2}\left(L_3 - 1 + \dfrac{2((1-F_2)^{L_3} - 1)(F_2 - 1)(\rho^{L_1+L_2} - 1)}{F_2} \right. \\[2ex] + \dfrac{((1-F_2)^{2(L_3+1)} - 1) + ((1-F_2)^{2L_3} - 1)(F_2 - 1)^2 \rho^{L_1+L_2}(\rho^{L_1+L_2} - 2)}{(F_2 - 2)F_2} \\[2ex] + \dfrac{\rho^{L_1+L_2+1}(\rho^{L_3} - 1)(\rho(\rho^{L_1+L_2} + \rho^{L_1+L_2+L_3} - 2) - 2)}{(\rho^2 - 1)} \\[2ex] \left. + \dfrac{2\rho^{L_1+L_2+1}(F_2 - 1)((\rho - F_2\rho)^{L_3} - 1)(1 - \rho^{L_1+L_2})}{1 + (F_2 - 1)\rho} \right) \end{array} \right)}
$$

$$
\tag{11.12}
$$

Due to the rather unwieldy expressions of the objective functions, further analytical investigations are difficult to present. Thus, numerical investigations will be exploited.

Numerical investigations

In this section, the three scenarios with two lead-time settings $L_1 = 2$, $L_2 = 2$, $L_3 = 3$ and $L_1 = 1$, $L_2 = 3$, $L_3 = 3$ will be investigated numerically, $\sigma_\varepsilon^2 = 1$ is assumed. By using equations 11.9 and 11.12, the values of J_{S2} have been plotted in Figure 11.1 and the values of J_{S3} in Figure 11.2 and Figure 11.3 with the restriction that $0 < F_1 < 2$ and $0 < F_2 < 2$, when $\rho = -0.7$, 0.0 and 0.7 for both lead-time settings. From these figures, it can be seen that J_{S2} and J_{S3} have a unique minimum value for the given values of ρ, L_1, L_2 and L_3. The optimum values of the proportional controllers, F_1^* and F_2^*, to minimize the objective functions, J_{S2} and J_{S3} respectively, are obtained by using the cylindrical algebraic decomposition algorithm (Collins, Johnson and Krandich 2002). J_{S2}^* and J_{S3}^* will be used to represent the minimized values of J_{S2} and J_{S3} respectively.

Benefit of Scenario 2

Table 11.1 and Table 11.2 show the results of Scenario 1 and Table 11.3 and Table 11.4 highlight the results for Scenario 2. From the four Tables, the following insights can be obtained:

- $J_{S2}^* < J_{S1}$ for all values of ρ and all lead-time settings. This means that the generalized OUT policy supply chain always outperforms the traditional OUT policy supply chain.
- Both F_1^* and F_2^* never have unit value.
- The value of F_n^* ($n = 1, 2$) is affected by both the value of ρ and the lead-time settings.
- $J_{S2}^* < J_{S1}$ is achieved by altruistic behaviour in the first-level player, by accepting a greater level of net stock to achieve a predetermined customer service level. That is accepting $\sqrt{V[\overline{\overline{NS_1}}]} > \sqrt{V[\overline{NS_1}]}$.
- In almost all parameter settings, the second-level player enjoys the benefit, that is $\sqrt{V[\overline{\overline{NS_2}}]} < \sqrt{V[\overline{NS_2}]}$. The only exception in the points of the solution space we have chosen is the case when $L_1 = 1$, $L_2 = 1$, $L_3 = 3$ and $\rho = 0.9$.

Figure 11.4 shows ΔJ_{S2}, a measure of the benefit of altruistic behaviour described as $(J_{S1} - J_{S2}^*)/J_{S1}$. The average values of the ΔJ_{S2} are 26.1 per cent and 22.7 per cent for the lead-time settings $L_1 = 2$, $L_2 = 2$ and $L_3 = 3$ and $L_1 = 1$, $L_2 = 3$ and $L_3 = 3$ respectively. If it is assumed that ρ is positive as in

202

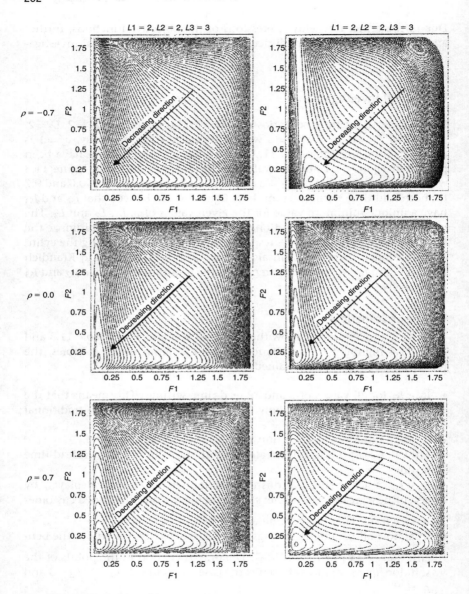

Figure 11.1   The values of J_{s2}

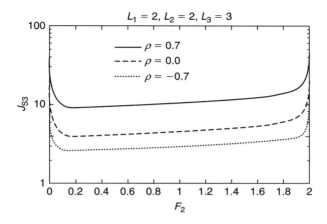

Figure 11.2 The values of J_{s3} when $L_1 = 2$, $L_2 = 2$ and $L_3 = 3$

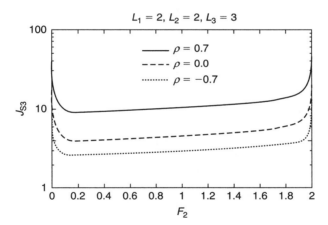

Figure 11.3 The values of J_{s3} when $L_1 = 1$, $L_2 = 3$ and $L_3 = 3$

Lee, So and Tang (2000), then the average values become as high as 26.9 per cent and 23.7 per cent respectively.

Benefit of Scenario 3

Tables 11.5 and 11.6 provide the results of the numerical investigation. In Scenario 3, since the value of F_1 is constant ($F_1 = 1$), only the optimum values of F_2^* are shown in these tables. In this scenario, the first-level player's standard deviation of the net stock level is identical to $\sqrt{V[\overline{NS}_1]}$ because of the unit value of F_1.

Table 11.1 Values of J_{S1}: $L_1 = 2$, $L_2 = 2$ and $L_3 = 3$

ρ	$\sqrt{V[\overline{NS}_1]}$	$\sqrt{V[\overline{NS}_2]}$	$\sqrt{V[\overline{NS}_3]}$	J_{S1}
−0.9	1.005	0.928	1.169	3.102
−0.8	1.020	0.902	1.079	3.000
−0.7	1.044	0.908	1.071	3.023
−0.6	1.077	0.935	1.105	3.117
−0.5	1.118	0.976	1.164	3.258
−0.4	1.166	1.031	1.240	3.437
−0.3	1.221	1.098	1.333	3.652
−0.2	1.281	1.182	1.444	3.906
−0.1	1.345	1.286	1.575	4.206
0.0	1.414	1.414	1.732	4.560
0.1	1.487	1.570	1.924	4.982
0.2	1.562	1.759	2.165	5.486
0.3	1.640	1.985	2.472	6.097
0.4	1.720	2.252	2.871	6.844
0.5	1.803	2.565	3.401	7.769
0.6	1.887	2.929	4.111	8.926
0.7	1.972	3.348	5.069	10.390
0.8	2.059	3.830	6.366	12.255
0.9	2.147	4.378	8.120	14.646

Table 11.2 Values of J_{S1} : $L_1 = 1$, $L_2 = 3$ and $L_3 = 3$

ρ	$\sqrt{V[\overline{NS}_1]}$	$\sqrt{V[\overline{NS}_2]}$	$\sqrt{V[\overline{NS}_3]}$	J_{S1}
−0.9	1.000	0.933	1.169	3.102
−0.8	1.000	0.924	1.079	3.002
−0.7	1.000	0.956	1.071	3.027
−0.6	1.000	1.017	1.105	3.122
−0.5	1.000	1.097	1.164	3.261
−0.4	1.000	1.192	1.240	3.433
−0.3	1.000	1.302	1.333	3.636
−0.2	1.000	1.428	1.444	3.871
−0.1	1.000	1.570	1.575	4.144
0.0	1.000	1.732	1.732	4.464
0.1	1.000	1.917	1.924	4.842
0.2	1.000	2.130	2.165	5.294
0.3	1.000	2.373	2.472	5.844
0.4	1.000	2.652	2.871	6.523
0.5	1.000	2.971	3.401	7.372
0.6	1.000	3.337	4.111	8.448
0.7	1.000	3.755	5.069	9.825
0.8	1.000	4.232	6.366	11.598
0.9	1.000	4.773	8.120	13.893

Table 11.3 Values of J_{S2}^*: $L_1 = 2$, $L_2 = 2$ and $L_3 = 3$

ρ	F_1^*	F_2^*	$\sqrt{V[\overline{\overline{NS_1}}]}$	$\sqrt{V[\overline{\overline{NS_2}}]}$	$\sqrt{V[\overline{\overline{NS_3}}]}$	J_{S2}^*
−0.9	0.07346	0.10481	1.035	0.845	0.934	2.814
−0.8	0.09560	0.14682	1.104	0.731	0.654	2.489
−0.7	0.10825	0.17411	1.200	0.640	0.499	2.339
−0.6	0.11694	0.19493	1.314	0.564	0.424	2.302
−0.5	0.12391	0.21274	1.441	0.500	0.398	2.339
−0.4	0.12979	0.22753	1.576	0.449	0.403	2.427
−0.3	0.13482	0.23843	1.717	0.412	0.425	2.554
−0.2	0.13911	0.24527	1.863	0.395	0.459	2.717
−0.1	0.14270	0.24865	2.014	0.400	0.505	2.918
0.0	0.14562	0.24952	2.169	0.434	0.561	3.164
0.1	0.14796	0.24890	2.327	0.504	0.632	3.463
0.2	0.14988	0.24776	2.489	0.618	0.725	3.832
0.3	0.15146	0.24678	2.653	0.785	0.853	4.291
0.4	0.15277	0.24629	2.819	1.013	1.037	4.869
0.5	0.15388	0.24631	2.987	1.310	1.310	5.608
0.6	0.15482	0.24678	3.156	1.684	1.721	6.562
0.7	0.15564	0.24762	3.327	2.143	2.336	7.806
0.8	0.15638	0.24874	3.498	2.694	3.246	9.439
0.9	0.15708	0.25011	3.670	3.347	4.570	11.587

Table 11.4 Values of J_{S2}^*: $L_1 = 1$, $L_2 = 3$ and $L_3 = 3$

ρ	F_1^*	F_2^*	$\sqrt{V[\overline{\overline{NS_1}}]}$	$\sqrt{V[\overline{\overline{NS_2}}]}$	$\sqrt{V[\overline{\overline{NS_3}}]}$	J_{S2}^*
−0.9	0.76356	0.13470	1.029	0.927	0.968	2.924
−0.8	0.52431	0.16327	1.137	0.784	0.767	2.688
−0.7	0.35779	0.16386	1.305	0.608	0.651	2.564
−0.6	0.27910	0.17316	1.443	0.501	0.562	2.506
−0.5	0.22998	0.18930	1.567	0.425	0.505	2.497
−0.4	0.19440	0.21008	1.688	0.367	0.473	2.527
−0.3	0.16710	0.23270	1.807	0.332	0.461	2.600
−0.2	0.14897	0.24737	1.904	0.351	0.472	2.727
−0.1	0.14191	0.24474	1.947	0.459	0.509	2.915
0.0	0.14054	0.23656	1.956	0.638	0.566	3.161
0.1	0.14049	0.23072	1.956	0.866	0.641	3.464
0.2	0.14058	0.22772	1.956	1.140	0.738	3.834
0.3	0.14060	0.22679	1.956	1.463	0.870	4.289
0.4	0.14055	0.22724	1.956	1.843	1.060	4.858
0.5	0.14048	0.22856	1.957	2.287	1.339	5.583
0.6	0.14043	0.23043	1.957	2.804	1.757	6.518
0.7	0.14043	0.23264	1.957	3.402	2.379	7.738
0.8	0.14048	0.23505	1.957	4.089	3.297	9.343
0.9	0.14060	0.23762	1.956	4.873	4.630	11.459

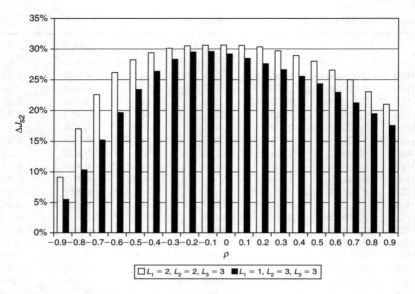

Figure 11.4 ΔJ_{S2} objective function reduction (%)

Table 11.5 Values of J_{S3}^*: $L_1 = 2$, $L_2 = 2$ and $L_3 = 3$

ρ	F_2^*	$\sqrt{V[\overline{\overline{NS}}_1]}$	$\sqrt{V[\overline{\overline{NS}}_2]}$	$\sqrt{V[\overline{\overline{NS}}_3]}$	J_{S3}^*
−0.9	0.13673	1.005	0.978	0.956	2.939
−0.8	0.17795	1.020	1.019	0.703	2.741
−0.7	0.19758	1.044	1.089	0.571	2.704
−0.6	0.20904	1.077	1.170	0.514	2.760
−0.5	0.21693	1.118	1.254	0.502	2.874
−0.4	0.22213	1.166	1.343	0.517	3.026
−0.3	0.22508	1.221	1.443	0.548	3.211
−0.2	0.22644	1.281	1.559	0.591	3.430
−0.1	0.22689	1.345	1.698	0.645	3.688
0.0	0.22694	1.414	1.867	0.709	3.990
0.1	0.22698	1.487	2.073	0.788	4.348
0.2	0.22724	1.562	2.325	0.889	4.776
0.3	0.22783	1.640	2.628	1.025	5.293
0.4	0.22877	1.720	2.990	1.218	5.929
0.5	0.23005	1.803	3.420	1.501	6.724
0.6	0.23165	1.887	3.924	1.921	7.732
0.7	0.23351	1.972	4.511	2.546	9.029
0.8	0.23560	2.059	5.188	3.466	10.713
0.9	0.23788	2.147	5.963	4.801	12.911

Table 11.6 Values of J_{S3}^*: $L_1 = 1$, $L_2 = 3$ and $L_3 = 3$

ρ	F_2^*	$\sqrt{V[\overline{\overline{NS_1}}]}$	$\sqrt{V[\overline{\overline{NS_2}}]}$	$\sqrt{V[\overline{NS_3}]}$	J_{S3}^*
−0.9	0.13632	1.000	0.983	0.956	2.939
−0.8	0.17592	1.000	1.040	0.701	2.741
−0.7	0.19295	1.000	1.135	0.566	2.700
−0.6	0.20129	1.000	1.247	0.503	2.750
−0.5	0.20594	1.000	1.367	0.484	2.851
−0.4	0.20817	1.000	1.495	0.491	2.987
−0.3	0.20868	1.000	1.634	0.515	3.150
−0.2	0.20827	1.000	1.789	0.552	3.341
−0.1	0.20768	1.000	1.964	0.599	3.563
0.0	0.20740	1.000	2.166	0.658	3.824
0.1	0.20774	1.000	2.399	0.733	4.132
0.2	0.20880	1.000	2.672	0.829	4.502
0.3	0.21055	1.000	2.992	0.962	4.954
0.4	0.21289	1.000	3.365	1.151	5.517
0.5	0.21570	1.000	3.801	1.431	6.232
0.6	0.21884	1.000	4.307	1.850	7.156
0.7	0.22219	1.000	4.892	2.473	8.364
0.8	0.22567	1.000	5.564	3.391	9.955
0.9	0.22921	1.000	6.332	4.726	12.058

From Table 11.5 and Table 11.6, the following insights may be obtained:

- $J_{S3}^* < J_{S1}$ for all values of ρ and lead-time settings. This means that the generalized OUT policy supply chain always outperforms the traditional OUT policy supply chain.
- F_2^* never has unit value.
- The value of F_2^* is affected by both the value of ρ and the lead-time settings.
- $J_{S3}^* < J_{S1}$ is achieved by altruistic behaviour of the second-level player. That is by accepting $\sqrt{V[\overline{\overline{NS_2}}]} > \sqrt{V[\overline{NS_2}]}$.

By using a measure of benefit of $\Delta J_{S3} = (J_{S1} - J_{S3}^*)/J_{S1}$, the benefit of Scenario 3 has been plotted in Figure 11.5. The average benefit in Scenario 3 is 11.9 per cent and 13.2 per cent for the lead-time settings $L_1 = 2$, $L_2 = 2$ and $L_3 = 3$ and $L_1 = 1$, $L_2 = 3$ and $L_3 = 3$ respectively. With the assumption of positive values of ρ, these average benefits will increase to 13.0 per cent and 14.8 per cent respectively.

Conclusion

By using a three-level supply chain model, three different scenarios have been investigated and some interesting insights have been obtained. To obtain

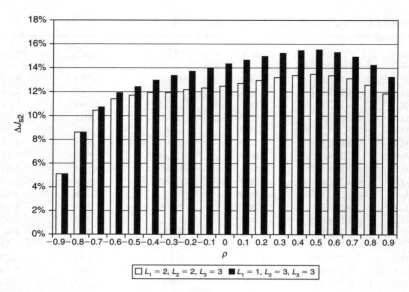

Figure 11.5 ΔJ_{S3} objective function reduction (%)

analytical expressions of the variances of the end-period net stock levels at each level in the generalized OUT policy supply chain, a newly developed method is exploited. The traditional OUT policy supply chain has been used as a benchmark for performance in Scenario 1.

In Scenario 2, two proportional controllers were incorporated, one at the first level and the other at the second level. By adjusting the values of the proportional controllers properly, a significant amount of benefit can be obtained. Neither of these two controllers takes unit values; however, $\sqrt{V[\overline{\overline{NS_2}}]}$ is less than $\sqrt{V[\overline{NS_2}]}$, and only altruistic behaviour of the first level is required to enjoy such a benefit, in almost all parameter settings. The quantified benefits are quite large, and it is shown that such *benefits come from each player in the supply chain doing what is the best for itself and the supply chain, rather than doing what is the best for its own selfish interests.* In other words, a sequence of optimum policies does not provide a global minimum cost of a supply chain.

Scenario 2 has shown the lowest cost function in the model settings; however, to enjoy the benefit, the altruistic behaviour at the first level must be accepted. But this is usually where the most expensive inventory holding costs are incurred. In addition, the redistribution of the inventory costs among players might be a barrier to implementation of Scenario 2, as we discussed in the literature review. Some additional incentives for the first-level player may be necessary, since the overall benefit completely depends on the degree of altruistic behaviour given by the first-level player.

To overcome incentive conflict issues in a supply chain, Scenario 3 is considered. Scenario 3 may be a case of a three-level supply chain that is governed by two organizations: the first-level inventory is managed by a retailer, and both second- and third-level inventories are managed by a supplier, for example. The retailer's concern is to minimize its own inventory-related costs. The supplier's interest is to minimize the sum of the inventory-related cost at both second and third levels. The retailer can help the supplier by providing up-to-date market demand information. To achieve the goal independently, the retailer may use the traditional OUT policy, which minimizes its own standard deviation of net stock level, and the supplier incorporates F_2 into the OUT policy at the second level and employs the traditional OUT policy at the third level to minimize its total inventory related costs. Having worked in the real business world, the two-organization three-level supply chain in Scenario 3 might become realistic. Since the supplier behaves altruistically and it is the supplier who enjoys the benefit from Scenario 3, it may be more acceptable to a real business world than Scenario 2. Therefore, Scenario 3 could bring a 'win-win' situation in a supply chain easily with less difficulty in implementation and operation.

There might be some challenges to enjoy the benefit. The results shown herein depend on a crucial assumption that all necessary information is shared without delay and exploited in a proper manner to obtain optimum values of F_n. To share the information without delay, the use of information technologies such as the internet and/or EDI might be essential. For the latter point, since the value of the objective function is not so sensitive to the value of F_n (see Figures 11.1–11.3, for example), even if the values of proportional controllers actually used in a supply chain are slightly different from the optimum values, the supply chain still can reduce its total costs by exploiting the generalized OUT policy.

Appendix

To optimize supply chain costs, analytical expressions of a cost function are essential. In this research, analytical expressions of variances are exploited. These expressions are able to be obtained through the following steps (Hosoda 2005).

Step 1: Express the end-period net stock level process as an ARMA(1,q) process, where q is a non-negative integer.

Step 2: Obtain the analytical expression of the variance of the ARMA(1,q) process.

The most significant advantage of this method is that it is not necessary to specify the value of the lead times in a supply chain to gain analytical expressions.

From now, the details about how to obtain $\sqrt{V[\overline{\overline{NS}}_1]}$ will be shown. By following the same steps, $\sqrt{V[\overline{\overline{NS}}_2]}$ is also obtainable.

In our model, the order placed by the first-level player is expressed as:

$$O_{t,1} = \tilde{D}_t^{L_1} + F_1(DIP_{t,1} - (WIP_{t,1} + NS_{t,1})) \tag{A.11.1}$$

It is assumed herein that $NS_{t,1}$ can be described as:

$$NS_{t,1} = NS_{t-1,1} + O_{t-L_1,1} - D_t$$

From above equation

$$O_{t,1} = NS_{t+L_1,1} - NS_{t+L_1-1,1} + D_{t+L_1} \tag{A.11.2}$$

can be obtained. $WIP_{t,1}$ can be expressed as:

$$WIP_{t,1} = \sum_{i=1}^{L_1-1} O_{t-i,1} \tag{A.11.3}$$

Consider first the case when L_1 is greater than one. Substituting equation A.11.2 into equation A.11.3, another expression of $WIP_{t,1}$ is:

$$WIP_{t,1} = NS_{t+L_1-1,1} - NS_{t,1} + \sum_{i=1}^{L_1-1} D_{t+i} \tag{A.11.4}$$

After incorporating equations A.11.2 and A.11.4 into the LHS and the RHS of equation A.11.1 respectively, some algebraic simplification yields:

$$NS_{t+1,1} = (1-F_1)NS_{t,1} + (\tilde{D}_{t+1-L_1}^{L_1} - D_{t+1}) + F_1\left(DIP_{t+1-L_1,1} - \sum_{i=1}^{L_1-1} D_{t+1-L_1+i}\right) \tag{A.11.5}$$

Now, D_{t+1} can be expressed by using D_{t+1-L_1}:

$$D_{t+1} = \rho D_t + \varepsilon_{t+1}$$

$$= \rho(\rho D_{t-1} + \varepsilon_t) + \varepsilon_{t+1}$$

$$= \cdots$$

$$= \rho^{L_1} D_{t+1-L_1} + \rho^{L_1-1}\varepsilon_{t+2-L_1} + \rho^{L_1-2}\varepsilon_{t+3-L_1} + \cdots + \rho\varepsilon_t + \varepsilon_{t+1}$$

Thus, since $\tilde{D}_{t+1-L_1}^{L_1} = E[D_{t+1} \mid D_{t+1-L_1}]$, $\tilde{D}_{t+1-L_1}^{L_1}$, is given by:

$$\tilde{D}_{t+1-L_1}^{L_1} = \rho^{L_1} D_{t+1-L_1}$$

Therefore, $\tilde{D}_{t+1-L_1}^{L_1} - D_{t+1}$ can be written as:

$$\tilde{D}_{t+1-L_1}^{L_1} - D_{t+1} = -\sum_{i=0}^{L_1-1} (\rho^i \varepsilon_{t+1-i}) \tag{A.11.6}$$

$\sum_{i=1}^{L_1-1} D_{t+1-L_1+i}$ described as:

$$\sum_{i=1}^{L_1-1} D_{t+1-L_1+i} = D_{t+2-L_1} + D_{t+3-L_1} + \cdots + D_t$$

$$= \rho D_{t+1-L_1} + \varepsilon_{t+2-L_1} + \rho(\rho D_{t+1-L_1} + \varepsilon_{t+2-L_1}) + \varepsilon_{t+3-L_1} + \cdots$$

$$+ \rho^{L_1} D_{t+1-L_1} + \rho^{L_1-2} \varepsilon_{t+2-L_1} + \rho^{L_1-3} \varepsilon_{t+3-L_1} + \cdots + \varepsilon_t$$

$$= \frac{\rho(\rho^{L_1-1} - 1)}{\rho - 1} D_{t+1-L_1} + \sum_{i=0}^{L_1-2} \sum_{j=0}^{L_1-2-i} (\rho^j \varepsilon_{t+2-L_1} + i)$$

And DIP_{t+1-L_1-1} is:

$$DIP_{t+1-L_1-1} = E\left[\sum_{i=1}^{L_1-1} D_{t+1-L_1+i} \mid D_{t+1-L_1}\right] = \frac{\rho(\rho^{L_1-1} - 1)}{\rho - 1} D_{t+1-L_1}$$

Thus, an expression for $F_1\left(DIP_{t+1-L_1,1} - \sum_{i=1}^{L_1-1} D_{t+1-L_1+i}\right)$ becomes:

$$F_1\left(DIP_{t+1-L_1-1} - \sum_{i=1}^{L_1-1} D_{t+1-L_1+i}\right) = -F_1\left(\sum_{i=0}^{L_1-2} \sum_{j=0}^{L_1-2-i} (\rho^j \varepsilon_{t+2-L_1+i})\right) \tag{A.11.7}$$

By substituting equations A.11.6 and A.11.7 into equation A.11.5, the final expression of the end-period net stock level process at the first level can be expressed as:

$$NS_{t+1,1} = \eta_1 NS_{t,1} - \lambda_{0,1}\varepsilon_{t+1} - \lambda_{1,1}\varepsilon_t - \cdots - \lambda_{L_1-1,1}\varepsilon_{t+2-L_1}$$

$$= \eta_1 NS_{t,1} - \sum_{i=0}^{L_1-1} \lambda_{i,1}\varepsilon_{t+1-i}, \tag{A.11.8}$$

where $\eta_1 = 1 - F_1$ and $\lambda_{i,1} = \rho^i + \frac{F_1(\rho^i-1)}{\rho-1}$.

From equation A.11.8, it can be seen that $NS_{t,1}$ follows ARMA(1, $L_1 - 1$) process with AutoRegressive (AR) coefficient η_1 and moving average (MA) coefficients $\lambda_{0,1}, \ldots, \lambda_{L_1-1,1}$. It should be noted that in the case of the traditional OUT policy where $F_1 = 1$, the AR coefficient η_1, becomes zero and $NS_{t,1}$

follows ARMA(0, $L_1 - 1$) process. This result coincides with Gilbert (2005). Generally, the variance of ARMA($1,q$) process at level n can be expressed as:

$$\frac{\sigma_\varepsilon^2}{1 - \eta_n^2} \left(\sum_{i=0}^{q} \lambda_{i,n}^2 + 2\eta_n \sum_{i=1}^{q} \left(\lambda_{i,n} \sum_{j=0}^{i-1} (\eta_n^{i-1-j} \lambda_{j,n}) \right) \right) \qquad \text{(A.11.9)}$$

After substituting the AR and the MA coefficients into equation A.11.9, some algebraic simplification yields equation 11.6. The same conclusions can be obtained for the case of $L_1 = 1$, where $WIP_{t,1} = 0$, by following the same steps described herein.

Notes

1. It should be noted that several researchers adopt an alternative expression for the OUT policy that exploits a time varying OUT target (see Lee, So and Tang 2000, for example); however, the dynamics given by these two expositions is identical, as shown in Hosoda and Disney (2006b).
2. Readers are encouraged to visit our website, <http://www.bullwhip.co.uk/bwExplorer.htm> to see how altruistic behaviour brings benefits to a supply chain.
3. For the details of an MMSE forecasting, see Box, Jenkins and Reinsel (1994).

References

Aviv, Y. and Federgruen, A. 1998 'The operational benefits of information sharing and vendor managed inventory (VMI) programs', working paper, Washington University, St Louis, MO.

Bellman, R. 1957 *Dynamic Programming*, New Jersey: Princeton University Press: 83.

Box, G.E.P., Jenkins, G.M. and Reinsel, G.C. 1994 *Time Series Analysis: Forecasting and Control*, 3rd edn, New Jersey: Prentice Hall.

Collins, G.E., Johnson, J.R. and Krandick, W. 2002 'Interval arithmetic in cylindrical algebraic decomposition', *Journal of Symbolic Computation*, 34: 145–57.

Disney, S.M. and Towill, D.R. 2003a 'The effect of vendor managed inventory (VMI) dynamics on the bullwhip effect in supply chains', *International Journal of Production Economics*, 85: 199–215.

Disney, S.M. and Towill, D.R. 2003b 'Vendor-managed inventory and bullwhip reduction in a two-level supply chain', International *Journal of Operations and Production Management*, 23: 625–51.

Gavirneni, S. 2006 'Price fluctuations, information sharing, and supply chain performance', *European Journal of Operational Research*, 174: 1651–63.

Giannoccaro, I. and Pontrandolfo, P. 2004 'Supply chain coordination by revenue sharing contracts', *International Journal of Production Economics*, 89: 131–9.

Gilbert, K. 2005 'An ARIMA supply chain model', *Management Science*, 51: 305–10.

Graves, S.C. 1999 'A single-item inventory model for a nonstationary demand process', *Manufacturing and Service Operations Management*, 1: 50–61.

Hosoda, T. 2005 'The principles governing the dynamics of supply chains', PhD dissertation, Cardiff University, UK.

Hosoda, T. and Disney, S.M. 2006a 'The governing dynamics of supply chains: The impact of altruistic behavior', *Automatica*, 42: 1301–9.

Hosoda, T. and Disney, S.M. 2006b 'On variance amplification in a three-echelon supply chain with minimum mean square error forecasting', *OMEGA: The International Journal of Management Science*, 34: 344–58.

Hosoda, T., Naim, M.M., Disney, S.M. and Potter, A. 2008 'Is there a benefit to sharing market sales information? Linking theory and practice', *Computers and Industrial Engineering*, 54: 315–26.

Kim, H. and Ryan, J.K. 2003 'The cost impact of using simple forecasting techniques in a supply chain', *Naval Research Logistics*, 50: 388–411.

Lee, H.L., Padmanabhan, V. and Whang, S. 'Information distortion in a supply chain: The bullwhip effect', *Management Science*, 43: 546–58.

Lee, H.L., So, K.C. and Tang, C.S. 2000 'The value of information sharing in a two-level supply chain', *Management Science*, 46: 626–43.

Luo, J. 2007 'Buyer-vendor inventory coordination with credit period incentives', *International Journal of Production Economics*, 108: 143–52.

Raghunathan, S. 2001 'Information sharing in a supply chain: A note on its value when demand is nonstationary', *Management Science*, 47(4): 605–10.

Tsay, A.A. 1999 'The quantity flexibility contract and supplier–customer incentives', *Management Science*, 45(10): 1339–58.

Vassian, H.J. 1955 'Application of discrete variable servo theory to inventory control', *Journal of the Operations Research Society of America*, 3: 272–82.

Weng, Z.K. 1995 'Channel coordination and quantity discounts', *Management Science*, 41: 1509–22.

Part III

Knowledge Management-Led Supply Chain Management: Innovations and New Understanding

12
Electronic Integration of Supply Chain Operations: Context, Evolution and Practices

Aristides Matopoulos, Maro Vlachopoulou and Vicky Manthou

Introduction

Successful companies seem to be, nowadays, those that have carefully linked their internal processes to external suppliers and customers in unique supply chains (Frohlich and Westbrook 2001, Boyer, Frohlich and Hult 2004). In this effort towards linking internal processes to external suppliers and customers, the sharing of information among enterprises is absolutely critical. Electronic data interchange (EDI) in the past and the internet in the last decade have enabled supply chain partners to act upon the same data (Christopher 2005). This reality explains much of companies' initial enthusiasm regarding the introduction of the internet and internet-based application in the early 1990s. Companies' ultimate goal of process integration across the entire supply chain was now much more feasible than ever before.

In the literature, the role and the potential impact of the internet on companies and on supply chain operations are not questioned and have received significant attention. However, in many cases the role of the internet in integrating supply chain operations has been approached in a quite generic way (Cross 2000, Croom 2000, Auramo, Kauremaa and Tanskanen 2005). Moreover, most of this research focuses on knowledge and information high-intensive sectors. In addition, much of the confusion regarding the internet's role in integrating supply chain operations derives from the fact that the notion of integration is not very clearly defined yet. The complex nature of supply chains and the different levels of operations integration that exist add significant difficulties and complexity to understanding the internet's true contribution. Consequently, the role and the contribution of internet in integrating supply chain operations is not fully explored and understood. As a result, in many cases companies' initial enthusiasm has been transformed into scepticism and in some cases even in negativism, as companies often find difficulties in quantifying or even clarifying the role and the benefits of the internet. This chapter intends to increase the understanding of electronic integration and its impact on supply chain operations. The objective is initially to propose an overall framework for supply chain integration, based on which the role of the internet is further examined in different business sectors, since most research focuses on a specific business sector, which often limits the applicability of the findings and the ability to generalize the results. Through secondary data research and literature review, the following research questions are going to be investigated:

* RQ1. What is the context of supply chain integration?
* RQ2. What is the contribution of the internet in integrating supply chain operations in different sectors?

In other words, the chapter will try to empower the understanding regarding the real value of the internet for companies and, particularly, whether or not and in what way this value appears in different sectors.

The context of supply chain integration

The concept of supply chain integration, although not a new one is still receiving significant attention in the literature (Harland *et al.* 2007, Van der Vaart and van Donk 2008). As many authors argue (Gunasekaran and Ngai 2004a, Pagell 2004) the integration of all activities that add value to customers, starting from product design to delivery, is the cornerstone of supply chain management, and the performance of a supply chain is dependent to a great extent on its level of integration (Stock, Greis and Kasarda 1998, van der Vaart and van Donk 2008). However, a survey by Bagchi and Skjoett-Larsen (2005), in more than 100 European firms, revealed that while performance seems to have improved as a result of collaboration with suppliers, and in some cases with customers, the nature and extent of integration has been a bit selective. Despite the importance of supply chain integration, the concept is not very well defined and difficult to measure empirically (Frohlich and Westbrook 2001). Much of the confusion is due to the fact that researchers tend to pay attention to specific sectors or specific companies, which are performing much better than the majority of companies.

In this paper, the approach followed regarding supply chain integration is the one proposed by Matopoulos *et al.* (2007). Their framework consists of three dimensions:

* Direction of integration
* Width of integration and
* Levels of integration

The first dimension in this framework is the direction of integration. It refers to the multitude of the entities and their place in the supply chain, in relation to the focal company. Based on the categorization provided by Stevens

(1989), and Fawcett and Magnan (2002), three type-levels of integration exist, namely backward, forward and complete integration. Backward integration involves integration with valued first-tier suppliers or even second-tier suppliers. Analogously, forward integration involves integration with valued first-tier customers or even second-tier customers. Finally, complete integration, includes forward and backward integration from the 'suppliers' supplier to the customers' customer'. Managers who are responsible should first examine the characteristics of their supply chain in terms of the type of product moved and the type of entities participating. Product or partner constraints may put significant limitations on the direction of integration.

The second dimension in the framework refers to the extent of operations involved in the integration (width of integration). Fawcett and Magnan (2002), suggest that one way of dealing with the diversity of definitions is to concentrate on some of the core processes and functions related to the management of supply chains. Drawing from the literature (Cooper, Lambert and Pagh 1997, Ross 1998, Mentzer *et al.* 2001) these key business processes include not only basic operations, such as procurement, inventory management, production planning, transportation, order processing and customer service but also marketing, promotion, sales, product design and new product development, processes that expand the organizational boundaries of individual companies. It is clear, that integration may not be applicable to all supply chain operations and, moreover, may not be applicable in the same way for different sectors. Therefore, managers who are in charge should be in position to evaluate the strengths of each participant in their supply chain and to identify and prioritize integration opportunities based on the feasibility criterion.

The third dimension in the framework considers the level of integration based on one of the most widely accepted classifications of decision-taking levels: strategic, tactical and operational. At the strategic level it is important to identify what the long-range aspects of integration are, for example, if the competitive strategy of a firm has changed due to the integration of operations. The tactical level includes medium-term aspects. Finally, the operational level includes day-to-day decisions and actions. Managers should be able to identify what the appropriate level of commitment and involvement of each partner in the supply chain is. For example, companies that focus on the operational aspects of integration are less likely to invest in technologies that may alter their way of conducting business (new business models apart from the traditional).

Electronic integration

In this section the origin of electronic integration is presented and, furthermore, it is attempted to provide understanding regarding the evolution of the concept and the potential impact on supply chain integration.

Context and evolution

The concept of electronic integration has been approached in many different ways in the literature. According to Kambil and Short (1994), electronic integration refers to 'strategic choices made by firms to exploit EDI and Inter-Organizational System platforms to transform business processes and relationships, the business network or the firm's business scope' (p.60). Another approach, less strategic, is the one by Zaheer and Venkatraman (1994). They take a more process-based view of electronic integration, which is defined as 'the interconnection and integration of the business processes of two or more independent organizations through information technology applications' (p.594). In other words, electronic integration refers to a business model that combines the application of new technologies to the matching of supply and demand, collaborative partnering and/or outsourcing and coordinated logistics (Walters 2004, Power and Singh 2007). Electronic integration is by no means something new for companies. For more than 20 years, EDI application was enabling companies to exchange information and data so as to bridge supply chain integration gaps. In particular, EDI enabled direct computer-to-computer transfer of information between independent organizations, providing numerous benefits such as reductions in data transmission error, clerical paperwork and inventory investment; and increased flexibility of response to rapidly changing customer demands and market environments (O'Callaghan, Kauffmann and Kosynski 1992, Peters 2000, Weber and Cantamneni 2002). Although the EDI approach achieved integration at the data level, it did not provide process integration. The development of the internet, particularly over the last decade, has provided an additional tool in an effort to deal with the incompatibility, the complexity and the increased development and installation costs of EDI (O'Callaghan, Kauffmann and Kosynski 1992, Peters 2000, Harrison and van Hoek 2008). Before the internet, achieving real-time demand information and inventory visibility was impossible and most supply and demand integration involved a patchwork of telephoning, faxing and EDI (Frohlich 2002).

Benefits and types of electronic integration

In the internet era, widely available web-based technologies now permit, more efficiently than ever before, strong customer and supplier integration for numerous intra-enterprise operations, such as inventory planning, demand forecasting, order scheduling, new product development and customer relationship management. The development of the internet has brought new ways of dealing with old supply chain problems. Its role in the evolution of supply chains has been already recognized in the literature (Gecowets and Bauer 2000, Lancioni *et al.* 2000). A significant body of literature has emphasized the benefits of electronic integration, often from different perspectives. Mukhopadhyay and Kekre (2002), for example, examined the strategic and operational benefits of electronic integration for industrial procurement. Sethi, Pant and Sethi (2003) emphasized the role of web-based integration on the new product development process. Grean and Shaw (2002) examined the impact of electronic integration on inventory and demand management. Benefits of electronic integration, however, are not always clear or direct and this is very much related to specific characteristics of the sector where it is applied. The research by Forster and Reagan (2001), for example, revealed that there was no direct impact of electronic integration in the US air-cargo industry.

According to Harrison and van Hoek (2008) supply chain partners can integrate electronically in three ways: transactional, information sharing and collaborative planning. Transactional integration refers to less complex and more operational business processes, such as purchase orders, invoices and advanced shipping notices. This type of electronic integration focuses on the automation aspect of these processes and the benefits are more relevant to the intra-organizational level. Information sharing is about transmitting and receiving information regarding pricing, promotional, inventory and shipment track and tracing issues. These processes are more at the tactical level than at the operational, and the benefits span the boundaries of the single firm. Finally, collaborative planning is the most sophisticated form of electronic integration, since it involves intense interaction and collaboration for long-term or even strategic processes such as new product development, joint demand forecasts, and replenishment planning. In this case, each piece of information needed by a supply chain participant is entered only once, through an automated process. Subsequent use and dissemination of that information is managed through software programs, without the need of manual intervention or translation. Communication of this information across geography, among facilities within a firm and between firms is accomplished seamlessly (White, O'Connor and Rowe 2004). The benefits at this level are not limited to the single firm, but are realized more in the supply chain as whole. In the following figure (Figure 12.1) the electronic integration ladder is presented, which is based on the overall research framework for supply chain integration suggested earlier and the types of electronic integration proposed by Harrison and van Hoek (2008).

Electronic supply chain integration: Evidence from various sectors

In this part of the chapter, an identification of the role of the internet and its impact on supply chain integration is attempted in an industry-specific context. Based on the overall integration framework presented earlier and based also on the context of electronic integration, an exploration of the internet's contribution follows. The industry-specific context facilitates the identification of the real weaknesses and strengths of the internet in different sets of business environment and the type of integration that has been

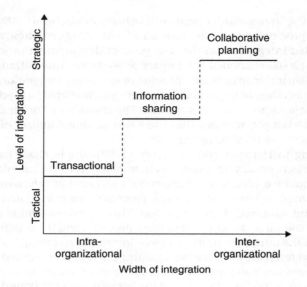

Figure 12.1   The electronic integration ladder

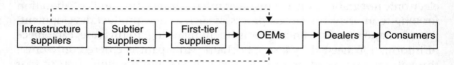

Figure 12.2   The basic automotive supply chain

achieved. The business sectors that have been selected for exploration are: the automotive sector, the computer sector, the grocery sector and the apparel sector. The logic behind this selection was initially to include sectors with economic importance. Additionally, all four sectors are, to a great extent, global and represent both high- and low-intensive knowledge and information sectors. Finally, the availability of relevant data for those sectors was another important element.

Evidence from the automotive sector

The automotive supply chain consists of many different entities: numerous mainly small suppliers, a few, but very large, original equipment manufacturers (OEM's), numerous dealers and final consumers (Figure 12.2).

During the last decade the automotive industry has been in the process of globalization in an effort to confront global over-capacity, rising stock levels and low profitability (Palm and Sihn 2005). Speed has also become a crucial issue in the development process, with manufacturers aiming to achieve significant reduction in the time-to-market cycle. In addition, most of the manufacturers faced the challenge of extending their production plans to different places than the traditional US—Japan–Europe triad (Lung 2000). These changes have resulted in an undisputed need for integrating supply chain operations beyond companies' boundaries, and the role of the internet in supporting this integration has been rather important.

In particular, regarding the direction of integration in the automotive industry, the internet has allowed for forward integration, with customers (for example dealers) getting more knowledge than even before regarding products and services they are considering purchasing (Handfield and Nichols 2002). Most automotive manufacturers have built powerful websites allowing customers to reach any of their products. Backward integration is more feasible in the automotive industry due to the use of the internet, which enables not only first-tier suppliers (as in the past with the use of EDI), but also second- and third-tier suppliers to have access on production schedules and plans (Handfield and Nichols 2002). Regarding the width of integration, the internet has extended the processes upon which suppliers and customers do collaborate. Over recent years, first-tier suppliers have risen in status, and their roles in the supply chain have been extended from the traditional activities related to material flow and sourcing to more complex activities, such as new product design (Palm and Sihn 2005, Neto and Pires 2005). Customers from this tier also not only can have access to prices, but, in some cases, become active parts in the manufacturing process by selecting colour, type of seat covers etc. For example, BMW allows customers to make changes to their vehicle, even within six days of final assembly (Gunasekaran and Ngai 2004b).

Even the level of integration in the automotive industry has been shifted from operational and tactical to strategic, with manufacturers communicating via the internet with executives from divisions all over the world, taking decisions on product development, market and pricing issues (Handfield and Nichols 2002). The clearest example in the automotive industry is the online marketplace, which was launched in 2000 by some of the major companies in the sector in their effort to manage their complex networks of suppliers, dealers, distributors and service providers (for example 3PLs). This global collaboration platform, with powerful dashboards and EDI interconnectivity, delivers information and applications, and facilitates processes such as collaborative forecasting and planning, order management, sales and service support and scheduling functions by linking each supply chain link. Potential benefits as a result of increased electronic integration include improvements of the delivery reliability for customers, reduction in delivery times for customer-specific vehicles and, of course, cost reductions (Wolff and Geiger 2000). Indeed, the survey by White *et al.* (2004), regarding communication methods in automotive firms revealed that automotive firms prefer EDI as the main communication method. EDI is followed by paper/fax and only a small number of communications is conducted with the use XML/Internet. The survey also revealed that automotive firms were using the same methods with the same frequency whether they were communicating with suppliers or customers.

Evidence from the computer sector

The computer sector is a very complex one, requiring interaction and coordination among industry participants throughout the manufacturing process. Computers consist of thousands of discrete components, systems and accessories, which are designed and manufactured by numerous companies across the world. In the following figure (Figure 12.3) a representation of the computers supply chain is presented, along with the major product flows.

The computer industry is a very competitive one with powerful manufacturers competing on a global basis and being probably the most important players of the industry. Similar to the automotive industry, time pressures are also characteristic, perhaps even more crucial. Time-based competition has emerged as the winning strategy in the fast-cycle computer industry, where product life cycles are relatively short (two years or less) and computer products become obsolete in even less time than before (Rosas-Vega and Vokurka 2000). Apple, for example, was unable to fill orders for its new high-end line of G4 computers because of delays in the supply of chips, thus experiencing a devastating 14 per cent drop in revenue in 1999 (Gunasekaran and Ngai 2004b).

The main characteristic of the computer industry is the fact that most OEMs are using more or less the same components (for example, there are only two companies in the semiconductor business) and, thus, the competition game is mainly played on the basis of cost and customization, rather than on service and innovation, since OEMs can not realize unique value from common suppliers. As a result, OEMs continue a relentless pursuit of cost reductions and operational improvements, to drive supply chain efficiencies and to confront the continuing drop in retail prices and distributor margins. In their effort to achieve integration and improvements, the internet has been quite important. In fact, the computer industry has moved much further along the path towards efficient supply chain integration than the automotive sector, most notably through the efforts of industry-wide consortia like NEMI and RosettaNet (White, O'Connor and Rowe 2004). RosettaNet, for

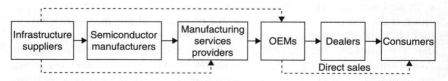

Figure 12.3   The basic computer supply chain

example, is a global consortium of major computer and consumer electronics, electronic components, semiconductor manufacturing, telecommunications and logistics companies working to create and implement industry-wide, open e-business process standards with the aim of aligning processes between supply chain partners on a global basis. The basis of the RosettaNet standard is Extensible Markup Language (XML). Despite the development of such a platform, much of the integration in the sector refers mainly to backward entities, although there are many cases of OEMs that have achieved forward integration, with Dell and Gateway being successful and well-known cases (Boyer, Frohlich and Hult 2004). In addition, regarding the width of integration, this is limited to less complex supply chain operations such as automating ordering and distribution.

Evidence from the grocery sector

The grocery industry is one of the most important industries and presents some interesting characteristics. Groceries are perhaps the most universal commodity; thus competition, along with varying customers' tastes and the perishable nature of products, often spurs retailers to go to great lengths to develop new technologies and methods of streamlining their supply chain efforts (Boyer and Hult 2005). Another characteristic of the sector is its diversity, since it is comprised of companies ranging from very small manufacturers to global retailers. In the following figure (Figure 12.4) a representation of the grocery supply chain is provided.

A number of changes have occurred in the last decade in this sector. The entrance of global retailers, industry's consolidation, changing consumer consumption attitudes and the existence of stricter regulations and laws regarding food production as a result of the recent food crises (Hughes 1994, Kaufman 1999, Fearne, Hughes and Duffy 2001) have altered the business environment for most of the companies operating in the sector, encouraging a positive attitude towards integration and improvement. Despite the specific characteristics of the sector, it is one where pioneering work for electronic integration has been conducted (Harrison and van Hoek 2008). Similar to the automotive and the computer sector companies, even competitors decided to invest on electronic integration. For example, in 2000 17 international retailers founded the Worldwide Retail Exchange (WWRE) to

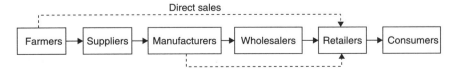

Figure 12.4   The basic grocery supply chain

enable participating retailers and manufacturers to simplify, rationalize and automate supply chain processes, thereby eliminating inefficiencies in the supply chain. The WWRE is the premier internet-based business-to-business exchange in the retail e-marketplace, which enables retailers and manufacturers to substantially reduce costs across product development, e-procurement and supply chain processes.

The impact of the internet on supply chain integration has been very important, particularly integration between food manufacturers and retailers. Forward integration has been more intense at the retailer level, given the size of these companies, but not at the consumer level, which essentially remains at a distance and isolated from food production (Kaufman 1999, Fearne, Hughes and Duffy 2001, GMA 2000). Backward integration has been weak, as most of their suppliers are small to medium-sized companies, such as farmers, producer groups and cooperatives, which have not adopted internet-based applications (E-business Watch 2006). The width of integration has not been very extensive, with companies using the internet mainly for logistics activities, rather than for new product development and relevant activities (King 2001). This is also due to the fact that innovation and new product development is still conducted at the manufacturer level and has not been passed to its suppliers, which are usually growers and cooperatives. With regard to electronic integration, it seems, in most cases, to be limited to transactions, particularly at the supplier–food manufacturer level. However, some big manufacturers have established links with the retailers and have moved towards an increased level of electronic integration. For example, in many cases manufacturers are scheduling in the short- or mid-term, planning forecasts and promotion plans (for example, the use of the CPFR platform), in collaboration with the retailers. Sainsbury, one of the biggest UK retailers, developed a package that aims at reducing new product development time by up to a third of the traditional time by linking over its website a number of entities involved in the new product development process (e.g chefs, concept developers, manufacturers, nutritionists, marketers, design studios, artwork and reproductive houses, and product safety and legal experts). For example, a technologist on a supplier visit to South America can log on and approve packaging details online, keeping the project on time (Sainsbury 2002). The system enables all parties to access the data (same versions) online as needed. For example, if an ingredient was changed by the chef, an e-mail would be sent to the packaging designer alerting them to alter the packaging, too, which results mistake reductions (Sainsbury 2002).

Evidence from the apparel sector

The apparel sector is also a sector with various segments. The apparel supply chain (Figure 12.5) consists of many diverse entities, which results in complexity. The sector has witnessed many changes since the 1990s. A large segment of the sector started to compete on low cost and this resulted in many

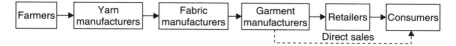

Figure 12.5 The basic apparel supply chain

manufacturers sourcing and producing from abroad. The apparel sector is very competitive and time-sensitive due to the fact that product life cycles are shortening and product proliferation is accelerating, even in the most basic garments. These trends have created increasing demand uncertainty, which has changed radically the basis of competition in the textile—apparel–retail channel (Hammond and Kohler 2000).

In such a competitive sector integration was an absolute necessity, and was facilitated over the last 20 years by the use of EDI. However, due to the globalization of the sector, integration with the use of EDI was made difficult because of companies operating across borders with different languages, tax systems and document requirements (Mossinkoff 2006). In particular, regarding the direction and the width of integration, EDI at the beginning allowed mainly backward integration; however, this was restricted to less complex and more operational business processes, such as purchase orders, invoices and advanced shipping notices. Recent results from the survey of Teng and Jaramillo (2006), regarding the integration of the US textile and apparel supply chain with small companies in South America, reveal that it is difficult to achieve complete integration. This is mainly due to the inability of small supply chain partners to streamline their own internal processes. As a result, integration is limited to a few supply chain members and electronic integration focuses on the automation aspect of these processes; the benefits apply more to the intra-organizational level. Information sharing is about transmitting and receiving information regarding pricing, promotional, inventory and shipment track and tracing issues. The problematic past EDI connectivity resulted in companies trying to invest on web-based platforms that would enable more integration, with more entities and more processes. Similar to other sectors and in an effort to overcome EDI inefficiencies, many marketplaces have been established since the early 2000s. These marketplaces were expected to enable and support linkages between retailer and apparel manufacturers, but also between apparel manufacturers and their suppliers, offering planning, procurement, product development and order fulfilment support. However, after the dot.com crisis, most of these marketplaces were abandoned. In most recent years, however, it is evident that big garment manufacturers are building powerful websites in an effort to achieve links directly with the final consumer. With regard to backward integration, they invest in EDI applications in order to achieve higher levels of integration in their already vertically integrated supply chain (Mossinkoff 2006).

Conclusions

This chapter has investigated the issue of supply chain and electronic integration. The literature revealed that the concept of supply chain integration is not well defined. For this reason, an overall framework was presented with the aim of contextualizing the concept in a more structured way, so as to provide a basis for analysis. The framework proposes three major dimensions: width, depth and direction of integration, which should be taken into account when trying to assess and indentify supply chain integration. The framework served as a basis to explore the role of the internet in supply chain operations in an industry-specific context. Assessing the real value of the internet on supply chain operations is particularly important since, in many cases, it may be overestimated as a result of internet 'euphoria'. Kanter (2004) very accurately argues that it is only now, as the unrealistic hype about the internet passes away, that the potential of the internet can emerge. Driven by this suggestion the chapter examined four business sectors with the aim of identifying the uptake of internet-based applications, as well as the impact that has been reported. The sectors selected were: automotive, computer, grocery and apparel. In some of the sectors explored, the contribution of the internet to the integration of supply chain operations proved to be more of a theoretical ideal than a business reality. This was particularly the case in the apparel industry, where companies, due to the specific characteristics of the sector and the way it is segmented, have achieved supply chain integration, but this is rather limited to transactions. On the other hand, in the automotive, computer and grocery sectors there seems to be a more intense integration, particularly backward integration. In these sectors companies seem to have also achieved higher levels of electronic integration, but still they are far away from being truly integrated. For example, a comprehensive site-based study by Towill, Childerhouse and Disney (2000) of the European automotive sector found that only 10 per cent of supply chains could be regarded as fully integrated. A more recent survey by Poirier and Quinn (2003) similarly concluded that 10 per cent of supply chains in the USA had achieved external integration. In general, it seems that integration very often fails due to conflicting interests of the supply chain members, their specific characteristics and because of the lack of commonly accepted information technology and process standards (Nagy 2006). In fact, managers should bear mind that achieving supply chain integration involves many more things than just deploying electronic applications; the role of these applications should be supportive (Sanders 2005). This research has several constraints related to availability of data, which limits the ability to generalize the findings and conclusions. A more in-depth analysis of the sectors examined, as well as further analysis of other business sectors may be also needed. This will allow for generalizations to be drawn and more accurate and measurable assessment of the internet's contribution to supply chain integration.

References

Auramo, J., Kauremaa J. and Tanskanen, K. 2005 'Benefits of IT in supply chain man-agement: An explorative study of progressive companies', *International Journal of Physical Distribution and Logistics Management*, 35(2): 82–100.

Bagchi, P.K. and Skjoett-Larsen, T. 2005 'Supply chain integration: A European survey', *International Journal of Logistics Management*, 16(2): 275–94.

Boyer, K.K. and Hult, T.G. 2005 'Extending the supply chain: Integrating operations and marketing in the on-line grocery industry', *Journal of Operations Management*, 23(6): 642–61.

Boyer, K.K., Frohlich, M.T. and Hult, T.G. 2004 *Extending the Supply Chain: How Cutting Edge Companies Bridge the Critical Last Mile into Customers' Homes*, New York: American Management Association.

Bowersox, D.J. and Daugherty, P.J. 1995 'Logistics paradigms: The impact of information technology', *Journal of Business Logistics*, 16(1): 65–80.

Cooper, M.C. Lambert, D.M. and Pagh, J.D. 1997 'Supply chain management: More than a new name for logistics', *International Journal of Logistics Management*, 8(1): 1–14.

Christopher, M. 2005 *Logistics and Supply Chain Management: Creating Value- Adding Networks*, 3rd edn, London: Pearson Education Limited.

Croom, S.R. 2000 'The impact of web-based procurement on the management of operating resources supply', *Journal of Supply Chain Management*, 36(1): 4–13.

Cross, G.J. 2000 'How e-business is transforming supply chain management', *The Journal of Business Strategy*, 21(2): 36–9.

E-business Watch 2006 'ICT and e-business in the Food, Beverage and Tobacco Industry', Sector report.

Fawcett, S.E. and Magnan, G.M. 2002 'The rhetoric and reality of supply chain integration', *International Journal of Physical Distribution and Logistics Management*, 32(5): 339–61.

Fearne, A., Hughes, D. and Duffy, R. 2001 'Concepts of collaboration-supply chain management in a global food industry', in J.F. Eastham, L. Sharples and S.D. Ball (eds), *Food and Drink Supply Chain Management Issues for the Hospitality and Retail Sectors*, Oxford: Butterworth-Heinemann: 55–89.

Forster, P.W. and Regan, A.C. 2002 'Electronic integration in the air cargo industry: An information processing model of on-time performance', *Transportation Journal*, 40(4): 44–61.

Frohlich, M.T. 2002 'E-Integration in the supply chain: Barriers and performance', *Decision Sciences*, 33: 537–56.

Frohlich, M.T. and Westbrook, R. 2001 'Arcs of integration: an international study of supply chain strategies', *Journal of Operations Management*, 19: 185–200.

Gecowets, G. and Bauer, M. 2000 'The effect of the Internet on supply chain and logistics', *World Trade*, 13(9): 71–80.

GMA 2000 'Food manufacturers take first step toward real B2B e-commerce for grocery industry', accessed 5 July 2005, <http://www.gmabrands.com/news/docs/News Release.cfm?DocID=615&>

Grean, M. and Shaw, M.J. 2002 'Supply-chain integration through information sharing: Channel partnership between Wal-Mart and Procter & Gamble', Center for IT and e-Business Management, University of Illinois, Urbana-Champaign, IL: 21, accessed 21 November 2007, <http://citebm.cba.uiuc.edu/IT-cases/Graen-Shaw-PG.pdf

Gunasekaran, A. and Ngai, E.W.T. 2004a 'Information systems in supply chain integration and management', *European Journal of Operational Research*, 159(2): 269–95.

Gunasekaran, A. and Ngai, E.W.T. 2004b 'Build-to-order supply chain management: A literature review and framework for development', *Journal of Operations Management*, 23(5): 423–51.

Hammond, J. and Kohler, K. 2000 'E-commerce in the textile and apparel industries', working paper, Harvard Business School.

Handfield, R.B. and Nichols Jr, E.L. 2002 *Supply Chain Redesign: Transforming Supply Chains into Integrated Value Systems*, Upper Saddle River, NJ: Prentice Hall.

Harland, C.M, Caldwell, N., Powell, P. and Zheng, J. 2007 'Barriers to supply chain information integration: SMEs Adrift of E-Lands', *Journal of Operations Management*, 25: 1234–1254.

Harrison, A. and van Hoek, R. 2008 *Logistics Management and Strategy*, 3rd edn, Harlow: Pearson Education: 238.

Hughes, D. 1994 *Breaking with Tradition: Building Partnerships and Alliances in the European Food Industry*, Wye: Wye College Press.

Kambil, K. and Short, J.E. 1994 'Electronic integration and business network redesign: a roles-linkage perspective', *Journal of Management Information Systems* 10(4): 59–83.

Kanter, R.M. 2004 'How to evolve: Leading change in the digital age', Foreword in S. Tonchia and A. Tramontano, *Process Management for the Extended Enterprise*, Berlin-Heidelberg: Springer-Verlag.

Kaufman, P. 1999 'Food retailing consolidation: Implications for supply chain management practices', *Journal of Food Distribution Research*, 30(1): 6–11.

King, R.P. 2001 *The New Logistics*, Minnesota: The Retail Food Industry Center, University of Minnesota.

Lancioni, R., Smith, M. and Oliva, T. 2000 'The role of the Internet in supply chain management', *Industrial Marketing Management*, 29(1): 45–56.

Lung, Y. 2000 'Is the rise of emerging countries as automobile producers an irreversible phenomenon?', in J. Humphrey, Y. Lecler and M.S. Salerno, *Global Strategies and Local Realities: The Auto Industry in Emerging Markets*, London: Macmillan.

Matopoulos, A., V. Manthou, A. and Vlachopoulou, M. 2007 'Integrating supply chain operations in the internet era', *International Journal of Logistics Systems and Management*, 3(3): 305–14.

Mentzer, J.T., De Witt, W., Keebler, J.S., Min, S., Nix, N.W., Smith, C.D. and Zacharia, Z.G. 2001 'Defining supply chain management', *Journal of Business Logistics*, 22(2): 1–24.

Mossinkoff, M.R.H. 2006 'Implementation of web-based electronic data interchange in the apparel industry: Evidence from the Netherlands', *Proceedings of the International Conference of the International Foundation of Fashion and Textile Institutes (IFFTI)*.

Mukhopadhyay, T. and Kekre, S. 2002 'Strategic and operational benefits of electronic integration in B2B procurement processes', *Management Science*, 48: 1301–13.

Nagy, A. 'Collaboration and conflict in the electronic integration of supply networks', *Proceedings of the 39th Hawaii International Conference on System Sciences*: 1–10.

Neto, M.S. and Pires, S.R.I. 2005 'Production organization, performance and innovations on the supply chain management within the brazilian automotive industry', in P. Ketikidis and L. Koh (eds), *Proceedings of the 3rd International Workshop on Supply Chain Management and Information Systems*, Thessaloniki, Greece, 6–8 July: 101–10.

O'Callaghan, R., Kaufmann, P.J. and Kosynski, B.R. 1992 'Adoption correlates and share effects of electronic data interchange systems in marketing channels', *Journal of Marketing*, 56 (April): 45–56.

Pagell, M. 2004 'Understanding the factors that enable and inhibit the integration of operations, purchasing and logistics', *Journal of Operations Management*, 22: 459–87.

Palm, D. and Sihn, W. 2005 'Agility in the automotive supply chain', in P. Ketikidis and L. Koh (eds), *Proceedings of the 3rd International Workshop on Supply Chain Management and Information Systems*, Thessaloniki, Greece, 6–8 July:13–20.

Peters, L.-R.R. 2000 'Is EDI dead? The future of the internet in supply chain management', *Hospital Material Management Quarterly*, August: 42–7.

Poirier, C.C. and Quinn, F.J. 2003 'A survey of supply chain progress', *Supply Chain Management Review*, 7(5): 40–8.

Power, D. and Singh, P. 2007 'The e-integration dilemma: The linkages between internet technology application, trading partner relationships and structural change', *Journal of Operations Management*, 25: 1292–310.

Rosas-Vega, R. and Vokurka, R. 2000 'New product introduction delays in the computer industry', *Industrial Management and Data Systems*, 100(4): 157–63.

Ross, D.F. 1998 *Competing Through Supply Chain Management*, New York: Chapman and Hall.

Sainsbury 2002 'Food products to be developed on the internet', accessed 5 July 2002, <http://www.j-sainsbury.co.uk/index.asp?pageid=322&subsection= news_releases&Year=2002>

Sanders, N.R. 2005 'IT alignment in supply chain relationships: A study of supplier benefits', *Journal of Supply Chain Management*, Spring: 4–12.

Sethi, R., Pant, S. and Sethi, A. 2003 'Web-based product development systems integration and new product outcomes: A conceptual framework', *Journal of Product Innovation Management*, 20: 37–56.

Stevens, G.C. 1989 'Integrating the supply chain', *International Journal of Physical Distribution and Materials Management*, 8(8): 3–8.

Stock, G.N., Greis, N.P. and Kasarda, J.D. 1998 'Logistics strategy and structure: A conceptual framework', *International Journal of Operations and Production Management*, 18(1): 37–52.

Teng, S. and Jaramillo, H. 2006 'Integrating the US textile and apparel supply chain with small companies in South America', *Supply Chain Management: An International Journal*, 11(1): 44–55.

Towill, D.R., Childerhouse, P. and Disney, S.M. 2000 'Speeding up the progress curve towards effective supply chain management', *Supply Chain Management: an International Journal*, 5(3): 122–30.

Van der Vaart, T. and van Donk, D.P. 2008 'A critical review of survey-based research in supply chain integration', *International Journal of Production Economics*, 111: 42–55.

Walters, D. 2004 'A business model for the new economy', *International Journal of Physical Distribution and Logistics Management*, 34(3/4): 346–57.

Weber, M.M. and Cantamneni, S.P. 2002 'POS and EDI in retailing: An examination of underlying benefits and barriers', *Supply Chain Management: An International Journal*, 7(5): 311–17.

White, W.J., O'Connor, A.C. and Rowe, B.R. 2004 'Economic impact of inadequate infrastructure for supply chain integration', *Planning Report 04–2*, prepared for National Institute of Standards and Technology, US Department of Commerce.

Wolff, S. and Geiger, K. 2000 'The e-supply chain of the future in the automotive industry', white paper of SAP AG and the ZLU Logistics and Management Consulting.

Zaheer, A. and Venkatraman, N. 1994 'Determinants of electronic integration in the insurance industry: An empirical test', *Management Science* 40(5): 549–66.

13

Collaborative Cultural Space: Disciplines for Inter-Organizational Collaborative Learning Behaviour

Peter Y. T. Sun and Paul Childerhouse

Introduction

In the present environment of rapid change, organizations collaborate in order to rapidly deploy resources, and the extant literature acknowledges that increased inter-organizational learning is a beneficial consequence of such collaboration (Chen, Paulraj and Lado 2004, Simchi-Levi, Kaminsky and Simchi-Levi 2003). Such collaborative learning strengthens the development of joint capabilities (Lane and Lubatkin 1998, Lui and Ngo 2005, Selnes and Sallis 2003), provides a constant stream of innovation (Hall and Adriani 1998) and ensures a greater balance of bargaining power (Hall and Adriani 1998).

This chapter will provide the practitioner with guidance on the appropriate personnel to deploy in the boundary-spanning roles. Further, mechanisms to capture and disseminate new knowledge gained from the day-to-day inter-actions with such personnel are discussed. Researchers will benefit from the concise literature review of organizational learning in the context of supply chain management. More specifically, our proposed conceptual model highlights the key interactions and provides the reader with clear avenues of further research.

The type of collaboration in view is long term. The partners pool resources and activities in order to reach common goals, while maintaining their autonomy and independence (Grant and Baden-Fuller 2004). This type of collaboration is commonly seen in supply chains between customers and their suppliers, for example, between manufacturers and their key suppliers, an excellent example of this being Toyota's supplier association (Dyer and Nobeoka, 2000). Taking the organizational learning perspective, this chapter focuses on acquisition of new knowledge through interactive learning, which is aimed at enhancing partners' distinct and separately owned competencies (Grant and Baden-Fuller 2004). In taking this view, we exclude the possibility of partners moving upstream or downstream of the supply chain with a future competitive intent, as such an intent causes asymmetries in inter-organizational behaviours (e.g. Hamel 1991, Inkpen and Crossan

1995, Kale, Singh and Perlmutter 2000, Khanna, Gulati and Nohria 1998, Mody 1993).

Does this mean that asymmetric behaviours cannot occur in the view taken in this chapter? They can if there is the fear of loss of firm-specific knowledge. For example, in situations where a manufacturer deals with multiple suppliers for the same raw material, a supplier in the dyad can fear the transfer of knowledge to other suppliers by the manufacturer. This fear can give rise to protective strategies by the supplier, reducing collaborative learning (Simonin 1999).

While situating our discussion on such types of collaborations, this chapter explicitly focuses on the social arrangements and the interactive learning behaviours between boundary-spanning individuals, which is lacking in current literature (Sense and Clements 2006). We specifically look at key disciplines that would continue to encourage collaborative learning behaviours in such partnerships.

In the sections to follow, we first look at literature that discusses organizational factors that encourage collaborative learning. We then introduce the concept of a *collaborative cultural space* for the types of partnership that we intend to explore, and the disciplines that encourage collaborating learning in such a space.

Organizational factors affecting learning behaviour

What are the critical dimensions that affect learning behaviours? Larsson *et al.* (1998) suggest two dimensions that explain inter-organizational learning behaviours in a dyadic relationship: the level of *transparency*, which is a behavioural component; and the level of *receptivity*, which is a capability component. Partners can choose to be more or less transparent in their behaviour, for example, by withholding or diluting information transfer (Huber 1991), which has implications for learning. The capability to learn is the absorptive capacity of individuals to acquire, assimilate and exploit new sources of knowledge (Cohen and Levinthal 1990), and is dependent on the existence of some degree of prior knowledge.

Many studies have looked at organizational factors that influence learning and knowledge transfer. These organizational factors can be assumed to influence transparency and receptivity, although the direct link has not been explored. A brief review of the literature suggests eight broad categories of organizational factors: mutual goals; relationships; trust; common knowledge; interface facing systems and structures; learning intent; organizational culture; and asset specificity.

Inter-organizations having *mutual goals* and being involved in joint decision-making, where both partners' perspectives are equally considered, have been empirically established to give superior collaborative performance (e.g. Cachon and Lariviere 2001, Kim and Oh 2005).

Relationship between boundary-spanning actors, where there is greater awareness of each other's skills and capabilities, and opportunities exist to work together, enables collaborative learning behaviour (Dyer and Singh 1998, Hall and Adriani 1998, Lane and Lubatkin 1998).

However, such mutual goals and relationships are built on a foundation of *trust*. Trust is fundamental for effective dyadic relationships and is critical to the formation and continuation of collaborative learning behaviours (Bowersox, Closs and Cooper 2002, Handfield and Nichols 2002, Harrison and van Hoek 2005, Lui and Ngo 2005, Selnes and Sallis 2003). Inter-organizations that continuously collaborate can be considered as an ideal, at one end of a continuum. This end of the continuum is when organizations are in collaborative equilibrium, where the actions of each other reinforce the implicit and explicit collaborative guidelines (Lui and Ngo 2005). Inter-organizational trust has been empirically established to maintain such collaborative partner behaviours. It has been shown to encourage partners to consider others' economic and social well-being and refrain from negative reciprocal behaviours (Luo and Ngo 2005). However, Selnes and Sallis (2003) caution against high levels of trust between boundary-spanning individuals. High levels of trust can create situations where sensitive and negative information is not shared because it might hinder good relations, or it might create similarities in mental models that are counterproductive to creativity. At the other end of the continuum, there is complete avoidance between organizations in a dyadic relationship caused by the breakdown of trust. However, finding organizations that continuously operate in these two extremes is not common; what is commonly seen is organizations that operate between the extremes.

Common knowledge, or knowledge that overlaps (Carlile 2004, Dyer and Singh 1998), is a determinant of the receptivity of the partners. Zahra and George (2002) suggest that diverse new knowledge, although containing some extent of commonality with existing knowledge sources, is more easily received by the organization. The availability of common knowledge creates shared language, and helps actors to manage differences that may arise across the organizational boundaries (Lane and Lubaktin 1998, Mowery, Oxley and Silverman 1996).

Interface facing systems and structures are the IT systems as well as the implicit and explicit guidelines governing inter-organizational interactions. Malhotra, Gosain and El Sawy (2005) provide empirical evidence for the influence of interface facing IT systems on the learning behaviours of supply chains. An effective interface facing IT system reduces information load by effectively managing and transferring relevant information, creates a structure where common knowledge is well exploited and enables transfer and interpretation of rich information, all of which positively influence collaborative learning behaviour. Apart from IT-based interface systems, the implicit and explicit guidelines governing the interactions in the supply chain relationship are important (Luo 2002, Poppo and Zenger 2002). It is these guidelines that maintain the repetitive sequence of interactions creating a sense of equilibrium in the partnership (Lui and Ngo 2005).

The *learning intent* is the partners' explicit desire to learn from the partnership, and not to be focused narrowly on the tangible economic benefits that the partnership brings (Hamel 1991), as such a narrow focus can blind a partner to learning opportunities.

Studies have shown that a similarity in *organizational culture* can increase firms' cooperation and synergy, having a positive influence on organizational trust (Luo and Ngo 2005) and collaborative learning (Simonin 1999). The study by Lane and Lubatkin (1998) provides greater detail on how similarity of organizational cultures can positively influence inter-organizational learning behaviour. They empirically establish that inter-organizational learning can be enhanced if the two firms have similar knowledge-processing systems and similar dominant logic, increasing their capacity to assimilate and commercialize new learning. The knowledge-processing systems and dominant logic of the organization are formed by, and perpetuate, organizational culture.

The two organizational factors that are used as a proxy for the less visible knowledge-processing system are the compensation policies and the organizational structure. Organizations that have similar compensation policies may tend to have similar problem-solving and innovative abilities (Henderson and Cockburn 1994) and may tend to share similar risk behaviours, which explains why collaborative learning behaviour is easier between two such organizations. The organizational structure is the extent of formalization and centralization in their allocation of tasks and decision-making. Organizations that have similar organizational structure may exhibit similar learning behaviours, increasing their chances of collaborative learning.

Lane and Lubatkin (1998) (see also Simonin 1999) suggest that the dominant logic is the beliefs and preferences of the organization towards certain strategic orientation, nature of problems, size of projects and specific ways new information is viewed and processed. Similarity in such dominant logic aids in the exploitation of new learning, increasing the commercial potential for collaborative learning behaviours. A similar study by Inkpen and Crossan (1995) on North American-Japanese JVs comes to a similar conclusion. The differing perception of the partners on the way business is run (e.g. views on capital infusion), and dissimilarity on the tolerance of time-horizons for financial payback, hinder learning transfer to the JV parents.

Asset specificity (i.e. the extent of investment made that is specific only to the inter-firm partnership), increases interdependence between partners. This increase of interdependence is said to increase relational performance and hence stimulate greater relational learning (Selnes and Sallis 2003). Lui and Ngo (2005) conducted an action-packed research that looked at interactive partner behaviours. This study considered the roles that inter-organizational trust and similarities in firms (i.e. similarities of cultures) play in interactive learning behaviours, and how the asset specificity has a moderating relationship on these interactive behaviours.

Although studies in the extant literature deal with factors that influence collaborative learning behaviour, they have focused primarily on larger organizational factors, such as common goals; relational rents; joint decision-making; establishing proper forms of governance and IT systems; cultural similarities; and asset specificity. However, the day-to-day or operational interactions of the boundary-spanning individuals has not been given due consideration (Sense and Clement 2006). We suggest that this is critical as inter-organizational issues can start within the space of interactions of the boundary-spanning individuals and then escalate to the organizational level, with several twists added depending on the level of mutual trust. Such information contamination escalates to management, who are usually distant from operational involvement of the dyad. Their interpretation and corresponding action, if viewed negatively by their partner, can have a detrimental effect on future collaborative behaviour. There can also be situations where the boundary-spanning individuals work well together. However, any learning is confined within their space of interaction and not translated across the organizations. Management who are distant from the operations may not be aware of the informal learning taking place, and may make certain strategic decisions that destroy the efficiencies and learning gained. To explicitly focus research on this space of interaction, we introduce the concept of the *collaborative cultural space* (CCS)

In order to reinforce the concepts that would be discussed, we used some interview data collected by one of the authors with merchandizers in an apparel manufacturing organization (referred to as Unichela). Merchandizers are boundary-spanning individuals in the apparel manufacturing organization who coordinate with key retailers such as GAP, Nike, Marks and Spencer etc. Their role involves pricing of garments, ordering raw materials from fabric and trim suppliers (who are usually nominated by the major retailers) and monitoring and coordinating garment production and delivery.

Collaborative cultural space

The concept of CCS is similar to Nonaka and Konno's (1998) concept of 'ba', which is a 'shared space for emerging relationship' (p. 40). This shared space, which can be a combination of physical and virtual, as well as mental (Nonaka and Konno 1998), represents patterns of interactions among boundary-spanning individuals, and can endure over time. With proper ongoing disciplines, created and supported by the inter-organizations, this shared space can evolve into a context that harbours rich meaning (Walsh and Ungson 1991) and a forum where learning occurs and where new knowledge is created (Nonaka and Konno 1998).

An indirect support of this is seen in one hypothesis of Luo and Ngo (2005), which was not empirically supported in their study. Similarity of firm cultures was hypothesized by the authors to smooth temporary imbalances, share ambiguous information and not reciprocate in their behaviour towards each other. This hypothesis deals more with day-to-day ongoing boundary spanning interactions. However, this was not supported in their empirical findings. This suggests that it is not the larger organizational factors such as culture of the organizations that matter, but perhaps the *ba* where ongoing interactions take place.

How does the CCS originate? CCS originates through repetitive interactions between boundary-spanning individuals around a set of common work goals and objectives. These repetitive interactions can occur when dealing with boundary-specific operational issues, through telephone conversations, visits and face-to-face meetings. These repetitive interactions create shared language among the boundary-spanning individuals (Barker 1999) and, when enduring over time, would create common cognitive maps. Such common cognitive maps give rise to shared understanding with regards to the boundary operations, leading to implicit guidelines and more explicit control systems and processes (Laughlin 1991). The characteristics of CCS are identified and discussed below:

- It is a cultural space with a shared belief system between the boundary spanning individuals. As one merchandizer commented, 'We [referring to the CCS] have a great understanding when it comes to pricing a garment. We know the maximum reduction we can get off each other without adversely affecting our profit margins, and we always seem to go to our fabric and accessory suppliers with the same message in order to get further price reduction.'
- It is a space imbued with meaning and it preserves memory. Such memory is preserved in the cognition of boundary-spanning individuals, preserved in the interface facing implicit guidelines and the explicit systems and processes, and preserved in its culture (Selnes and Sallis 2003, Walsh and Ungson 1991). Selnes and Sallis (2003) propose a similar idea, describing this as relationship memory, where 'relationships develop idiosyncratic routines in the form of encoded formal and informal procedures and scripts for how the parties have learned to do things ... In customer–supplier relationships each party develops beliefs related to common frames of reference, norms and symbols, or what others [e.g. Walsh and Ungson 1991] refer to as culture' (p. 83). One merchandizer talked about the implicit guidelines that shaped their boundary spanning interaction, 'When we discuss garment pricing, we have unwritten rules regarding fabric and trim shrinkage and wastages depending on who the fabric and accessory suppliers are. These are accounted for as wastage or shrinkage factors in calculating garment pricing and placing purchase orders. We

do not always follow the shrinkage and wastage formulas that are there.' For this to occur, boundary-spanning individuals must be in their role for sufficient length of time.

• It has a distinct social identity of its own, which can impact on the boundary-spanning individuals in their operations. In many of the interviews we have had with the merchandizers, there was constant usage of the term 'we,' indicating their identification with a distinct boundary-spanning social group.

The way the CCS can impact on the boundary-spanning individuals depends on how the inter-organizations treat such roles. If the organization emphasizes and rewards individuals based on the performance outcome of their boundary-spanning roles, and membership in such a role is invariable over time, it is likely that such categorization gives meaning to the boundary-spanning individuals (Ellemers, Gilder and Haslam 2004). There would be a greater tendency for such individuals to identify with the CCS and compare themselves with other functions in the organization when it comes to boundary-sensitive operations (Ellemers, Gilder and Haslam 2004). One merchandizer, who works with the GAP account, described the frustration she felt in not getting on-time and accurate production figures from the Production department, 'I'm increasingly frustrated trying to work with Production. We [identifying herself with the CCS] get quantities from Production, but, when it comes to the final shipped quantity, there is almost 10 per cent–15 per cent discrepancy, causing havoc in the planned store deliveries.'

The extent of identification with the CCS is likely to be influenced by factors such as the status of the boundary-spanning role in the organization, the extent of the trusting relationship between boundary-spanning individuals and the individual's commitment to the role and the organization. Such issues have not been given due consideration in literature, especially from the perspective of inter-organizational collaborative learning.

The CCS shares conceptual affinity with communities of practice (COP). Wenger, McDermott and Snyder (2002, p. 4) defines a COP as 'groups of people who share a concern, a set of problems, or a passion about a topic, and who deepen their knowledge and expertise in this area by interacting on an ongoing basis (over a substantive timeframe)'. Such COP within an organization emerges more easily, as in the case of technical personnel (Brown and Duguid 1991). For such COP to emerge, there must be conditions in place such as a social group who share a common knowledge set, who are passionate about a shared objective or shared sets of problems, and whose interaction is constant and intense (Brown and Duguid 1991). However, there are challenges for such conditions to emerge between boundary-spanning individuals as they can be hindered by physical distance, by adversarial attitude, by limited interactions and by the temporal longevity of boundary-spanning individuals in their role. However, if disciplines are in place to ensure such conditions, a COP can emerge between boundary-spanning individuals (Sense and Clement 2006) and such COP gives rise to the CCS.

CCS is therefore a subcultural space where ongoing inter-firm interactions take place and it can overlap existing organizational cultures. In an ideal scenario, when there are similarities in organizational culture, the CCS need not be a separately fragmented subcultural space. It can seamlessly integrate with existing organizational cultures, increasing inter-firm cooperation and trust (Luo and Ngo 2005) and inter-organizational learning (e.g. Inkpen and Crossan 1995, Lane and Lubatkin 1998).

However, it is not always possible to find two organizations for an inter-firm partnership that share similar cultures, which are also strong in other necessary technical and structural criteria. Firms may not have much of a choice in choosing their partners based on cultural similarities. Such misfit of cultures has led to decreased receptivity towards new learning and knowledge (Lane and Lubatkin 1998), decreased organizational trust (Luo and Ngo 2005), and behaviour that began as collaboration moving towards avoidance or compromise (Larsson *et al.* 1998).

Such failures, we suggest, are because of a lack of practical as well as academic attention to the CCS. This requires academics and practitioners to move from 'hard systems thinking approach towards supply chains to one which focuses on the social arrangements/worlds between members in a supply chain' (Sense and Clements 2006: 6). CCS needs to be developed through proper disciplines and can be insulated, to some degree, from any negative effects of existing organizational cultures. We would attempt to elaborate on the disciplines that encourage collaborative learning behaviours in the section to follow.

Disciplines for collaborative learning behaviour in the CCS

The disciplines for collaborative learning behaviour must exist at all levels of learning: individual, group and organizational. Within CCS, learning occurs at the individual and group levels between the boundary-spanning individuals; however, this learning must also connect with the larger organizations to form a greater '*ba*' described by Nonaka and Konno (1998) as '*basho*' (p. 41). *Basho* is necessary for learning to be exploited and institutionalized at the organizational level, resulting in a tightening of supply chain partnership over time.

We suggest that the work of Senge (1990) on the five disciplines of a learning organization (i.e. mental model, personal mastery, team work, shared vision and systems thinking), provides a good framework of disciplines for boundary-spanning individuals working in the CCS. However, we add two more disciplines at the organizational level (i.e. senior management commitment and *basho* governance), needed to integrate with the larger

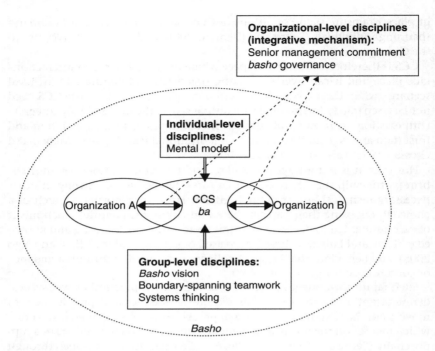

Figure 13.1   Basho and the key disciplines

organizations. These organizational-level disciplines come from Inkpen and Crossan's (1995) suggestions that leader and artefact integration is needed to facilitate integration with the larger organization. These are illustrated in Figure 13.1 above. Prior to the elaboration of the disciplines, a brief narrative of organizational learning and learning organization will be presented.

Organizational learning and learning organization

Some literature makes a distinction between organizational learning and the learning organization (e.g. Garvin 1993, Sun and Scott 2003, Tsang 1997), while others do not (e.g. Harvey and Denton 1999). In this chapter we take the former view, that organizational learning describes the socio-psychological processes of learning (e.g. Argyris and Schön 1978, Crossan, Lane and White 1999), while learning organization deals with prescriptions necessary for organizations that learn (e.g. Garvin 1993, Senge 1990). We now present the work of Crossan, Lane and White (1999) from organizational learning and Senge (1990) from the learning organization strands.

Crossan, Lane and White (1999)

Crossan and colleagues synthesize previous work and describe four socio-psychological processes of organizational learning spanning the individual, group and organizational levels: intuition, interpretation, integration and institutionalization.

Intuition is uniquely an individual process, happening in the subconscious, and involves some sort of pattern recognition. Behling and Eckel (1991) suggest two types of intuition. An expert intuition involves past pattern recognition, developed through many years of experience (Prietula and Simon 1989), while entrepreneurial intuition is the ability to make novel connections and discern new possibilities by breaking out of the constraining effect of the individual's cognitive framework or mental model. It is the entrepreneurial intuition that is more likely to initiate double-loop learning (Crossan, Lane and White 1999), which is learning that alters underlying beliefs and assumptions.

The process of *interpretation* focuses on the conscious element of learning, and is the process of ascribing language to what has been intuited. Individuals use metaphors to evolve, and make explicit, their entrepreneurial intuition, in order to achieve a shared interpretation with the group (Crossan, Lane and White 1999, Nonaka 1994). This occurs through a process of dialogue, where the cognitive map or the mental model of the individual is both influenced by, and influences, the domain or the environment where the process takes place (Crossan, Lane and White 1999, Isaacs 1993). Interpretation is, therefore, a process that moves beyond the individual and becomes more embedded in group work (Crossan, Lane and White 1999).

While interpreting is the process of making the preverbal intuition more verbal, the process of *integration* focuses on developing a new shared understanding, resulting in a collective and coherent action by the group. The process of integration is crucial, as it is the bridge that translates the shared understanding from the group level to the organizational level (Crossan, Lane and White 1999, Vera and Crossan 2004).

Institutionalization is when a new shared understanding develops across the organization and the underlying beliefs and assumptions of the organization change. The new behaviours must be institutionalized or embedded into systems, structures, routines and practices (Crossan, Lane and White 1999, Levitt and March 1988). This institutionalization process takes place uniquely at the organizational level.

The socio-psychological learning processes of intuition, interpretation, integration and institutionalization describe the feed forward learning flow of the organization from the individual to the organizational levels (Crossan, Lane and White 1999). However, due to barriers in the feed forward learning transfer (Sun, Scott and McKie 2005), stocks of learning can be built at the individual and group levels (Bontis, Crossan and Hulland 2002). In this chapter, learning stock is narrowly defined as the accumulated amount of learning. For example, capable individuals in the organization can be effective with the socio-psychological learning processes of intuition and interpretation, increasing individual-level learning stock. However, due to poor teamwork and an insular organizational culture, learning would remain largely at the individual level. Similarly, organizations may have good teamwork, increasing the stock of learning at the group level. However, an insular organizational culture can prevent learning being transferred to the organization. Therefore, stocks of learning can be built at the individual and group levels with little transfer to the organizational level, de-motivating individuals and adversely affecting business performance in the longer term (Bontis, Crossan and Hulland 2002).

Senge (1990)

Learning organization (LO) was popularized by Senge (1990) with his book *The Fifth Discipline: The Art and Practice of the Learning Organization*. Senge (1990) suggests five disciplines of LO: team learning, mental model, personal mastery, shared vision and systems thinking.

Team learning places emphasis on social relationships. It is through the foundation of good social relationships that dialogue takes place, involving a process of reflection and enquiry. Through dialogue, deeply held beliefs and assumptions can surface and the *mental models* can be reframed (Isaacs 1993). This is referred to as generative learning (Senge 1990) or double-loop learning (Argyris 2004). However, when this transition does not occur, learning results in the beliefs and assumptions remaining unchanged. This type of learning is adaptive learning (Senge 1990) or single-loop learning (Argyris 2004).

Personal mastery, shared vision and systems thinking could be viewed as resources necessary for learning. *Personal mastery* is the individual's ability to continuously develop his or her own capacity to learn, and is a catalyst in the continuous attempt to reframe the mental model. *Shared vision* is an organizational resource, whereby individuals in teamwork share an image of the future they wish to create. The primary purpose of the shared vision is to build a sense of commitment and common direction. *Systems thinking* is considered as the discipline that binds all the other disciplines together. It is the understanding of how a change can affect the intricate inter-relationships of the system as a whole.

These five disciplines are inherently considered as the levels of learning. Personal mastery and mental models are at the individual level, team learning and shared vision are at the group level, while systems thinking is at the organizational level.

The four socio-psychological processes of intuition, interpretation, integration and institutionalization can be used to explain learning at the boundary-spanning interfaces and its integration with the larger organization. Proper learning organization disciplines would ensure ongoing collaborative learning behaviour. We expand the framework presented in Figure 13.1 and consider the interaction of CCS with one partner firm (the interaction of CCS with the other partner firm is the mirror image). This is illustrated in

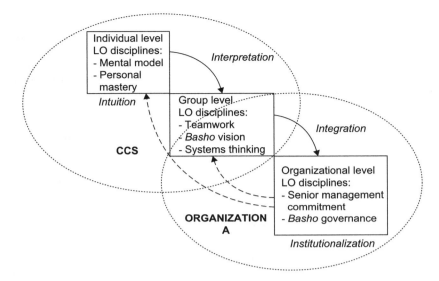

Figure 13.2   Interaction of CCS with one partner firm

Figure 13.2. We now discuss learning within the CCS at the individual, group and organizational levels.

CCS: individual-level learning

Due to the difficulty that exists in building partnerships with customers and suppliers, literature has discussed the importance of selecting the right partners (e.g. Das and Teng 2003, Saxton 1997). However, literature has paid little attention to selecting the right type of individuals for playing the boundary-spanning role. In Unichela, the overriding criterion in selecting merchandizers is the capability to communicate. Although this is a critical capability, the mental model and the personal mastery are important individual disciplines for boundary-spanning individuals (Senge 1990).

Mental models or cognitive maps are the worldviews of the individuals (Kim 1993). They act as a lens where certain external knowledge and information is privileged and therefore acquired (Cohen and Levinthal 1990, Zahra and George 2002), and also act as filters in processing and interpreting external knowledge and information (Senge 1990). Individuals form multiple cognitive maps through multiple experiences, and such cognitive maps act as efficient filtering and processing systems in dealing with myriad information.

However, mental models can be counterproductive if they are ingrained, so that the individual is unable to suspend their beliefs and assumptions in dealing with contradictory knowledge and information. As a result, any learning stays within the prevailing beliefs and assumptions of the individual and is referred to as single loop (Argyris and Schön 1978) or adaptive (Senge, 1990). Having individuals who possess entrepreneurial intuition as receptors to the external environment helps organizations go beyond adaptive learning (Crossan, Lane and White 1999). Such individuals possess more complex forms of cognitive processing (Hale and Jansen 1994), they tend to violate the given beliefs and assumptions and come up with frame-breaking insights (Tierney, Farmer and Graen 1999). They generally seek unfamiliar situations to access new and diverse experiences (Feist 1999). Therefore, the diversity of individuals' backgrounds and knowledge, coupled with their innovative characteristics, enables them to make novel associations and linkages.

Such a type of individual, we argue, is critical for the boundary-spanning role for two reasons. First, working across boundaries presents opportunities to access differentiated knowledge and information, which is often the source of new learning (Carlile 2004). Within the CCS, actors from across organizational boundaries would possess their unique domain-specific knowledge and hence difference or novelty exists at the boundary. However, due to continuous interactions between boundary-spanning actors and the development of shared understanding within the CCS, the actors develop a degree of common knowledge and shared language, which would help in the interpretation of such domain-specific knowledge (Carlile 2004, Cohen and Levinthal 1990), potentially generating many new insights.

Second, cultural differences between the organizations, especially with regards to knowledge management, can pose significant barriers to learning (Inkpen and Crossan 1995). For example, if one organization focuses on 'know-what' or explicit knowledge with focus on codifying such knowledge (Hansen, Nohria and Tierney 1999), while the other organization focuses on 'know-how' or tacit knowledge, with socialization as the means of managing knowledge, the differences in such knowledge focus can be a hindrance to learning (Inkpen and Crossan 1995). However, by being able to suspend beliefs and assumptions (i.e. mental model) about what constitutes valid knowledge, differences can be negotiated within the CCS and learning is enhanced.

Personal mastery is another individual discipline that is useful in negotiating such differences within the CCS. While the mental model deals primarily with the cognitive aspect of learning, personal mastery influences the behavioural aspect of learning. An individual with personal mastery would be more disposed to seeing areas of weakness in their work, more aware of critical issues and have a desire to learn and grow (Senge 1990). Even if discrepancies in mental models hinder initial change in cognition, such an individual would be willing to experiment, and through experiential learning a change in cognition can eventually occur (Inkpen and Crossan 1995).

Therefore, the two disciplines of mental model and personal mastery would enable boundary-spanning individuals to potentially generate many new insights for their respective organizations, insights that are able to break out of the traditional mindsets of the organizations, thus enriching the individual-level learning stock. Bontis, Crossan and Hulland (2002) empirically established that such individual-level learning stock has the potential for improving business performance if acted upon. Therefore:

Proposition 1: Having the disciplines of mental model and personal mastery for boundary-spanning individuals operating in the CCS increases the individual-level learning stock.

CCS: group-level learning

Although Proposition 1 above suggests the generation of many new frame-breaking insights at the individual level, such insights need to be interpreted and understood in the context of the collaboration (especially if they have inter-firm implications). This necessitates the boundary-spanning individuals to work together as a team within the CCS to interpret the many insights that originate at the individual level.

Effective teamwork requires dialogue, where individuals are able to expose their mental model and subject it to scrutiny and debate (Senge 1990). Such a process of reframing a mental model can be heated, with emotions of individuals involved (Isaacs 1993), and requires a foundation of trust and positive emotional engagement between individuals in the team (Druskatt and Wolff 2001, Isaacs 1993). Trust is often developed in the CCS by frequent visits, joint vendor summits and seminars, which we noticed in Unichela, and day-to-day interactions that reinforce trusting behaviour.

Although physical face-to-face interactions in teamwork facilitate dialogue, such interactions are not as common between boundary-spanning individuals, who are often physically distant from each other. However, technology-assisted communication is available to facilitate communication between boundary-spanning individuals. For the process of dialogue, where messages can be equivocal at first and knowledge sharing is complex, a technology-assisted rich media source, such as video conferencing, is necessary where face-to-face interaction is facilitated and allows for immediate feedback (Murray and Peyrefitte 2007).

However, such interactions must be supported by the disciplines of systems thinking. Systems thinking requires boundary-spanning individuals in the team to understand the complex interdependencies of the system as a whole and the implications created by any new learning (Senge 1990). For example, certain actions when implemented would create a self-reinforcing loop, when productive could be virtuous and when counterproductive could be vicious (Senge 1990). This was evidenced in one merchandizer, who gave a good example of a vicious self-reinforcing loop:

When we squeeze our suppliers to reduce fabric price, it is counterproductive for us, as in the end it costs us more. The more we squeeze prices, the less stringent the fabric mill becomes in quality assurance. For example, the fabric mill is supposed to do a physical inspection of the fabric rolls. To reduce costs, they would use less manpower to do the test on the inspection machine and run the machine much faster. This would result in some physical defects on the fabric not being caught. At the end, we suffer.

The CCS is, therefore, a forum where the boundary-spanning individuals develop a degree of common knowledge and shared language, especially with regards to each other's operations, and would be the platform to expand systems thinking from organizational to inter-organizational. It is a forum where the boundary-spanning individuals come to understand each other's idiosyncrasies and nuances. The understanding of systems implications would enrich the interpretation and solution-finding process, and would minimize future implementation barriers.

In such face-to-face interactions between boundary-spanning individuals, whether physical or technologically assisted, there is the possibility of identity clash (i.e. 'them' versus 'us'). Such identity clash can be minimized in the CCS by embracing a shared *basho* vision, which is a positive motivational factor to increase collaborative learning behaviour. For this, the *basho* vision must encompass a scope beyond mere economics or profit maximization; it should be broad enough to induce a collaborative commitment to learn, and must be part and parcel of the shared vision of the organization. The shared vision of Unichela is an excellent example of this *basho* vision: 'We are committed to striving for excellence, to be world class in apparel manufacturing, and we would achieve this by collaborating with our valued partners.'

What impact does the *basho* vision have for the organization? When such a *basho* vision is engaged for a period of time, it can give an organization multiple identities. As in the case of Unichela, it has an identity of a world-class lingerie apparel manufacturer, and a separate identity of being successful in partnerships and collaborations. When we interviewed one of their partners and asked what made them collaborate with Unichela, the response was that they could be trusted as partners. Apart from being known as an excellent lingerie manufacturer, Unichela was also known in the industry for their success in collaborative partnerships. Such an organization is said to be ideographic (Albert and Whetten 1985, Pratt and Foreman 2000).

Such multiple identities impact on boundary-spanning individuals in their teamwork within the CCS. While the identity of the CCS are more salient to the boundary-spanning individuals in their day-to-day boundary-spanning interactions (Pratt and Foreman 2000), they are also able to simultaneously identify with their larger respective organizations. This brings greater synergy between the identities and ensures that the decisions made are productive for all parties concerned. They are able to reconcile the economic and social well-being of their partners as well as their respective organizations, and minimize self-seeking identity clashes. This facilitates the socio-psychological process of integration and a shared understanding is more easily evolved between the boundary-spanning individuals.

Therefore, it can be argued that the disciplines of team learning, systems thinking and *basho* vision facilitate the group dynamics within the CCS and the development of shared understanding. This enables the individual insights to be richly interpreted, and shared understanding to be reached for new learning, enriching the group-level learning stock. Therefore:

Proposition 2: Having the disciplines of teamwork, systems thinking and basho *vision increases the group-level learning stock of the CCS.*

CCS: organizational-level learning

Group-level learning stock must transfer to the organizational level in order to enhance separately owned organizational competencies. For this transfer to take place, organizational-level disciplines are needed as integrative mechanisms.

An important issue arising from transfer of learning is the acceptance that such a learning transfer can enhance the competency of the organization. Often the transfer can be hindered by a 'not invented here' attitude. This poses a challenge in trying to escalate the shared understanding that is developed within the CCS around the new learning to the wider organization. This escalation of shared understanding from the CCS to the organization level requires the socio-psychological learning process of integration. Organizational leadership plays a crucial role in this socio-psychological process of integration and is therefore an important integrative mechanism (Inkpen and Crossan 1995).

Senior management commitment is an important leadership discipline needed to provide this integrative mechanism. Senior management commitment comes in two forms: cognitively, to develop receptivity towards new learning; and behaviourally, to dismantle formal as well as informal protective barriers that arise.

No new learning at the organizational level can occur if management's existing beliefs are ingrained. Such strong ingraining can result in organizational defensive routines that prevent questioning of established systems and processes (Argyris 2004). Therefore, it is important that senior management are receptive to new ideas, and inculcate a more open organizational culture (Steiner 1998, Watkins and Marsick 1996). While being cognitively receptive to new learning, management must also dismantle barriers that impede a new shared understanding developing across the organization. For this, management must have the discipline of reaching across hierarchies and interacting with the middle- and lower-level management, in order to challenge existing ingrained beliefs, dismantle any concerns for the new learning and connect the new learning with the *basho* vision of the organization. Vera and Crossan (2004) suggest that transformational leadership style is better able to work with such leadership disciplines, as such a style of leadership is usually inspirational, questions existing beliefs and leads through enthusiasm and vision.

An important prerequisite in collaborative learning is that such learning enhances the joint performance of the organizations. However, there is the tendency for the individuals/departments to maximize their own benefit at the expense of joint collaborative performance (Kim and Oh 2005), hindering learning transfer. Such tendencies can happen intentionally or unintentionally. Intentionally, learning transfer can be hindered if such learning affects performance parameters of some individual/department within the organization. For example, in Unichela there was the suggestion by the merchandizers to set up a rapid-response team dedicated to manufacturing garment orders involving smaller quantities. Such a rapid-response team was to be set up using the Japanese Toyota Production System. However, small orders affected manufacturing efficiency and therefore the effective production time was reduced. This was never viewed positively by the manufacturing department. This was a major barrier in learning transfer and the project did not successfully get off the ground. Barriers can also be raised unintentionally. Such unintentional barriers may arise if one party is not aware of the overall positive implication the learning has for the joint collaborative performance. To overcome such barriers, we suggest the implementation of *basho* governance as an important organizational-level discipline.

Such governance, we suggest, must incorporate two disciplines: *basho* organizational performance measures; and joint decision-making. A *basho* organizational performance measure considers the collaborative nature of the organization. To implement such a measure, we suggest that the inter-organizations embrace common sets of measures aligned with the overall objectives and purpose of the organization. Such measures must be an important constituent of the overall sets of organizational performance measures, and must influence the reward and recognition of individuals within the organization. With the saying 'What gets measured gets done', such *basho* organizational performance measures can facilitate collaborative behaviour and learning transfer to the organizational level.

However, such *basho* organizational performance measures must be supported by the discipline of joint decision-making (Kim and Oh 2005). Leadership of the organizations must set up explicit guidelines for joint decision-making between the partners. Such joint decision-making should not be only restricted to strategic-level decision-making, but also the more operational-level decision-making. The guidelines act as a guiding mechanism that prompts the boundary-spanning individuals, as well as others within the organization, when to consult their partners for a decision to be made. However, such explicit guidelines must be flexible and allowed to change as demands of the end customers evolve. Joint decision-making, when successfully implemented, tends to improve trust between organizations and improve information transparency across the organizational boundaries. Such increase in trust and information transparency inhibits any intentional or unintentional tendency to maximize benefit for self, and would facilitate transfer of learning to the organizational level. Therefore:

Proposition 3: The organizational-level disciplines of senior management commitment and basho *governance increases the learning transfer from CCS to the organizational level.*

What happens if there is a lack of such organizational level discipline as suggested above? In such situations, the boundary-spanning individuals within the CCS would evolve their own sets of implicit guidelines, or 'ways of working', in response to individual- and group-level learning, as long as such 'ways of working' do not impact on the systems and processes of the larger organization. They would find ways around the current limitations of their organization, increasing the number of non-documented guidelines. However, such a scenario can be detrimental to the organization, especially when the boundary-spanning individuals are changed or leave their role. Valuable tacit knowledge gained can be potentially lost. Therefore:

Proposition 3a: The absence of organizational-level disciplines increases implicit and non-documented guidelines within the CCS.

Dependence and complexity: moderating learning stocks

We suggest the extent of dependence between the partners and rate of change of the external environment as moderating the extent of individual, group and organizational levels of learning.

Greater dependency increases the need for boundary-spanning individuals, as well as the larger organization, to take each other's action into account. However, because of imperfect knowledge between actors across the organizational boundaries, increased dependency can increase the complexity at the organizational boundary (Carlile 2004). This is compounded when there are rapid changes in the external environment. Such rapid environment change would make existing knowledge less relevant, creating knowledge ambiguity (Simonin 1999) and further increasing complexity at the organizational boundary (Carlile 2004). Such factors would tend to increase the survival anxiety of the organization (Schein 1993), inducing greater learning in collaborative behaviour (Carlile 2004, Selnes and Sallis 2003). Therefore:

Proposition 4: The extent of dependence between the inter-organizations and the rate of change of the external environment moderates the individual-, group- and organizational-level learning stocks.

Conclusions

The extant literature on supply chain collaboration has looked at larger organizational factors such as common goals, relational rents, joint decision-making, establishing proper forms of governance and IT systems, cultural similarities and asset specificity. Such factors do not consider the social arrangements between boundary-spanning employees (Sense and Clements 2006). Research, and indeed most organizations, is not fully exploiting the learning opportunities from boundary-spanning employees. New knowledge created through the operational interactions of the boundary-spanning individuals is typically overlooked and lost. When the boundary-spanning individuals behave in a transparent and receptive manner, a positive collaborative cultural space (CCS) is created. The review of the literature, plus our case example, has illustrated how this space can yield significant inter-organizational learning and new knowledge to both parties.

A thorough review of the organizational learning literature, in the context of supply chain management, has led to the identification of seven disciplines to maximize the new knowledge created in the CCS. Individuals with entrepreneurial intuition and personal mastery are most suitable for the boundary-spanning roles in order to enhance new knowledge creation. New insights can then be captured and disseminated to the group and then wider organization through a *basho* vision and performance measurement system. The *basho* vision creates a dual identity, where the welfare of the partnership and the larger organization seamlessly merge, and enhance group dynamics within the CCS. A *basho* organizational performance measurement system would then facilitate shared inter-organizational measures, which are interwoven with the rest of the organizational objectives.

This chapter provides multiple avenues for further research. First, by proposing the concept of the CCS, more research is needed to delineate this space. Second, longitudinal studies can be conducted to analyze the formation of such a space, what factors influence and impact on the space and how such a space can impact on (or be impacted by) the larger organizational culture. Third, the set of propositions that we give in this chapter, suggesting how the seven disciplines can impact collaborative learning, needs to be empirically tested and verified.

References

Albert, S. and Whetten, D. 1985 'Organizational identity', *Research in Organizational Behavior*, 7: 263–95.

Argyris, C. C. 2004 *Reasons and Rationalizations: The Limits to Organizational Knowledge*, Oxford: Oxford University Press.

Argyris, C. and Schön, D.A. 1978 *Organizational Learning: A Theory of Action Perspective*, Reading, MA: Addison-Wesley.

Barker, J.R. 1999 *The Discipline of Teamwork: Participation and Concertive Control*, Thousand Oaks, CA: Sage.

Behling, O. and Eckel, N. 1991 'Making sense out of intuition', *Academy of Management Executive*, 5: 46–54.

Bontis, N., Crossan, M.M. and Hulland, J. 2002 'Managing an organizational learning system by aligning stocks and flows', *Journal of Management Studies*, 39: 437–69.

Bowersox, D.J., Closs, D.J. and Cooper, M.B. 2002 *Supply Chain Logistics Management*, Boston: McGraw-Hill.

Brown, J.S. and Duguid, P. 1991 'Organizational learning and communities-of-practice; Toward a unified view of working, learning and innovation', *Organization Science*, 2: 40–57.

Cachon, G.P. and Lariviere, M.A. 2001 'Contracting to assure supply: How to share demand forecasts in a supply chain', *Management Science*, 47(5): 629–46.

Carlile, P.R. 2004 'Transferring, translating, and transforming: An integrative framework for managing knowledge across boundaries', *Organization Science*, 15: 555–68.

Chen, I.J., Paulraj, A. and Lado, A.A. 2004 'Strategic purchasing, supply management, and firm performance', *Journal of Operations Management*, 22: 459–87.

Cohen, W. and Levinthal, D. 1990 'Absorptive capacity: A new perspective on learning and innovation', *Administrative Science Quarterly*, 35: 128–52.

Crossan, M.M., Lane, H.W. and White, R.E. 1999 'An organizational learning framework: From intuition to institution', *Academy of Management Review*, 24: 522–37.

Das, T.K. and Teng, B.S. 2003 'Partner analysis and alliance performance', *Scandinavian Journal of Management*, 19: 279–308.

Druskatt, V.U. and Wolff, S.B. 2001 'Building the emotional intelligence of groups', *Harvard Business Review*, 79: 81–90.

Dyer, J.H. and Nobeoka, K. 2000 'Creating and managing a high-performance knowledge-sharing network: the Toyota case', *Strategic Management Journal*, 21(3): 345–67.

Dyer, J.H. and Singh, H. 1998 'The relational view: Cooperative strategy and sources of interorganizational competitive advantage', *Academy of Management Review*, 23: 660–79.

Ellemers, N., Gilder, D.D. and Haslam, S.A. 2004 'Motivating individuals and groups at work: A social identity perspective on leadership and group performance', *Academy of Management Review*, 29: 459–78.

Feist, G.J. 1999 'The influence of personality on artistic and scientific creativity', in R. Sternberg (ed.), *Handbook of Creativity*, New York: Cambridge University Press.

Garvin, D.A. 1993 'Building a learning organization', *Harvard Business Review*, 71: 78–91.

Grant, R.M. and Baden-Fuller, C. 2004 'A knowledge accessing theory of strategic alliances', *Journal of Management Studies*, 41: 61–84.

Hale, S. and Jansen, J. 1994 'Global processing-time coefficients characterize individual and group differences in cognitive speed', *Psychological Science*, 5: 384–9.

Hall, R. and Adriani, P. 1998 'Management focus: Analyzing intangible resources and managing knowledge in supply chain context', *European Management Journal*, 16: 685–97.

Hamel, G. 1991 'Competition for competence and inter-partner learning within international strategic alliances', *Strategic Management Journal*, 12: 83–103.

Handfield, R.B. and Nichols Jr, E.L. 2002 *Supply Chain Redesign: Transforming Supply Chains into Integrated Value Systems*, Upper Saddle River, NJ: Prentice Hall.

Hansen, M., Nohria, N. and Tierney, T. 1999 'What's your strategy for managing knowledge?', *Harvard Business Review*, 77: 106–16.

Harrison, A. and van Hoek, R. 2005 *Logistics Management and Strategy*, 2nd edn, Harlow: Prentice Hall.

Harvey, C. and Denton, J. 1999 'To come of age: The antecedents of organizational learning', *Journal of Management Studies*, 36: 897–918.

Henderson, R.M. and Cockburn, I. 1994 'Measuring competence? Exploring firm effects in pharmaceutical research', *Strategic Management Journal*, 15: 63–84.

Huber, G.P. 1991 'The contributing processes and the literatures', *Organization Science*, 2: 88–115.

Inkpen, A.C. and Crossan, M.M. 1995 'Believing is seeing: Joint ventures and organization learning', *Journal of Management Studies*, 32: 595–618.

Isaacs, W.H. 1993 'Dialogue, collective thinking, and organizational learning', *Organizational Dynamics*, 22: 24–39.

Kale, P., Singh, H. and Perlmutter, H. 2000 'Learning and protection of propriety assets in strategic alliances: Building relational capital', *Strategic Management Journal*, 21: 217–37.

Khanna, T., Gulati, R. and Nohria, N. 1998 'The dynamics of learning alliances: Competition, cooperation and relative scope', *Strategic Management Journal*, 19: 193–210.

Kim, B. and Oh, H. 2005 'The impact of decision-making sharing between supplier and manufacturer on their collaboration performance', *Supply Chain Management: An International Journal*, 10: 223–36.

Kim, D.H. 1993 'The link between individual and organizational learning', *Sloan Management Review*, 35: 37–50.

Lane, P.J. and Lubatkin, M. 1998 'Relative absorptive capacity and inter-organizational learning', *Strategic Management Journal*, 19: 461–77.

Larsson, R., Bengtsson, L., Henriksson, K. and Sparks, J. 1998 'The interorganizational learning dilemma: Collective knowledge development in strategic alliances', *Organization Science*, 9: 285–305.

Laughlin, R.C. 1991 'Environmental disturbances and organizational transitions and transformations: Some alternative models', *Organization Studies*, 12: 209–32.

Levitt, B. and March, J.G. 1988 'Organizational learning', *Annual Review of Sociology*, 14: 319–40.

Lui, S.S. and Ngo, H. 2005 'An action pattern model of inter-firm cooperation" *Journal of Management Studies*, 42: 1123–53.

Luo, Y. 2002 'Contract, cooperation, and performance in international joint ventures', *Strategic Management Journal*, 23: 903–19.

Malhotra, A., Gosain, S. and El Sawy, O.A. 2005 'Absorptive capacity configurations in supply chains: Gearing for partner-enabled market knowledge creation', *MIS Quarterly*, 29: 145–87.

Mody, A. 1993 'Learning through alliances', *Journal of Economic Behaviour and Organization*, 20: 151–170.

Mowery, D.C., Oxley, J.E. and Silverman, B.S. 1996 'Strategic alliances and interfirm knowledge transfer', *Strategic Management Journal*, 17: 77–91.

Murray, S.R. and Peyrefitte, J. 2007 'Knowledge type and communication media choice in the knowledge transfer process', *Journal of Management Inquiry*, 19: 111–33.

Nonaka, I. 1994 'A dynamic theory of organizational knowledge creation', *Organization Science*, 5: 14–37.

Nonaka, I. and Konno, N. 1998 'The concept of "ba": Building a foundation for knowledge creation', *California Management Review*, 40: 40–54.

Poppo, L. and Zenger, T. 2002 'Do formal contracts and relational governance function as substitutes or components?', *Strategic Management Journal*, 23: 707–25.

Pratt, M.G. and Foreman, P.O. 2000 'Classifying managerial responses to multiple organizational identities', *Academy of Management Review*, 25: 18–43.

Prietula, M.J. and Simon, H.A. 1989 'The experts in your midst', *Harvard Business Review*, 67: 120–4.

Saxton, T. 1997 'The effect of partner and relationship characteristics on alliance outcomes', *Academy of Management Journal*, 40: 443–61.

Schein, E.H. 1993 'How can organizations learn faster? The challenge of entering the green room', *Sloan Management Review*, 34: 85–92.

Selnes, F. and Sallis, J. 2003 'Promoting relationship learning', *Journal of Marketing*, 67: 80–95.

Senge, P. 1990 *The Fifth Discipline: The Art and Practice of the Learning Organization*, New York: Doubleday/Currency.

Sense, A.J. and Clements, M.D.J. 2006 'Ever consider a supply chain as a "community of practice"? Embracing a learning perspective to build supply chain integration', *Development and Learning in Organizations*, 20: 6–8.

Simchi-Levi, D., Kaminsky, P. and Simchi-Levi, E. 2003 *Designing and Managing the Supply Chain: Concepts, Strategies, and Case Studies*, 2nd edn, Boston: McGraw-Hill.

Simonin, B.L. 1999 'Ambiguity and the process of knowledge transfer in strategic alliances', *Strategic Management Journal*, 20: 595–623.

Steiner, L. 1998 'Organizational dilemmas as barriers to learning', *Learning Organization*, 5: 193–201.

Sun, P.Y.T. and Scott, J.L. 2003 'Exploring the divide: Organizational learning and learning organization', *Learning Organization*, 10: 202–15.

Sun, P.Y.T., Scott, J.L. and McKie, D. 2005 'Reframing and engaging with organizational learning constraints', in A. Rahim and R.T Golembiewski (eds), *Current Topics in Management (Vol. 10)*, New Jersey: Transaction: 51–76.

Tierney, P., Farmer, S.M. and Graen, G.B. 1999 'An examination of leadership and employee creativity: The relevance of traits and relationships', *Personnel Psychology*, 52: 591–620.

Tsang, E.W.K. 1997 'Organizational learning and the learning organization: A dichotomy between descriptive and prescriptive research', *Human Relations*, 50: 73–89.

Vera, D. and Crossan, M.M. 2004 'Strategic leadership and organizational learning', *Academy of Management Review*, 29: 222–40.

Walsh, J.P. and Ungson, G. 1991 'Organizational memory', *Academy of Management Review*, 16: 57–91.

Watkins, K.E. and Marsick, V.J. 1996 *In Action: Creating the Learning Organization*, Alexandria, GA: American Society for Training and Development.

Wenger, E., McDermott, R. and Snyder, W.M. 2002 *Cultivating Communities of Practice: A Guide to Managing Knowledge*. Boston, MA: Harvard Business School Press.

Zahra, S.A. and George, G. 2002 'Absorptive capacity: A review, reconceptualization, and extension', *Academy of Management Review*, 27: 185–203.

14

Innovative Information and Communication Technology for Logistics: The Case of Road Transportation Feeding Port Operations and Direct Short Range Communication Technology

Adrian E. Coronado Mondragon, Etienne S. Coronado Mondragon and Christian E. Coronado Mondragon

Introduction

In the 21st century, logistics has emerged as a leading and complex field. Logistics deals with everything involving planning, organizing and managing activities that provides goods or services (Logistics World 1997). Main factors that have contributed to the emergence and complexity of logistics include: globalization, outsourcing, contract manufacturing, shortened product life cycles, pressure to reduce carbon-emissions, multichannel distribution and the need for adequate return channels.

Information and communication technology (ICT) plays a key role in managing today's logistics operations. For example, data availability has become a principal element to the responsiveness of an organization. Therefore the supply chain and its associated logistics operations have become 100 per cent dependent on ICT, both at the intra-organizational and inter-organizational levels. ICT has made it possible to build communication links between enterprises and for many organizations around the world the global, web-linked environment of today has emphasized the importance of ICT in logistics.

ICT has become a visible element of the required infrastructure of companies, regions and nations. Today, ICT is at the same level of importance as traditional infrastructure developed to provide essential functions to society and the economy such as transportation, water and energy. Moreover, the interaction of different actors and networks is dependent on the state of the ICT infrastructure. Hence, an ICT infrastructure in optimal conditions is key to facilitate the development of economic activities.

In recent times, governments and private organizations all over the world have come across rejuvenation and business plans where infrastructure is a major component, and ICT is no exception. For example, in Northern Europe, the European Commission in 2007 (Motorways of the Sea 2007) recognized the importance of short sea routes between neighbouring countries; these routes offer high quality regular services that can be combined with other transport modes to provide efficient alternatives. According to the European Commission, these efficient alternatives involve principal infrastructure elements such as port infrastructures, infrastructures for direct land and sea access, as well as facilities comprising electronic logistics management systems, facilities to ensure and enhance safety and security and facilities to simplify administrative and custom procedures.

The widespread recognition of ICT as an important element of the infrastructure required to support complex supply chain management and logistics operations has motivated investigating new solutions and tools in the form of innovative developments that will be able to overcome the limitations of the technology associated with solutions currently in use. On the other hand, new solutions based on innovative ICT have to be able to guarantee meeting the changing needs of organizations.

This chapter includes a brief summary of ICT developments in supply chain management/logistics. Then, it introduces particular supply chain/logistics arrangements in the form of road transport feeding port operations and, more specifically, the case of finished vehicle logistics. Direct short range communication (DSRC) technology is presented as an innovative ICT technology capable of meeting the specific requirements associated with road transportation feeding port operations. That is followed by the implications of the technology in terms of visibility in the supply chain and its impact on logistics. Conclusions on innovative ICT and its role in the infrastructure required to support logistics and supply chain management appear at the end of the chapter.

ICT developments that have impacted supply chain management and logistics

The last decade of the 20th century witnessed the development of software based on object-oriented technology, as well the widespread use of applications and technologies related to operational modelling, enterprise integration, intelligent sensors, active agents, virtual reality, advanced process control, e-commerce using the internet, B2B (business to business) and B2C (business to customer).

Early efforts to support supply chain management and logistics through ICT have centred around the management of demand uncertainty though inventory demand forecasting and reduction of inventory and transportation costs and/or cycle times through optimization techniques (Kumar 2001). Generally described under the umbrella term 'advanced planning systems' (APS), these applications provide decision support by using operational data to analyze and optimize the flows through the supply chain (Kumar 2001). Techniques deployed in APS include forecasting and time series analysis, optimization techniques (linear programming, mixed integer programming, location-allocation techniques, and genetic and rule-based algorithms), and scenario planning ('what-if' analysis and simulations) (Kumar 2001).

Another technology that has made a significant impact on logistics is radio frequency identification (RFID). RFID technology has been useful for precisely identifying objects (Borriello 2005). In the supply chain, RFID tags are used in pallets and crates of goods, enabling 100 per cent traceability from the manufacturer through the global transportation system and into retail stores worldwide.

An ICT development that has had a major impact on logistics and supply chain management is enterprise resource planning (ERP) software which can be seen as an evolution of manufacturing resource planning (MRP) systems. ERP systems enable collaboration and information sharing between the functions of an internal supply chain. ERP systems such as SAP, via extranets, connect not only different functions within a firm but also among the firm's supply chain partners (i.e. suppliers, distributors and third-party logistics providers), enabling the partners to share information such as order status, product schedules and sales records, to integrate major supply chain processes and to plan production, logistics and marketing promotions (Gunasekaran and Ngai 2004). ERP systems have been conceived to deliver benefits such as: improved demand visibility, which translates into inventory reduction; a contribution to an increase in profitability; reduction of cycle times; improved information availability; a contribution to costs reduction; and better synchronization between separate functions (APICS 2006).

It is worth mentioning that modern ERP systems include additional modules that provide functionality to address specific logistical requirements. For example SAP's advanced planning and optimizing (APO) tool includes a supply network planning capability which determines a permissible short- to medium-term plan for fulfilling the estimated sales volumes (Basan 2003). With the use of such a tool, organizations are able to generate a plan that covers the quantities that must be transported between two locations and the quantities to be produced and procured, while comparing all logistical activities against available capacity.

Today, in logistics the use of internet-based applications such as web services, and technologies such as RFID, cellular networks, GPS-enabled devices, Wi-Fi and 3G, among others, have made it possible to experience levels of visibility, control and connectivity never experienced before. In road transportation, applications based on WiMax, cellular infrastructure, Bluetooth and Wi-Fi have been adopted to provide certain connectivity. For example, by using the cellular infrastructure to reach the internet network, an embedded mobile phone in a given vehicle can get access to the network by using GPRS from a network operator.[1]

Despite major technological achievements in recent years, still there are several limitations associated with current ICT solutions in logistics. For example, in road transportation one main problem is that available services have to hop between different technologies like cellular networks, Wi-Fi, UMTS, 4G and WiMax, resulting in reliability and connectivity problems, not to mention problems associated with limited range, scalability and security. Therefore, by using heterogeneous ICT there is a high risk of experiencing performance downgrade to the solutions designed to manage road transport logistics. It is expected that the creation of innovative supply chain and logistics arrangements will demand the implementation of innovative ICT solutions able to support new logistical arrangements and overcome previous shortcomings.

The growing interaction and collaboration between organizations reflected in increasing flows of materials and information, the creation of complex networks, plus the strain on existing infrastructure such as roads and ports, demand the use of more sophisticated ICT solutions capable of dealing with the ever-rising complexity of modern day supply chain management and logistics tasks.

Opportunities and challenges for ICT presented by innovative logistics arrangements impacting modern supply chains: the case of road transportation feeding port operations

The worldwide economic environment has put pressure on companies, government and countries to maintain an up-to-date infrastructure and, hence, consider the implementation of innovative ICT solutions. Indeed, in a dynamic, demand-driven environment an organization requires connectivity enabled by ICT, cooperation and coordination between players within an industry – horizontal coordination – and across industry and firms – vertical coordination (Basan 2003).

Complex logistics arrangements can result from the combination of different types of transportation. For example, port operations are a complex arrangement (combining sometimes road, rail and sea) with a significant impact on the economy of a region. A schematic representation of road transportation feeding port operations and related infrastructure is depicted in Figure 14.1.

According to the European Commission (Motorways of the Sea 2007), in 2005, port operations related to short sea shipping in the North Sea region totalled some 591 million tonnes, with regular liner services and ferries operating fast, reliable and flexible connections carrying a wide range of cargos in a wide range of vessels, including charter vessels transporting bulk steel and construction materials between terminals in the region, as well as roll on-roll off (RO-RO) operations. In the view of the Commission, the

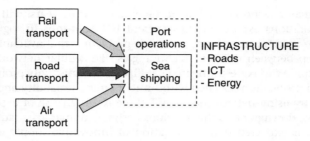

Figure 14.1 Representation of road transport feeding port operations and infrastructure

established benefits of short sea shipping as a sustainable part of the logistics chain creates demand for the extension of the North Sea short sea network.

In port operations road transportation can be seen as a feeder to sea transport. Moreover, sea transportation is heavily dependent on road transportation and that may represent a problem. In 2007, the European Commission (*Coia* 2007) identified road congestion in Europe as a major issue affecting the efficiency of short sea transport. Therefore, the European Commission highlighted that there is a need to upgrade the infrastructure used by road transportation to make short sea shipping more efficient. On the other hand, the interaction between different types of transport provides unique opportunities to generate and exploit synergies in logistics. Moreover, the logistics associated to road transportation and port operations can be seen as an example of a business sector that can benefit from the adoption of innovative ICT solutions.

Finished vehicle logistics: an example of complex logistical arrangements

Following up on the previous section, an example of the importance of North Sea short sea network operations can be found in finished vehicle logistics in England's North East. Finished vehicle logistics has emerged as a principal business activity in the automotive industry and it has a significant impact in the economy of the North East of England. Generally speaking, finished vehicles can be transported by ship, truck, rail and, in extreme cases, by air. In the case of transportation of finished vehicles by sea, this area is expected to experience substantial levels of growth in the coming years. According to *Coia* (2007), of the 65 million new cars built in 2005, 15 million were exported by ship. By 2015 the number is expected to grow to 20 million cars. Also according to the same publication, the European Sea Ports Organization (ESPO) has found that the increasing movements and global shifts of car flows have led to traffic in ports and a shortage of car carriers. The latest reports suggest there is a 10 per cent shortage of car carriers today. Other problems involve the use of older vessels, which are not adequate for vehicle transportation. *Coia* concludes that the situation has been aggravated by the importance of emerging markets, as growth and production in Asia, South America, Eastern Europe and Russia are leading sea trade to put more focus on these markets.

Sea transportation of finished vehicles is classified as deep sea and short sea. In Northern Europe, short sea transportation of finished vehicles is a major transportation route, connecting the UK, Germany, the Benelux and the Nordic countries. In a business activity such as finished vehicle logistics comprising sea and road transportation, having up-to-date infrastructure becomes critical not only to the profitability of the operations but also because of the implications it has on the entire supply chain. Moreover, finished vehicle logistics have a significant impact on the economy of a region.

Innovative information and communication technology for opportunities, challenges and innovative logistics arrangements impacting modern supply chains

In the foreseeable future it has become evident that the use of new technologies will be required, on the one hand, to gather the benefits associated to the high potential growth of short sea routes and, on the other hand, deal with the reliance of port operations' logistics on road transportation. In the particular scenario of road transportation feeding port operations, novel ICT has the potential to solve many of the challenges faced today, guarantee the future sustainability of logistics operations in a specific geographic area and contribute to the generation of synergies that may lead towards better use of resources and waste reduction. In Europe, organizations like ERTICO (2007) have recognized that the use of intelligent transport systems and services (ITS), combined with the appropriate investment in infrastructure, will result in reduced congestion and accidents, while making transport networks more secure and reducing their impact on the environment.

It has been mentioned before that road transportation acts as a feeder for port operations and sea transport. Road transportation logistics have specific needs in terms of ICT solutions. According to the 2007 Commercial Vehicle Telematics Conference (2007), some ICT-related issues affecting the sector include:

- An infrastructure where data and security layers ensure that all business critical data is not destroyed or corrupted
- Integrated application in replacement of commercial telematics with limited range and reliability
- For all fleet managers, the elimination of expensive roaming and administered multicarrier agreements

- Increased visibility and productivity of a supply chain through integration with on-board GPS tracking systems leading to routing and traffic solutions
- The creation of a seamless supply chain where planning and replenishment activities will be completely automated
- Becoming a true interlinking technology that facilitates seamless interoperability
- Providing in-vehicle integration comprising location-enabled services, communication capabilities, safety and security solutions, routing information and detailed management reporting
- Helping fleet managers adhere to anti-idling rules.

To address the issues listed above and in order to be able to run road transport logistics without the problems that have plagued current technologies in use, there is one wireless solution that promises to be more reliable and that is still under development and subject to standardization for massive deployment: direct short range communication (DSRC). DSRC promises to overcome the limitations associated to the use of heterogeneous technologies such as security, breakdown in internet protocol (IP) mobility and lack of seamless handover.

DSRC is a promising technology based on the standard IEEE 802.11p, which is designed to handle different types of service applications, including the transmission of both safety and non-safety messages into two modalities: vehicle to vehicle (V2V) and vehicle to infrastructure (V2I). DSRC is allocated at the 5.9 GHz frequency band and is designed to support high vehicular velocities in a radio transmission range up to 1,000 metres, with a data rate up to 27 Mbps (DOT HS 809 859 nhtsa, 2005) per channel, including two control channels and seven service channels. Within this technology two types of messages are transmitted: Wireless Access for Vehicular Environment (WAVE) short messages (WSM) and IPv6 traffic. WSM involves low latency and critical safety-related messages assuming a real-time propagation, while IPv6 traffic is generally related to commercial services such as download or streaming of data. To allow IP traffic, the discovery of IP addresses (WAVE 2005) is performed by generating a global IP address with the media access control (MAC) address and the IP prefix advertised by the current roadside infrastructure. A timer value is assigned to this IP address, so when the timer expires the IP address is no longer valid. If the vehicle attaches to a new roadside infrastructure, a new IP address based on the new IP prefix must be generated. According to the vehicle-to-infrastructure integration VII report (Farradyne 2005), the main network elements are briefly described as follows:

On-board unit (OBU). This element comprises a hardware module installed within the vehicle, which includes a 5.9 GHz DSRC transceiver; a GPS location system; a processor for application services; and a human machine interface (HMI). A wide range of applications generated at the OBU can be formatted as IP traffic and propagated by using an available DSRC service channel.

Roadside unit (RSU). This element is considered to be the gateway between the fixed infrastructure and vehicles. RSUs comprise a DSRC transceiver (RSU), a GPS location system, an application processor and a router that is attached to the fixed network. The RSU periodically broadcasts advertisement messages within its radio transmission range to alert neighbouring vehicles to its presence. Any exchange of information coming from a vehicle is verified at the RSU's processor and forwarded by the router to reach the core network.

Message switch (MSW). Its main function is to handle and parse all the data intended to reach any network element. It also performs message management and subscription operations according to the message's priority for efficient bandwidth distribution. All RSUs must be registered with their assigned MSW and associated to a specific region.

Network management (NM). The management of the network will be carried out by centralized entities known as network operation centres (NOC). These centres are responsible for the analysis of all the information retrieved from the MSW, as well as operation and maintenance of the vehicular network infrastructure.

Certification authorities (CA). All messages passing through the network must be digitally signed so the CA is responsible for the distribution of key certificates to secure all the exchange of information and minimize the risk of a network attack.

Map server (MS). The function of the MS consists of maintaining the accuracy of map databases and it is logically connected to the MSW. Once an update in the position parameters has been performed in the map database, the updated information is released and sent back to the MSW, RSU and OBU.

Figures 14.2 and 14.3 show the components of a DSRC vehicular network.

The exchange of messages between vehicles and the fixed infrastructure can be implemented in either broadcast or geocast transmission modes. In the broadcast protocol, periodic messages advertise to neighbouring vehicles via the roadside unit, with its radio transmission range. In the geocast protocol messages are transmitted according to specific geographical regions. This latter is suitable when the message needs to be propagated beyond a limited radio transmission range. Moreover, the exchange of information can be performed in a single-hop- or in a multi-hop-based routing. For the first case, the communication is carried on exclusively between the OBU and the RSU, while the second involves the collaboration of vehicles to propagate the message.

In Europe, the Cooperative Vehicle-Infrastructure Systems (CVIS) project (CVIS 2007), funded by the European Union, has been investigating the capability to link vehicles to the roadside infrastructure through seamless communications channels. According to CVIS, the fundamental enabling

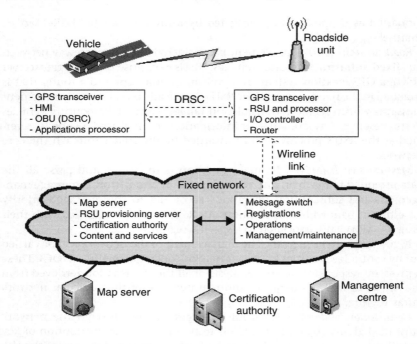

Figure 14.2   Vehicular network components

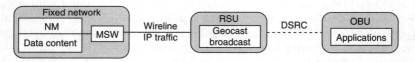

Figure 14.3   Communication diagram

technology for cooperative systems is a 'universal communications module' that can interface to existing in-vehicle systems, and to existing roadside installations, and that can maintain a continuous wireless high-capacity data channel. ERTICO – ITS Europe and the UK Department for Transport had organized workshops on Policy Implications for Cooperative Vehicle Infrastructure Systems with the aim to exchange ideas regarding the impact new applications may have on transport policy and to consider the policy environment required to support the widespread deployment of cooperative systems and services.

The implementation of DSRC has the potential to provide an environment with the highest degree of security, reliability and quality to manage road transport logistics acting as feeders of port operations. Total visibility, seamless inter-operability and vehicle integration are some of the characteristics provided by DSRC that will facilitate the generation of the required synergies to run logistics operations in a way that can contribute to an increase of short sea transportation and ensure future sustainability of road transportation/port operations, as well as securing a positive impact on the regional economy. Also DSRC may help fleet operators to adhere to anti-idling rules set by government initiatives.

The eventual implementation of innovative ICT solutions such as DSRC might involve looking simultaneously at the technical and human aspects of the technology. Technical aspects related to the technology include mobility and systems integration, which require a high-level of technical expertise. On the other hand, non-technical (human) aspects, such as people and interactivity, might include human–computer interaction, and how users deal with new ICT can provide them with the required information.

Adopting DSRC technology

Prior to committing to the purchase of ICT equipment to adopt DSRC to support logistics operations, a number of actions must be considered to ensure the success of DSRC. For example, the adoption of DSRC to support logistics operations can be assisted by the use of tools such as value stream mapping in order to provide a picture of the flow of materials/goods and the flow of information in the supply chain analyzed. Also any implementation plan will require the identification of the functionality provided by current ICT solutions and the support given to the exchange of information 'messages' between vehicle transporters and port operators. This exercise will help to generate a list of requirements that will have to be considered in the design of a DSRC-based logistics solution.

The adoption of a DSRC network entails defining the specification and topology of DSRC required to adopt the technology within a road transport environment serving a port site. This step requires defining the technical characteristics of the main network elements, as well as estimation costs on the design of the network, documentation, deployment, testing, evaluation, training, scalability and maintenance. Additionally, since the implementation of DSRC is envisioned for massive deployment, governmental authorities are required to play a key role in establishing certain control regulations and public policies, as DSRC networks will be part of the roadside infrastructure.

Also adopting DSRC requires the use of a modelling tool to simulate the configuration required for the proposed DSRC network. This action is highly recommended prior to the purchase of equipment, as the elements required to install a DSRC network such as OBU, RSU, MSW, NM, CA and MS are costly. A modelling tool that uses the IEEE 802.11p standard can be used to simulate the behaviour of a DSRC network serving road transport and port operations. A tool useful for that purpose is OPNET's Modeller Wireless Suite, which allows wireless network modelling and simulation. According to OPNET (2007), the use of this suite provides 'the industry's most flexible and scalable wireless network modelling environment, and includes a broad range of powerful technologies for accelerating simulation run-time'. The software offers full protocol stack modelling capability with the ability to model all aspects of wireless transmissions, interference, transmitter/receiver characteristics, including RF propagation, node mobility, including handover, and the interconnection with wired transport networks (OPNET 2007). Adopting DSRC is a high-magnitude project that demands the commitment not only of the companies involved in its implementation and operation, but also of government agencies, as DSRC becomes part of the regional infrastructure and an asset that can provide a competitive advantage over other geographical regions without DSRC.

Direct implications associated with novel ICT in logistics: DSRC-enabled visibility capabilities

The adoption of novel ICT solutions such as DSRC in logistics and supply chain management might have further implications well beyond its original intention of improving communications reliability. An example of further implications of novel ICT is visibility in the supply chain. The concept of visibility has been addressed by several researchers in recent years because of the direct impact it has on the performance of logistics and the supply chain. In fact, access to information that enables visibility has been identified behind the mitigation of demand visibility problems such as excess inventory levels, poor supply chain synchronization and the bullwhip effect. For example, DSRC technology can be used to provide accurate figures on stock on transit in real time.

Several industries, in particular the automotive, have experienced significant benefits from visibility, such as the implementation of synchronized/sequenced deliveries of components/subsystems, which translates into the elimination of finished goods inventory and the mitigation of demand amplification. Benefits of visibility have been identified mainly in upstream tiers of the supply chain. In finished vehicle logistics, visibility has implications downstream in the supply chain. For example, DSRC in finished vehicle logistics can have a direct contribution on:

- Access to more reliable information for better forecasts on the use of specific and general road transporters for each OEM served by the finished vehicle
- The creation of synergies by bringing together different manufacturers for a better use of logistical resources (e.g. sharing general road transporters from assembly plants to shipping site).

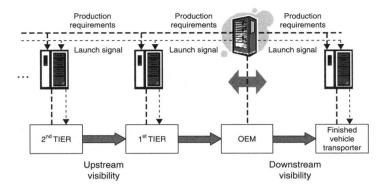

Figure 14.4   Information visibility upstream and downstream

Figure 14.4 illustrates the concept of visibility in an automotive supply chain, downstream and upstream. Upstream visibility has been associated to deliveries of components/subsystems all the way to the OEM. Downstream visibility has implications in the operation of finished vehicle logistics; from the point a car leaves the assembly line to the shipping port to the vehicle dealer.

Having access to visibility downstream in the supply chain can be used to address issues on finished vehicle logistics such as:

• Postponement operations (e.g. fitting accessories to vehicles that have already left the assembly line and are sitting in parking lots)
• Use collected data to anticipate the trend of the type of vehicles that will be manufactured in the future and, hence, define the design of future vessels for vehicle transportation.

The adoption of novel ICT such as DSRC gives the possibility of looking at efficiencies associated with information visibility/sharing, from the OEM to the finished vehicle supplier, as shown in Figure 14.5.

The use of a DSRC solution in road transport logistics serving port operations and, in particular, the logistics of finished vehicles gives the opportunity to look into the benefits of information visibility downstream in the supply chain. The use of this approach can contribute to expanding the knowledge of the principles of information visibility in a growing business sector such as finished vehicle logistics.

Conclusions

Logistics is an infrastructure-dependent economic activity that has become critical for the long-term profitability and sustainability of many industry

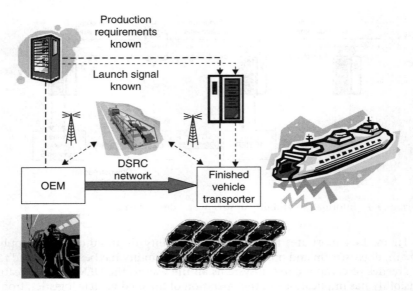

Figure 14.5   Information visibility from the OEM to the finished vehicle transporter

sectors. However, the success of logistics operations relies heavily on the state of infrastructure available where ICT plays a principal role. Nowadays, and for the coming years, drivers such as climate change and outsourcing will continue to shape the face of logistics and supply chain management. Hence, new technologies and designs play a key role in the modernization and revitalization of the infrastructure required to support the needs of logistics operations. The importance of ICT will continue to grow in coming years, as ICT is critical to ensure the future operation and sustainability of logistics operations in geographic regions.

Road transport logistics represent the most important mode of transportation, ahead of sea, rail and air. Hence, the implementation of novel ICT such as DSRC has the potential to provide an environment with the highest degree of security, reliability and quality to manage road transport logistics acting as feeders of port operations. Total visibility, seamless inter-operability and vehicle integration are some of the characteristics provided by DSRC.

On the one hand, the use of a DSRC solution in road transport logistics has the potential to improve the capability of inter-organizational information systems and therefore be adopted as a routine platform. On the other hand, adopting DSRC is a high-magnitude project that demands the commitment not only of the companies involved in its implementation and operation but also of government agencies, which have to be committed to the support and construction of the required infrastructure.

One of the main implications of developing an ICT infrastructure that makes use of innovative developments such as DSRC to support logistics operations is visibility in the supply chain. This element has serious repercussions in the responsive capabilities of a supply chain, not to mention a reduction in inventory costs, mitigation of demand amplification and better decision-making. One key contribution of DSRC to practice is the possibility of expanding the implications of visibility to the supply chain by including together the upstream and downstream components of it.

Finished vehicle logistics was used as an example of the potential benefits of using innovative ICT such as DSRC. Several other logistics arrangements in different industry sectors can benefit from the use of DSRC. Future lines of research will have to look at using DSRC in the logistics arrangements of various industry sectors. Another issue to be investigated involves linking the ICT infrastructure with current and new logistics software tools.

Note

1. http://www.onstar.com

References

APICS 2006 'Using information technology to enable supply chain management, 4, Section B: ERP in supply chain management',*Certified Supply Chain Professional*, 4: 63.

Basan, S. 2003 'Theory and practice of advanced planner and optimizer in supply chain domain', *Proceedings of the 2003 Winter Simulation Conference*, ed. by S. Chick, P. J. Sánchez, D. Ferrin and D. J. Morrice: 1424–32.

Borriello, G. 2005 'RFID: Tagging the world', *Communications of the ACM*, 48(9): 35–7.

Coia A, 2007. 'Demand for ro-ro capacity outstrips supply', *Finished Vehicle Logistics*, September, 58–61

Commercial Vehicle Telematics (CVT) USA 2007, <http://www.telematicsupdate.com/pastevents/2007/cvtusa2007/> accessed December 2007

Cooperative Vehicle-Infrastructure Systems (CVIS), 2007 <http://http.cvisproject.org>

Department of Transport 2005 *Identify Intelligent Vehicle Safety Applications Enabled by DSRC*, Vehicle Safety Communications Project Task 3 Final Report, DOT HS 809 859 nhtsa, March.

ERTICO – ITS Europe 2007, <http://www.ertico.com>

Farradyne, P.B. 2005 'Vehicle Infrastructure Integration (VII), Architecture and Functional Requirements, version 1.0', *FHWA. ITS-US Department of Transportation*, April.

Finished Vehicle Logistics 2007 'Demand for ro-ro capacity outstrips supply',*Finished Vehicle Logistics*, September: 58–61.

Gunasekaran, A. and Ngai, E.W. 2004 'Virtual supply-chain management', *Production Planning and Control*, 15(6): 584–95.

Kumar, K. 2001 'Technology for supporting supply chain management', *Communications of the ACM*, 44(6): 58–61.

Logistics World/MDC 1997 LogLink. http://www.logisticsworld.com/logistics.htm, accessed December 2007

Motorways of the Sea 2007 Projects in the North Sea Region, notification of a joint call for tender, <http://www.dft.gov.uk/162259/165226/jointcallnorthseamos2007fin1. pdf>

OPNET 2007 Network Wireless Modeller, <http://www.opnet.com/solutions/network_rd/modeler_wireless. html>, accessed December 2007.

Wireless Access in Vehicular Environments (WAVE) 2005 *Networking Services*, Draft IEEE P1609.3/D13, April.

15

An Evaluation of Electronic Logistics Marketplaces within Supply Chains

Yingli Wang, Andrew Potter and Mohamed Naim

Introduction

The growth in e-business over recent years, driven by developments in information and communication technology, has resulted in the increased use of electronic marketplaces (EMs) for business-to-business transactions. Potentially, EMs can have a significant influence over the way that transactions are carried out, relationships are formed, supply chains are structured and profit flows are operated (Kaplan and Sawhney 2000). While many aspects of supply chain management have been considered, there are only a few studies that investigate the development of these EMs in logistics (Grieger 2003). In this chapter, we focus upon these electronic logistics marketplaces (ELMs), which are electronic hubs that use web-based systems to link shippers and carriers together for the purpose of collaboration or trading. At a basic level, an ELM involves three main parties – the shipper of goods, the carrier and a technology provider. While any of these parties can lead the ELM development, it is usual for the leader to be the shipper.

As ELMs have developed, so two main formats have emerged: open and closed systems (Skjøtt-Larsen, Kotzab and Grieger 2003). The former have no restrictions on entry, with carriers and shippers free to use the system as much as they like. Commonly, such systems take the form of online exchanges, where transport services are sourced on a spot hire basis (Diaz Jiménez 2007). These are more similar to generic electronic marketplaces studied in the literature and particularly focus upon trading. Closed systems require participants to be invited into the marketplace. Therefore, they are more commonly used in conjunction with longer-term relationships underpinned by formal contracts. A key element is information sharing throughout the transportation process, and this knowledge can then be used to manage the supply chain more effectively. To date, there has been only limited research investigating this form of marketplace (Cruijssen, Cools and Dullaert 2007).

The aim of this chapter is to critically review the use of closed ELMs within knowledge-driven supply chains. In doing so, consideration is given to the operational models currently in use, motivations behind their use and the costs and benefits that arise from their use. The findings are based on a study of six exemplar ELMs conducted during 2006 and 2007.

The chapter proceeds with a brief review of the literature relating to ELMs, before outlining the research method adopted. The main operational models are then examined. Next motivations, benefits, barriers and costs are evaluated before, finally, conclusions are drawn. These include potential future directions for ELMs, from both practical and research perspectives.

Previous research

Early ELMs, such as www.teleroute.com, are open platforms and hence have similar characteristics to generic open EMs. They adopted many-to-many transactions and utilized fixed and/or dynamic pricing (Gosain and Palmer 2004). Despite, the benefits of lower search and coordination costs, companies, and particularly shippers, increasingly need to retain their linkages with preferred business partners (Dai and Kauffman 2002). Consequently, closed ELMs are emerging. These are based on relational lines, emphasizing the extent of services. The operational scope provided by closed ELMs goes beyond basic load posting and matching services, and shifts to complex offerings that might encompass complete order fulfilment services. Table 15.1 compares open and closed ELMs.

Previous academic research in ELMs has largely focused upon open marketplaces, and consequently overlaps with generic EM research. Focusing on the latter area, Lynagh *et al.* (2001) found there is limited adoption of closed ELMs in industry, but their study focuses only on the perspective of logistics service providers. Rudberg, Klingenberg and Kronhamn (2002) examine

Table 15.1   Comparison of open and closed ELMs

Open ELM	Closed ELM
• Unlimited number of companies involved	• Limited number of companies involved
• Simple functionality and long reach	• Complex functionality and short reach
• Spot trading of transport services	• Prices based on pre-agreed contracts
• Little information sharing and collaboration	• High degree of information sharing and collaboration
• Focus on selection and identification of potential buyers/suppliers	• Focus on collaboration and execution

Sources: Adapted from Grieger 2003; Skjøtt-Larsen, Kotzab and Grieger 2003.

different collaborative supply chain planning scenarios using EMs, one of which is specifically related to an ELM. However, the scope is only limited to planning and does not cover execution or reporting. Helo and Szekely (2005) track historical developments in logistics information systems, up to ELMs while Kale, Evers and Dresner (2007) demonstrate that shippers may benefit by establishing a closed ELM, using a theoretical model to do so. Finally, Caplice (2007) examines the use of closed ELM for the strategic procurement of carriers and the planning of transportation. As with Rudberg, Klingenberg and Kronhamn (2002), there is no consideration of execution and reporting.

Wang and Naim (2007) propose a conceptual model that categorizes and traces different inter-organizational information control and coordination mechanisms observed in the logistics domain. This model combines control architectures originating from control manufacturing systems (Dilts, Boyd and Whorms 1991) and coordination theories based around transaction cost economics and resource-based governance (Malone and Crowston 1994). Three types of closed ELM architectures are identified and shown in Figure 15.1:

- A *private ELM* focuses on vertical integration. A dominant player (usually the shipper) creates an ELM for its own use. This type of ELM uses authority and other procedural coordination processes instead of a pricing mechanism.
- In the *shared ELM* model, a number of shippers start to share one single platform to get connected with their carriers. Some horizontal collaboration is introduced along with more value-added elements.
- A *collaborative ELM* is characterized by great level of horizontal collaboration between shippers. This network is normally a web-based and web-hosted platform, and enables high level of information sharing and joint activities. This encourages the reduction of empty running by identifying synergies within product flows and sharing the capacity of carriers. The ownership of such a network is usually via a consortium group. The network is designed and highly customized in servicing the consortium's specific needs.

Overall, there is a lack of understanding of the business models for closed ELMs. In fact, it is argued that the logistics dimension of EM has been largely neglected and there is a very real need for empirical research to fill the gap (Grieger 2003).

Research approach

This research adopts a multiple case study approach. To select appropriate cases, relevant companies were identified through the Transport and Logistics

Private marketplace

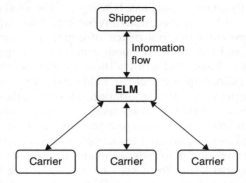

Shared marketplace

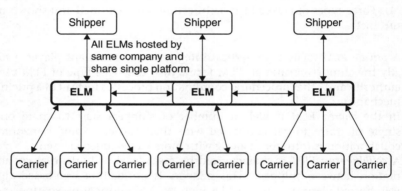

Collaborative marketplace

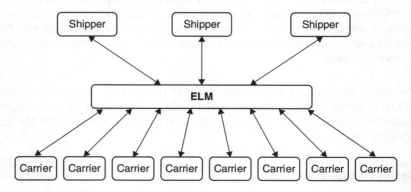

Figure 15.1 System architectures for closed ELMs
Source: Adapted from Wang and Naim 2007.

directory at Business.com (2006) and recommendations from industry peers. Initial contact was made by e-mail, with follow-up telephone calls as appropriate. Out of ten companies contacted, six agreed to participate. Details on each of the cases can be found in Table 15.2.

The main data collection instrument was a semi-structured interview. Generally, the interviews were carried out with staff of the technology provider, although with case E the opportunity to collect data in more depth existed, leading to interviews with both shippers and carriers. In most cases, interviews were carried out with at least two members of the company. In total, 30 interviews were carried out. The interviews typically last two hours and covered the company background, opportunities and challenges in the market, the ELM business model and the factors behind why companies sought to use the marketplace. The interviews were transcribed and cross-checked both between the researchers involved and with interviewees.

Operational models

In examining the operational models, three key areas are studied: process, technology and collaboration, reflecting Baeza-Yates and Nussbaum (2006). We note that the process functions for each case study have similarities, so to generalize our findings we have developed a generic operational scope template as given in Figure 15.2. This splits the transportation process into three elements: planning, execution and reporting. Planning covers all activities associated scheduling the load and communicating this information with carriers. Execution relates to the actual movement, while reporting covers activities once delivery has occurred. Because of operational differences, the unit of analysis is the information architecture type.

Private marketplaces

Technology

Both ELM solutions are traditional client-server systems but with web-based functions for communication with carriers and shippers. Orders can be imported automatically from the shipper's information system or be inputted manually via the web. Large carriers can afford to build automatic linkages with the system, while all carriers can use the web to input or output data. Access is obtained with a username and password. Only an internet connection and a browser are needed. Case A does not charge for data transactions but requires a one-off fee to cover the costs associated with system integration. As a fourth-party logistics provider (4PL), they also look to share in any transport cost savings they identify and achieve. In Case B, it is the shippers who buy the solution and pay most of the charges. As with Case A, carriers are occasionally asked to pay one-off charges to cover system integration costs.

Table 15.2 Overview of case ELMs

Architecture type	Case name	Country of origin	Industry	ELM ownership	Owner description (all figures from 2006)	Number of interviews
Private	Case A	UK	Cross-industry	Independent	A small to medium-sized fourth-party logistics provider established within the European logistics sector. Customers from automotive, retail, electrical, pharmaceutical and packaging industries. Around 30 employees. Annual revenue unknown.	4
	Case B	US	Cross-industry	Independent	A major supply chain software provider with a particular focus in the retail industry. 1,856 employees and a customer base of 5,500 companies in 60 countries. Annual revenue: US$277.5 million.	1
Shared	Case C	US	Cross-industry	Independent	One of the top ten software providers in the world. Over 8,100 employees with offices in 100 countries and 70,000 customers worldwide. Annual revenue: US$2.1 billion	2
	Case D	Canada	Cross-industry	Independent	A leading provider of on-demand logistics solutions with two specific target customer groups: transportation/logistics providers and manufacturers, retailers and distributors. Over 3,000 customers in more than 60 countries globally. Annual revenue: US$52.0 million.	2

					Created by three FMCG manufacturers:	19
Collaborative	Case E	UK	FMCG	Shippers' consortia	• Shipper 1 specializes in confectionary, main meal and petcare products, with operations in 65 countries. Annual revenue: US$18 billion.	
					• Shipper 2 manufactures beauty, home and healthcare products. Annual revenue: US$68.2 billion.	
					• Shipper 3 is a major soft drinks manufacturer with 74,000 employees worldwide. Annual revenue: US$19.8 billion.	
	Case F	Spain	FMCG and chemical	Shipper-oriented consortia	Created by three companies:	2
					• A leading beer company in the Spanish and European markets. Employees and annual revenue unknown.	
					• A global management consultant and technology. Operations in 49 countries with 158,000 employees. Annual revenue: US$16.7 billion.	
					• A global provider of communications solutions operating in 170 countries with 106,000 employees. Annual revenue: US$37 billion.	

Source: Adapted from Wang 2008.

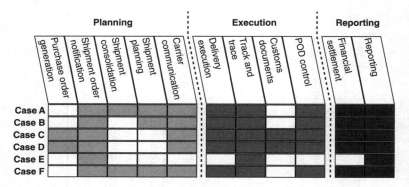

Figure 15.2   Functionality of the ELMs studied
Source: Adapted from Wang, Potter and Naim 2007a.

Process

As can be seen from Figure 15.2, there are only slight differences between Case A and Case B in terms of functionality. In Case A, load consolidation takes place within the ELM. By contrast, Case B requires orders to be consolidated by the in-house transport management system before being imported into ELM. Another difference is that in Case B, carriers can input which routes they would like to undertake, as well as their capacity and rates. Therefore the transport planner has visibility of each carrier's availability before finalizing the schedule. In Case A the schedule is created and then sent to carriers. The transport scheduler will fine-tune the plan if there are any rejected loads. Both systems track the status of shipments and alert relevant parties should delays occur. Once a delivery occurs, the proof of delivery (POD) can be uploaded onto the system for financial settlement and performance reports generated.

Collaboration

In both cases there is a great degree of vertical integration between carriers and shippers. Case A is facilitated by the 4PL, while in Case B there is a direct link between shippers and carriers. By contrast, horizontal levels of collaboration are very limited. In Case A, shippers themselves do not collaborate with each other, nor do the carriers. This is due to the fact that they operate in an environment where there is no requirement for collaborative arrangements. However, the 4PL does act as an intermediary and understands both parties' requirements. They can mediate between partners with potentially conflicting interests. Therefore, though there is a low level of horizontal collaboration, the whole ELM community benefits from both economies of scope and scale. The Case B solution is enabled via vertical integration, which is a more traditional approach to communication between shippers and carriers.

Shared marketplaces

Technology

Both Case C and Case D are web-based solutions, deploying the 'on-demand' model. No desktop installation is required as they are browser-based systems. A single database ensures that all data is located in one place, which improves transaction speed and information visibility. The system can be integrated with a range of legacy enterprise systems. As with the private marketplaces, shipment status can be inputted in various ways, including EDI-, web- and e-mail-based methods or mobile phone.

In both cases the technology provider hosts the marketplace and is responsible for creating communities based on the ELM leader's requirements. Such leaders may be either shippers or carriers. Different homepage configurations are possible for users, based around standard data forms. Usually it is the ELM leader who takes the initiative and pays for all services. Both cases deploy the pay as you go (PAYG) pricing model. For Case C the fee is charged annually, based on predicted transaction volume ranges, while in Case D there is a charge per transaction.

Unlike Case C, Case D's system adopts a modular approach. Participants subscribe to the functions required based on their individual needs. The central data bus is the key function of this ELM, where customers, shippers and carriers are connected and data transferred. Based on this, the hosting company creates a number of databases for specific purposes.

Process

Compared to private marketplaces, the operational scope is extended (Figure 15.2). It is not only the shippers and carriers that get involved but the customers can also be integrated into the system. Customers can either generate purchase orders (Case C) or have the visibility of inbound delivery through (Case D).

One distinct feature of both cases is that they support global logistics. Therefore import and export functions are built-in and the systems provide global trade compliance checks and customs clearance assistance. The ELM communities also benefit from value-added services provided by the hosting company, such as currency converters and cross-boundary legal advice.

Collaboration

Through the hosted system, there are many private ELM communities sharing one single platform. Despite this, there is currently no horizontal collaboration between those community leaders or participants. Horizontal collaboration is possible given the technology used, but has yet to be required by users. Compared with private marketplaces, there is a greater level of vertical integration in Case C and Case D. Shippers, carriers and customers are all integrated together through sharing the same system. This leads to enhanced speed of communication and the full audit trail of all shipment changes. Because the shippers can get spot quotes from the connected carriers, these systems also incorporate some limited features of open ELM.

Collaborative marketplaces

Technology

Both ELMs are hosted by the technology provider and are web-based systems. Shippers share a single database and website, and are charged based on transaction volume. The technology provider is responsible for setting up homepages for each participating company. The carriers do not need to pay any transaction fees, or any for system integration. However, in Case E, real-time tracking and tracing is deployed and so carriers need to buy telematics equipment and pay to download the data to the ELM.

Process

Although the underlying technology is the same, there are large differences between Case E and Case F in terms of functionality, as shown in Figure 15.2. In Case E, as currently deployed, the ELM provides only three functions; real-time tracking and tracing, exception alerts and performance reports. Other functions, such as transport planning, tendering and financial settlement, are conducted through legacy systems. In the future, functions such as joint scheduling and delivery would be included if current functionality sustains performance and fulfils shippers' needs. We can see from Figure 15.2 that Case F provides shipment consolidation by identifying back haulage opportunities and enabling joint deliveries between shippers. In both Case E and Case F customers are not integrated into the ELM system.

Collaboration

In contrast to the other architectures, there is a greater degree of horizontal collaboration between shippers and carriers. Not only do they share the same ELM infrastructure, they may also share the same carriers and deliver to the same customers. This involves a certain level of information sharing.

However, the collaboration between shippers and their carriers through ELM has some issues and conflicts. In Case E it has been found that carriers are reluctant to join due to the heavy investment required to buy and maintain telematics, and this has created tension. In Case F, the lack of synergies of loads between shippers failed to create a critical mass of loads because of the very different products being delivered. As a result of this, Case F has been disbanded.

The above section has shown that there is some diversity between the three information architectures in terms of technology, function and collaboration. We now move on to consider the motivations for the use of an ELM. Because of similarities between the findings, there is no distinction between the architectures.

Motivations to use an ELM

Kärkkäinen *et al.* (2007) identify three main drivers for the inter-firm use of information systems in the supply chain: transaction processing, supply chain planning and coordination, and order tracking and delivery coordination. However, their discussion does not explicitly address the specific motives for the companies to join a closed ELM. Howard, Vidgen and Powell (2006) conducted empirical research looking at the motivations and barriers in automotive EMs, where they discovered the main motives are material cost reduction, supply base reduction, common sourcing, transaction efficiency, product quality, delivery lead time and skills and knowledge. A more comprehensive category of motives behind EMs is developed by Standing *et al.* (2006), including economic, relational, service and community motives.

Motivations are closely linked with benefits. Many benefits discussed in the literature are based on open systems. The research most closely related to the benefits of the closed system consists of studies like McLaren, Head and Yuan (2002) and Easton and Araujo (2003). Large similarities exist, including efficiency and effectiveness gains, risk reductions and improvement in time-based performances. Therefore, building on previous studies and considering logistics applications, our research probes further the benefits for both shippers and carriers. Based on the above discussion, we develop evaluation criteria as listed in Table 15.3, which also shows whether each factor is a motivation for ELMs, based on our research.

From the shipper's perspective, all of the motives proposed were identified during the course of the interviews. Given that the shipper is normally the main driving force behind the adoption of an ELM, this finding is perhaps to be expected. However, it should be noted that not all motivations existed in each case, and that the relative importance of each also differed. By far the biggest motivation was the opportunity to reduce cost through improved efficiency. Another important factor was the increased visibility offered by the marketplaces. This was particularly so for the two cases involved in global supply chains, where there can often be difficulties in tracking the containers before they arrive at the port. Community motivations were less important, and were only present in Case E. Because of the requirements for telematics equipment and the size of the shippers, the ELM could lead to the introduction of industry standards.

From the carrier's perspective, there are fewer motivations for becoming involved in an ELM. Again, economic motives are more prevalent, as ELMs offer the opportunity to reduce costs through eliminating empty running. There may also be relational motivations, in order to understand the requirements of the supply chain more. Surprisingly, there are few service motivations, with only reliability and responsiveness being identified.

Table 15.3 Motivations for using ELMs

Generic motivation factor for an electronic marketplace	Key references	Motivation for ELM Shipper	Carrier
Economic motives			
a) Productivity gains through process automation, improved visibility and quick information exchange	Kumar and Van Dissel (1996), Martinez *et al.* (2001), McLaren,	✓	✓
b) Cost savings through effective scheduling (labour and assets) and critical mass gained from cross-company collaboration	Head and Yuan (2002), Standing *et al.* (2006),	✓	✓
c) Secure market competitiveness	Howard, Vidgen and Powell (2006), Silveira and Cagliano (2006)	✓	✓
Relational motives			
a) Shippers exert influence to 'lock in' carriers, or vice versa	Kumar and Van Dissel (1996),	✓	
b) Desire to coordinate and collaborate in exchanging information and conducting transactions	Martinez *et al.* (2001), Gosain, Malhotra and Sawy (2004)	✓	✓
c) Reduce uncertainties in the supply chain		✓	✓
Service motives			
a) Increasing pressures on delivery performance	McLaren, Head and Yuan (2002),	✓	✓
b) Uniform visibility of pipeline information to manage and monitor each consignment	Folinas *et al.* (2004), Silveira and	✓	
c) Reliability and responsiveness	Cagliano (2006), Howard, Vidgen and Powell (2006)	✓	✓
Community motives			
a) Desire to impact on industry sector as a whole	McLaren, Head and Yuan (2002),	✓	
b) Try to promote the development of policy and industry standards	Standing *et al.* (2006)	✓	
Environment motives			
a) Reduce impact by minimizing empty running, improving fill rate and dynamic vehicle scheduling	Hesse (2002)	✓	✓

Source: Adapted from Wang, Potter and Naim 2007b.

Benefits from using an ELM

Closely aligned with motivations are the benefits that arise from the use of an ELM, and often these are dependent upon the functionality of the individual marketplace. Figure 15.3 summarizes the main benefits that can be achieved.

Improved process efficiency is achieved through reducing the administration associated with handling information and providing the supply chain with more accurate information. Information is transmitted electronically between all parties involved in the ELM. This increases the speed of information transfer, as well as improving its accuracy. In an ELM, all shipments are recorded, along with details of which carrier transported the load. Further, tracking and tracing allows confirmation that a load has been collected, its location en route and when delivery has occurred. In many cases this information is linked to a self-billing function, where the shipper calculates how much they have to pay the carrier. This replaces the more traditional approach of the carrier providing an invoice. Therefore, any disputes relating to whether a delivery has been made or if the carrier actually undertook the movement can be resolved quickly and easily.

Another area of benefit is through cost savings. While improved process efficiency contributes towards this, there are other benefits accrued by both the shipper and carrier. For shippers, there is the opportunity to simplify the day-to-day management of carriers, as all information is transmitted through a single interface. Equally, where the marketplace permits horizontal collaboration, it is possible for the shipper to benefit from improved flexibility in the provision of transport services, and therefore gain economies of scope. From a cost perspective, the range of different ELMs available makes it possible for the shipper to avoid significant setup costs through the use of a hosted system. Shipper benefits may also extend beyond the transport journey, with the opportunity to improve warehouse operations through greater visibility of loads. From the carrier's perspective, a key benefit is the better use of resources. The greater visibility of loads and their progress enables scheduling to be more effective and avoids the knock-on effect of delays. In addition, because of the nature of closed ELMs, once a carrier joins, there is the potential for them to receive more loads and therefore gain economies of scale.

A third area of benefit is in more proactive management of deliveries. The track and trace facility within ELMs enables managers to see where loads are. Should a delay occur, the improved visibility offered by the ELM enables this to be detected earlier and, therefore, decisions can be taken to ensure customer service is maintained. This may involve rerouting the vehicle or, if the ELM is being used within a global supply chain, possibly choosing an alternative mode of transport. Inventory control in these long supply chains can be improved by identifying where stock is and when it is likely to arrive.

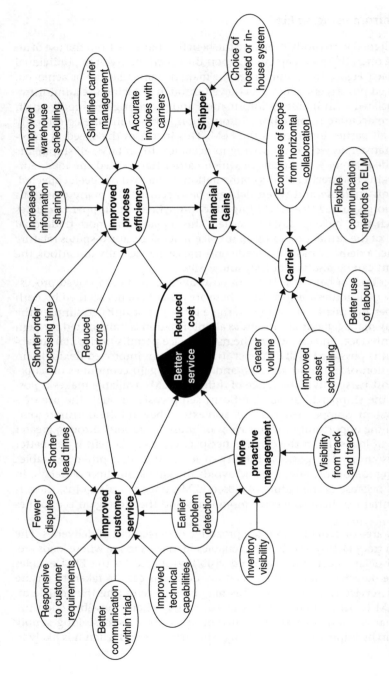

Figure 15.3 Benefits from using an ELM
Source: Adapted from Wang, Potter and Naim 2007b.

Finally, ELMs can deliver improved customer service, with proactive management being just one part of this. A shipper can be more responsive to customer requests, especially if they can draw on a large pool of different transport options. They can also reduce order-to-delivery time as information flows between shippers and carriers are faster. When delays occur, the shipper has earlier notification of this and so can contact the customer to warn them of the delay, while, if a dispute should arise on delivery performance, it is possible for more accurate information to be obtained to identify the root causes of the problem. The fact that in some circumstances the ELM is neutral can further enhance this benefit, as there can be less suspicion that the data is distorted. Finally, from a carrier's perspective, being able to participate within an ELM improves their capabilities, and therefore competitiveness in delivering a solution that meets the needs of the shipper.

As can be seen from the discussion above, a wide range of benefits can be obtained for both the shipper and carrier participating in the ELM. In particular, the increased knowledge as to activities within the supply chain improves the scope for effective management. However, many of the benefits are specifically related to the delivery of improved service to the shipper's customer while maintaining efficiency. While the exact benefits will vary between applications, it appears that there may be greater benefits in adopting an ELM for the shipper rather than the carrier.

Barriers to using an ELM

As well as benefits, it is also possible to identify a number of barriers to adoption of an ELM. Being often developed by shippers, an ELM can be very biased towards to their needs and provide lower incentives for carriers. An asymmetry of cost/benefits allocation can disturb the smooth implementation of an ELM. This supports earlier findings by Wilson and Vlosky (1998) in the context of information systems that the more unbalanced the benefits, the greater the open resistance from exchange partners. The shipper-related costs can vary according to the type of ELM used. If the system is operated in-house, a suitable IT infrastructure needs to be provided. The level of expenditure needed depends upon the capacity required for the ELM and current provision. The other main setup cost is for the software, which is then supplemented by an annual maintenance fee. If using a hosted system, then the most popular approach was for the marketplace to charge on a PAYG basis. A fixed amount is charged for each shipment, with the term 'shipment' being defined within each contract. For carriers, the level of cost depends on information requirements. If the ELM is driven by event-based monitoring, then relatively low cost communication methods (such as mobile telephone or internet forms) can be used. For real-time monitoring, telematics equipment needs to be fitted to each vehicle – a significant investment.

We also found that the misalignment between needs of the shippers and a lack of synergies can lead to failures in the adoption of closed ELM, even though the system technically functions well. The fear of sharing information is another factor that inhibits the potential of ELM. For example, between shippers there are opportunities for joint scheduling of deliveries for better fleet utilization and transport cost reduction. However, shippers do not want to disclose commercial information like transport rates. Therefore, optimization efforts are restricted to supply chains rather than networks.

Another potential barrier is the technological capabilities of the companies involved, particularly the carrier. It would be expected, given the shipper is normally the driver within the supply chain for the adoption of an ELM, that they would have the capabilities to adopt the technology. However, the range of different methods for communicating with the ELM makes this less of a barrier. In many cases, the minimum requirement is a computer with internet connection. A recent survey found that 93 per cent of UK road hauliers had such facilities, although 13 per cent did not use them (Davies, Mason and Lalwani 2007). Technological barriers emerge if advanced technologies are required. Case E requires telematics, a capability only 33 per cent of UK road hauliers have (Freight Transport Association 2005).

Finally, people issues arise from the individual user's willingness and skills in using ELM. For example, all ELMs require in-house training for the staff in various functions. The more complex the functionality, the more time and effort are needed. The change of processes or procedures can generate resistance. Using in-cab systems for communication with drivers also leads to a fear in drivers of being watched.

Conclusions and future directions

Recent years have seen the growth of electronic intermediaries introduced into the supply chain in order to improve visibility and speed the flow of both physical products and information. One such development within the information flow has been the ELM. While there has been some research into open systems, closed ELMs have been less well researched. This chapter has focused upon this type of system, which is underpinned by relationships rather than trading. A key element is information visibility, and this enhanced knowledge can then be used to manage the supply chain more effectively.

This chapter has filled a specific gap in the current know-how regarding the logistics application of electronic marketplaces. Specifically the chapter defines the architectures and characteristics of three types of closed ELMs; namely, private, shared and collaborative. The benefits, barriers and motivations to ELM adoption have been highlighted through case studies of six

ELM implementations, two in each type. Hence, this chapter has filled in the gaps in previous research by considering:

- the perspective of ELM providers and shippers in addition to that of the logistics service provider
- the execution and reporting functionality of closed ELMs as well as procurement and planning aspects
- empirical evidence of the application of closed ELMs
- testing conceptual models of three types of closed ELM.

The main technologies, processes and collaborative arrangements have been identified. While the private and shared marketplaces appear relatively well developed, collaborative marketplaces are still at a formative stage and need to demonstrate their long-term sustainability. Of the two cases studied, one currently has limited functionality (Case E), while the other only lasted for a limited time before being disbanded (Case F). There is a wide range of motivations for adopting an ELM, reflecting the more generic EM literature. In terms of benefits, the overall outcome is improved service and reduced cost in the supply chain. Many of the benefits are derived from the increased knowledge afforded through the use of an ELM. There are also a number of barriers, relating to technology, costs, collaboration, processes and people.

The main barrier to ELM adoption is the asymmetry of cost/benefits allocation, with ELMs primarily driven by shippers. A major consideration is the setup costs, especially for small to medium-sized transport operators. Hence, many of the motivations are driven by the shippers looking for benefits directly impacting on their operational performance in light of their requirements to satisfy their customer requirements. Closed ELMs have the main benefit of increasing knowledge access, through information transparency, among the key ELM stakeholders, leading to increased service levels and reduced total costs.

In terms of future directions for industry, there appears to be significant scope for collaborative marketplaces to develop further. Because these marketplaces offer the opportunity for optimization across distribution networks, there is the potential for achieving significant economic and environmental performance improvements. However, there are still significant barriers due to the high level of collaboration required. One way around this could be for regional marketplaces to be developed, supported by government. An example of such a system is e-Freight Logistics, which was established in Scotland with the support of regional development agencies (Gardner 2001). Run as a commercial organization, this marketplace was formed in 2001 but had ceased trading by the end of 2002. This highlights the risks associated with developing ELMs.

There are a number of future directions for academic research. While this chapter has particularly looked at the economic implications associated with adopting an ELM, there is also scope for considering the human and environmental issues that may arise. Furthermore, there is scope for studies looking at how the knowledge obtained from ELMs can be effectively exploited by the supply chain to improve performance. Finally, this chapter has only examined six ELMs, typically from the perspective of the technology provider. Larger-scale surveys to ascertain wider awareness, application and impact of ELMs within industry would enhance the findings presented.

References

Baeza-Yates, R. and Nussbaum, M. 2006 *The Information Architect: A Missing Link?* <http://www.dcc.uchile.cl/~rbaeza/manifest/infarch.html.> accessed 12 February 2007.

Business.com 2006 *Transportation and Logistics Management Companies*, <http://www.business.com/directory/transportation_and_logistics>, accessed 2 June 2006.

Caplice, C. 2007 'Electronic markets for truckload transportation', *Production and Operations Management*, 16: 423–36.

Cruijssen, F., Cools, M. and Dullaert, W. 2007 'Horizontal cooperation in logistics: Opportunities and impediments', *Transportation Research Part E*, 43: 129–42.

Dai, Q. and Kauffman, R.J. 2002 'Business models for internet-based B2B electronic markets', *International Journal of Electronic Commerce*, 6(4): 41–72.

Davies, I., Mason, R. and Lalwani, C.S. 2007 'Assessing the impact of ICT on UK general haulage companies', *International Journal of Production Economics*, 106: 12–27.

R. Diaz Jiménez, C.S. 2007 'Working together to win', *Logistics and Transport Focus*, 9(9): 46–8.

Dilts, D.M., Boyd, N.P. and Whorms, H.H. 1991 'The evolution of control architectures for automated manufacturing systems', *Journal of Manufacturing Systems*, 10: 79–93.

Easton, G. and Araujo, L. 2003 'Evaluating the impact of B2B e-commerce: A contingent approach', *Industrial Marketing Management*, 32: 431–9.

Folinas, D., Manthou, V., Sigala, M. and Vlachopoulou, M. 2004 'Evolution of a supply chain: Cases and best practices', *Internet Research*, 14: 274–83.

Freight Transport Association 2005 *Telematics Guide*, Tunbridge Wells: Freight Transport Association, http://www.fta.co.uk/information/otherissues/telematics/pdf/ telematics_guide.pdf, accessed 5 June 2006.

Gardner, D. 2001 'Eureka moment that launched e-Freight on the road to riches', *The Sunday Herald*, 11 March, <http://findarticles. com/p/articles/mi_qn4156/is_2001 0311/ai_n13956148>, accessed 7 May 2006.

Gosain, S. and Palmer, J.W. 2004 'Exploring Strategic Choices in Marketplace Positioning', *Electronic Markets*, 14: 308–21.

Gosain, S., Malhotra, A. and Sawy, O.A.E. 2004 'Coordinating for flexibility in e-business supply chains', *Journal of Management Information Systems*, 21(3): 7–45.

Grieger, M. 2003 'Electronic marketplaces: A literature review and a call for supply chain management research', *European Journal of Operational Research*, 144: 280–94.

Helo, P. and Szekely, B. 2005 'Logistics information systems: An analysis of software solutions for supply chain co-ordination', *Industrial Management and Data Systems*, 105: 5–18.

Hesse, M. 2002 'Shipping news: The implications of electronic commerce for logistics and freight transport', *Resources, Conservation and Recycling*, 36: 211–40.

Howard, M., Vidgen, R. and Powell, P. 2006 'Automotive e-hubs: Exploring motivations and barriers to collaboration and interaction', *Journal of Strategic Information Systems*, 15: 51–7.

Kale, R., Evers, P.T. and Dresner, M.E. 2007 'Analyzing private communities on internet-based collaborative transportation networks', *Transportation Research Part E*, 43: 21–38.

Kaplan, S. and Sawhney, M. 2000 'E-hubs: The new B2B marketplaces', *Harvard Business Review*, 78(3): 97–103.

Kärkkäinen, M., Laukkanen, S., Sarpola, S. and Kemppainen, K. 2007 'Roles of interfirm information systems in supply chain management', *International Journal of Physical Distribution and Logistics Management*, 37: 264–86.

Kumar, K. and Van Dissel, H.G. 1996 'Sustainable collaboration: Managing conflict and cooperation in interorganisational systems', *MIS Quarterly*, 20: 279–300.

Lynagh, P.M., Murphy, P.R., Poist, R.F. and Grazer, W.F. 2001 'Web-based informational practices of logistics service providers: An empirical assessment', *Transportation Journal*, 40(4): 34–45.

Malone, T.W. and Crowston, K. 1994 'The interdisciplinary study of coordination', *ACM Computing Surveys*, 26: 87–119.

Martinez, M.T., Fouletier, P., Park, K.H. and Favrel, J. 2001 'Virtual enterprise: Organisation, evolution and control', *International Journal of Production Economics*, 74: 225–38.

McLaren, T., Head, M. and Yuan, Y. 2002 'Supply chain collaboration alternatives: Understanding the expected costs and benefits', *Internet Research*, 12: 348–64.

Rudberg, M., Klingenberg, N. and Kronhamn, K. 2002 'Collaborative supply chain planning using electronic marketplaces', *Integrated Manufacturing Systems*, 13: 596–610.

Silveira, G.J.C.D. and Cagliano, R. 2006 'The relationship between interorganisational information systems and operations performance', *International Journal of Operations and Production Management*, 26: 232–53.

Skjøtt-Larsen, T., Kotzab, H. and Grieger, M. 2003 'Electronic marketplaces and supply chain relationships', *Industrial Marketing Management*, 32: 199–210.

Standing, C., Love, P.E.D., Stockdale, R. and Gengatharen, D. 2006 'Examining the relationship between electronic marketplace strategy and structure', *IEEE Transactions on Engineering Management*, 53: 297–311.

Wang, Y. 2008 'Electronic logistics marketplaces for tailored logistics', PhD thesis, Cardiff University.

Wang, Y. and Naim, M.M. 2007 'B2B e-business reference architecture for customised logistics', *International Journal of Services Operations and Informatics*, 2: 253–66.

Wang, Y., Potter, A. and Naim, M.M. 2007a 'Electronic marketplaces for tailored logistics', *Industrial Management and Data Systems*, 107: 1170–87.

Wang, Y., Potter, A. and Naim, M.M. 2007b 'Evaluating the reasons for using electronic logistics marketplaces within supply chains', *Proceedings of the 12th Logistics Research Network Conference*, Hull: 137–42.

Wilson, D.T. and Vlosky, R.P. 1998 'Interorganisational information system technology and buyer-seller relationships', *Journal of Business and Industrial Marketing*, 13: 215–34.

16
Environmental Management in Product Chains

Michael Søgaard Jørgensen and Marianne Forman

Introduction

The product chain – the chain of interacting suppliers and customers, which together make up the activities from raw material extraction to handling of waste connected to a product – plays an important role in the shaping and management of environmental aspects connected to the production and consumption of a product, for example, a piece of clothing. To illustrate, with lack of environmental focus, a retail chain may only be willing to pay a certain price for the product because their business strategy focuses on price competition with the other retailers. Therefore the retail chain does not care about the environmental protection measures taken by their suppliers and the retail chain procurement persons do not control the environmental aspects of the manufacturing at the suppliers' facilities. In contrast, as an example of proactive environmental management, a manufacturing company may initiate direct supply of organic cotton from a number of small farmers in order to be able to protect their own workers during the manufacturing of T-shirts from the cotton.

Different notions are used for this kind of environmental management in product chains. 'Life cycle management' is a notion where focus is on the environmental aspects in the whole product chain from 'cradle to grave' (see e.g. Garcia-Sanchez, Wenze and Jørgensen 2004), while Kogg (2002) uses the term 'environmental supply chain management' in almost the same way about efforts initiated by companies to improve and/or control environmental performance upstream and/or downstream in their supply chains. However, the term 'supply chain management' is primarily used by some authors to describe demands directed upstream in the supply chain (which means towards the suppliers) (see e.g. Schary and Skjøtt-Larsen 2002).

De Bakker and Nijhof (2002) use the term 'responsible chain management' to describe a continuous alignment of different internal and external expectations in a company. This term signals that today not only are environmental demands in focus in product chains, but sometimes also issues like social conditions, occupational health and safety, child labour etc. Some companies have started using the term 'sustainability management' and reporting guidelines have been developed. An example is the Global Reporting Initiative (www.globalreporting.org).

In this chapter, 'environmental management in product chains' is used as the general term. Environmental management in a product chain is defined as an attempt to:

- Address environmental problems in a product chain
- Convert the understandings of problems and the management hereof into changed practices in the individual companies in the product chain and/or the product chain as a whole.

The chapter aims at giving background to companies, consultants, governmental regulators, NGOs etc. for the analysis and planning of environmental management in specific product chains through:

- A framework for understanding environmental management in product chains as shaped by the interaction between existing resources, norms and values *and* external pressures for environmental management (second section).
- A model for the types of corporate network relations that need to be mapped and understood in order to analyze and/or develop environmental management in a product chain (third section).
- An overview of examples from our own research and from literature of the type and the role of environmental issues and initiatives in product chains (fourth section).
- A typology for characterizing corporate strategies as part of environmental management in product chains and characterizing those competencies that are developed or need to be developed as part of environmental management in a product chain (fifth and sixth sections).
- A framework for understanding, in particular, environmental management in product chains involving companies from different countries with different regulatory frameworks and some international schemes and standards that may be applied as part of this kind of environmental management (seventh and eighth sections).

A conceptual framework: a social shaping perspective on environmental management in product chains

Traditionally analyses of changes of corporate practice are based either on a resource-based perspective, with focus on the development of routines and resources inside the company, or on a contingent perspective with focus on the corporate uptake of external demands and discourses. The chapter combines the two perspectives into a social shaping perspective, where the focus is on the co-shaping of companies and societal discourses during the emergence and stabilization of new issues inside companies and how this changes routines and resources within the involved companies (Forman and Jørgensen 2001a, b).

The focus on the shaping of environmental management practice in product chains implies that the environmental activities in a product chain are seen as shaped by the interaction between existing technical and organizational resources, norms and values within the companies and among the companies in a product chain, *and* the external pressures on the companies to introduce environmental efforts. This pressure may come through environmental requirements from external and internal actors, including governmental regulation.

Also Bowen, Cousins and Lamming (2001) stress the importance of focusing on corporate environmental activities as well as strategic purchasing and supply when analyzing the shaping of what they call 'green supply'.

Existing traditions in a product chain and in the companies include:

- The strategic orientation in the companies
- The division of labour and communication in and among companies
- The methods of control companies use to achieve the fulfilment of the requirements to their suppliers, such as quality, delivery etc.

Analyses from a social-shaping perspective of the environmental management practice focus on:

- The change processes
- The background (the triggers of the changes)
- The interaction with the present business strategy and the product chain
- The outcomes of the change processes.

The outcomes of the change processes are assessed as:

- Environmental changes, which means changes in environmental aspects and the impacts related hereto
- Organizational changes, which means changes in knowledge resources, values, routines and/or organizational structures in one or more of the companies in a product chain.

Changes in environmental aspects and impacts can be described through the following dimensions:

- Extension in space: whether the focus is on environmental impacts in the whole product chain or mainly related to the direct impact of the company that raises demands.

- Prevention: whether an environmental problem is solved as close to its source as possible, for example, by reducing environmental impacts from a production facility through changes in raw materials, routines etc. Other types of environmental initiatives reduce environmental impacts through handling of waste, for example, recycling of waste into new raw materials.
- Time perspective: whether the focus is on management of existing problems or prevention of future problems by integration of environmental concerns in product design.
- Holistic orientation: whether there is focus on the connection between environmental problems and other concerns, such as quality and work environment. With a holistic approach, several problems can be solved during the same process, while ensuring that new problems are not introduced.
- Types of environmental impacts: whether the focus is on resource consumption and the scarcity of resources, including energy consumption, wastes and emissions and their impacts on toxicological impacts, water pollution with nutrients, greenhouse impact and so on, land use etc.

The organizational changes should be seen as offering potential for embedding a new practice as the future practice. Also the organizational changes can have different extension in space in relation to the product chain.

Network relations in and around product chains

In order to understand environmental management in product chains, a broader network analysis is necessary. The broader societal 'selection environment', which creates the earlier-mentioned pressures on one or more of the companies in a product chain, is not captured with a product chain analysis alone. Other types of networks around a single part of the product chain, or networks addressing the whole product chain, can also contribute to the development of the selection environment. Inspired by Holm, Kjærgård and Pedersen (1997) and Søndergaard, Hansen and Holm (2004), a distinction is made between four types of networks, which companies, consciously or unconsciously, are part of:

- The business network – here called the product chain: the flow of material, capital and information from cradle to grave between suppliers and customers and users.
- The developmental network – sometimes also called the knowledge network: focuses on the development of new processes and products and can include parts of the product chain, universities and other types of knowledge institutions.

- The regulatory network: includes public authorities from the local to the international level, but also civil society organizations that directly or indirectly address how companies should or ought to act.
- The local network: consists of the local supply of natural resources, infrastructure, staff, local governmental regulation, etc.

This combination of focus on innovation, product chain and network approaches contributes to the analysis of the environmental management in a product chain as co-shaped by processes in and among the companies in the product chain and in other types of networks, where the companies are involved. Figure 16.1 shows the combined focus on the four different types of networks related to companies in product chains.

In the analyses of the product chain relations and their interaction with environmental management practice Schary and Skjøtt-Larsen (2002) can be used as background for characterizing customer–supplier relations in product chains. According to Schary and Skjøtt-Larsen, product chain relations can be found on a continuum between market conditions and hierarchies. Market conditions imply that materials, services etc. are bought, from time to time, looking for the best price, and hierarchies imply that a company takes over or integrates a certain competence into its own organization. In between these extremes are a number of so-called hybrid forms with some kind of competence hold by the supplier and some kind of specificity of the materials, services etc. the supplier offers.

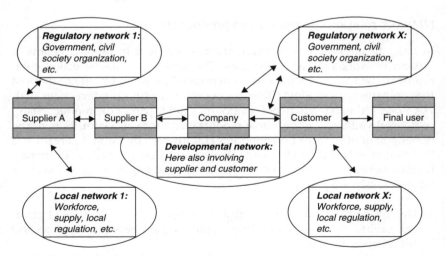

Figure 16.1   A conceptual model

Note: The model is for the network relations in the product chain, the developmental network, the regulatory network and the local networks. The arrows show the complex pattern of flows among the different networks of natural resources, information, capital, etc.

Table 16.1 shows an overview of different relations to suppliers with increasing strategic importance of the relationship when going from top to bottom in the table. The overview is based on Andrew Cox's typology for supply relations and sourcing approaches (Cox 2004).

According to Cox, Schary and Skjøtt-Larsen, it should be expected that the closer a certain competence of a supplier is to the core competence of a company, the more likely it is that this competence becomes integrated into the dominating company in the product chain. A company has often, however, a portfolio of product chain relations at different levels of integration. A number of factors influence the break away from past practice of simple procurement at market conditions: increased outsourcing, global sourcing, JIT purchasing, information technology development and increased focus on environmental supply chain management (Schary and Skjøtt-Larsen 2002).

The role of environmental issues in product chains

Jørgensen *et al.* (2008) analyze 25 case studies with environmental initiatives in product chains, collected in (Bauer and Ettrup 2002), and conclude that environmental initiatives in product chains can be of very different types. Some initiatives mainly aim at collecting information and may be present for customers, while other initiatives involve development of new products and development of strategic relations between a company and a supplier

Table 16.1 Typology of relationship to suppliers

Type of relationship to supplier	Characteristics of the relations to the supplier
Ongoing supplier selection	Frequent 'shopping' among potential suppliers based on price comparison between suppliers. Demands multiple potential suppliers and stable market conditions.
Preferred suppliers	More long-term contract periods with a limited number of suppliers and some exchange of planning information.
Single or parallel sourcing	Supply by a single supplier for a period for a certain good or service. Relevant with goods and services linked directly to the core competencies of the company. If there is more than one supplier within an area the practice is called 'parallel sourcing'.
Strategic alliances	Focus on voluntary arrangements with exchange of staff, sharing of information and/or co-development of goods and services. Relevant with high specificity of demands for goods and services or, when suppliers complement the customer's capabilities.

Sources: Schary and Skjøtt-Larsen 2002: 183–93; Cox 2004.

or a customer. The analyses in (Jørgensen *et al.* 2007) show that demands mostly are passed upstream in product chains from a customer towards the suppliers. Demands passed downstream (to customers) are only seen in a few cases. One of these concerns the distribution of chemicals, where a multinational company demands of its customers that they audit their distribution companies. This can be seen as a kind of extended producer responsibility from the chemical manufacturer based on the inherent hazardous properties of the chemical products and an attempt to avoid critique of the products the company manufactures.

Foster and Green (2000) analyze in nine companies how environmental issues influence R&D in companies. Focus includes the role of consumer demand, university research and governmental regulation. According to Foster and Green (2000), English companies seem only to develop so-called greener technologies if they are under regulation or if customers further down the product chain demand them. This is borne out by examples of companies that have Scandinavian customers who demand greener products. Foster and Green (2000) argue that environmental innovation could assume a bigger role if suppliers encouraged their customers to become more involved in dialogue about environmental potential.

In Steward *et al.* (2000) the role of broader societal 'demands' and concerns for technology development and environmental innovation have been analyzed. Broader social concerns are mentioned to be of increasing importance for innovation. Because of their less direct influence, terms such as the 'selection environment' and 'indirect stakeholder influence' have been used in this context. These broader concerns are harder to demonstrate since the concerns are often more complex and involve several technical traits, links are indirect between, for example, NGOs and the company, and the consideration of the concerns is often not traceable in the company. Also Madsen and Ulhøi (2001) see environmental innovation as the result of a very complex process involving not only suppliers and customers, but also a broad group of societal stakeholders or actors.

Hall (2000) refers to small companies as less responsive to general or indirect environmental concerns, whereas large and high-profile companies are more inclined to address their environmental image in public. One reason why it may be more difficult to trace the responses in small firms, is the lack of someone with environmental responsibility or a formulated environment policy etc. Hall also refers to small firms as attracting less criticism, because they are small. He uses the notion of 'channel power' to describe the ability of a company to raise demands to its suppliers or customers.

Stranddorf *et al.* (2002) conclude, in a study of Danish textile companies and their environmental demands to suppliers, that whether a company chooses to address an environmental issue depends on a number of factors, including the present product chain relations and possible ways of integrating the topic into the business strategy. There may be different triggers for environmental initiatives in the same company. The triggering factors include:

- Governmental regulation of chemicals and materials
- Governmental regulation as public–private sector-based dialogue forum (developing plan for eco-labelled collection of garments)
- Governmental funding, including funding for eco-labelling and for joint development projects with suppliers in developing countries
- Public debate, especially in relation to child labour
- Customer demands
- Expectations of market opportunities.

Stranddorf *et al.* (2002) show how the environmental initiatives involving suppliers may focus on different parts of the product chain and for different reasons. Some companies are concerned about the conditions at the suppliers' facilities, while others are concerned about the conditions at their own facilities. However, the latter type of concern may also imply demands to suppliers in order to prevent problems at their own facilities. Examples of the two types of concerns from the textile sector are:

- Demands regarding conditions at the suppliers' facilities:
  - Pollution from cotton growing (either purchasing organic cotton or restrictions on pesticide residues, a requirement for eco-labelling)
  - Child labour
  - Chemicals for dyeing (requirement for eco-labelling)
- Demands on suppliers in order to improve conditions at their own plants:
  - Buying organic cotton in order to improve occupational health and safety in their own plants
  - Demands for supply with less hazardous chemicals (due to requirement from local environmental authorities about the environmental load of the waste water).

A typology of corporate environmental management strategies in product chains

This section discusses how environmental initiatives in product chains are organized. Hall (2000) discusses environmental supply chain dynamics and highlights the importance of buyer–supplier relations, including the degree of collaborative buyer–supplier relations and the degree of one actor's ability to control the decisions of the other actors, so-called *channel power*. For the analyses of product chain relations Goldbach (2002) describes two extremes of relations in product chains: one characterized by cooperation, incentives, trust and win-win solutions and another characterized by confrontation, control, power and win-lose solutions. Kogg (2002) identifies two aspects of environmental supply chain management approaches from two case studies. One aspect concerns whether environmental measures take place through direct interaction with each of the suppliers upstream or by approaching the nearest supplier, whom then is supposed, if necessary, to approach its own suppliers, which could be called a kind of 'mediated environmental management' with the product chain as arena. The other aspect concerns whether the initiatives are taken by a company alone in order to position itself on the market or collaboration is established with competitors in order to increase the pressure on the suppliers.

In a study of environmental management in product chains in the Danish textile sector, three different types of environmental management in relation to suppliers are identified (Stranddorf *et al.* 2002, Forman and Jørgensen 2004). The aspects, which showed the need for differentiating between different practices, were:

- The degree of proactivity in the corporate environmental strategy
- The tradition for short- or long-term relationships and for control and/or cooperation with the suppliers
- The concepts used by the companies to plan and monitor demands to the suppliers
- The organizational impact of environmental initiatives on the product chain in terms of development of the competencies of the company itself and/or the supplier(s).

The three environmental supply chain management practices are:

- *The wake strategy*, where the company does not place requirements on suppliers, but follows in the 'wake' of organizations, which already place these requirements.
- *The asymmetrical partnership*, where a company wants long-term relationships with a supplier. The customer dominates the relationship, builds up a lot of competence itself and controls the fact that the supplier meets the requirements.
- *The symmetrical partnership*, where a company wants long-term relationships with a supplier and enters a mutual partnership with the supplier(s) and builds the strategies in dialogue.

A company might have different supply chain strategies and different environmental management practices in relation to different suppliers, depending on the competence of the supplier. If a supplier is easy to substitute, which, for example, sewing companies in the textile industry in some cases seem to be, the environmental supply chain management practice is an asymmetrical partnership. If the company is more dependent on the competence of a supplier, it is more likely that there will be symmetrical partnerships.

The aspects of stabilization of these three product chain practices can be viewed both from a customer and a supplier perspective (Forman and Jørgensen 2004). The wake strategy can make it easy for a company to switch to new suppliers, when, for example, the market for eco-labelled products has become mature. However, companies might face problems at that stage in finding suppliers due to potential suppliers' agreements about not selling to more customers, because existing customers want to secure their own market position.

The most important reason why suppliers decide to enter agreements to provide environmentally improved products or improve processes is that they can see competitive advantages in participating in these partnerships and a direct link to customer demands. An international retail chain is, for example, a potentially large customer for suppliers. Therefore, it is attractive to suppliers and they are more willing to cooperate with the company. It is, however, not only the size of the company that makes it attractive as customer. A strategic alliance with suppliers of chemicals may be developed, because the customer buying the chemicals is well known for its in-depth testing of new chemicals.

Companies that have outsourced their production activities are likely to need to pay attention to how they ensure their market position, as the essential competence-building is undertaken by the supplier.

With respect to asymmetrical and symmetrical partnerships, the more complex customer–supplier relations are, the more resource saving it might be to develop more long-term and close customer–supplier relations. The focal company will have to expend time and human resources if it frequently has to develop new customer–supplier relations, with implications for aspects of quality, environment and occupational health and safety. Forman and Jørgensen (2004) report the same dilemmas for customers and suppliers connected with these types of relations as Hall (2000) in his literature review of environmental management in product chains. The customer is sure to have qualified suppliers, but might find it difficult to shift suppliers due to the dependency of the supplier being developed, for example, if external conditions like currency rates change and make it more profitable on a short-term basis to find other suppliers. The supplier has more stable planning conditions, but might also be pushed by the customer to take the burden of a number of new activities, like obtaining eco-labelling.

Asymmetrical partnerships are not necessarily capable of disseminating advanced environmental competence along a supply chain and developing a multiplier effect, as a company may make demands that its supplier build up its own environmental competencies, but does not expect the supplier to be able to develop similar competencies. Seen in a long-term perspective, this might make the supplier very dependent on the customer, with the customer taking all of the responsibility for updating knowledge about more environmentally sound opportunities. (Schary and Skjøtt-Larsen 2002) refer to the fact that, in some cases, multinational companies urge preferred suppliers also to have other customers in order to ensure more dynamic suppliers.

Competencies in environmental management in product chains

The management of an environmental issue in a product chain demands knowledge resources and structures for the translation and evaluation of the environmental initiatives and their results. Jørgensen *et al.* (2007) show how such knowledge resources and structures can be built by a number of very different stakeholders:

* A company itself
* A product chain (with different types of partnerships between suppliers and customers)
* Business initiatives for sourcing companies like BSCI (Business Social Compliance Initiative – promoting a common monitoring and factory development system)
* NGOs and NGO initiatives, for example Save the Children
* International institutions, for example the ILO
* Multistakeholder initiatives like FSC (Forest Stewardship Council) involving businesses and NGOs.

Organizational structures and routines inside a company might change as part of the development of environmental management in a product chain. Lenox and Ehrenfeld (1997) suggest the following organizational elements as necessary for a company to be able to handle environmental issues:

* *Knowledge resources:* information and expertise residing in individuals, groups and technical artefacts inside or outside the company
* *Communication channels, formal and informal, as well as external and internal:* the channels through which information flows and is exchanged
* *Interpretive structures:* structures that can help create mutual understanding and values among the involved stakeholders, because the stakeholders need to find the information meaningful in the context of their own work.

From the earlier-mentioned case studies about Danish textile companies and their interaction with suppliers, five different competencies involved in the environmental management in product chains were identified (Stranddorf *et al.* 2001, Forman and Jørgensen 2004). These competencies are developed within the companies in the product chains as a part of the planning, the implementation and the monitoring of the initiatives in the environmental supply chain management. Depending on the environmental supply chain management practice, the various competencies are developed and anchored at (1) the company that sets the requirements, (2) the supplier and/or (3) a third party (e.g. an advisor or a certifying organization):

- *Interpretation competence:* Partly the competence to understand external requirements from, for example, environmental agencies and customers, and partly the competence to translate those requirements into practice within the organization itself – such as converting the requirements into actual practices for purchasers, production workers, designers, suppliers etc.
- *Technical environmental competence:* The insight into technical and chemical processes, etc., which is a prerequisite for the adjustment or reorganization of a production process or a design scheme in order to meet environmental requirements.
- *Documentation competence:* The knowledge about how to build and operate documentation systems and document handling routines etc.
- *Control competence:* Refers to knowledge about monitoring systems, management systems, auditing, etc., and the responsibility or empowerment to maintain control. This competence can reside with the company, the supplier, or a third party – for example, a certification agency.
- *Network competence:* The ability to create changes in a product chain through networking among customers and suppliers, including the ability to motivate the companies in the chain to enter a dialogue, as well as the ability to transfer technology and knowledge in or among product chains.

De Bakker and Nijhof (2002) have developed a capability assessment framework for responsible chain management, where they distinguish between internal and external capabilities and talk about four types of capabilities in a so-called capability cycle: interpretation, integration, monitoring and communication. The circular process, inspired by the 'plan—do—act' cycle, is too sequential, since the processes of interpretation, integration, monitoring and communication often occur in a more interwoven manner, but the four types of capabilities and the focus on internal and external capabilities seem relevant. The four competencies identified by De Bakker and Nijhof (2002) correspond to those presented above, although Stranddorf *et al.* (2002) identify a more detailed range of integration competencies: part of the interpretation competence, technical environmental competence and network competence.

Environmental management in transnational product chains

More and more product chains are transnational, which in most cases implies that there is a different level of environmental protection in countries along the product chain. Hansen (1999) argues that transnational environmental management typically will have at least the following elements:

- General principles for the environmental activities of the entire corporation
- More specific policies and programmes applicable throughout the corporation
- A cross-border environmental management system with procedures for monitoring and controlling the practice of the foreign affiliates
- Training, education and information exchange programmes and activities
- A formal organization where responsibilities and functions are delineated and allocated between different entities and persons – for example, between headquarters, affiliates and suppliers.

Hansen (1999) argues that corporate environmental management practice in transnational product chains falls within the range from adaptation to the local regulation and practice in developing countries to global integration where a company is practising the same level of concern and responsibility as in the home country. Hansen (1999) refers to two types of product chains: management of controlled affiliates and management of non-controlled foreign entities (organized through franchising, licensing, subcontracting or strategic alliances). With reference to Bartlett's and Ghoshal's ideal types of cross-border organization in transnational corporations, Hansen (1999) describes four ideal types of cross-border environmental management: decentralized environmental management, international compliance, centralized environmental management and globally integrated environmental management. The most elaborate and environmental ambitious cross-border environmental functions are seen in the centralized and globally integrated types. Table 16.2 gives an overview of the four types of practice.

According to Hansen (1999) the types of forces, which shape the environmental management in transnational product chains between local adaptation and global integration, seem to be:

- *Regulatory forces:* the type of environmental regulation shaping the cross-border practice: international regulation, home country regulation and host country regulation
- *Market forces:* the quality and environmental orientation of the markets and the value chains
- *Industry-specific forces:* collaboration in the specific industry
- *Company-specific forces:* the nature of the production technology, the environmental history from the home country, the international orientation of the company.

Table 16.2 A typology of corporate environmental management in transnational product chains

	Decentralized environmental management	International compliance	Centralized environmental management	Globally integrated environmental management
Environmental management focus	Local adaptation	Host country legislation (country where facility or subsidiary is localised)	Home country legislation (country of headquarters) and global company standards	Internationally oriented company standards
Concept of environmental management	Environmental management the responsibility of local managers. May take advantage of weak implementation of local environmental regulation	Affiliates around the world take the necessary measures to operate in accordance with laws and regulations of the host countries	The environmental regulation of the home country as the basis, regardless of the local requirements. Fear the regulation of the host countries is not sufficient	Initiatives for new measures from different facilities in the company. Networking among local environmental managers. Adaptation to local conditions allowed, within the corporate principles

Source: Adapted from Hansen 1999.

International schemes and standards in environmental management in product chains

Environmental management may involve the use of national or international schemes and standards for planning and maybe also certification of the environmental management. In their book *Living Corporate Citizenship*, McIntosh *et al.* (2003) analyze a number of initiatives that aim at supporting the development of socially responsible businesses, including environmental management, such as:

- The UN Compact – with focus on nine UN principles within social and environmental problems, and rights and commitment to improve and report
- The Global Reporting Initiative – a scheme for corporate sustainability reporting
- OECD Guidelines for Multinational Enterprises – a broad focus with local practice in a host country, rather than international principles, as norm
- ILO Conventions – a set of core labour standards and a number of more specific conventions on health and safety and child labour
- The ISO 14000 Series – a set of international standards with focus on corporate environmental management and some of the tools within this area, for example, eco-labelling
- AccountAbility 1000 – with a focus on organizational learning in combination with social and ethical accounting
- Social Accountability 8000 – an auditable standard on working conditions.

McIntosh *et al.* (2003) point to a number of gaps and problems in these initiatives:

- Numerous issues are being ignored, such as animal welfare and indigenous rights
- There is a lack of definition and consensus on several major terms, for example, 'the precautionary principle' and how a company should define its potential for influence on suppliers and customers
- The initiatives are voluntary and companies vary dramatically in their levels of commitment
- The schemes seem to favour large companies
- If the various initiatives are to gain legitimacy, societies will also have to benefit through enhanced social and environmental development and better access to information
- There are unintended consequences, such as initiatives trying to curtail child labour leading to children being fired and resorting to begging or prostitution.

The initiatives may be divided into principles and standards, where principles are more overarching values that underpin behaviour (e.g. ILO Conventions) and can be used as reference in the management of a certain area. Standards, for example ISO 14001: 2004, can be very different, with more or less focus on process, performance and certification.

The ISO 14001:2004 standard contains a number of demands on a company that follows the standard. However, core elements of the standard also demonstrate loopholes allowing a large degree of interpretative flexibility in how it is implemented (Behrndt 2002), here cited from (Jørgensen 2003). These potentially weak elements are:

- The scope or boundaries of the activities covered
- The identification of environmental aspects and impacts of company activities
- The legal requirements to be recognized by the company
- The policy priorities of the company
- The extended focus in relation to suppliers, products and design.

These issues become even more complex when they are part of the dynamics in transnational product chains with very different national cultures, regulatory systems and levels of environmental and social awareness and responsibility.

ISO 14001: 2004, section 4.3.1 (about procedures for identifying environmental aspects), says:

> The organization shall establish, implement and maintain a procedure(s)... to identify the environmental aspects of its activities, products and services within the defined scope of the environmental management system that it can control and those that it can influence taking into account planned and new developments, or new or modified activities, products and services.

This paragraph leaves it more or less up to the company to define its environmental scope, since it may decide to say that it cannot control or influence suppliers' or users' activities.

ISO 14001 2004,section 4.4.6 (about operational control), says:

> The organization shall identify and plan those operations that are associated with identified significant environmental aspects consistent with its environmental policy, objectives and targets, in order to ensure that they are established under specified conditions, by ... establishing, implementing and maintaining procedures related to the identified significant environmental aspects of goods and services used by the organization and communicating applicable procedures to suppliers, including contractors.

This paragraph demands that a company focuses on environmental aspects related to the activities of its suppliers. However, through ISO 14001, section

4.3.1, the company may decide that it is not possible to control or influence suppliers and contractors and it may leave out these aspects in its choice of aspects to focus upon. Whether this is accepted depends on the role of the involved certifiers, auditors and stakeholders that may request insight into the practice of the company.

The Ethical Trading Initiative (ETI) is a joint initiative between retailers, trade unions and environmental NGOs in the UK. The report from the ETI members' meeting on 16 November 2006 indicates several problems experienced by companies sourcing in transnational supply chains, but also gives examples of good practice. Some problems seem to be the result of limited auditor skills, whereas others involve cases where fraudulent supplying companies try to hide their real labour practice. Analysis of the background to these issues also points, however, to the practices of the customer companies themselves as part of the problem. If a customer company demands a very short lead time (from the time of ordering products to the time their delivery is requested), it is likely to be more difficult for a supplying company to find the time to adapt to conditions required by the customer, therefore the risk of fraud becomes bigger (ETI Forum 2006).

Concluding remarks

The chapter has presented a number of frameworks and models for the analysis and development of environmental management in companies and other types of organizations involved in product chains and networks related to product chains, and has shown how the level and the focus in time and space of the environmental management in a product chain is influenced by:

- The strategic interpretations made by the involved companies of the necessary level of environmental protection and the perspective on competence development in the different parts of a product chain.
- The international and national regulation and its enforcement in relation to companies, foreign investments, products and materials etc.
- The pressure for transparency and control in product chains from customers, public debate and NGOs.

Growing globalization of production and consumption is very relevant to environmental management in a company as it considers its role in the direct and indirect product chain relations with suppliers (and their suppliers), with customers and with the final users of products and services. It is also important that companies in product chains consider their responsibility in the shaping and the management of resource consumption and environmental impact related to products, waste and emissions.

There is increasing public focus and increasing focus in business-to-business relations on environmental aspects of the sourcing of materials in other countries with different social and regulatory frameworks, and the distribution of products to countries with social and regulatory frameworks that differ from those where the products originally were developed for use. This has initiated development of conventions and standards that companies may refer to in their environmental management planning and documentation. However, the complexity and the geographic distances in the product chains also make it difficult to control the actual practice of the involved companies. Reports from companies about their management of environmental issues, and other aspects of sustainability, are often not very transparent and concrete in their actual documentation of corporate initiatives and the results of these initiatives. It is often difficult to differentiate between good intentions and actual efforts and results. It is a future research need and challenge for the public debate to consider the role of companies, especially multinationals, in securing more reliable documentation regarding the shaping and the results of environmental management in product chains.

References

Bauer, B. and Ettrup, B. 2002 *Miljøledelse i produktkæder – en eksempelsamling* (in Danish) (Environmental Management in Product Chains), Environmental Project No. 41, Danish Environmental Protection Agency.
Behrndt, K. 2002 ' "Hot spots" in the interpretation of the ISO 14001 standard to ensure continual improvements', paper for the Greening of Industry Conference, Gothenburg, June.
Bowen, F.E., Cousins, P.D. and Lamming, R.C. 2001 'The role of supply management capabilities in green supply', *Production and Operations Management*, 10(2).; 174–89.
Cox, A. 2004 'The art of the possible relationship management in power regimes and supply chains', *Supply Chain Management – An International Journal*, 9: 346–56.
De Bakker, F. and Nijhof, A. 2002 'Responsible chain management: A capability assessment framework',*Business Strategy and the Environment*, 11: 63–75.
ETI Forum 2006 *Getting Smarter at Auditing: Tackling the Growing Crisis in Ethical Trade Auditing*, Report from ETI members' meeting, 16 November.
Forman, M. and Jørgensen, M.S. 2001a 'The social shaping of the participation of employees in environmental work within enterprises: Experiences from a Danish context', *Technology Analysis and Management*, 13(1): 71–90.
Forman, M. and Jørgensen, M.S. 2001b 'Corporate environmental competence: The effects of networking, organisational learning and preventive strategies', edited version of paper for 5th Nordic Environmental Research Conference, Aarhus, 14–16 June.
Forman, M. and Jørgensen, M.S. 2004 'Organising environmental supply chain management', *Greener Management International*, 45 (Spring): 43–62.
Forman, M., Hansen, A.G. and Jørgensen, M.S. 2003 'The shaping of environmental concern in product chains: Analysing Danish case studies on environmental aspects in product chain relations', paper presented at EGOS (European Group on Organisation Studies) Conference 2003, Copenhagen Business School, 3–5 July.
Foster, C. and Green, K. 2000 'Greening "the Innovation Process"', *Business Strategy and the Environment*, 9: 287–303.

Garcia-Sanchez, I., Wenzel, H. and Jørgensen, M.S. 2004 'Models for defining LCM, monitoring LCM practice and assessing its feasibility', *Greener Management International*, 45(Spring): 9–25.

Goldbach, M. 2002 'Organizational settings in supply chain costing', in S. Seuring and M. Goldbach (eds), *Cost Management in Supply Chains*, Heidelberg: Physica-Verlag: 89–108.

Hall, J. 2000 'Environmental supply chain dynamics', *Journal of Cleaner Production*, 8: 455–71.

Hansen, A.G. 2001 *Regulation: Promoting or Limiting Biotechnology? New Genetics and Society*, Technical University of Denmark.

Hansen, M.W. 1999 'Cross border environmental management in transnational corporations: An analytical framework', Occasional paper no. 5, Copenhagen Business School, Department of Intercultural Communication and Management.

Holm J., Kjærgård, B. and Pedersen, N.K. (eds) 1997 *Miljøregulering – tværfaglige studier* (in Danish) (Environmental Regulation – Cross-Disciplinary Studies), Roskilde: Roskilde Universitetsforlag.

ISO 14001:2004 2004 *Environmental management systems – Requirements with guidance for use*, International Organization for Standardization.

Jørgensen, M.S., Jørgensen, U., Hendriksen, K., Hirsbak, S. and Thorsen, N.N. 2007 'Modes of environmental management in transnational product chains', paper presented at GIN 2007: International Conference of the Greening of Industry Network: Sustainable Ecosystem and Social Stewardship, Wilfrid Laurier University, Waterloo, Ontario, 15–17 June (available on conference CD-rom).

Jørgensen, M., Forman, M. and Hansen, A.G. 2008 *Environmental Management in Product Chains: Theoretical and Regulatory Perspectives Based on 25 Danish Case Studies*, Copenhagen: Danish Environmental Protection Agency.

Jørgensen, U. 2003 'The "hidden" networks of practice in ISO 14001', paper for the Greening of Industry Conference, San Francisco, October.

Kogg, B. 2002 'Power and incentives in environmental supply chain management', in Seuring, S., M., Müller, M., Goldbach, M. and Scheidewind, U. (eds), *Strategy and Organization in Supply Chains*, Heidelberg: Physika-Verlag, 65–81.

Lenox, M. and Ehrenfeld, J. 1997 'Organizing for effective environmental design', *Business Strategy and the Environment*, 6: 187–96.

Madsen, H. and Ulhøi, J.P. 2001 'Integrating environmental and stakeholder management', *Business Strategy and the Environment*, 10: 77–88.

McIntosh, M., Thomas, R., Leipziger, D. and Coleman, G. 2003 *Living Corporate Citizenship: Strategic Routes to Socially Responsible Business*, London: Prentice Hall.

Schary, P.B. and Skjøtt-Larsen, T. 2002 *Managing the Global Supply Chain*, Copenhagen: Copenhagen Business School Press.

Steward, F., Garcia, G., Hansen, A.G., Joly, P.B., Bailey, P. and Yearley, S. 2000 'Environmental networks and societal management of technological innovation in the food sector (EC DGXII Environment programme)', Brunel University, University of Carlos III, Technical University of Denmark, SERD/INRA Grenoble, The Stockholm Environment Institute, University of York.

Stranddorf, H., Forman, M., Nielsen, A. and Søgaard, M. 2002 *Miljø-, etik og arbejdsmiljøkrav i tekstilproduktkæden: En udredning om erfaringer, strategier og handlemuligheder* (in Danish) (Environmental, Ethical and Work Environmental Demands in the Textile Product Chain: A Survey of Experience, Strategies and Possibilities for Action), Danish Environmental Protection Agency, Environmental Project no. 681, <http://www.mst.dk>

Index